Frugal Innovation and Innovative Creation

To

F & G
L & O
07 12 26 – 20 12 20 21

Smart Innovation Set

coordinated by
Dimitri Uzunidis

Volume 40

Frugal Innovation and Innovative Creation

Paul Bouvier-Patron

iSTE

WILEY

First published 2023 in Great Britain and the United States by ISTE Ltd and John Wiley & Sons, Inc.

ISTE Ltd
27-37 St George's Road
London SW19 4EU
UK

www.iste.co.uk

John Wiley & Sons, Inc.
111 River Street
Hoboken, NJ 07030
USA

www.wiley.com

Library of Congress Control Number: 2023937228

British Library Cataloguing-in-Publication Data
A CIP record for this book is available from the British Library
ISBN 978-1-78630-697-5

Contents

Introduction

In order to innovate, the frugal approach meets the dual objective of seeking a competitive advantage while lowering the costs of innovation, and a new potential for innovative creation (see Chapter 7) likely to promote innovation (see Chapters 5 and 6) that respects the Natural Environment (NE) (see Chapter 1). In this book, therefore, it is not a matter of addressing, per se, frugality or the circular economy, or even the figures (the subject of numerous publications) of pollution, waste or recycling, which are staggering in their volumes, even though, when it is possible, the recovery of existing waste, at best and on average, does not exceed 50%. This invites us to reflect on the need to produce and consume differently. The point of view adopted is to place ourselves halfway between economics and management. The key actor is the company or companies, but more specifically, innovative companies in their interactions with the NE. Taking into account NE can be perceived *a priori* as a costly constraint, especially in an innovation process that is already intrinsically very costly. Technological innovation, which is very popular in the West, always comes at a very high cost. Therefore, is it possible to produce an innovative product that respects the NE at an acceptable cost? This question will be addressed throughout the book and can be answered or solved as long as we accept a questioning of the classic scheme of innovation in business while adopting a consequentist approach (see Chapter 1 and Appendix 2; Bouvier-Patron 2014, 2015a).

The first positive response in this sense, found by the companies themselves, is to operate in a network (*network of companies*: NoC) generally articulating complementary skills. Each company in the network is refocused on its business and, potentially, a leader in its field (by concentrating its resources, skills and efforts, particularly in terms of innovation) on its distinctive specificity.

The coordination of distributed competences is a clever way of controlling the costs of innovation of a good produced within a network. This decisive inter-organizational dimension is not, however, sufficient to deal with the question of the NE and is therefore only one step in the process.

The second positive response is potentially the mobilization of technology (via ICT and DT, respectively: information and communication technologies or ICT; digital technology or DT) favoring fluid interactive coordination, more or less virtual, and drastically reducing the costs of design by the FabLab while relying on a mutualization of exchanges of information, skills and knowledge through innovation communities (extending beyond and/or transversing the companies). The communitarization of innovation with a decentering towards design/conception is an original and adaptive device, but one that does not necessarily yet integrate the question of the NE while accelerating the technological race.

The third positive response, still in the making, consists of moving towards a technical–organizational reappraisal through a form of frugality likely to promote innovation, but integrating from the outset the consideration of the NE.

Frugality is a recent concept, but is no longer a new concept in its classical terminological sense (for the classical version, see Basu et al. (2013)). One contribution of the present work is to insist on the possible articulation of frugality with the consideration of the NE: hence, the advanced concept of *frugal environmental innovation* (FEI) (see Bouvier-Patron 2017b, 2020). From then on, by crossing frugality and taking into account the NE, the nature of the innovation induced comes back to questioning technology insofar as it is, finally, a matter of being interested in the *satisfactory technological level* (in the sense of satisficing (Simon 1976, 1978)). Far from being anecdotal, this new look refers to a reflection on the usefulness of an unbridled recourse to technology in western or westernized societies.

In order to understand the process towards this *frugal environmental innovation* or FEI, it is necessary to go back to the foundations of innovative creation (Chapter 7) and to unveil its fundamental forces. Of course, both technology and an appropriate form of organization (some forms of organization being more conducive than others) contribute to innovation; but the latter is incorporated into innovative creation, the two key drivers of which are elementary practices (radiating whatever the more or less technological and/or more or less organized modality): *bricolage*[1] and *improvisation* (Chapter 7).

1 The primitive form of *responsible bricolage* is explained by Levi-Strauss (1962a).

Thus, bricolage and improvisation are two crucial levers that operate, regardless of the type of innovation, the place, or the time, both in the design of the product and in the very functioning of an organization or inter-organization. Bricolage and improvisation are thus essential as cogs in the dynamic complexity of organizations: whether we are engaged in an expensive technological approach or in a frugal practice and whether or not we integrate the NE.

In order to allow the path followed to succeed, it is necessary to break down the problems and present them one after the other until the solution is possible through FEI, but this relies, like all innovative solutions, on two essential springs: bricolage and improvisation.

The specific form of frugality sought, the FEI, examined in Chapters 5 and 6, must take into account the NE (Chapter 1), long considered a free resource and which turns out to be an exhaustible good: this is a characteristic with multiple consequences on the societal level and which proves to be, from a strictly rational point of view, a new constraint to be managed in the business equation. It is therefore also a new challenge for the company, even though the problem has been pointed out for a long time. Recycling at the end of the chain (never guaranteed) is necessary to mop up the existing but (beyond the imperfections and problems of such a practice) must be revised. The challenge must now be to innovate products and technologies that respect the environment from the outset, while thinking *ex ante* (through design) about the end of life. The path is stimulating but not easy. Theoretically, the necessary revolution in thinking for this paradigm shift is reflected in the dual concept of *positive private good* (PPG) and *consequentism* (see Chapter 1). To achieve this type of PPG, given the accepted practice in the West, a technological response is possible through the coupling of ICT and DT from FabLab (Chapter 2). The FabLab is a means that mobilizes ICT and DT, assuming a collaborative and open interactive organization with decentralized expertise oriented towards experimentation for the creation or innovative design and then the conduct of projects (with or without a commercial purpose) where technological bricolage and improvisation are essential. The 3D printing used in the FabLab is an increasingly effective support tool, but its impact on the NE is still unknown. The same is true for the ICT and DT that allow for dematerialization and virtualization (thus minimizing a form of impact on the NE) but that induce the use of elements that are not very respectful of the NE: instruments (computing machines, networks of machines, portable terminals, connected objects, sensors, batteries, relays, systems and transmission flows, such as 5G), dynamic interactive storage of the Cloud linked to Big Data (multimedia mass digital data) and the energy needed to power and manage the overall operation.

The technological combination of ICT and DT is accompanied (Chapters 3 and 4) by a new way of innovating through the communitarization of upstream (community of practice; see below) and downstream (community of use) innovation. Innovation is affirmed as a collaborative, open process, and associates use from the design stage. The organization of innovation mobilizing resources and means in this collaborative and open framework is a crucial issue, especially as the design approach invites multidisciplinarity and the need to perceive complexity, hence the innovation platform dedicated to a project and/or specialized in a field. Innovative creation and innovative design actively mobilize, in this context, the bricolage and innovation so vital for the maker or hacker.

The resulting downstream use (Chapter 4), through the tools available (for the user via the Internet – essentially the smartphone and the laptop – as well as the frequentation of social networks) generates a creation of value increased by the virtual in an expanding bubble that is limited only by the imagination of those who offer and seek it. Let us note that classical marketing or online marketing, whether strategic or operational, can rely on artificial intelligence (AI) to articulate the collection, processing and use of mass data for all kinds of commercial (or other) purposes. AI, in a multidisciplinary perspective, consists of implementing a certain number of techniques and/or technologies, allowing machines to imitate the human brain and/or to create a form of intelligence by elaborating usable knowledge. The degree of machine expertise is correlated to the evolution of the technologies themselves: from imitation/reproduction by predefined programming at the beginning, we are now moving on to Deep Learning which aims, through learning by mobilizing Big Data, at a form of autonomization of artificial creation and decision-making. The fields of application of AI are numerous. One of the most striking, in everyday life, is, for example, facial recognition. The growing use of AI touches various and sometimes unexpected fields. We will illustrate the question of the use of AI by marketing (conclusion of Chapter 4) by addressing a symptomatic case, that of the virtual influencer. The issue of virtual influencers, far from being marginal, deserves great attention as a point of intersection: technology (or often combinations of technologies including AI and social networks); strategic marketing; consent (permission marketing; see below); experiential (experiential marketing proposing the immersion of the prospect and/or customer, in an attractive interactive sensory and emotional universe, providing an unforgettable experience where the individual pilots their real, augmented, virtual or simulated experience), which can also make sense within the framework of a communal referential of the post-modern tribe type (see Chapter 4).

The media noise about a particular application (e.g. TikTok) concerning potential abuses (or risks of abuses), in terms of the use of personal data, is not the exception but the norm. The risk (potential or proven) is present. Only the ethical rules (notably of the provider or of a brand), when they exist and are respected, are a remedy to abuse, but the technology allows this abuse. Beyond the ethical stakes and the use of personal data (with or without user/client consent[2] as a dividing line as well as a new way of marketing), the power of commercial potential is multiplied.

Whatever the criticism or relativization to be made, the technological means engaged (from the most basic to the most advanced) are still based on *human innovative creation* approaches (at least as long as the machines are not at the origin of the creation, because, to this day, all machine creations result from algorithms programmed by humans and, eventually, allowing the machine to understand with the help of the supplied databases): human creation where bricolage and improvisation have their place.

The level of value to be elaborated does not contravene this rule as long as humans control the system and the communitarization of innovation is based on the interweaving of levels where enlightened amateurism, decentralized expertise or strong professional expertise are side by side, intermingled and fructified by mutually supporting each other.

Also, in the face of technological excess (or technological hubris), a return to common sense through frugality (Chapter 5) can be an alternative without sacrificing anything to the desired result. Obviously, frugality in its basic definition is not enough to develop an alternative, especially when the alternative sought must incorporate consideration of the NE: hence, the concept of the FEI. This specific frugality to be convoked, the FEI (Chapter 6) as a specific EI, represents a dosage or *satisfactory technological level*, as it is adapted to innovation, which respects the NE in a consequentist approach.

The key problem is therefore to find the *satisfactory technological level* (in the sense of satisficing (Simon 1976, 1978)) within an open interactive collaborative organization based, in particular, on serendipity (discovery by chance), trial and error, or resourcefulness (or system D).

2 Permission marketing consent was developed for Internet commerce by Seth Godin in the 2000s. The other related term is inbound marketing, which refers to the collection of information flows from customers, especially end customers, with permission (explicit authorization). The aim is to establish and build a personalized, qualitative, trusting and high value-added relationship with the customer (i.e. one that can be commercially valued), including permanent and interactive follow-ups based on the co-construction of a service (between the brand and the customer). The implicit objective is, if possible, to generate ambassadors (lead users). This also explains the importance of community management for online companies.

In the end, this raises the essential question (Chapter 7) of the basis of innovation, whose roots and very dynamics are based on the springs of bricolage and improvisation in an open, interactive and collective organizational framework. The proposed focus revisits the very understanding of innovation.

For now, let us emphasize the very nature of the dynamic complexity of organizations (Bouvier-Patron 2001, 2014) as a receptacle for innovation and for carrying out the necessary transformation and/or change.

The organization, itself a complex entity, enables innovation through a dynamic ability to create, interact, open up, learn, be agile, discover by collaborating and, if necessary, redeploy. A complex innovative project mobilizes a lot of resources in a time frame that may or may not be under control. If, for an expected result (with no guarantee of success), time is constrained, the resources to be committed will be much greater, with a high number of trial and errors and waste or losses, and this is the general case in competitive situations. Apart from NASA (a public agency coordinating its private suppliers) with a substantial budget in the 1960s, only a few rare for-profit organizations (e.g. SpaceX, but again with public funds) venture to plan innovation on very complex projects; this also presupposes a form of innovative monopoly (in Schumpeter's sense), having a head start, with potential competition being sufficient to stimulate the effort without being able to threaten the project. However, as a general rule, in a hyper-competitive world, the company finds it impossible to plan innovation. At best, the company can create favorable organizational and technological conditions to stimulate the innovative effort (e.g. 3M). In any case, both the cost of access (in terms of means to be put in place, investment in machinery, skills and knowledge, training of people) and the intrinsic cost of carrying out an innovation before it is put on the market are high, without even prejudging the subsequent commercial success.

In a competitive situation, the ability to be proactive is the organizational breath that also gives the company an adaptive capacity to adapt to the context, whatever the path taken in the past, and to anticipate the future (not in a planned way, as this is generally impossible, but at least by not closing off options that could prove useful later).

At the abstract level, this factor of permanent evolutivity while preserving a core corresponds to a dynamic complexity close to self-organization (see below).

We will first discuss the evolutionary logic of organizational forms before underlining the bases of dynamic complexity that allow us to understand uncertainty and the need to renew skills.

I.1. Organization of the company and organization of the form

The National Institute of Statistics and Economic Studies (INSEE[3]) mainly classifies companies or enterprises by size, according to the number of employees (individual enterprise (IE); x < 25, very small enterprise (VSE); x < 250, small- and medium-sized enterprises (SME); x < 5,000, intermediate (ISE); x > 5,000, large enterprise (LE)). However, the underlying assumption of homogeneity of behavior according to size is questionable for the analysis of competitive strategy and/or value creation (where what matters most is the ability to create a nontrivial and/or innovative product). Size, taken as an explanatory variable of success, is in fact an *ex post* observation, which does not integrate the choice for any organization to grow (or not), and is neglecting the fact that success is always relative to the success criterion used. Moreover, starting from the different sizes does not allow us to explain the transition process from small to large companies. Especially because, for a given size, sector specificity can play a role as a key explanatory variable of success. Moreover, the contextualized singularity of a particular market imposes itself on each company present on that market, regardless of size. The only intangible rule identified is that, within the organization, codification and formalization (of procedures, rules, skills, processes, products) are essential for growth (Chandler 1962). In a population of companies (taken at random), a correlation may exist between age and size but this is not always proven. In this same population, for a given size, several different *organizational forms* are generally present. Historically, from a timeline since the beginning of the European industrial revolution (noted IR*), from 1770 onwards (and rather 1790 in France), we can see a trend in the evolution of forms through choices of adaptation to new phenomena (more or less brutal) or to different circumscription parameters (contingency). The trend is the reflection of decentralized behaviors that converge in the same direction. The dynamics of evolution and decentralized change are initiated by each company as a proactive or adaptive entity in an environment that is co-constructed and shared by all and that can be subject to sudden external shocks. A historical overview allows us to understand that a company can be born at the beginning of the industrial revolution, transform itself as its market expands (quantitatively, qualitatively, geographically) and reform itself (or adapt in the event of a crisis or problem) in order to avoid disappearing without this being a general rule.

Thus, a company born in the industrial revolution can still exist today (e.g. DuPont de Nemours, a company founded in 1802 by a French nobleman who emigrated to the United States of America) or can have completely disappeared. The creation of companies has been numerous in all eras, but mortality has also been high in all

3 INSEE is the abbreviation of the French government agency "Institut national de la statistique et des études économiques".

eras. A major question remains that of the growth of the company, by transition, from the individual company or the start-up to the large enterprise (LE) when its deliberate choice is to grow (some choose not to grow). The corollary of this analysis is the speed of transition from one form to another.

The diachronic perception of the dynamics does not prevent a synchronic perception, at a given moment, with a cross-sectional view showing a diversity of sizes (IE, VSE, SME, Int., LE) of enterprises – which are not at the same stage of evolution and/or do not want to grow (enterprise keeping a small size to maintain a limited production and quality to preserve knowledge, a know-how, an authenticity) – but also a diversity of forms.

Comparing implies taking companies of the same age, in the same sector, on a particular market, in the same cultural context and in a homogeneous geographical area (within the Organisation for Economic Co-operation and Development (OECD), for example, as it is delicate and anachronistic to compare European and Chinese companies).

We can also try to detect a general law of the demography of the organizational forms of companies (apart from the temporal dimension and historical anchoring) rather than looking for criteria of birth, evolution and disappearance of companies (beyond even a particular case of company).

The concept of the company, in the modern sense, makes sense with the industrial revolution. Any company, at this origin, marries the *simple* form (which today corresponds to the IE, the SME or the start-up). The economic life not being an eternal homogeneous ether, the evolution is permanent. Any historical transformation has an irrevocable character (Georgescu-Roegen 1971). Permanence seems to be that of the socio-ideological substratum of market transaction (relatively immutable) since at least A. Smith with his famous book, published in 1776. Each period of time is affected by a combination of specific variables and requires appropriate responses from companies, not taking into account the anticipations of the most proactive actors (the latter will be ahead of others and will do better than others but will not escape the general context of the moment).

It would then be futile, beyond the birth of a form (a form espoused by symbiosis or impelled by necessity at one period), to predict the death of the form:

– on the one hand, because the forms coexist synchronically, through a distribution of roles in the economic and managerial universe;

– on the other hand, because, at the diachronic level, the required evolutions telescope the forms and produce mutations from one form to another without ever liquidating the previous form or forms.

Over the period 1790–2010, the simplified typology of the organizational forms of industrial companies can be broken down as follows: simple (S), functional (F), divisional (D), matrix (M), network (N) and virtual (V). The holding form (H), which is excluded here, allows for lubrication and flexibility of the economic machinery, via legal and fiscal advantages, but at the risk of emptying the company of its industrial substance for the management of a financial portfolio (which is denounced by Chandler 1977), one possible role of which is the conservation or transmission of patrimony. We can therefore attempt to establish a *theoretical table of the demography of the organizational forms S, F, F', D, M, N, V of companies*. The evolution is not automatic, but merely shows a trend. It would take a long time to explain the phases of transition from one form to another. Each pure form represents a typical model. Each typical model is the result of reflections and/or managerial practices, at a given period, taking into account the experience acquired from previous forms, in order to respond to unmet structural needs. Each model is associated with academic authors (who generally observe rather than anticipate evolution). Only practitioners (such as Ford for the F-form or Sloan for the D-form) were designers, practitioners and anticipators.

The simple S-form (from the IE to the SME) is emblematic of the original capitalism of the beginning of IR (IR*), which persists today and which Knight (1921) defends.

The functional form F was set up at the end of the IR by: Taylor (1911) in terms of the organization of work (through parceling out with the aim of productivity); Fayol (1916) in terms of hierarchical rationalization; Ford in terms of supply, via a business model[4] (a model for all based on the productive efficiency of volume and standardization) as well as, at the commercial level, via the creation of a solvent demand (purchasing power through an attractive salary). This is perfectly in line with a project emblematic of the industrial revolution, namely the democratization of the product, i.e. the sale to all of a good previously reserved for the elite (for instance, the automobile in the case of Ford as a company).

These last three creators provide complementary contributions from an efficiency perspective (at the risk of excessive verticality and task specialization leading to staff exhaustion and demotivation). The reforms implemented to correct the excess of the F-form, based on the work of E. Mayo (whose initial objective was to seek, by means of environmental factors, the conditions that would allow

4 The business model can be defined, in understanding, by a few main characteristics: a fine analysis of the external and internal value chain; a perception of the key moment and the nature of the value creation generating a specific offer; a mobilization of dedicated and relevant resources to do so; an operationalization inducing a martingale (of success, via a cash machine) to generate revenues.

productivity to be increased), led, later on, to the hierarchical-functional Staff & Line form, denoted here as F', where expertise, the quality of the work environment and the reintegration of laterality into the organization made it possible to improve the functioning of the F-form, but did not transform it into its substance.

The divisional form (D), introduced by Sloan (head of General Motors and Ford's competitor) to promote product differentiation as early as the 1930s (and even more so with the advent of pull marketing after World War II), was later theorized by Chandler (1962, 1977) as an essential key to the growth of the company open to the world. This form is still one of the most widely used by companies today.

The matrix form (M) emerges at a singular moment in the history of humanity to carry out a particularly complex project, unprecedented on the scale of the planet, articulating complex complementary sub-projects: to make humans walk on the moon (requiring the solving of so many problems: the rocket, its propulsion, the lunar landing module, the diving suit, the return to the Earth, etc.).

NASA was the instigator of this M-form. Only a few private companies, resolutely oriented towards innovative projects that are technologically, commercially or culturally complex, have adopted this M-form today.

The forms mentioned so far refer to an intra-organizational logic. A significant evolution has been to no longer simply consider the intra-organization but to consider the inter-organization following the example of the network form. The N or network form (*network of companies* or NoC) has imposed itself by being inspired by the Japanese *J* resilient customer–supplier industrial network organization, which makes it possible to offer high-quality products at a price that was then inaccessible to other western firms, as well as to innovate at distributed costs. This *J* model, theorized by Aoki (1986), constitutes a major evolution in industrial organization by systematizing the pairing of business refocusing and outsourcing (which implies strategically defining the business and outsourcing all activities that are not part of it, while preserving, if possible, secondary activities that are useful for the renewal of the business); the outsourced parts remain necessary for the realization of the final product. With each company being refocused on its core business, networks of complementary activities are formed. The network, around a coordinating actor, brings together competent and innovative complementary actors.

Outsourcing takes place outside the company's borders in the local or national space. If outsourcing takes place outside the national framework, it is referred to as delocalization. Delocalization is increasingly disputed, but the return of products to western countries is to be distinguished from inversion and from reversion (see Chapters 5–7). Depending on the needs of the *business model* chosen, no function can escape *a priori* to outsourcing (e.g. outsourcing research and development (R&D) is no longer necessarily a marginal phenomenon (Bouvier-Patron 2009; Appendix 3).

The turn taken by companies in the 1980s, consecrating the network form (N), generates a more open organization crossed by a widespread innovation. Basically, there is a new economic and social dynamic referring to a possible new industrial revolution. The network form can give rise to a bifurcation on a variant: the virtual form (V). The virtual form corresponds to an extension of the network form in a dematerialized way by first mobilizing ICTs (then the DTs): the Internet in particular. The abolition of the physical and/or geographical and cultural frontier of the enterprise is the most visible characteristic of this form, in addition to the preponderant role taken by technology at all levels. This is obviously true beyond the lone *start-up*.

Recent developments, incorporating ICT and DT, tend to associate a geographical place of collective creation and a geographical virtualization to extend the community and the exchange of information or practices: a network form incorporating an open FabLab is an illustration. All organizations are concerned, the only question being whether the FabLab is outside the walls or within the walls of the company. *Innovation platforms* (Merindol and Versailles 2017), specialized by major innovative project (thus reviving the matrix form but beyond the intra-organization), make it possible to geographically localize and mobilize skills (from various horizons and specialties), as well as methods (ICT and DT technologies; FabLab-type organizational methods; test centers; showrooms) in a spirit of communitarianization of innovation.

Everything here seems to be focused on fluidity, agility, adaptation, experimentation, learning and evolution, relying on the structuring concepts of bricolage and improvisation, within the framework of an open community and mobilizing the technological means of ICT and DT as the key to innovative creation. If the ICT and DT dyad is a promising combination that should be valued, three-dimensional printing (or 3D printing within DT) will play a growing role in the industrial organization and the organization of the firm because it generates a revolutionary way of designing and producing. 3D printing emerged in the early 1980s for rapid prototyping.

The major characteristic of 3D printing (Berchon 2014) is the method of *additive manufacturing* (AM) – adding material layer by layer – as opposed to the usual *subtractive manufacturing* method known in the processing industry since the beginning of IR (IR*) – by progressive removal of material or deformation of material. All known 3D printing technologies today are based on the formation of the virtual 3D object in successive 2D thin layers: the layers are deposited one after the other, by fixing them to the previous ones, to constitute the final real object. Three main 3D printing techniques, which appeared successively, coexist today:

– *Fuse deposition modeling* (FDM) where a filament of synthetic material, usually plastic, is melted through a nozzle. Trademarked by the Stratasys company, this process was improved in 2005 with the *Replicating Rapid Prototyper*: the first printer with documentation freely available on the Internet and a machine itself under GNU GPL license[5]; and others are now available in open source.

– *Stereolithography apparatus* (SLA) using in general a special resin sensitive to ultraviolet (UV) treatment. The patent was filed in 1984 by the founder and director of 3D systems.

– *Selective laser sintering* (SLS), a technique similar to the previous one, but where a laser agglomerates a powder rather than resin. Intended for R&D, these printers have the advantage of allowing the choice of printing materials as long as they can be reduced to a homogeneous powder.

This last process is also valid for metal (*Direct Metal Laser Sintering*, DMLS), a key area of research and development. Boeing and EADS are now using the technique to build aircraft parts.

3D printing, initially adapted to specific local unit production, is seeing its limits being exceeded at all levels:

– reduction in the cost of machines and raw materials;

– choice of the size of the series (small or large);

– increase in precision, quality and speed of printing, as well as in the choice of materials or colors;

– the possibility of printing any type of object by its nature or size (the technique of contour crafting, via a 3D printer larger than the desired object, makes it possible to build a house, for example);

– design software that is less and less complex to use and/or recourse to scanning or to digital model files available on the Internet;

---

5 The GNU GPL (GNU for *Gnu's Not Unix*, an operating system inspired by Unix but with an open source code; GPL for *General Public License*) dates from 1989, but its origin dates back to 1983 with the *GNU Manifesto* of the hacker Richard Stallman establishing the first rules for the use of Free Software (from the *GNU* project, which can be considered as the basis of Linux – designed and released under the GPL by Linus Torvalds in 1991). Stallman, in 1985, actively participated in the creation of the Free Software Foundation (the term *free* being, however, contested because it is fraught with ambiguity) before Eric Raymond proposed, in 1998, that the *Open source* project widely accepted and diffused today.

– for objects linked to combinations of ingredients that cannot be printed in one piece, each ingredient can be made alone and then assembled.

The network-virtual-FabLab-3D articulation is a powerful economic vector with immense potential for transforming industrial organization (but the health and NE impact of 3D printing has yet to be assessed). The breakdown between industrial production in companies (in whatever form: S, F, F', D, M, N, V) and domestic production (household, family, artisanal: traditional and/or virtual) and/or henceforth also in open collectives or even in solidarity and social forms can play like a cursor that can call into question the founding model of development known since the beginning of the industrial revolution (IR*). The division between this new mode of production and the old one may be sectoral (due to the importance and necessity, or not, of equipment or infrastructure industries; or for collective or voluminous objects) or according to the typicity sought and/or the small series for micro-markets. The company will remain as a physical place of production, but it may be reserved for certain productions of equipment or intermediary goods or downstream, as an interface with the final customer (unless we are betting that the latter will replace everything else and become its own producer in all fields).

The network form, by its flexibility, and without specifying its morphology *a priori*, can be sufficiently generic to think of its deformations, by decomposing/recomposing the enterprise organization in different ways. The superimposition of the virtual form on that of the network completes its protean character. 3D printing opens new perspectives in terms of the design and production of artifacts.

On the demand side, if the former customer becomes the designer, producer and user of their own needs, and if everyone has ICT- and DT-related means at home or in a shared place, the whole production–distribution–sales chain will be modified.

Individualism, an essential value in the West, already at the center of political revolutions at the end of the 18th century, the concern to differentiate ourselves socially and economically in the 19th century, and then the rise of the consumer society in the 20th century, now sees a technical, practical and ethical solution with ICT and DT. The individual can envisage a project and/or a specific fabrication, alone at home (Do It Yourself, DIY) or in a collective (Do It With Others, DIWO) at the FabLab, generally by joining a *community of practice*[6].

---

6 As a first approximation, the *community of practice* is defined as *a collective of individuals who are passionate about an activity (related to technology), who are involved in a common approach through the practice of the activity and who communicate regularly with each other.*

The network form extended to the *virtual* form generates a new potential of creation/production/distribution through ICT and DT.

The brakes to the hyper-decentralization generated are rather physical constraints measurable in terms of health risks (still to be evaluated), space (to install and carry out the desired production), human–machine cohabitation, nuisances (storage, sensitive nature of inputs, upstream or downstream pollution of inputs or outputs, noise pollution, health risks). This is why IE, VSE and SME companies are still led to play a key role as an interface: through design/production, upstream, with final customer downstream.

The current period is a potential source of a new economic and social dynamic that can be drawn around three main scenarios (and a possible evolution from one to the other) depending on the intentionality of the actors and their effective actions:

– continuation of the current trend where large key companies have large R&D center(s) operating within classical customer–supplier networks and/or feeding a nebulous virtual quasi-network to ultimately serve the end customer (whose role is rather passive);

– dominance of a few large technological companies, upstream of other (large or small) dependent ones, the former piloting a real and virtual nebula, leaving a superficial congruent portion to individual initiative; with relay SMEs serving the final customer;

– decomposition and/or sustainable splitting up of large companies (at least in the OECD), except around a few technological cores driving the virtual economy (e.g. the GAFAM, Google, Apple, Facebook, Amazon, Microsoft or Intel), to the benefit of a complex and decentralized nebula shaped by the in-built dynamics of technology and the virtual economy, where all the individual or collective actors become entrepreneurial-bricolagers.

At the industrial level, the S, F, F', D, M, N, V forms of enterprise will remain. The probability of each scenario occurring will depend on the progress of technology, especially 3D technology, and its dissemination to the end customer, as well as on access, via the Internet, to the democratization of 3D modeling. This raises the recurring question, since the beginning of the Internet and digital technology, of the management of proprietary solutions and, alternatively, of the possible use of free software through open source. In any case, each form corresponds to a pivotal point in the evolution of the historical context. The proposed summary Table I.1 is indicative and can be read in columns.

The company in the modern sense appears with the industrial revolution (in the phase: IR*), and any company, at this origin, is an IE that marries the simple form.

The non-liquidation of the previous form (immortality of the form but potential mortality of a singular enterprise) is tangible even for the functional form (F) announced as dead at the end of the 1960s in the West (because it was rendered bloodless by its organization), is present today in growing countries such as China, India, Bangladesh or Brazil and can find a new youth in Japan with the very advanced robotization (labor substitution by capital).

Forms	S (IR*)	S	F, F'	D	M	N	V
Birth trend	(1790)	Creation	1900	1950	1970	1980	1990
Evolution: growth	(1850)	If ≥ 5 years	1914	1980	Possible but rare	1990	2000 Internet bubble
Evolution: transformation	1900	Choice to maintain or Δ form	1960	1990	Possible (return to D or to N)	Potential and permanent	2010
Stabilization	If life and if choice	If life and if choice	1940	1960	1980 (as well as punctual)	2000	?
Death of the form	Never	Never	2030 for BRIC? … but pursued with robots in Japan	Never	Never	Never	Never
Mortality company associated	High but creation and after 1900 where concentration	Raised (bankruptcy) … but creations	Raised from 1970 onwards bankruptcies	Low and/or redemption or merger	Low Abandonment for reversion	Low Recombined (mortality = nonsense)	Raised But other issues: redemption

Table I.1. *Table of demographics of organizational forms (source: author)*

Japan, with a declining demography (and not compensated by immigration, voluntarily, for the sake of cultural identity), can find its economic salvation via the functional form by using massively in the near future robots (instead of people), which can constitute, in addition to the return to the myth of the flexible company without people, an essential competitive advantage (strong decrease of the wage bill and/or of the charges on the personnel or even decrease of claims or conflicts, of accidents and professional diseases).

Japan is at the forefront of the design and development of robots and does not hide its ambition to replace people with them whenever possible. In this context, there is no reason not to (re)mobilize the purely functional form to produce goods.

The organizational question is then settled from a certain point of view, with the same causes producing the same effects; this perspective engenders even more of the systematic exhaustion of resources (once all people have been mobilized, all other economic factors are exploited (and/or wasted) and all natural resources are destroyed). The search for a viable alternative is the subject of this book.

However, before this new perspective, in order to capture the essence of change, now going back to a more abstract level, it seems essential to us to seek in order to characterize the complexity and the organizational dynamics.

I.2. Increasing interactions between firms

Economic dynamics are characterized by the complexity of growing and evolving interactions (intra- and inter-firms) within a competitive as well as cooperative environment through open innovation, the adoption of rival technological options, spatiotemporal contextualization, the key role of the inter-organizational network, contingencies and customer demand. The managerial issue is the articulation of complexity and the stability/dynamic dyad; this generates change.

I.2.1. *Complexity and stability/dynamics dyad*

Simon (1947, 1957, 1969, 1980, 1982) is one of the great architects of the organizational complexity sciences, whose flagship concept is that of the open system.

At the basis of complexity theory, we find Von Bertalanffy's systems theory (1968) (where any system is composed of five elements: inputs, process, output, environment, objective), as well as Wiener's (1948) science of systems (or cybernetics, a concept coined in 1938), which explains the system as a set of interacting elements, the whole having properties (characterizing the dynamics of the system) that each element does not have in isolation. A distinction is made between a closed system and an open system: the difference between the two is the openness to the environment. The *system* can then be defined as a *set of elements in dynamic interactions forming an entity (with an external limit) organized according to a goal*. We also obtain, as a joint product, the definition of the organization (by specifying that the goal is intentional and emanating from a human collective) and even, at the same time, of the company (by specifying, moreover, that the goal is lucrative).

The properties of an open system are as follows: finality (a goal); equi-finality (different ways are possible to reach this goal); complexity (see below); feedback (existence of feedback and acting information); homeostasis (the capacity to reach an equilibrium despite the turbulence of the environment); and non-summability (the whole is greater than the sum of the parts).

For the rest, we will remember that complexity is constituted by a large number of elements (potentially varied in nature) in interaction, generally open to the environment, in a dynamic process that can be unpredictable.

A fundamental law of complexity, established by the neurologist and engineer Ashby (1958), in the footsteps of Wiener (1948), is *the law of required variety of the system*. "Variety" is the count of the number of different behaviors and states measured for a given system.

This law states that the *more complex a system is, the more complex the system's control system must be* in order to respond to the multiple potential disturbances (from the environment, for example). It is therefore imperative to preserve the internal variety of an organization in interaction with an environment (potentially infinitely complex) in order to allow regulation. Moreover, Ashby (1952, 1958) proposes the distinction between adaptation and learning where learning is the strong concept: the system first treats a perturbation as minor (single loop) and then, if it leads to failure, it learns and treats it as major, generating a modification of the action pattern (double loop).

There are therefore two forms of feedback according to Ashby (1952): single loop to avoid repeating the error made; and double loop to significantly modify the action pattern. Machine learning, through the programming that follows, aims to imitate the functioning of the human brain (which will lead to AI).

The combination of the two effects at a higher level, the triple loop (mobilized for organizations by Argyris and Schön (1978)), makes it possible to insist on the importance of the operational proposition of learning to learn as a generic skill. The limit of the approach lies in the trial-and-error selection procedure through answers drawn from a prior reservoir and through an automatic procedure. Organizational learning, in the absolute sense, should be a controlled process (whether the change is internally generated or externally initiated by positive capture or forced import), inherent to the functioning setup in a particular organization and allowing for adequate management in the face of uncertainty and for any source of uncertainty. In other words, the art of steering under uncertainty cannot normally be linked to pure luck but should result from the intuitions and procedures learned (and, logically, regularly updated by the collective of actors constituting the organization under consideration), experimentation, learning, bricolage and improvisation.

Opportunities are offered by the economic environment, regardless of the weight of the past, the trajectories or the orientations chosen, but on condition that they can be seized. The ability of firms to reposition themselves and/or capture new opportunities is essential in the framework of strategic management (Ansoff et al. 1976; Ansoff 1979) and/or in competitive positioning strategy (Porter 1980, 1985). However, this is only fully possible with open (and proactive) organizations, which think in terms of skill renewal and learning (Penrose 1959).

Everything moves, but decision-making implies the existence of relative stability (useful for creating value) at a given moment: hence the stability/dynamics dyad. Simon (1980, pp. 52–57) explains this clearly: the process of evolution leads to global qualitative leaps from simultaneous adaptations of each element that is at the basis of it; however, this is only possible because there are stable principles that ensure and preserve the potentiality of this evolution. It is a question, for example, of the genes in biology (Simon 1980, p. 56)[7].

In economics and management, finding the equivalent principle is very difficult, but it could well be (Simon 1980) organizations and markets (which are always regulated in one way or another – the more they are deregulated, the more the state is the guarantor of the last resort – to restore stability, even when there are profound changes in the system, often perceived as crises). North (1990) and the institutionalist current have explored this axis. Moreover, Simon (1980), Powell (1990) and others reject the market-organization dichotomy[8] (initially established by analytical convenience as well as by neglecting the essential role of the environment and interactions).

In a dynamic framework where interactions are increasing between actors, within organizations and between organizations, coordination configurations are renewed through bifurcations. We must therefore consider the dynamics of business organizations (generally in cooperative interactions: Ring and Van de Ven 1992, 1994)[9]. In this context, the role of interaction, self-organization, learning and renewal plays a major role. If we take a closer look, the trade-off to be made is a double consideration (apparently contradictory), which can be summarized as the stability/dynamics dyad. This is in line with the intuition of Weick (1979, p. 215),

7 Simon (1991, 1993) insists on resistance or weighting factors and/or altruistic attitudes, which stabilize the environment and therefore do not generate a population *equilibrium* based on individual and selfish behaviors (generally favored in economics).

8 Contrary to an idea that has gained ground in economics and management since the work of Williamson (1975, 1985), which took up and systematized Coase (1937). On the whole of this problem, see Bouvier-Patron (1993).

9 In the context of noncooperation, we return to more classical and static debates opposing market and organization, as in Imai and Itami (1984).

for whom the need for the firm to function requires a trade-off to be found between stability and flexibility: the stability/dynamics dyad.

Simon (1976) suggests using procedural rationality in the context of bounded rationality, where it is important to insist on the fundamental character of the processes of stabilization of the environment[10], as well as of the moments of rest (suspensory) between two search procedures (launched by the company) when we accept the idea that the firm is subject to a bounded rationality of the actors since Simon (1972, 1976, 1978, 1979, 1982, 1986). The clarification concerning stabilization is of great importance, because by sometimes focusing on sectors of the economy that are subject to rapid rates of change and to the weight of permanent disequilibria, we often come to consider that there is a perpetual search.

First of all, the existence of a search should not be confused with the statement of the obvious that it is not possible to predict, locally or globally, the future behavior of the economic system (even though we try to build possible scenarios). Secondly, it is even more important to remember that the setting of objectives, their attainment and their possible revision are inescapable phenomena of human activity requiring the formation of anticipations and conjectures about the future, and that this attitude contributes to what tomorrow will be like. The close interweaving between the necessary principles of stabilization so that organizations can function, and dynamics so that they can evolve obliges us to consider a rereading of the firm. Naturally, the field covered, in order to envisage new angles of analysis and with the help of tools linked to new approaches, is vast, and we propose to explore a necessarily restricted domain: that of the firm and its economic environment, or rather, in order to avoid remaining in this misleading dichotomy, which is the source of many misunderstandings, that of the firm in interaction with other firms in a given environment. This interactive dimension is not thought of in a static way and is necessarily based on dynamic reasoning in which the dimensions of learning and change play a full part. Let us look at the foundations of a first alternative paradigm to the standard approach, then at the hinges of the evolution of thinking about the firm, before tackling the contributions of complexity to the theory of the firm and of organizations.

I.2.2. *Reform of the standard framework*

The positioning of standard analysis (or reference analysis) in economics has the merit of clarity and efficiency by relying on robust analytical and mathematical bases with the search for the necessary and sufficient conditions for the existence and stability of an equilibrium, from the microeconomic point of view (producer and/or consumer), as well as from the macroeconomic point of view: with n agents

10 Simon (1958, pp. 389–392) emphasizes the role of institutions in stabilizing the environment.

supplying and buying *x* goods (products and/or services) that can be exhaustively counted (in understanding), on *m* markets and *p* prices; these prices allowing, via the markets, the coordination of the *n* agents between them through their exchanges on the *x* goods, the vector of prices having to be such that it allows the supply–demand equilibrium. This initial framework is called *pure and perfect competition*. The refinements made to incorporate observed facts, while maintaining more or less the reference framework, lead to a more open variant of *imperfect competition*, to take account, for example, of *imperfections* in competition (Cournot 1838; Chamberlin 1933), *outsourcing* (Marshall 1890; Pigou 1920; Samuelson 1954; Coase 1960), *indivisibilities* and *returns to scale* that disrupt marginalist reasoning (Sraffa 1926).

The question of the existence of *collective goods* also arises[11] (Samuelson 1954), of *information asymmetries* (Knight 1921; Akerlof 1970) or, more recently, the recognition of the importance of the existence of *network infrastructures* and *network outsourcing* (Katz and Shapiro 1985; Farrell and Saloner 1986).

Developments on *information asymmetries* are absolutely central to contemporary analysis, and it is interesting to note that they result from pioneering work that was initially little considered (Akerlof 1970) or has been relatively forgotten since its publication (Knight 1921).

It is not advisable to link information asymmetries and agency theory because taking into account information asymmetries has a meaning and a usefulness in itself (whereas agency theory[12] is a particular reading of the implementation of the management of a contract on the insurance model). The question of informational asymmetries reveals its full importance in strategic interactions via game theory (where it is even more important to take into account the relational symmetry/asymmetry: (Bouvier-Patron 1995)) than in a hierarchical and fixed reading of a relationship (as established by the principal–agent or agency theory).

The agency theory is closely linked to the insurance question[13] where the premium that can be paid, once the participation constraint has been met, is conditional on the revelation of information and/or a private characteristic. The insurer seeks to have as many insureds as possible so that the premium to be paid is as small as possible while remaining acceptable, if not attractive. The premium must

11 Public goods are difficult to divide and, *a priori*, are available to all without generally reducing competition for access to them; these goods are nonexclusive, therefore, non-reservable and nontransferable against private payment.

12 For an in-depth presentation, see Sappington (1991).

13 The insurance principle is based on the calculation of the risks incurred by a population likely to be affected but not *a priori*, on the basis of risks and risk factors previously listed by the insurer.

not be too high so that people can continue to insure themselves (participation constraint); unlike in certain medical specialties where the cost for the doctor to insure themself is too high (or for art museums with their paintings). The agency theory is useful, provided that its limits are understood and that no attempt is made to generalize the approach to any situation.

In the case of *adverse selection*, the principal's satisfaction depends on hidden information known by the agent but not observable by the principal (or even observable but not verifiable): the objective is therefore to induce the agent to reveal this information. The contract is thus designed in such a way that the agent reveals the desired private information (the most cited example being that where the employer (principal) is unaware of the productive characteristics of the employee (agent) and must set up a contract with the appropriate incentive constraint).

In the case of *moral hazard*, the variable hidden from the principal is the agent's own action (and no longer information): thus, for any job proposal, the employer is taking a risk because the employee may not make the effort (a "shot in the dark") but receive the wage (at least as long as they are not detected, because the risk for them would then be dismissal). The level of the wage (and the risk of losing it) can be the incentive to reveal the effort.

The principal–agent model intends to apply to the intra- (e.g. employer/ employee) as well as to the inter-organization (e.g. principal (DO)/subcontractor (ST) where the principal gives a task to the ST agent who performs it). We can define subcontracting as a situation of *two distinct decision-making entities in an economic relationship – called the principal – where we delegate a task (more or less complex) to the other – called the agent (who performs it) and is therefore unable to know or estimate without error the characteristics of the agent and/or their actions, while their income depends on it.* The principal therefore implements a contract that incorporates a participatory and incentive mechanism in order to encourage the signing of the contract, on the one hand, and the revelation of hidden information by the agent and/or to encourage them to undertake the best action on the other. However, the agency model intends to govern all client–supplier relationships, whereas it should only apply to a marginal fringe of the spectrum reduced to DO/ST relationships (thus to quasi-integration (Houssiaux 1957)) because it stumbles on the strategies, *bargaining power* and *skills* of providers (see Bouvier-Patron 1994a, 1998b, 2002, 2011a, 2013, 2017a). Moreover, as soon as subordination has to give way to strategic inter-actions, game theory eliminates the idea of *economic agents* to retain only *actors* whose strategic role is restored, at least partially, by noncooperative games.

Contemporary contract theory, at the heart of important advances in economic science, also often favors agency theory, whereas the primary orientation of the logic of contractualization (since Coase 1937), and the most interesting one at that, is based on *incomplete long-term contracts*.

The dual prism of game theory and incomplete contracting has led to particularly remarkable advances in industrial economics and the theory of the firm (Tirole 1988; Holmstrom and Tirole 1989). Nevertheless, game theory is designed to search for computed solutions (unique and stable) in an abstract way with an effort of realistic contextualization. It is rarely about forging and exploiting strategic tools that model the functioning and real life of organizations. However, real actors make bets in a context of radical uncertainty. This is not captured by pure standard theory, revisited or enriched by postulating that firms maximize their profits (or earnings) and survive, sequentially, only by respecting this rule. In the real world, an organization is born, lives and can die, with more or less success in its development and its business, in a variable temporality and sometimes suffering very significant failures without ever being able to maximize and, what is more, in an immediate way.

The evolutionary theory (two of whose main roots are to be found in Schumpeter (1939) and Penrose (1959)) undoubtedly represents, since the publication of Nelson and Winter (1982), an alternative path to the standard theory. Nevertheless, it must be considered as an ambitious but rather incomplete and imperfect attempt. At the outset, two key arguments are put forward, as a basis for the alternative, to explain evolution and change:

– instead of optimization, individual behavior (and then, at the higher level, inter-individual interactions relies on the *level of satisficing* (Simon 1976, 1978, 1979, 1980, 1982), as well as on *routines* and the *tacit character of knowledge* to be able to innovate (March and Simon 1958; Polanyi 1966);

– the *survival* of a firm in a market is possible without its conduct being governed by the (profit) maximization rule.

These are two important breaks with standard theory. Perhaps paradoxically, it is also the treatment of interactions and routines that deescalates a very serious limit to the approach proposed by Nelson and Winter, as interactions are simply ignored (because they are locked in the black box of routines already retained) and any significant intra-organizational conflict remains within certain limits and follows a certain trajectory consistent with the routine in progress[14].

Strategic interactions and conflicts disappear in the framework of evolutionary theory in favor of general principles of *selection* (which comes exclusively from the environment with an induced causality that brings us back to a crude contingency

14 Nelson and Winter (1982, p. 110): "Manifest conflict follows largely predictable paths and stays within predictable bounds that are consistent with the ongoing routine".

theory at the organizational level) and *adaptation* (concerning organizations comprising individuals walled up in their firms and their routines within a trajectory). The evolutionary edifice, as it stands (and even conceding that it is not a finished theory), thus ignores degrees of strategic freedom and conflict.

It is particularly unfortunate that the evolutionary paradigm suggests that individual free will disappears in favor of a naturalistic logic in terms of biological robot species. Biological robots (of evolutionary theory) are replacing mechanical optimizing robots (of standard theory), thus ignoring the importance of strategic interaction and conflict in organizational functioning, complexity and dynamics. Thus, the evolutionary and standard paradigms constitute useful reference points for analysis without being very convincing (Paulré 1999; Bouvier-Patron 1999). An important point, however, has been the explicit recognition by the evolutionary current of the greater validity, in economics, of the Lamarckian hypothesis in relation to the Darwinian hypothesis concerning evolution[15]. The example generally used is that of the giraffe's neck. In Darwin's explanation, all neck lengths exist at the outset, but selection favors the long neck that allows giraffes to grab foliage from above (inaccessible to other herbivorous animals) in a context of scarcity of foliage in the African bush and with the benefit of being able to eat in safety, stabilized on all four legs, while being able to retaliate if necessary or to flee. In Lamarck's explanation, the need to grasp foliage from above implies an animal intentionality. This intentionality, linked to a vital need, implies a push of the neck in time (from generation to generation by continuous improvement) where each useful organ develops.

In any case, in view of the increasing interactions (notably because of the relations between organizations), conflicts, complexity and dynamics in the observable economic universe, there is a general disqualification of the standard economic or even evolutionary explanatory framework.

In both cases, there is determinism: the mechanistic scheme of standard theory or the selection scheme by the environment in evolutionary theory. The useful framework must integrate interactions, conflicts, complexity and dynamics.

In fact, the standard approach was renewed by the theory of imperfect competition (as early as Cournot in 1838, but which was rediscovered late) with market imperfections (through, in particular, *outsourcing* with Marshall in 1890 and *information asymmetries* with Akerlof in 1970). If everything is reduced to

---

15 Saviotti (1996, p. 36): "Firm Strategy and search activities imply a degree of intentional behavior in the presence of uncertainty. While it is true that the outcomes achieved differ, sometimes considerably, from the goals pursued, it is also true that *ex ante* adaptation of firms to their external environment to firm requirements are essential components of firm behavior".

individual maximizing behavior, the theory of contracts (*first* or *second* rank), used within the theory of agency, can mechanically deal with the problems of moral hazard and adverse selection, when the interest of game theory is, precisely, to insist on strategic interactions (by preserving maximization). Evolutionary theory refutes maximization but eliminates strategic interactions. For more realistic behaviors, the theory of organizations is not out of the field but is much more used in management than in economics. Here, Simon (1947) opened the way to a better construction of an economic and managerial theory of organizations, much more mobilizable than the one linked to the neo-institutionalist current à la Coase–Williamson, which is a very particular, albeit widespread, part of it (contemporary institutionalism being better represented by North (1990)). The fundamental contribution of Coase (1937) is indeed the highlighting of the incompleteness of contracts, which is still an open and fruitful paradigm today; mobilized by Williamson (1985) in the coordination of specific assets but taking up work on strategic interaction, such as that of Schelling (1956, 1960) concerning a relational model (with *hostages* and *hold-ups*). To muzzle interactions, authors close to standard microeconomics (Klein et al. 1978; Grossman and Hart 1986; Riordan 1990), invoke the *difficulty of writing a contract that should lead to internalization* (or *vertical integration*). This is a denial of reality. As for Hart and Moore (1990), they develop a contractual axiomatic around *complementarity*[16] of *essential assets*[17] and the question of *replaceability* (indispensable versus dispensable)[18].

16 *Complementarity* (Hart and Moore 1990, p. 1135): "Two assets a_m and a_n are strictly complementary if they are unproductive unless they are used together" (pp. 1144–1145); "If asset a1 and a2 are strictly complementary, then integration always dominates non-integration. [...] In words, suppose that two assets are (at the margin) unless used together, but they are owned by two different people. Then making one of these people the owner of both assets will help outside agents, who have to negotiate with only one person rather than two people in order to use them". Transaction costs will be mechanically reduced in case of integration (but by whom on whom?): the *bargaining power* of each party is the key and, in such a case, would rather argue for a partnership.

17 *Essential* (Hart and Moore 1990, p. 1138): "An asset a_n is essential to an agent if the marginal product of investment for the agents in a coalition will not be enhanced by agent unless the coalition controls a_n".

18 *Indispensable* (Hart and Moore 1990, p. 1133): "An agent is indispensable to an asset a_n if, without agent in a coalition, asset a_n has no effect on the marginal product of investment for the members of that coalition"; Proposition 6, "If an agent is indispensable to an asset, then he should own it [...]" (p. 1134); "What happens if a whole group of agents are indispensable to an asset? In this case, one (or more) of the group should always be given control over the asset. In the extreme, when all the agents are indispensable to all the assets, the control structure is unimportant". *Dispensable* (p. 1136): "If agent k were not a member of a coalition, the coalition members could hire an outside agent to replace him".

Let us distinguish between *ex post* complementarity and *ex ante* complementarity, because Hart and Moore's definition of complementarity can only be used *ex post*, i.e. once coordination has been achieved between several firms. This coordination makes it possible to have at our disposal all the skills required to develop a product (through client–supplier relations between, on the one hand, the firm that wishes to develop the product, called the *coordinating actor*, and, on the other hand, the other firms that provide the other required skills). This idea is translated by the generic concept of *specific relationship* (in Williamson, for example): as a result, complementarity exists (as a consequence) of the construction of relationships linked to the joint elaboration of the product. Once this construction has been made, the definition of complementarity in the sense of Hart and Moore is applicable. Hart and Moore's concept of *replaceability* applies only to an agent towards an asset, but not to an asset towards another asset. For Hart and Moore, this makes it possible to distinguish a productive structure composed of asset(s) with individuals that are, or are not, replaceable from the point of view of access to these asset(s). However, it is even more important to study the *replaceability* of an asset with respect to another or other assets, and if we replace asset by *skill*, we obtain the key idea of the *replaceability, or not, of a skill*. With the idea of the *non-replaceability of skills in the broad sense*, we arrive, at the same time, at the strategic idea (as opposed to the technical angle adopted by Hart and Moore) of *ex ante* complementarity in the sense of Richardson (1972): a coordination of complementary skills, distributed in distinct firms, in order to produce a common product at a later date. However, it is not *ex ante* and/or from a logical or technical point of view that *non-replaceable skills in the strict sense or essential skills* (by analogy with Hart and Moore's (1990) definition of *essential asset*) are identified, but rather according to the competitive context and the power relations in presence.

These power relations are expressed by the respective *bargaining power* of the different actors (Porter 1980; Aoki 1986; Asanuma 1989; Bouvier-Patron 1994a, 1998b, 2002, 2011a, 2013, 2017a)[19]. Several cases can be envisaged: firstly, that of a complementary skill that is engaged but difficult to substitute by another. This is what the situation of the monopolistic upstream service supplier accounts for; as opposed to competition in skills, which leads us to consider their substitutability by others, depending on the existence of several firms capable of supplying these skills.

Richardson (1972) contrasts similar activities with complementary activities and thinks of industrial organization through inter-firm relations based on the necessary articulation of complementary activities distributed in distinct firms to produce a product.

---

19 Thus, *bargaining power* (Bouvier-Patron 1994a, 1998b, 2002, 2011, 2013) is positively related to the *level of skill* held, the *scarcity of that skill* and the *difficulty of replacing that skill* (non-substitutability) with a competing one.

In summary, we can retain Hart and Moore's (1990) concept of complementarity as *ex post* complementarity. On the other hand, we will oppose *complementarity of skills* (in the sense of Richardson and expressed in a similar way in Hart and Moore (1990), by the idea of *non-replaceability*) to *replaceability of skills*. With regard to the competition of skills, we can consider the substitutability of each of them according to the existence, or not, of firms that are substitutable from the point of view of their respective skills.

The choice between several suppliers *ex ante* often leads, once the relationship with one of them has been established, to the constitution of a *specific relationship* by the effect of *first mover advantage* (Lieberman and Montgomery 1988). The established relationship is a source of learning and mutual enrichment. Of course, potential competition is always latent (and acts as an incentive before, during and after): a pro-tendering procedure remains possible and actionable in case of problems. However, if a supplier already has *ex ante* a strong skill (*ex ante* complementarity of essential skills between customer and supplier), the substitutability of this skill becomes very difficult. This more or less amounts to an upstream situation of monopolistic supply. Potential competition only becomes possible again via an *ex post* bidding procedure if there is the same level of skills available but at a cost that is generally much too high (due to the loss of relationships, without even considering the cost of establishing a new relationship with the new selected supplier).

In short, a firm must produce a product based on the synthesis of several ingredients required to obtain this product. Each ingredient is realized with the help of one or more skills not necessarily existing within the firm realizing the product (especially as the massive tendency to refocus on the business of the 1980s and the generalization of the network form) and must call upon providers whose skills are based on specific knowledge held by particular individuals or groups of individuals. There is *idiosyncrasy*[20] in the sense that the use of specific knowledge is impossible without the actor(s) who hold(s) this knowledge.

A set of skills organized in a firm, at a given moment, is called the firm's *business* if there is an identification between these skills and the strategic image chosen by the firm's management team. This choice, sometimes strongly dependent on the past, defines a specific knowledge and/or know-how on which the *reputation* is based (Kreps and Wilson 1982a). The business is based on some or all of the

20 The concept of *idiosyncrasy* was developed earlier by Hayek (1945). Hart and Moore (1990, p. 1133): "An asset is idiosyncratic for one agent if for all other agents the asset is irrelevant to their marginal benefit".

skills held: any skill belonging to the business is such that if it were removed, the company would lose its reputation. This would have the consequence of considerably damaging its turnover, as a result of the eviction of its clientele towards competitors with a stable reputation.

There are therefore also skills that are essential for the development of the product and that are not part of the business, on the one hand, and/or are not held by the same firm, on the other hand. In this case, this means that, since they are not held by the firm and although they are indispensable to the development of the product, they must be provided through client–supplier relations, provided that they have access to them. Thus, some of these skills are said to be *essential* (by analogy with the definition of Hart and Moore (1990)) insofar as the final product cannot be produced without access to the skill, and this within the framework of coordination between the client and the supplier (with, potentially, a control that can be strengthened by *property rights*): vertical integration can therefore be posed concerning skills that are essential to the development of the product but that are not held by a single firm. The inter-firm relationship can be based on a wide range of possibilities (from ST to partnership), or it can be based on mutual control (in the case of a joint-venture) or unilateral control (if one of the parties takes control through property rights, from an equity stake to influence, to direct or to decide, to vertical integration).

All skills belonging to the business are normally held by the firm, but not all the skills required to develop the product are. Thus, theoretically, the question of vertical integration potentially arises for those skills that are indispensable to the development of the product but that are not held by the firm that wishes to develop the product. However, the actual practice is different.

Analytically perceived by Hart and Moore (1990)[21], the customer–supplier relationship is envisaged on a more pragmatic level by Richardson (1972) and is at the basis of resilient functioning (Aoki 1986) when, on the other hand, beyond even the theoretical eventuality, vertical integration is sometimes promoted, *a priori*, as a necessity (see Williamson (1985)) without much linkage to observable reality.

It is true that the potentially integrating firm may ask itself the question of acquiring an additional skill belonging to the business of another firm, but without

---

21 The customer–supplier relationship is the necessary non-integration (Hart and Moore 1990, p. 1142, p. 1146) if the two *assets* are independent (Proposition 10) where each agent is indispensable (without it, we cannot use the *asset*) and/or provides a significant level of investment.

this leading to the vertical integration of the target firm. External core or *essential* skills (by analogy with Hart and Moore) are not integrated for strategic reasons linked to two causes: *the non-integration of skills into the business of the potentially integrating firm and/or the insufficient bargaining power of the potentially integrating firm*[22] vis-à-vis the third party holding the skill.

Vertical integration is often impossible. This is due to the difficulty of circumventing the *bargaining power* of the supplier, which is based on the skill level held, and the difficulty of replacing it. To appropriate such a skill is only feasible here at an exorbitant internal organization cost and dissuasive *a priori*.

In the case of vertical integration (i.e. when the two causes above, which have become clauses, are waived or not applicable), Hart and Moore (1990) indicate the possibility (for the integrating firm) of keeping, in whole or in part, the skills of the integrated firm and/or of keeping (or firing) the management team of the integrated firm. In practice, this will be done without any assurance *a priori* of the efficiency of the operation once the integration is complete.

The article by Hart and Moore (1990) is the only reference, after Coase (1937), capable of providing a lasting basis for a general analysis of vertical integration by keeping open the alternative of internalization/contractualization, even though their obvious preference seems to be for integration and *property rights*.

It is interesting to note that the analytical approach covers, more or less, the intuitions of Richardson (1972) based on common sense (and without recourse to sophisticated analytical appraisal) by the dichotomy of complementary versus similar activities in order to analyze the relations between firms while explaining, indirectly, the logic of the firm's operation. Other complementary works, such as those by Teece (1980, 1988), Dosi et al. (1990), or Prahalad and Hamel (1990), have insisted on the *importance of the core skills* held by the company in order to think and strategically delimit the core business, to base the global strategy and the evolution of the company. Then comes the question of *renewing skills* (Doz 1994)[23]: the coexistence of several activities within the company, where secondary activities (but generally complementary to the main ones) tend to serve as a support point to gradually develop a new business for the firm. The importance of secondary activities (i.e. outside the firm's core business) as a means of improving and/or mutating skills and as an entrepreneurial response to complexity and change was

22 The integrating client firm assumes that responsibility for coordinating the relationship does not mean that it necessarily exercises a dominant position (far from it) over the supplier.

23 For a comprehensive review of the concept of *competence*, see Doz (1994).

mentioned by Weick (1977). Dosi et al. (1990) have analyzed the dynamics of this process particularly well. Interactions, the nature of interactions, the capture of external opportunities, dependence on the past, path constraints, skill renewal and learning are key factors in analyzing this dynamic, and we shall now examine them. Non-reversibility or irreversibility is a crucial element, notably through the concept of path dependence (Arthur 1989) linked to the historical time and to decisions taken previously, to explain trajectories. Moreover, the phenomena of the *reputation* of individuals or firms (Selten 1978; Kreps and Wilson 1982a; Axelrod 1984) are recognized. These phenomena often counteract the determination of equilibria conceived by standard theory. The phenomenon of reputation is sometimes relativized in relation to an irreversible (and *a fortiori* irrevocable (Georgescu-Roegen 1971)) process. The reform of the standard framework always comes up against the problem of taking into account irreversible temporality and radical uncertainty. We have to decide under radical uncertainty (Knight 1921) in an irreversible open temporal dynamic. The organization operates through the stability/dynamics dyad to stabilize the environment, without ever being able to freeze it, in order to reach the fixed objectives.

Weick (1979) emphasizes that the functioning of the firm imposes *an arbitration to be found between flexibility* (to anticipate and be adaptive) and *stability* to decide with a possibility of implementation; this supposes first of all a *convention* and *anticipations* in the sense of Keynes (1936). In the industrial logic, anticipations are only possible by relying on acquired and to be acquired skills. Upstream of anticipations (Bouvier-Patron 1999), a prerequisite is the coordination (of knowledge, actors, activities, skills, organizations) through the elaboration of a common knowledge (necessary cement to build, develop and renew a profession) within a collaborating and/or cooperating inter-organization. This common knowledge is based on:

– the existence of specific private information useful to the community as promoted by Hayek (1945) and an adequate organizational weld to allow everyone to *reveal* private knowledge;

– the *tacit* and/or *explicit* character of knowledge (Polanyi 1966) and skills (Teece 1980, 1988; Dosi et al. 1990);

– the need to *reduce uncertainty* (Knight 1921; Bouvier-Patron 1996a) through organization, to combine elements (individual and collective) of knowledge, know-how, skills or techniques, as well as to create (and/or *capture* (Cohen and Levinthal 1990)), and then use new information;

– *the functioning or creation of institutions*[24], as soon as $n \geq 2$ (n individuals or organizations), in order to organize what is otherwise unmanageable: Knight (1921); Simon (1958)[25]; Bouvier-Patron (1996a, 1999).

I.2.3. *Milestones in the evolution of the firm*

The roots of the theory of the firm are already old (Cournot 1838; Knight 1921; Schumpeter 1939)[26], but its evolution is the result of jumps not mastered by the standard framework:

---

24 Schotter (1981, pp. 9–12) considers that a convention in the sense of Lewis (*social convention*: "regularities in behavior which are agreed to by all members of a society and which specify behavior in specific recurrent situations") can only ensure a weak coordination of actions in a game, because conventions have the disadvantage of requiring an external guarantee that behavior will go in the same direction; otherwise, it is impossible to prevent a unilateral deviation by an actor. As a result, Schotter (1981) develops the concept of *Social Institution* where a deviation can lead to a stable configuration producing a regularity accepted by all (convention) until the next deviation. Thus, conventions are stabilizing moments between two deviations, as Keynes (1936) already stipulated. From one stability appears one or more deviations that can be transformed again into regularities accepted by all (conventions) until the next deviation. This makes it possible to establish a procedure for the endogenization of institutions (see the concept of *plan* in Appendix 1).

25 See above. Simon (1958) discusses the role of institutions in stabilizing the environment.

26 Cournot (1838) explained a continuum existing between *indefinite competition* or *perfect competition* and *imperfect competition* (oligopoly, duopoly, monopoly). In perfect competition, there are a large number of equally small firms and the actions of each do not affect the overall supply of goods in the market. As Cournot sought to propose a coherent and formalized approach, he took, as a first approximation, the size of the firm as an explanatory variable for the formation of the market price. Moving from one polar situation to the other (perfect competition or monopolism) means making a conceptual leap between the *price taker* and the *price maker*. Walras (1874) systematized perfect competition to characterize the general economic equilibrium or GEE (whereas Marshall (1890), who was more descriptive, favored partial equilibrium and market imperfections such as outsourcing), where firms are price takers (or representative agents). On the other hand, Chamberlin (1933) and Robinson emphasized imperfect competition due to asymmetric size and the *market power* of firms that become players (asymmetric size becoming a strategic variable). Radical uncertainty (Knight 1921) and the time to innovation (Schumpeter 1939) are two other major variables of the imperfect economy. The privileged link between market power and size is a debatable hypothesis except in the monopoly case. *Bargaining power* (introduced by Porter (1980): the five forces diagram) is, in the upstream relationship, more explanatory and relevant because it is based on the skill held and its difficulty of replacement (Aoki 1986; Asanuma 1989; Bouvier-Patron 1994a, 1998b, 2002).

– Knight (1921) focuses on the capacity to decide and undertake in radical uncertainty while providing the basis for the modern analysis of the firm and organizations;

– the Knight–Coase debate, based on Knight's question (i.e. *why shouldn't a single firm do all the activities?*), initiated the invention of the theory of the firm and organizations specified by Coase (1937) with the incompleteness of contracts, as well as the make-or-buy principle (basis of the *transactional paradigm*[27]) and by Knight (1921), Hayek (1945) and Akerlof (1970) concerning the consideration of information asymmetry;

– Simon (1947), Ashby (1952), March and Simon (1958) and/or Cyert and March (1963) examine the development of a modern theory of organizations based on complexity, bounded rationality, learning, routines and conflicts;

– Penrose (1959) insists on the construction of the firm as a set of skills in a long structuring and the necessity of rapid evolutions; this approach – in terms of capacities and skills – has been rediscovered by Teece (1980, 1988);

– Schelling (1956, 1960) analyzes strategic interactions integrating the crucial parameter of contextualization and, later, Selten (1978) models these specific temporal strategic behaviors;

– Burns and Stalker (1961) propose developments on the variety and dynamics of the organizational forms of firms, according to the state of the environment;

– Ansoff (1965), starting from the strategic positioning (by preserving the intra-organization and the dichotomous firm/environment dyad), sets up (Ansoff 1979) the strategic management as the art of choosing and deciding;

– Polanyi (1966) shows the tacit character of knowledge;

– Georgescu-Roegen (1971) examines the irreversibility and irrevocability of the processes of economic life;

– Richardson (1972) emphasizes the importance of the complementarity of activities (the basis of inter-organization) in order to think about industrial organization (through the distinction similarity/complementarity);

– Caves and Porter (1977) propose the identification of strategic groups and barriers to mobility in the dynamic process of creating competitive advantages (beyond the static barriers to entry and exit of Bain (1956));

27 Comparative *make-or-buy* analysis of the activity internally versus by market transaction (with hypothesis of commensurability and measurement); then knowing the *specificity* (*non-transferability on the market*) of what is done within the firm.

– Von Hippel (1976) shows the role of usage and users in the conception of innovation;

– Weick (1977, 1979) imposes the collective and collaborative interpretative construction of situated action (or *enaction*) among a set of possibilities;

– Nelson and Winter (1982) stipulate the importance of routines and the principle of selection in the evolution of firms; Jacquemin (1985, 1988) subsequently represents industrial organization on the basis of evolutionary and cooperative selection;

– Kreps and Wilson (1982a) consider the importance of the phenomenon of reputation in the strategy of actors;

– Katz and Shapiro (1985) or Farrell and Saloner (1986) explain the adoption process at work through *network externalities*;

– David (1985) and Arthur (1989) are interested in the diffusion and selection of technological options through *path dependence* and *lock-in*: firms promoting these options as innovators or adopters;

– Porter (1985) insists on the essential role of the customer's perceived value;

– Rosenberg (1982), Kline and Rosenberg (1986), then Abernathy and Clark (1985) and Henderson and Clark (1990) renew Schumpeter's typology of radical/incremental innovation by incorporating the commercial dimension; a process integrated in Aoki's resilient network *J* functionary (1986, 1988); subsequently, the importance of uses is enshrined in Bower and Christensen's (1995) *disruptive innovation*;

– Aoki (1986, 1988) analyzes a major evolution in industrial organization: the networked operation of complementary players, each specialized in its own field;

– Brown and Duguid (1991) show the essential role of communities of practice in the diffusion and evolution of technologies.

Staying with David and Arthur, and before examining the fundamental question of complexity, in a changing universe where interactions between actors are increasing, we can glimpse a major explanatory mechanism for the current phenomena of adoption and diffusion of technological options (Arthur 1989) via *path-dependency*, *increasing returns of adoption* and *small historical events*. *Small historical events* are comparable to grains of sand that, through a cumulative effect, end up having a structuring effect leading to irreversibility (through *path-dependency* and *increasing returns of adoption*). This is linked to the *small world* argument (Milgram 1967): we do not exhaust all possible connections to reach a result because, whatever the size of a given space, we use only a few essential and structuring interactions, by proximity, to reach an objective[28]. More generally, the adoption of a standard by each individual depends on the adoption behavior of others and on convergence: hence, the notion of *network externalities* (Katz and Shapiro 1985; Farrell and Saloner 1986) linked to direct *positive effects* (as a function of the size of the community of adopters/users) and indirect effects (as the supply of compatible and complementary services – products and/or services – increases and thus extends the service provided to adopters in a spatial and temporal dynamic). This is what explains the diffusion of an innovation as well as and above all the selection between several competing technological options up to the point of technological closure or *lock-in* (Arthur 1989). In addition, David (1985) has clearly shown that the option chosen and adopted is not systematically the best one, but results above all from a convergent effect of closure (or *lock-in* (Arthur 1989)) by a critical mass of adoption.

Many efforts have been made to interpret Arthur's work: Dalle (1995), for example, proposes a model in which the choice is made between two techniques, according to the locality and the increasing returns to adoption, with mutating paths. Synthesis and overcoming work is rarer: Auriol and Benaïm (2000) study in detail the question of dependence and its emergence in the adoption phenomenon. The introduction of the *tolerance of incompatibility* variable in individual adoption and its result on the community then considerably modifies the central role played by the phenomenon of *path dependence*. Indeed, if the tolerance of incompatibility is a constitutive vector of the emergence of a *lock-in*, it engages a process of adoption that is not systematically predictable – the choice can also be made for dominated/outdated standards. Incompatibility tolerance implies that standardization (resulting from a *lock-in*) is uncertain but that the adoption process is highly predictable. Incompatibility neutrality leads systematically to the emergence of standardization (thus to an alignment with the dominant standard). The interpretation of the implicit coordination underlying these results remains open, even though the authors conclude that there is a game of myopic actors leading to unconscious maximizing behavior. Furthermore, in a dynamic model of adoption, to test the robustness of their analysis, Auriol and Benaïm (2001) show how the multiplicity of competing standards ($n > 2$) does not allow for convergence, but rather for an oscillation corresponding to a flaw in the standardization that could generate a major crisis of confidence for consumers (materialized by a critical drop in demand). In this case, there can be no form of self-organization.

28 The anecdote often cited to illustrate this concept is the one relating to the rather limited private network of contacts that a citizen of a large country like the United States has to mobilize in order to be able to transmit information to the White House.

Nevertheless, in strict accordance with David and/or Arthur, we can insist on the fact that local relations induce, through the effect of contagion (sequential transitivity), global effects (normally with feedback). There is then, in general, an orientation towards a standard among the competing options.

In complex spatial structures (such as those analyzed by the *percolation* process[29]), *the dependence on initial conditions is crucial*, thus referring rather to chaos theory. However, a system does not need to be chaotic to be complex (Morel 1999, p. 280), complexity being mainly linked to self-organization.

I.2.4. *Complexity and organizations*

Many authors propose a contextualized and precise examination of the arrangement of *small historical events* and conclude on the relevance of *small worlds* (Milgram 1967) and the *self-organized criticality* (SOC) phenomenon, highlighted by Simon (1955) and then by Kauffman (1995). Morel and Ramanujam (1999) explain and illustrate Simon's (1955) SOC concept, which corresponds to the law[30] 1/f, based on the *allegory of the avalanche*: it is only a few extra grains that produce an avalanche, and it is this quantity that should be assessed.

In simulations, it has been shown that the frequency of avalanches is inversely proportional to their size (a scarce event among time is less likely to occur today according to the law follows a 1/f distribution). Any system following this law is then called *self-organized critical* (or SOC). This SOC or 1/f principle is one of the main characteristics of complex systems. This type of work belongs to a relatively modern conception of self-organization as the emergence of a certain "spontaneous order".

Let us review each successively, to distinguish between chaos and self-organization.

29 The *percolation* consists of a slow passage through an organic sieve, or membrane, to extract the elements that are specific to this diffusion. The imitation (mimicry) of some by others, as in competitive universes, explains the generalization of the process and the possible convergence towards a place and/or an objective in an endogenous way. Diffusion, by percolation and mimicry, generates phenomena of self-organization.

30 Morel and Ramanujam (1999, pp. 281–282): "To explain the ubiquity of the 1/f distribution, Simon (1955) demonstrated that 1/f distributions correspond to the stationary state of stochastic processes where the probability of an event occurring is proportional to the number of times it has occurred in the past".

I.2.4.1. *Chaos*

For an application of chaos to the theory of organizations, we can refer to Thiétart and Forgues (1995, p. 19) who emphasize the contradiction of chaos as an apparent result of randomness but based on *a priori* deterministic behaviors. More generally, according to Cosnard (1991), chaos is expressed by a dependence and a sensitivity to the initial conditions in the sense that the imprecision of the initial conditions leads to the unpredictability of the system, which becomes chaotic. The characteristics of a chaotic system relate, at least *a priori*, quite well to what is at work in the economy:

– nothing is ever repeated identically;

– the very great sensitivity to initial conditions in the sense that a small change (in one of the initial conditions) can generate considerable effects at the macroscopic/macro-economic level;

– the determinism governing the system at the base (framework, laws, structures, rules) gives rise to unpredictable results which are at the origin of bifurcations[31].

Dooley and Van de Ven (1999) study chaos and *noise*. Thus, five models have been identified in the analysis of time series: the *static* model; the *cyclic* model (*periodic*); the *strange* model (*chaotic*); the *noises* (pink, brown, black); the *random* model (white).

The difference (Dooley and Van de Ven 1999) between *periodic* and *chaotic* is that periodic results from simple, independent linear interactions, while chaotic results from global level interdependencies. The random *white noise* model results from multiple causalities (i.e. numerous causalities that are independent of each other). When there are constraints, through interrelations and interdependencies between causes, for example, structures can then be revealed.

The random movements propagate, compared to the white structure, in the same direction (cases of *brown and black noise*) or in opposite directions (case of *pink noise*). The additional characteristic of pink noise is that it favors low frequencies.

---

31 This question is discussed without further elaboration in the appendix: see section A1.3.1 of Appendix 1. *Bifurcations* are treated theoretically by Prigogine and Stenger (1979) through *dissipative structures*. This work is conceptually inspired by Thom (1980): the *theory of catastrophes* expresses that a continuous process in evolutionary dynamics can generate discontinuity(s). The abrupt change of morphology (or singularity) is said to be catastrophic. Empirically, according to the phenomenon and the consequences of this induced change, the term catastrophic can then join the usual meaning.

I.2.4.2. *Self-organization*

However, the most important thing is not so much the periodic, chaotic aspect, the noise or the random patterns as the complexity itself.

Boisot and Child (1999) point out that, after Simon, Kauffman (1993, 1995) is the major author at the heart of the development of complexity approaches.

For Kauffman (Morel and Ramanujam 1999), two axes seem to stand out:

– the analysis of network interactions;

– self-organization on the basis of spatialized interactions.

I.2.4.2.1. Analysis of network interactions

Kauffman (1993), using the language of Boolean networks NK, proposes to study the relationships between the nodes of the network as a function of the varying degree of link density. As N represents the number of elements of the considered system, each element has a contributory share of adjustment depending on both the considered element and the K other elements. K thus represents the richness of the coupling within the network. With K = 0, there are no interactions. With K = N - 1, we have the maximum number of possible interactions (K represents the maximum number of interactions where each node is affected by each of the others). This is a general framework that is particularly useful for thinking about interactions as well as about self-organization in systems with dynamic interactions between neighboring sites (Morel and Ramanujam 1999, p. 283).

I.2.4.2.2. Self-organization on the basis of spatialized interactions

According to Kauffman (1995), a small change in behavior leads to too small a jump; the system may not evolve much (see Anderson 1999). In a chaotic universe, on the other hand, if small local changes lead to various and different peaks being reached, the system may either make evolutionary jumps without being able to stay at those reached levels, or it may end up in regions of no interest. This is because it is when the vertices tend to be close to each other that it is possible to follow a satisfactory continuous learning path (where the system can then reach higher vertices): hence, the importance of the *landscape* considered and its topology (for an application to organizations, see Boisot and Child (1999)). In space interactions, the state of a space is affected by its neighboring space(s) (see Morel and Ramanujam 1999, p. 283). Over time, the different neighboring spaces then lead to spontaneous self-organization, the number of interactions being a crucial parameter[32]. Self-organization is here relative to dynamic interactions between neighboring sites as pointed out by Morel and Ramanujam (1999).

Following Morel and Ramanujam (1999), let us draw the conclusions of the above concerning Kauffman's approach: large numbers are relevant in the experimental sciences to explain self-organization; the term large number is problematic in the social sciences because, in the case of the Internet with millions of Internet users, we are close to the experimental sciences but, within organizations, several hundred individuals must be considered as a large number; moreover, at the level of organizations, each individual plays several functional roles (while maintaining already very numerous and varied interactions with others). The number and variety of interactions do generate complexity (i.e. not everything in an organization is planned and prescribed). Organizations are complex and dynamic, depending on the number of intra- or inter-organizational interactions, learning, anticipation, the environment, internal and external changes, and the capture of external opportunities: these are the explanatory principles of self-organization and evolution. We can also consider the spatialization of the firm on a geographical level (unless it adopts the V form mentioned above) and beyond, through the peripheral circles of operation constituting a more or less structured relational network around a firm (e.g. the close environment with the network of suppliers, which is proven with the N form systematized after 1980; environment of strategic competitive interactions; sectoral environment; national macroeconomic environment; economic zone environment (e.g. EEC); globalized environment). This perspective imposes the rejection of a double cliché of the standard framework, sometimes taken up again in management: the *dichotomous firm/environment dyad*; the vision according to which the firm would be *an island in an ocean of market* (to use Richardson's expression (1972)). Thus, self-organization is the system's own capacity to develop, to learn, to acquire new skills and/or to modify its functioning from within, but always in an environment. Paulré (1997) evokes two conceptions of self-organization: 1) a system is self-organizing if it modifies its basic structure according to its experience and its environment (a pioneering approach with interactions); 2) a capacity to bring about the emergence, through local processes, of a global structure (which is thus neither imposed authoritatively by a higher authority, nor elaborated deliberately and unilaterally by the basic elements – pure emergence of a spontaneous order à la Hayek).

---

32 Weisbuch (1991) gives a more systematic presentation of the different modelings taking into account nonlinear interactions; in particular, by mobilizing *artificial neural networks* (imitating human neural learning). *Artificial neural networks* are useful for computer modeling, going beyond programmed *Machine Learning* to generate *Deep Learning*, whose purpose is to become autonomous through long and complex learning phases (according to the different layers between the input of processed information and the result produced), now relying on *Big Data*.

The synthesis proposed by Paulré (1997), in which self-organization is the capacity of a system to produce, of its own accord and not necessarily voluntarily or consciously, a structure, an organization, a new behavior and/or its own rules of operation, in relation to an environment, but where the endogenous and proactive character (with or without intentionality about a goal) prevails. In contrast, a reactive system adapts to an environment and can be, at best, resilient. What is important is the link established between complexity and self-organization.

I.3. Design, create, learn, build, modify and renew

In economics and management sciences, self-organization is essential to understand the organization and the relationships between organizations in their environment. In order to evolve, organizations depend on their capacity to adapt, on their degree of openness and on the choice of mutations which are sometimes driven by pure opportunities. The most accurate intuitive representation that we can have of an organization, at this stage, is that of a living cell in its environment, exchanging with other cells and evolving. Organizations are living, evolving entities, in their changing environment and faced with uncertainty. They learn and build to renew themselves.

I.3.1. *Organizations and uncertainty*

From the outset, it seems absurd to oppose the organization to an external environment, because the organization lives with and through this exteriority. This vision is fully reflected in the concept of *coevolution* (see Paulré 1997; and *Organization Science* 1999b): individuals or groups coevolve in the sense that not only do they structure and transform, collectively and individually, their common environment, but, moreover, because of competition, each one participates in the structuring of the environment of others. In management, Porter (1985) offers an elementary pragmatic illustration by envisaging an *articulation* of the internal/external link through a *value chain*. In fact, the success of the firm already depends, indirectly, on its competitive positioning (Porter 1980), as this is based primarily on the internal resources mobilized to achieve it (Wernerfelt 1984). The analysis of resources, thus conceived, is, however, rather static and, moreover, less perceptive than the analysis in terms of evolving capacities (Penrose (1959): *capacities*), which leads, quite immediately, to the concept of *skills*. In a dynamic framework where the multiplicity of interactions prevails, the dimension to be retained is that of complementary evolving skills between firms (Richardson 1972). To take up Simon's allegory (1991), the economic world that should be drawn from the perspective of an extraterrestrial observing human society would be that of a large collection of organizations linked together by flows that are not strictly economic.

Named the firm on the abstract level, the company is thus analyzed as an organization like any other organization, but with the particularity of buying and selling services while always striving to create a positive differential (profit) between what is sold and what is bought by it. This constraint generates an internal creation with the help of evolving skills based on coordination, a channel of which passes internally through a corporate culture, a *management style* and, externally, a *business practice*.

The operation, particular to each firm, is also the fruit of a history: this is what determines the *corporate culture* (see Kreps (1990) or Crémer (1990, 1993)); it is a question of *shared values*, see Ouchi (1981, 1984) and Peters and Waterman (1982)). The *corporate culture* is the foundation on which *a management style* (specific to the leader) will be built; the style can nevertheless be symbolized by an action verb linked to a type of organizational form: decide under informal uncertainty with the simple form "S"; command with the functional form "F"; motivate with the hierarchical-functional (*staff & line*) form "F'"; adapt-plan with the divisional form "D"; participate with the matrix form "M" as well as on which the *management* of the company (in the broad sense) is based. In addition, the qualitative arguments of *trust* (Breton and Wintrobe 1982) or *atmosphere* (Hakansson 1982, 1988, 1989), both internally and externally (in the context of business relationships), play a predominant role. In addition, corporate management is not immune to *trends* (which, at a given moment, impose themselves on managers as a matter of course). A company's trajectory is not strictly univocal and rectilinear (because of the sole weight of the past, for example) because (i) the constant interaction with the environment, (ii) the need to absorb shocks or hazards (as well as to deal with changes in the environment) and, finally the duty to anticipate (iii) future events (i, ii, iii constituting the factors of uncertainty) induce a more or less skillful *adaptive management* (depending on the know-how and the entrepreneurial mastery) and more or less brutal (depending on the severity of the impact and/or the extent of the correction/modification to be made). The uncertainty in question is indeed radical (Knight 1921): it concerns the difficulty, in a market economy, of estimating at *t0* the right decisions to be taken in order to anticipate future needs and taking into account current and future competition, the market being the natural vector of uncertainty. In an economy bathed in radical uncertainty, a particular organization is constructed as a stabilizing space, allowing the *reduction of uncertainty* (Knight 1921; Bouvier-Patron 1996a)[33] in a sufficient

33 It is this ability to anticipate future events in a context of non-reproduction of situations, each situation being unique, which Knight (1921) insists on (see Bouvier-Patron 1996a), and which characterizes the decision in a situation of radical uncertainty. The future is unknown (not objectively probable), which links Knight to Shackle (1979).

manner[34] to generate the creation of value. This reduction does not mean, however, that uncertainty has been eliminated.

In such a framework of uncertainty, Keynes (1936) insists on *anticipations* that are only possible by taking into account *conventions* (existing at t0 to orient what the possible field of the future will be). Anticipation depends, at t0, on the idea that we have of the future: hence, the importance of the question of the formation of *anticipations*, as actors can only think, at a given moment (t0), about the future according to the idea they have of it (at t0). Does this mean that they are self-fulfilling prophecies? The convergence results from mimicry (which is also at the origin of *speculative bubbles*) generates a spontaneous order via interactions. The driving force is the attempt to reduce radical uncertainty (which can be seen as a process of creation/destruction of *anticipations* and/or *conventions* of the moment). The revision of *anticipations*, to make them adaptive without breaking them, is a specifically managerial issue (Simon 1958).

In the total absence of objective information on what the future will be and/or even of a weight (objective or subjective) of a probabilistic type, orienting them in one direction rather than another, decision-makers act by "feeling", relying on the convention of the moment. The equiprobability of the situations envisaged, but without being able to envisage the consequences and scope, is a situation of indecision, as Keynes (1921) evokes, even supposing that all eventualities can be counted and apprehended by the decision-makers. The decision is made under radical uncertainty (on this issue, see Chapter 1).

When a possibility is so likely to appear or not appear and, as in the practice of industrial decision-makers, we must very often reason in pure strategy (and not in mixed strategy as a financial decision-maker does when they calculate the average expectation of profit). Nothing can be decided *a priori* and uncertainty remains. However, decision-makers always have some idea of what they want to do and what might happen (without being able to establish a subjective probability distribution). This is why the ability to construct a representation is fundamental, and this ability can go against the general opinion or, on the contrary, be merged with it by mimicry and conformity to the convention of the moment. Uncertainty can therefore be perceived as a surprise (Shackle 1961, 1979) as to the gap between the knowledge

34 For Knight (1921), the main method of *reducing uncertainty*, or *grouping*, consists of socializing uncertainty. By extrapolation, the idea of *grouping* can be analyzed as a structuring of the environment through *pooling* and common *procedures* in order to obtain an assurance on the means that can be mobilized when the uncertain entrepreneurial decision has to be executed. However, there is no reason to limit this assertion to the internal organization of the firm.

available and that needed to follow the path towards realization (and by reference to what has been conceived and/or adopted by simple mimicry).

Learning has its place on a path to be followed and/or discovered. If the repertoire of possible answers for the decision-maker is sufficient and/or satisfactory, the available knowledge base is robust in the sense that it allows for adaptability; the initial system of representations is sufficiently flexible. If this does not prejudge the potential obstacle of the limited rationality of the decision-makers or the intertemporal validity of a routine, imagination and creativity take precedence.

Internal stimulation is achieved through creativity methods: the most basic is that of *brainstorming* initiated by Osborn (1953), within the BBDO advertising agency (cofounded by Batten, Barton, Durstine and Osborn); and/or other more sophisticated methods articulating use–feasibility–viability, such as the *design thinking* popularized by the IDEO agency (founded in 1991 by Kelley and Brown; see Brown 2008). The latter concept is due to Simon (1969) and was developed at Stanford University in the United States by McKim (1972): the aim is to avoid, from below (decentralization), too great a bias towards the market (and at a reasonable cost), without, however, guaranteeing commercial success. A good decision will nevertheless always be taken on the basis of a good or rather a *satisfying* representation (in the sense of *satisficing* (Simon 1976, 1978)).

The decision is based on the representation and induces a friction between the impulse of a decision to change (no matter who initiates it at the moment) and the established routine. This is what motivates Weick (1979) to plead for the search for a trade-off between *flexibility* and *stability* (stability/dynamics dyad). The apprehension of the frictional shock is relative to both the exteriority and the organizational interiority since, in the latter case, the brakes on change or *resistance* (by reflex of fear, refusal or denial) aim to maintain the organizational functioning as it is while the impulse or impulses to change aim to reform the organization or its principles. Naturally, the source initiating the change is of great importance: internally (in this case, *who* and *where* in the hierarchy?) and externally (with the consideration of new parameters, new issues, etc.).

The *management style* must therefore encourage a process of change and accompany it (without necessarily initiating it). The management style (Doz 1994) must provoke a process of aggregation of knowledge internally without leading to standardization and the elimination of the gray areas essential to creation (Thiétart and Forgues 1995). The necessary expansion of knowledge implies preserving excellence (to satisfy, better and better, current and future needs) but enriching and combining (Doz 1994) skills to meet new needs. The management style depends on who has the power. Complexity may dilute but does not eliminate the issue of power. Simon (1947), then March and Simon (1958) and, in their own way, Cyert and March (1963)[35] show that the functioning of the organization is always based on decision-making power and conflicts of interest.

The internal strategies of the actors implemented aim to ensure that their own objectives prevail and/or to arrange for their interests to be best preserved. The overall organizational process aims to get everyone to adhere to a main objective, and this is only possible if the proposed incentive is satisfactory (participation is then preferable). The structure of the organization, depending on its flexibility or rigidity, does not respond in the same way to a request (internal or external) for change management and guidance.

The principles governing the functioning of the organization are the result of a history as well as of a permanent updating. The weight of history in the construction of *institutions* (North 1990) conditions the nature of the power in place. At the same time, new external conditions, which are not necessarily foreseeable, provide opportunities for change (sometimes as radical as they are unexpected), whether salutary or fatal, for an organization or a group of organizations.

The interactions between history, structure, culture and power, within the organization or between organizations in an environment, therefore, seem essential to understanding complexity. Change, whether proactive or by necessary adaptation (as well as *resistance to change*), is inescapable whether it is linked to an innovation or results, for example, from a merger operation (desired or experienced).

Managing to isolate the nature and source (who initiates it?) of change should not obviate the need to look at the consequences in terms of interactions in, on and around the organization, at several levels:

– the individual intra-organizational level;

– the organizational level of inter-individual exchanges (Simon 1947);

– the inter-organizational or inter-firm level (customer–supplier relations with Richardson (1972), Hakansson (1982), Aoki (1986), Farrell and Gallini (1988) and Farrell and Scotchmer (1988) on the one hand; alliances with Harrigan (1985a, 1985b) and Dussauge et al. (1988), and even external growth with Ansoff (1965) or Chandler (1977), on the other hand);

– the level of interactions with the wider environment (competitive, sectoral, macro with public policies, final customers, etc.).

35 It is the question of conflict of interest, through the formation of coalitions (notably the majority coalition) within the organization, which is dealt with by Cyert and March (1963), while singularly neglecting the analysis of change. However, the analysis of power issues linked to the analysis of change is essential.

Guidance in the face of radical uncertainty invariably leads to a questioning of the existing situation (which is itself linked, more or less, to a given trajectory), as well as of the internal capacities available (particularly in terms of R&D, as in Cohen and Levinthal (1990)).

Organizations have the capacity to resist selection principles or to anticipate in radical uncertainty thanks to the creation of an adequate level of uncertainty reduction (Bouvier-Patron 1999). At the same time, several different organizational forms coexist.

I.3.2. *Building within and between organizations*

The variety of organizational forms in the industrial organization, with the coexistence of several types of organizational forms, at the same time, ensures that the community, as well as each firm (by learning from the neighboring position), can adapt and respond to a variability of contexts: there is *coexistence* on a synchronous axis and *coevolution* on a diachronic axis.

The phenomenon allowing these forms can be summarized in the degree of decentralization of information processing (Radner 1992)[36], certain contexts or environments (e.g. those that are turbulent or change very quickly) induce the need for a strong decentralization. Less abstractly, Burns and Stalker (1961) envisage restoring this diversity by referring to states of the environment (E1 (stable); E2 (intermediate); E3 (unstable)).

However, from a logical point of view first (causality) and then from a contextual point of view (variety of situations), it is impossible to be locked into an overly deterministic reasoning.

In fact, if the environment induces the organizational form in the sense that the latter must adapt mechanically (and thus determine the evolution of the organization), as Lawrence and Losch (1967) do, this amounts to adopting a deterministic point of view. Every organization must adapt to the demands of the environment. This purely contingent approach (where the environment considered determines the organizational form) is similar to the evolutionary approach of Nelson and Winter (1982) where the environment acts as a selection process for organizations.

---

36 Radner (1992) sought to mobilize some knowledge about computer network architectures in an effort to show the relationship between the degree of decentralization of information processing and the reduction of organizational response time.

On the other hand, the opposite determinism advocated by Chandler (1962, 1977), that of the power of large vertically integrated firms dominating or forging their environment, may be true in individual cases but very excessive in the general case.

We therefore have the following opposition: a pure contingency approach[37], determinism also found in Nelson and Winter (1982) where the environment is the selection mechanism; a Chandlerian *organizational strategy push* approach, with decisional determinism.

The conceptualization proposed by Weber (1922) to analyze bureaucratic systems is still relevant (Kimberly and Bouchikhi 1995; Meyer 1995; Boisot and Child 1999). Is Max Weber's *ideal type* a tool or a norm? *A priori*, the argument that deviation from the ideal type leads away from efficiency locks the analysis into comparative statics. However, efficiency is not necessarily measured in relation to the *ideal type*[38] but in relation to its virtuality in action. This is what induces the possible existence of transitory forms. The challenge is to move from a static comparative to an effectively dynamic approach.

There are transitory inefficiencies between two ideals and that firms are, in real life, in the movement between two and never on an ideal type. Real firms are always evolving. Evolution is the possible consequence of at least one contingency factor (or, conversely, for Chandler, of the strategy pursued).

The theories of contingency are certainly widespread and diffused, and they have the merit of helping to take into account the diversity of organizational forms. However, certain simplifications reinforce a deterministic reading focused on an environmental causal factor. Thinking in terms of a post-bureaucratic model to go beyond contingent approaches to the organization is not new, since Weick (1979) very early on emphasized, on the one hand, the importance of the role of the environment on the organization, while insisting on the permanent interactions between the organization and the environment, and, on the other hand, the process by which leaders (the *enactment* process, see Chapter 7: decisions made in a situated way, in action and experimentation), select and eliminate and then appropriate and impose elements among many other possible ones.

---

37 This can be linked to Nelson and Winter (1982) for whom the environment acts as the selection mechanism.

38 For Lawrence and Lorsch (1967), there is no organizational ideal in the sense that each organization must adapt and be flexible to meet the demands of the environment.

Whether as the basis for a typological approach or as an analytical reference, the hypothesis put forward by Max Weber in 1922 (in opposition to Aristotelian thought) – and taken up by Burns and Stalker (1961) – has been fruitful, never invalidated and remains as modern as ever: Burns and Stalker (1961) distinguish, following Max Weber, between *mechanistic* (vertically hierarchical) and *organicist organizations*. Mechanistic organizations are represented first by the F-form (by three layers of contributions: Taylorist on the double separation of design and execution, centralization of decisions, division of work into compartmentalized tasks, disciplinarization; Fayolist on the unity of command; and Fordist on standardization to reduce costs in relation to the productive efficiency of the production chain and the commercial strategy). Then, they are represented by the form D (set up by Sloan and theorized later by Chandler). Organic organizations are represented by the M-form (matrix) where interactions and laterality prevail. This mechanistic/organistic dichotomy is very illuminating:

– the mode of coordination is hierarchical and pyramidal in the first case, thus of a strictly vertical type, while it is rather horizontal (favoring laterality) in the second case;

– the circulation of information is vertical in the first case, whereas it is horizontal in the second case;

– the decision structure is centralized in one case, while it is decentralized in the other;

– if the environment is codified (without any impacts or innovations likely to call into question the established routines of behavior and operation), the mechanistic model is relevant; on the contrary, when the environment is complex and changes rapidly – without reaching a breaking point – the organicist model will be more effective.

Following Burns and Stalker (1961), where three states of the environment are enviable (E1 stable, E2 intermediate, E3 unstable), Aoki (1991) makes these three states of the environment correspond to three levels of information affecting the organization's strategic plan: *i1* (no new information); *i2* (new information requiring an adaptation of the initial plan); and *i3* (new information requiring a revision of the plan). The idea of making the adaptability of the organization (*A* or *J*) to a state of the environment conditional was formalized by Itoh (1987): the *A* model (particularly well adapted to the E1 state) is opposed to the *J* model (particularly well adapted to the E2 state).

In fact, the organization with the most rigid skeleton (organization *A*) will find itself, due to its autonomy in relation to the environment, fairly well adapted to the latter if it is stable (E1) or unstable (E3). On the other hand, in intermediate situations (E2) where a continuous flow of new information requires a succession of adjustments, the most flexible organization (organization *J*) will be the most adapted (Bouvier-Patron 1994a).

The reason for this is due to the different types of variables that characterize the *A* and *J* modes of coordination: what will take precedence is the adequacy between the active variables of a given model in relation to the type of environment. If we follow Aoki (1986, 1988) on the opposition of the *A*/*J* forms, the circulation of information leads to the observation of a lack of reactivity of model A (vertical system of centralized decision that can only act too late or against time). This is an example of what can be detrimental to the management of a complex system.

Nevertheless, the reading of an organization chart could lead us to believe that the pyramidal hierarchy seems to predominate until today as a mode of coordination (within as well as between organizations). On a practical level, we can admit that the two models (vertical centralized versus horizontal decentralized) can coexist within the same organization: in the inter-organization and in the entire population of organizations. In reality, we have hybrid situations between these two management models, with, however, a domination of the mechanistic model for the majority of established companies (if we exclude start-ups, for example).

In periods when the information to be processed is of the *i2* type (as has been the case since the mid-1980s), the inter-firm dimension largely explains the efficiency of the organization of the *J* model. The vertical integration practiced by the *A* firm (Klein et al. 1978; Williamson 1985; Grossman and Hart 1986; Hart and Moore 1990; Riordan 1990) is abandoned by the *J* firm in favor of a policy of long-term contracting.

These ideas, taken up and synthesized by Aoki (1986, 1988, 1990a, 1990b, 1991), have an analytical basis for the intra-organization that is indebted to Crémer (1980) and Itoh (1987). Moreover, Crémer (1980), in the tradition of Knight (1921), shows that intra-organization with good coordination reduces uncertainty. Crémer (1990) insists above all on the necessity of the circulation of information in the organization considered as a collective process. This process is not necessarily hierarchical (due to the existence of lateral relations between the actors within the same organization). The unification of behaviors is based on taking into account the rules or even a more specific common culture (or *coding*) that is not necessarily formalized, which is also fundamental for the renewal of skills.

It can be established that hierarchy is essential in an organization, but this hierarchy is not necessarily vertical.

The *A* or *J* model (via the corporate culture and management style) is not neutral in terms of understanding uncertainty, managing complexity, organizational learning or change management. For example, Table I.2 can help classify organizations by isolating the two variables of uncertainty and complexity.

External uncertainty environment / Complexity	– Stable environment E1	+ Uncertain Dynamic environment E2
–	"F" (→ "D") Centralized bureaucratic mechanism with DT and standardization	"S" Centralized but more or less organic
+ Complex	"M" Internal decentralization by projects and sub-projects	"N" Intra/inter-decentralization and organicism

Table I.2. *Classification table of organizational forms*

Given the above, defining the concrete organization in an abstract and objective way is not so easy: the organization is *a specific coordination space – with an external limit – via a predefined hierarchical principle whose purpose is to achieve chosen objectives*.

We can be more precise: the organization is a set of rules, imposed or negotiated, to achieve objectives by mobilizing and coordinating, in a structured way, a collective of human actors (who do not necessarily have identical interests at first sight), as well as material and immaterial resources, while the organizational boundary is open; the greater the openness, the more interaction with other organizations is a determining factor in anticipating, adapting to and/or acting on the environment. The minimal implication of this last definition is that the organization is a collective entity and that the relevant space is no longer only the intra-organization as well as the inter-organization.

The double dichotomy (firm/environment and organization/market), which is always structuring in standard theory, obviously loses its meaning here. To be exhaustive, the organizational typology of firms is fairly comparable to that of Miles and Snow (1978, 1992) once the simple "S" form (e.g. SME) has been established:

– internal organization with pyramidal hierarchy (unitary or functional "F"; hierarchical–functional "F'"; divisional "D") with top-down information;

– internal hierarchical organization but with a decentralized information processing and decision-making circuit (*J* without its network (Aoki 1986));

– internal organization favoring a density of exchanges (between individuals, functions or skills) of the matrix type "M" (thus a complex internal network strongly connected); see Galbraith (1971);

– external organization, *star-shaped* inter-organization (coordination by a hub), with decentralization of information processing and decisions: "N".

In this last case[39], the hierarchy of the network is *horizontal* (for Richardson (1972) and Thorelli (1986)) but essentially *vertical* for Aoki (1986).

The "N" network form contains more or less complex configurations: depending on the number of actors involved, the degree of connectedness between them, as well as the hierarchical relationship. The "N" approach or network of firms (NoF (Bouvier-Patron 1993, 1994a, 1995, 1996b, 1998b, 2002)), although independent, confirms the work carried out by the marketing–purchasing current in management whose emblematic figures are Hakansson (1982, 1988, 1989), Valla (1982) and Thorelli (1986).

We thus obtain the typology of organizational forms of firms: S, F, F', D, M, N, V.

I.3.3. *Learning and renewal of skills*

Not all forms have the same capacities or abilities. The ability to change is based on at least two main generic factors: learning and renewal of skills.

Let us consider these two factors in turn.

---

39 In the upstream vertical relationship (customer–supplier) of complementarities of activities (Richardson 1972), the domination of one party over the other is not retained (except in Houssiaux (1957)) in the DO/ST framework and/or the theory of agency) while cooperation is prevailing (Thiétart and Koenig 1987): the hierarchical nature, in the relationship, is thus flat or horizontal (Bouvier-Patron 1994a) but this situation must be relativized according to the *bargaining power* of the supplier (Asanuma 1989). The existence of different ranks among the suppliers induces a rather vertical hierarchy in Aoki's *J*-network. The established flat/vertical hierarchy thus depends on the respective *bargaining power* of the protagonists (Asanuma 1989; Bouvier-Patron 1994a). *Bargaining power* is a different issue from that of *negotiation*, which is used in management and highlighted in economics by Zeuthen (1933).

I.3.3.1. *Learning*

The challenge is, if not to foresee, at least as far as possible, to be proactive (as opposed to defensive reactivity) and thus to get used to anticipating, or, in other words, to make decisions under uncertainty (Knight 1921; Keynes 1936).

The questioning of rules (by whom? For what interests? In which context?) that prevent the desired change induces resistance to change linked to the interests of those who rely on the prevailing routines. With a conflictual reading of change, we cannot speak of *organizational learning*[40]. In the broadest sense of the term, and to the extent that the logic of confrontation is the cause of an evolution (no matter which one) which, as a transitory result between two different states, will have enabled a learning situation to be qualified globally and roughly.

More positively, organizational learning, as discussed by Argyris and Schön (1978), is largely inspired by the ideas of Ashby (1952, 1958).

Naturally, the strength of conviction of the members of an organization, the common culture of the members, the importance of this organization in the higher reference system (economy, culture, society), the interest in the services offered (products and/or services), the ability to anticipate (permitted or hindered by the operating principles), the learning capacities, the renewal of skills, the management of the dynamic complexity of uncertainty, are all indispensable parameters for change. They are also, as far as possible, keys to bending the environment to the goals and needs of the organization when the change is driven internally and the anticipations are realized. Moreover, the potential macro-economic impact, driven by the micro-economic level, is a potential ambition of companies that want to become unavoidable (as in the case of GAFAMs, for example).

The will to initiate such an irreversibility can succeed in the context of an economic gamble, but such a success is by no means obvious. To rely on the strength of the leader's will or management style alone is a strong assumption, even though it should not be underestimated. On the other hand, we can be interested in the operating principles of an organization and evaluate whether these make it possible to manage uncertainty in an adaptive way. In essence, the problem is not to foresee what cannot be foreseen, but to have capacities and modalities of intra/inter-organizational functioning that favor proactivity and change in rules and routines, behaviors, skills and tools.

---

40 Since the work of Simon (1947), organizational learning is generally defined as the *discovery and development, through trial and error, of sets of new behaviors that form a system*.

We can therefore better understand the work of organizational psychosociologists, such as Weick (1979), who show the importance of representations and the way in which the organization manages to interpret and/or define/redefine constraints (much more, in the end, than to integrate them), as well as to take into account the difficulties or blockages initiated by the organization itself, which prevent it from achieving the goals it has set for itself or the strategies it is developing (while at the same time seizing the opportunities opened up by the more or less open and more or less changeable environment). Thus, most of the time, the company generates its own brakes or obstacles. The self-generated obstacle is a serious handicap, which makes it impossible to solve/overcome a problem or to manage a necessary change.

I.3.3.2. *Renewal of skills*

As we can understand, a real dilemma for the organization exists in the search for a stability/dynamic trade-off that is always difficult and fragile to obtain or preserve: too much uniformity prevents evolution and too much variety prevents coherent development (Doz 1994). This is particularly crucial in the case of innovation (product, technology, organization): there is a need to formalize, sometimes from scratch, what is intuitive and tacit in order to develop the necessary key skills.

At the same time, which is contradictory *a priori*, it is necessary to encourage the informal and the variety that allows for change. The development of a single core of skills maintained indefinitely is an apparent security (useful in certain sectors, such as arts and crafts or luxury goods) but which, on an industrial level, generates inertia and can prevent openings and access to future options or value creation. A trajectory is always necessary, as there is no zero-based strategy: what the organization can do tomorrow depends, to a very large extent, on what it knows how to do today, without forcing it to keep blinders on. There is therefore a certain relative determinism (what the organization can do today is the result of what was learned yesterday).

Core skills are the basis of a competitive advantage that must be built up and then developed, but they are also a potential source of inertia that can prevent responses to new situations: core skills increase the ability to deal with similar niches but, without evolution, can reduce the ability to deal with change.

It is therefore necessary to cultivate the existing core skills, as well as secondary skills. Thus, Weick (1977) insists on the importance of these secondary activities (outside the core) in order to respond to complexity and change. Linked to the primary ones, they allow the study of new combinations and avoid falling into a routine that is harmful in the long term: hence, the absolute necessity of *mobility*[41] outside of what we already know how to do. This is why the central question (Doz 1994) is indeed that of the *renewal of skills*, imposing itself in a perspective of self-organization open to the network (form N) while at the same time endowing itself with capacities of absorption (Cohen and Levinthal 1990) and/or to the business ecosystem (BE (Moore 1993, 1996, 2006); see Chapter 3).

Two things that are *a priori* in conflict must be reconciled:

– on the one hand, the codification of skills, which facilitates their internal diffusion, deepening and performance;

– on the other hand, to have skills (key and secondary), which are certainly exploited, but with a constantly broadened base (so that the competitive advantage built up can evolve and is not a source of inertia).

In terms of innovation, Henderson and Clark (1990) show the importance, for the firm, of its link to the market and the need for the process of *recombining* technologies and skills on a synchronic level (between those already existing) and on a diachronic level (between old and new), while at the same time valorizing them commercially: this is what leads these authors to speak of *architectural innovation*. This only confirms the preeminence of the success of incremental innovations over radical ones (Rosenberg 1982; Kline and Rosenberg 1986). The N form was the key to the success of Japanese companies in the 1980s before western companies reorganized and took up the challenge.

Thiétart and Forgues (1995) also insist on the need to experiment with new solutions (and therefore, at the base, on the possibility left by management to experiment with new solutions). Indeed, linear planning (rather than vagueness, intuition, free initiative) leads to a dead end. It is important to preserve variety, nonlinearity (inducing a complex amplifying feedback), the density of exchanges and therefore of interactions (internally as well as of internal/external interface). Thus, following Simon, Doz (1994) and Thiétart and Forgues (1995) suggest leaving a certain amount of flexibility and vagueness in internal procedures because exhaustive specifications and strict adherence to procedures stifle learning and openness to something else.

The *management style* can foster this necessary malleability (Doz 1994) through a process of aggregation without initiating hyperspecialization. The broadening of skills also induces the need to preserve expertise in order to satisfy, better and better, current needs, but by enriching it and combining it/recombining it permanently to

41 Such mobility is evident in a market: Caves and Porter (1977) and Porter (1979) show the existence of *strategic groups*, the mobility of firms and the need for *barriers to mobility* in a dynamic process of building a *competitive advantage*.

face new needs. Communities of practice (Brown and Duguid 1991, 1998; Wenger and Snyder 2000) are essential for this. The internal organization of the firm, whatever its form, is thus no longer the only possible vector for the valorization of knowledge. The continuous learning of communities of practice is at the heart of this vitality by allowing skills and practices to be built, developed, modified and, above all, to be acquired (by reappropriation and/or creation). A principle of self-organization of a new order emerges. It may even be a question of *unlearning in order to learn* (Doz 1994), so as not to be overwhelmed by routine but to always be in a position to question the dominant logic in order to overcome it and create or seize a new opportunity.

In short, the balance of the stability/dynamics dyad (Weick 1979) rests on its two feet: that of voluntary construction from the accumulation, over the long term, of incremental innovations reflecting an *organizational capacity to learn* (which is the ability least imitable by competitors), as well as that of the deliberate capacity to *learn to unlearn*.

Hence the importance of having a minimum internal capacity to learn (Cohen and Levinthal 1990) in order to understand the environment, to draw from it what is necessary and to stay in the race to innovate. The challenge therefore goes beyond the firm's R&D capabilities. It is a question of disseminating knowledge within the organization and/or the inter-organization by scanning all the possibilities and by building different paths that can be used to innovate. Thus, Nonaka (1991, 1994) proposes a systemic approach to the information circuit and the creation of knowledge leading to innovation.

The perspective of innovation and anticipation under radical uncertainty, at the center of which are the complexity and dynamics of the interactions of actors, is multiplied 10-fold at the intra/inter-organizational interface.

In order to innovate, the potential market embraces needs that are not yet satisfied (within the framework of existing technologies) or future needs via future technologies.

These needs cannot be durably dissociated from customer satisfaction; customers must be associated, upstream, to the innovation process (Von Hippel 1976).

Learning by Interacting (Von Hippel 1976; Lundvall 1988) is used to analyze the link between product innovation and customer(s) when mass production, more or less differentiated, was based exclusively on learning during product production (which originated in Arrow's *Learning by Doing* (1962b)).

If the fear of failure remains a powerful inhibitor in the decision, each enterprise seeks methods to dare to undertake at a lower cost, so that the trial leading, eventually, to a failure (from which we always learn something) is not done at a prohibitive cost prejudicial to the continuation. The trial can then reasonably be integrated into the strategy as a normal necessity. At the same time, it is also necessary to generate, internally, a facility to combine and recombine information and/or skills in order to try new bets that transcend the existing routine. Internally, the recombination of skills is favored, or not, by a culture of exchange, organization, teamwork, and an individual and collective capacity to question.

The main problem to be faced is the *internal myopia* that makes the available skills correspond too closely to the needs to be satisfied in the short term.

A restrictive perception of the market constitutes a self-generated brake or block (Weick 1979). On the contrary, an overestimation of the possibilities of transferring and/or renewing skills (or even the profession) creates a gap between discourse and reality, which is also potentially dangerous for the company.

It is probable that the short-term efficiency is reduced in case of a renewal strategy. Product improvements (minor or major) are the result of incremental adaptations and radical changes. The frequency of changes seems to accelerate. For a radical change, both the content and the trajectory are weakly predictable.

Evolutionary theory has attempted to respond by mobilizing the Darwinian paradigm and, more usefully in economics, by mobilizing the Lamarckian paradigm. Corporate behavior is then linked to previous experience (whereas turbulent environments only give an advantage to firms with the capacity to cope with what is new and/or to grasp radical changes).

Clarifications are proposed on the demographic processes of companies and on the effects of changing environmental conditions or of innovation without explaining the dynamic complexity of self-organized emergence of new organizational forms or their evolution through increasing interactions within open inter-organizations where co-creation of innovation takes place. Hence, the broader sweep made above.

Starting from the dynamic complexity based on self-organization, this book proposes to underline the importance of an innovation respectful of the NE by mobilizing the most adapted paths to envisage viable solutions, which passes (necessarily) by frugality, bricolage and improvisation.

I.4. From respect for the Natural Environment (NE) to frugality to innovate through bricolage and improvisation: seven chapters

The path proposed in the book consists of seven steps in seven chapters.

Chapter 1 aims to explain in detail the constraint linked to the respect of the NE as a challenge to be taken up by the company: to do so, we put forward the concept of positive private good (PPG), as well as our approach, called consequentism.

Chapter 2 focuses on the design by the technological means of the FabLab allowing *a priori* to rise to the level of the challenge. The technological ambition induced is the usual solution in the West but reveals the importance, in filigree, of bricolage and improvisation.

Chapter 3 visits the technological orientation and its exacerbation by looking at the communalization of innovation (upstream through communities of practice; downstream through communities of use) where bricolage and improvisation play a key role in creation as well as in use (through appropriation) where, nevertheless, the creation of value is shifting increasingly towards the symbolic.

Chapter 4 more precisely examines the consequences of a technological excess visible at the level of use (as well as of the offer that is at the origin of it and/or that makes it possible) and of its drifts. This does not prevent the bricolage and the improvisation of technological objects and/or their detour (among hackers and geeks, as well as, via communities, for everyone). The stake of the bricolage corresponds to a need in a claim of self by the marking. The techno-marketing that makes it possible orchestrates it when it can, unless it escapes. It relies on: places of creation; interactions between creative milieus (the informal and the links to artists and/or interlopers' worlds not to be neglected); socialization through online games (with the societal importance of *gaming*); the means of virtualization of entities (including ourselves through the avatar); objects; symbols; values; tools made available for use (mainly *smartphones* and laptops). All of this is done in connection with social networks (now structuring the technologized social life). What will not be analyzed in this book is the development of the digital by the *Cloud* linked to *Big Data* (i.e. the cloud of multimedia mass digital data whose relevant indicators of measurement are the five "V"s: volume, speed or velocity, variety, value, veracity) allowing us to treat (technically and commercially), simultaneously, a singular individual, a group, a community (or several) or the mass of the population.

In this work, either the existence of the energetic abyss of this technological mobilization will not be analyzed; what requires an exhaustive study in itself, notably as for the insufficiencies of the taking into account of the NE, as well as concerning the means in terms of renewable energies. This is already a field studied by many specialists from different disciplines.

What is important is the main observation: the universe of value dominates and technology is its power vector. Thus, artificial intelligence (AI) opens up an even wider spectrum of new possibilities (which will only be touched upon here through the question of virtual influencers at the end of section 4.3).

That said, the more technology structures social life, the more we see appropriations and/or detour (first by hackers and then by geeks), showing that bricolage and improvisation are key factors that manifest themselves both at the level of creation and at the level of use. All of these considerations lead to a plea for a counter-model likely to integrate the constraint with respect to the NE while putting the technology in its place (i.e. as a means and not as an end in itself or as a possible tool of enslavement).

Chapter 5 invites a return to common sense, after the excessiveness of technological use, and highlights frugality as a possible path to an alternative solution and as an approach likely to fully achieve PPG: this is possible by focusing the analysis on the concept of *frugal environmental innovation* (FEI), because frugality in itself does not intrinsically lead to the consideration of NE.

Chapter 6 reinforces the previous point by showing, among the *environmental innovations* (EI), the FEI as a possible business strategy based on an adapted degree of technological sophistication. FEI is the most likely potential candidate to lead to a viable solution consistent with a consequentist approach. Frugality, and frugality *a fortiori* respecting the NE like the FEI, fully integrates bricolage and improvisation.

Chapter 7, through the mentioned thread, intends to make explicit the key role of bricolage and improvisation as motivations to innovative creation. Consubstantial to any frugal approach, these springs, on closer examination, prove necessary for any form of innovation (including the most high-tech).

From a managerial point of view, admitting the importance of these factors is not self-evident, because the company is promoting a reasoning for conducting and controlling the processes involved. The aim of the discourse is to affirm that innovation is possible in the company by choosing the right methods, and even by claiming that innovation should be programmed. However, except under very specific conditions (and, in general, on the initiative of the public authorities, as in the United States: the Manhattan project for the first atomic bomb in the secret laboratory of Los Alanos; NASA's Apollo missions for the project and the unprecedented challenge of a man walking on the moon, carried out with Apollo XI in July 1969), this is very difficult, if not impossible, to achieve in the organizational framework of a company that is subject to competition and profitability requirements. This also applies to the innovative monopoly that is the key player in high tech (Bouvier-Patron 2011a, 2011b).

Unless the monopoly situation turns into an anti-competitive bureaucracy (a situation denounced by Schumpeter (1942)), as sometimes happens.

As soon as innovation is sought, the fundamental role of the mechanisms mentioned (bricolage and improvisation) is reinforced.

The key issue of the book is to make explicit the importance of PPG and consequentism leading, through frugal innovation, to the FEI, as well as the key role of the domains (bricolage and improvisation) in the innovative creation and the innovative process.

We cannot consider the envisaged progression without first insisting on the starting point of our reasoning (Chapter 1): innovating by taking into account, explicitly, the Natural Environment (NE).

1

Natural Environment, Positive Private Goods and Consequentism

Corporate social responsibility (private or public), or CSER (Corporate Social and Environmental Responsibility) of sustainable development (SD) – based on its three pillars (economic, social, environmental) – implies taking responsibility for decisions made. Taking responsibility for a decision opens up several possibilities for action, but the most widely used way of impacting the NE to date (hypothetically) consists of repairing *ex post* any harm or damage. This *ex post* approach is problematic in that it tries to ameliorate, while underestimating, the impact on NE. By focusing on private enterprise, our main objective is to show that an innovative private good could free itself from negative externalities detrimental to NE, not by repairing or compensating *ex post*, but by anticipating *ex ante*. In order to establish our point, let us recall the basic definitions of economic goods by getting to the heart of the matter.

Samuelson (1954) contrasts *public good* with *private good*. In this case, the *private good* is perfectly circumscribed by the double criterion of *exclusivity*[1] and *rivalry*[2]. However, public good is a much fuzzier term and is also a poor translation.

Translating *public good* to *collective good* (*public good* is not a term that can be reserved only for goods initiated and/or managed directly by the public authorities) seems more correct, but introduces a new potential bias unless we distinguish

1 Exclusivity: an individual is excluded from consuming the good until they pay for it; otherwise, it would be impossible to limit access exclusively and it would become difficult to charge anyone.

2 Rivalry or divisibility: what the individual consumes is no longer available to others (i.e. the availability of the good is diminished by the presence of an additional user); otherwise, the marginal cost of supplying the good to an additional consumer/user would be zero.

collective good from two other categories: i) *club good* (or *toll good*: a *club good* is a special case of a *collective good* whose consumption respects the principle of non-rivalry, but which may be excludable by a toll, because a fee must be paid to access it, as in the case of a *golf club*; but if the access fee is prohibitive, the good reverts to being almost private); ii) *common good* (Ostrom and Ostrom 1977).

Let us note incidentally that this last type of good occupies a central place in the current evolution of economic and managerial analysis, as well as for our purposes.

Collective good is mixed (both *non-exclusive* and *non-rival*). *Common good* (Ostrom 1977, 1990) is always a mixed category (between *collective good* and *private good*), but with the property of being renewable if the ecosystem remains preservable (and, if possible, through joint management within the community concerned).

There is certainly a complex intertwining, and no less complex interactions, between categories of goods in economics and/or management sciences. However, beyond this introduction, we will voluntarily focus exclusively on the link between private goods and NE.

In summary, the generally accepted categories of goods are the following: *private good* (Samuelson 1954), *collective good* (Samuelson (1954); in approximate opposition to *private good*), *public good* (defined by the government in the name of the general interest), *club good* (Buchanan 1965) and *common good* (Ostrom 1977, 1990).

By integrating Ostrom's approach[3] and by crossing the criteria of *rivalry* and *exclusivity*, the typology of expanded assets is presented in Table 1.1.

Criteria	Non-exclusive	Exclusive
Non-rivalry	*Pure Collective good* (Samuelson 1954)	*Club good* (Buchanan 1965)
Rivalry	*Common good* (Ostrom 1977)	*Private good* (Samuelson 1954)

Table 1.1. *Accepted asset typology (source: undifferentiated)*

3 Ostrom proposes a specific grid by replacing the term rivalry of consumption by subtractability of use; Ostrom's matrix results from the crossing of *subtractability of use* and *excludability* (exclusion by price), as well as by mobilizing a gradation (weak to strong) rather than a binary choice (present or absent).

Nevertheless, we can observe that this categorization classifies goods that are too heterogeneous. Moreover, a strong collinearity may exist, at least in the sense that any public or collective good managed by a *private market logic* will be treated as such, and if a *public service mission* is delegated to a private company, the management will generally be based on private performance criteria. Logically, the analysis should be split between private and public logic.

Thus, the *public* dimension (see Table 1.2) should be considered independently (without any link to Table 1.1) by cross-referencing, for example[4], *intrinsic physical decomposability* (of the good) and *individual appropriability;* knowing moreover that a potential additional axis (not materialized here), *compulsory/optional,* can improve the finesse of the analysis.

	Indecomposable	**Decomposable**
Non-appropriable	Criminal justice	Sanitation network
Appropriable	State University degree	Access to a public toll

Table 1.2. *Proposed categorization of a public good (source: author)*

We then retain that pure *public good c* is, *a priori*, indecomposable and non-appropriable (and non-transferable, therefore non-transferable except if a public decision imposes it)[5]. On the other hand, the pure *private good* is decomposable and appropriable for the very purpose of being assignable (and therefore transferable).

If we consider only private goods that can be transferred on a market, the efficiency of the market is not absolute and comes up against *market failures*: natural monopoly, information asymmetries, collective goods and externalities. Conversely, the existence of *market failures* is, in itself, a possible legitimization of public intervention (and thus makes it possible to define what can or must be a *public/collective good*); the boundary or limit of what is not private is a matter for political decision alone (which may or may not be based on an economic justification).

4 The criteria used here as possibilities are simple. More sophisticated analyses (notably, see Laffont (1988)) propose alternative categorization criteria.

5 In a liberal capitalist economy that primarily assimilates private goods, the eventual privatization of any *public c* or *collective good* (if this is not yet the case for this last type of good) can be established for the sake of homogeneity of functioning (without necessarily being desirable).

On these failures, let us stay with *externalities*[6] (a concept initially proposed, in its positive dimension, by Marshall (1890)).

To solve the problem of *negative externalities*, two main schools of thought (associated with two authors) have emerged, proposing the *internalization* of negative externalities by different means: Pigou (1920) by means of the *polluter-pays tax*, which is the responsibility of the public authorities; Coase (1960) by means of *property rights* and private market exchanges without public intervention.

Indeed, taxes are not systematically the means to be mobilized as, according to Coase, negative externalities can also be internalized by exchanges (see below), which also extends the scope of relevance of the private sphere. Moreover, the private good, anchored in *property rights*, generates a reasoning horizon (rather short term) on which an economic calculation (of profitability, for example) will be applied. Now, insofar as these private goods often generate negative externalities on a single collective good, sometimes at the international level (Kindleberger 1986), such as NE, this calls into question the calculation method usually used; and, even more so, if we associate negative externalities with the question (Georgescu-Roegen 1971) of irrevocability (e.g. the potential disappearance of NE). How, then, can private goods be produced without impacting NE or other categories? We can try to answer this question conceptually, based on a few key authors.

The link between the economy and NE is, however, complex. Before refocusing on our (private) firm and NE axis, it seems useful to outline the contours of the economy-NE nexus (for a detailed and applied view, see Cropper and Oates (1992); for an open and broad perspective, see Costanza et al. (1997a)). The issue is then mainly macroeconomic.

One possible starting point, which has received a lot of media attention, is the Meadows report (Meadows et al. 1972): this report expresses the view that with increasing population and industrial development, the depletion of natural resources is to be feared, with the possible consequence of the collapse of economic growth and, consequently, the need to slow down and/or stop its pace (hence the notion of *zero growth*).

This perspective, even though criticized and questioned, has at least led to the consideration of NE (Dasgupta and Heal 1974; Nordhaus 1974; Solow 1974a, 1974b) as a factor of production under the title of *natural capital* (alongside other factors such as capital, labor and even technical progress), and whose access price

6 An *externality* results from *an action that has a direct effect on the satisfaction or profit of a third party without going through the market*; therefore without going through the price system.

(independently of that of the exploitation of the resource itself) cannot be free. Solow (1974a, 1974b) draws on the seminal work of Hotelling (1931)[7] aimed at economically rationalizing the debate of the time (when the powerful radical conservation movement in the United States dominated): it envisages the possibility of *optimal growth* characterized (Dasgupta and Heal 1974) by the *optimal depletion of exhaustible resources*. The twofold hypothesis formulated is that of perfect substitutability between natural capital and man-made capital, as well as the transferability from one generation to another of the capital constructed by mobilizing/exhausting natural capital. Intergenerational optimality is ensured as long as the capital transmitted to the new generation ensures the same *well-being* from the point of view of satisfaction measured in terms of utility (i.e. extrapolating and in an imaginary way: always being able to feed, clothe and house ourselves, as well as consume desired and non-vital goods, move around, etc.), notwithstanding certain problems or uncertainties about the conditions (with air that is always healthy and breathable, soil that is not contaminated, the existence of flora and fauna, landscapes without concrete and water that is always drinkable). Is it a question of substituting (Pearce 1988; Pearce et al. 1989, 1993) the natural for the built, even though it is at the price of the sacrifice, more or less important, of the limited stock of non-renewable resources? Minimizing the sacrifice of substitution to consent may define a form of weak sustainability most favorable to economic growth.

However, what should prevail economically to preserve the NE is rather *Hartwick's rule* (see below), which aims to *reinvest the equivalent of what has been taken away*.

However, whatever its form, this sacrifice by substitution is unacceptable in a more pro-ecological view of the economy (see Daly (1990), Costanza and Daly (1992) and Gómez-Baggethun et al. (2010) for a more complete perspective), which favors, in absolute terms, the *non-sacrifice of the still available stock of non-renewable resources*. On the theoretical level, different reasons can be given for the decisional prudence of preempting the future (prudence being unrelated to risk aversion). Prudence applies in particular to an investment of an irreversible nature that could alter the preservation of a unique or rare asset: it is then appropriate to renounce or defer.

7 Hotelling's reasoning leads to what is known as *Hotelling's rule*. If, at a given time t, the market price $p(t)$ of a resource is available (i.e. extracted and ready to be sold) and $c(t)$ is the marginal cost of extracting this resource at that time, the value of the asset linked to this resource is $\pi(t) = p(t) - c(t)$. Taking, as a reference value, the interest rate (r), as is the case in any investment, and in order to capture the opportunity cost, the condition for reaching a market equilibrium value according to Hotelling is given by the equation: $\pi'(t) / \pi(t) = r$; *Hotelling's rule* follows on from this; see below.

The preference for preservation (or the action of deferring) can be linked to a motive of conservation (Krutilla 1967), of avoiding irrevocability (Georgescu-Roegen 1971) or of decisional flexibility (therefore versus irreversibility) in situations of uncertainty (Arrow and Fisher 1974; Henry 1974). Thus, Arrow and Fisher (1974) or Henry (1974a, 1974b) propose a form of option value (a term originally coined by Weisbrod (1964)), called *quasi-option*[8], intended to make a part of the value *forgotten* by the usual investment decision criterion explicit (based on the Net Present Value (NPV)). The quasi-option is the value conferred on the acquisition of information (knowing that the available information is, at least initially, incomplete) by the very fact of the expected benefit of preserving and/or deferring the investment decision. The decision-making here (not linked to risk aversion) is more a matter of *willingness to pay* (see below) to keep the option open. In concrete terms, the quasi-option thus represents the interest in preserving (or even deferring an irreversible investment that could affect and/or destroy the tangible or intangible asset under consideration), with a view to a hypothetical use[9] and/or the benefit of future maintenance without necessarily being able to immediately determine the importance of the asset in question.

This concept of quasi-option appears central to the relationship between the economy and NE and to the consideration of decision-making within sustainable growth. Sustainable growth can only be envisaged on the condition that non-renewable natural resources are preserved.

The debate will crystallize (according to the dichotomy proposed by Pearce et al. (1988, 1989, 1993)) between *weak sustainability* and *strong sustainability*[10]. The weak sustainability approach is mainly inspired by Hartwick (1977), who proposed a

8 In some respects, the quasi-option can be likened to an insurance premium against an irreversible decision.

9 This use is not utilitarian but can refer to the individual/collective interest of the intrinsic maintenance of the considered asset (specific remarkable or invaluable resource of a patrimonial, historical, aesthetic nature).

10 Martinez-Alier (1995, p. 6) defines weak versus strong sustainability by relying on the article by Pearce and Atkinson (1993), but essentially to take issue with the opposition made by the latter authors regarding the attitude to sustainability of poor and rich countries: "Sustainable in a weak sense if the ratio of savings to income (which allows investment) is larger than the sum of the ratios of depreciation of human-made capital and natural capital […] strong sense, i.e. maintaining critical natural capital constant." In precision, Cabeza-Gutés (1996, p. 147) points out, "Weak sustainability, as no restrictions on the degree of substitutability between natural and man-made capital are introduced."

decision rule concerning natural capital (*Hartwick's rule*: "Invest all profits or rents from exhaustible resources in reproducible capital, such as machines").

The concept of natural capital, promoted by a rather economic vision of ecology (Pearce et al. 1988, 1989, 1993), corresponds to a logic based on a principle of substitutability by equivalence. This is the idea of weak sustainability.

According to *Hartwick's rule*, the rent, equal to the difference between the selling price and the marginal cost of the depleting resource, is taken but must be reinvested in *constructed capital* (substituted from the depleting capital) in the sense that the investment to be made in constructed capital must be at least equal to the depreciated or destroyed natural capital. Accepting a sacrifice of natural resources (regardless of whether this exploitation generates direct or indirect pollution, or leads to subsequent consequences on NE through the use of products derived from this exploited resource) translates concretely into an investment made for the benefit of future generations, following the example of the Norwegian sovereign wealth fund for the exploitation of offshore oil deposits.

This is a dominant vision today, including in the criticism of the measurement of growth in order to integrate the question of a weak form of sustainability: thus, the recommendations (e.g. the report by Stiglitz et al. (2009)) do not advocate a ban on the depletion of nonrenewable resources or an exit from capitalism. They are adjustments to the emission limitation objectives, invoking realism and economic pragmatism, which can be considered as a form of regression compared to Meadows et al. (1972).

With the danger to the NE increasing – if we accept the results of the work of the Intergovernmental Panel on Climate Change (IPCC) since 1990 – the weak sustainability accepted in terms of economic policy does not imply, *a priori*, when considering drastic reforms.

However, as already mentioned, to *this economic vision of ecology*, we can oppose an ecological vision of the economy (Daly 1990; Costanza and Daly 1992) based on an idea of *strong sustainability*, mobilizing a principle of *impossibility of substitution* (non-substitutability). We are then essentially in a logic of complementarity (not substitutability), still contributing to the human socioeconomic dynamics that have led to the Anthropocene era (a new era in which human activity has a significant global impact on the Earth's ecosystem; to stay in the point of view of economic sciences, see Barnosky et al. (2011)).

Strong sustainability opens up to the consideration of the importance of the ecosystem and biodiversity with the Millennium Ecosystem Assessment (MEA since 2001), which emphasizes the dependence of economic activity on the ecosystem, even though it is increasingly degraded, or with The Economics of Ecosystems and Biodiversity (TEEB since 2007), which explains the value of the *services rendered* by the ecosystem and biodiversity, as well as the amenities[11]. Here, the measurement of (economic) value is aimed at the proper management of natural resources and not their commodification. Thus, biodiversity (Chevassus-au-Louis 2009) is now the subject of particular attention in that it is valued (if we place ourselves in a logic of economic equivalence) by the *ecosystem service rendered* (Daily 1997; Costanza et al. 1997b); sometimes, in this sense, with very ambitious projects (Sukhdev 2008).

The antagonism over weak or strong sustainability generates a form of indecision due to the respective contradictory double risk of a commodification of NE or, on the contrary, of a vision in terms of a non-renewable stock to be strictly conserved. Let us go deeper into the opposition between weak and strong sustainability.

– ***Weak sustainability?*** In a weak sustainability logic, NE would have a price that needs to be appreciated. This implies an economic evaluation of the value of the NE[12] and/or even appreciation of what is depreciated or destroyed by exploitation

11 Ribière (2010) specifies the etymological origin of the term amenity (from the Latin *amoenitas*: charm), as well as the historical attachment to the charm of the landscape during trips to France by rich Englishmen, for leisure. *Natural* amenities, services provided by the Natural Environment, are now recognized and necessary for local development. However, the question of their alteration or destruction during development is raised. The question raised refers to the value of an amenity (the theoretical link to be made to the quasi-options is obvious).

12 Hardelin et al. (2010) provide an overview of the methods for putting a monetary value on NE: direct cost according to the *environmental benefit* of the good considered, assuming that the good is portable through a transaction; avoidance cost by assessing the cost of an equivalent service to be put in place to hypothetically replace the *environmental service* provided that would be lost; price of harm and restoration; hedonic prices consisting of isolating, in the price of a good or service, the part attributable to its different characteristics with the aim of estimating the value of an *environmental service* on the basis of the price differences observed between two similar goods but located in different situations; contingent valuation based on surveys of the users of a natural area (or of local residents) in order to ask them, directly or indirectly, what value they place on it and thus their willingness to pay (i.e. *the maximum price that a purchaser is willing to pay for a given quantity of a good or a service*). This last concept is, today, widely used in experimental economics, but has been diffused in several fields of economics; its origin goes back to Drèze's article (1962) on the price of a human life (known as the Value of Statistical Life or VSL; see below).

and use, thus the corresponding monetary equivalence: hence the question of commensurability[13].

Commensurability aims to find a system of equivalence in the absence of a translation of exact equality between two different elements.

This is particularly necessary and recurrent in law in order to establish the value of a prejudice or damage suffered (in particular physical damage to a person).

This also refers to the hypothesis of substitution (mentioned above) in the case of prejudice(s) or damage(s), the cost of repair (correction, rehabilitation, restoration), (physical) replacement of the prejudice–damage on the NE and/or possible compensation (this last case, in particular, refers to a search for minimization of this cost – and thus comes under the heading of economic efficiency). More broadly, it refers above all to decision-making with a projection in time, by means of a cost/benefit approach[14]: the philosophy of use of this methodological tool makes it possible, in theory, to dispense with normative regulation imposed by the public authorities in favor of the alternative of a comparative calculation between the benefit of the decision and the cost that would have incurred if the decision had not been taken (with, however, all the approximations required to determine the elements necessary for the calculation; especially in an uncertain situation and with

13 Commensurability (versus incommensurability) is a rather difficult philosophical problem, dating back to ancient Greece, concerning a mathematical question in the case of the ability/inability to reduce the value of distinct objects to a common measure. This question has been revived relatively recently in philosophy, notably by Raz (1986) and Chang (1997). Raz (1986) uses the terms comparability (versus incomparability) and commensurability (versus incommensurability) in an undifferentiated way, whereas Chang (1997) distinguishes them. To get to the heart of the matter, comparability refers to concrete objects, while commensurability refers to abstract objects. Incommensurability makes it impossible to establish a relation of order between concrete objects, even if they can be evaluated by common criteria. Thus, to mobilize Raz's metaphor, let us take a musician's career and a lawyer's career: both can be evaluated in monetary terms, for example, but no absolute criterion can establish that a lawyer's career is superior to that of a professional musician. Incommensurability opposes abstract values that cannot be ranked and that cannot really be evaluated according to common criteria. Thus, for example, human life and economic activity and/or NE and economic activity: should activity be prioritized over the life of the employee? What would be the criteria to establish this prioritization? Whatever the measurement system, there are choices made, but not proven and indisputable solutions. Should we prioritize economic activity over NE?

14 For a critical view of this and the difficulty of taking ecological account by this method, see Bebbington et al. (2007); for the origins of the approach to the question of taking NE into account, see Krutilla (1961); for a complete perspective outside of taking NE into account in this approach with its economic foundations, see Guillaume (1972).

incomplete information or even limited rationality, while making the strong hypothesis already mentioned according to which all things have a market value). Moreover, this approach necessarily reflects an anthropocentric vision as soon as the applicative issue concerns living organisms (other than humans). Moreover, in use, there is almost a bias of decentralization of decision, potentially based on an unbridled utilitarianism, but, more certainly, (too) dependent on the individual ethics of the decision-maker (not to mention their total subjectivity). Should we therefore make it clear that, with this method, the integration of all the foreseeable *ex ante* effects in the decision is unlikely? The uncertainty that weighs on the future would imply the mobilization of the precautionary principle, which is absent from this calculatory logic. However, generally based on the cost/benefit approach, the decision taken by a private or public economic actor (with a micro/meso/ macroeconomic impact) always has an impact on reality.

An impact on the living and the NE concerns a reparation (correction, rehabilitation, restoration) and/or a physical replacement of the harm–damage related to a compensation.

It is necessary to be able to measure the impact and assess whether the decision will be effective and efficient (repair by correction, rehabilitation, restoration and/or physical replacement of the harm–damage on the NE, and/or compensation). Moreover, at what cost and for whom? Because, obviously, if the need for an economic project (debatable or not) induces a prejudice/damage (important or not), but the cost of repair, replacement or compensation is borne by the community, the gap is important. The question remains, especially when applying an ideal rule, from this perspective, of No Net Loss for the NE in terms of its intrinsic physical characteristics and/or services rendered.

– ***Strong sustainability?*** In a strong sustainability approach, should we take an NE that pre-exists human activity as a reference? How can we reason without taking into account the appearance of humans on planet Earth and the inextricable link, since this appearance, between the NE (*de facto* transformed) and human activity (existing since the beginning of humanity), even though we want to consider specifically, in an exhaustive way, the importance of the damage caused by the Anthropocene era (Barnosky et al. 2011)? The work on strong sustainability, where the ecosystem must have/recover a form of resilience (in the sense of Holling (1973, 2001)) to human influence, shows the complexity of the problems to be solved and the effects of nested scales.

The level of claim on a reference to an inviolate primitive nature (versus minimal preservation of what still remains) gives the key to the interpretation of the analysis and the spectrum of positions of the actors from economic ecology to pure ecology. We then enter into a fascinating debate, but one that is mainly concerned with the critical political analysis of capitalism or, indeed, of the exit from capitalism, taking us far from the opposition between economics or ecological management versus economic or managerial ecology.

For the following, we therefore formulate the hypothesis of a capitalist economic functioning that must take into account the constraint of respect for the environment. Also, on a macroeconomic level, the quality of the growth to be retained is important (Stiglitz et al. 2009), taking into account the impact of human activity on the NE (Nordhaus 1991, 1998) and the alarm launched by IPCC scientists since 1990 concerning the very worrying accumulation of greenhouse gases (GHGs, or GGEs for Greenhouse Gas Emissions), including CO_2 (carbon dioxide)[15], and their effects on global warming and the resulting climate change.

Thinking about responsible growth implies controlling global warming. However, the current negative dynamics can eventually be curbed, but cannot compensate for the inertia of the cumulative phenomenon (since about 1750) and the time lag between: i) the cumulative effect over 200 years already achieved (corresponding to a significant increase in the global average temperature) due to the sole effect of human activity (during the European industrial revolution from 1770 onwards, which was very intensive in fossil fuel coal, and then, in a second period after 1850, with oil and gas); and ii) the effects that can be measured today. This leads to a twofold approach: access to green growth as part of sustainable development (SD) in the sense of Bruntland (1987); and an ecological and energy transition towards this green growth, which is not instantly accessible. Green growth is not self-evident and is difficult to impose at the global level, even though it is relevant to the issue of global warming. And this, even though western countries refuse to sacrifice all or part of their way of life and developing countries are seeking to achieve the equivalent of the western way of life.

Attempts to envision a common global future have been made: the United Nations Conference on Environment and Development with the Bruntland Report (1987), which opened the debate on SD; the Earth Summit held in Rio de Janeiro in 1992, under the aegis of the United Nations, which promoted SD and concrete actions to be taken (but was limited to a declaration of intent); and regular international coordination efforts in this area (Conference of the Parties or COP). A COP leads, in concrete terms, to protocols, such as that of Kyoto in 1997, setting

15 CO_2, which is now also used as a reference to compare the emissions of different greenhouse gases (GHG) expressed in CO_2e (CO_2 equivalent). The conversion of GHG emissions into CO_2e is the 100-year GWP. The GWP or global warming potential is expressed as the ratio between the energy returned to the ground in 100 years by 1 kg of gas and that which would be returned by 1 kg of CO_2. This indicator is generally used at the international level.

emission reduction targets to be met by each nation and introducing the possibility of *negotiable emission permits*, also known as the *market for rights to pollute* (with the dual possibility of trading between companies with surplus rights and others with deficit rights, as well as the transferability of rights between countries); the public authority responsible for a given territory distributes these rights free of charge or makes them payable in whole or in part. The Kyoto Protocol was subsequently judged too ambitious by some (the United States) and not ambitious enough by others (the Europeans feared that free or cheap permits would discourage the efforts needed to curb the upward slope of global warming and that this would send a negative signal to developing countries).

These global agreements are always necessarily laborious to obtain and then to respect, given that they are non-binding commitments. These agreements are also incomplete and distorted, so that Nordhaus (2006) comes to prefer a Pigouvian tax to the chaos of the operation of the right to pollute.

In any case, the solutions envisaged for regulation can be based on three possibilities: taxes (e.g. the carbon tax (Nordhaus 2006)); market transactions (Coase 1960) attached to property rights (but valid for a small number of situations; see Cropper and Oates (1992)); and tradable emission permits (Dales 1968), as allowed by the Kyoto Protocol.

The macro vision of the problem, centered on macroeconomics and general principles, and despite its necessity and/or usefulness, does not solve the intrinsic problems of economic activity in the concrete negative externalities generated locally by the use of the good produced (after the thorny question of production, sale, logistics, consumption and recycling). Our objective is to consider this decentralization from the point of view of the decision to innovate private goods by proposing a specific approach, as well as a corporate accounting system that measures the impact on the NE generated.

We will first look (section 1.1) at the question of the usual management of negative externalities, then (section 1.2) at the *private consequentist approach*, consistent with the preservation of other *third categories*, by putting forward (section 1.3) the concept of *positive private good* (PPG) and the need for a *consequentist calculation*.

1.1. Management of negative externalities

The activity of private enterprise can generate externalities (weak or strong; positive or negative). Generally, on the NE, externalities are negative. Thus, private interests, even when regulated (Stigler 1971), have a direct impact (generally negative) on natural resources. In order to go beyond a Pigou-like logic of taxation, we can consider the management of negative externalities (section 1.1.1) through trade, the market or governance by going back to the history of economic theory and having significant points of reference.

Moreover, in examining the question of decision and irreversibility, a key question remains (section 1.1.2), that of the regulatory institution necessary to define the rights and/or implement the quotas of permits allocated within a given regulatory space.

1.1.1. *Managing irreversible negative externalities: trade and markets, governance and choice*

1.1.1.1. *Trade and markets*

By focusing only on the firms generating pollution and the goods produced (and associated markets) and on the market(s) for the pollution generated (but without taking into account the potential effects induced elsewhere: markets for inputs, factors or other goods; or the impact on the consumer whose relative wealth does or does not absorb the cost of a negative externality suffered), Coase (1960) envisages, under the above-mentioned conditions, that if property rights are perfectly defined, under the hypothesis of complete information and the absence of transaction costs (during bilateral negotiations between two polluting firms to reach an agreement that respects the interests of each party), the market can internalize externalities and thus correspond to an optimum (in the Pareto sense). This can be done without recourse to public power and without the establishment of a tax (recommended by Pigou to internalize the social cost of pollution), or without prejudging the initial distribution of property rights (the hypothesis of neutrality of the initial allocation of rights). This statement has been labeled the *Coase theorem* (since Stigler (1966)). For Coase (1960), the rights to pollute are thus not exchanged on a market, but are the subject of a bilateral negotiation between the person suffering the pollution (in a position to deliver a compensatory right) and the polluter, who must acquire the right to pollute. This situation is adapted to situations between polluters and the polluted, where the number of actors affected by the externality is limited.

Meade (1952) was the first to propose the introduction of rights associated with externalities, as well as the existence of markets on which these rights could be exchanged: this amounts, *de facto*, to creating rights to pollute. A right to pollute authorizes a certain number of pollution units. The counterpart of the purchase of these rights to pollute is paid to those who suffer the effects. The acquisition of rights (where the mere perception of the rights to be acquired in order to produce by polluting) obliges the polluter (actual or potential) to take externalities into account.

Ideally, the market equilibrium is Pareto optimal. However, who decides to issue the rights to pollute?

If it is the polluter themselves, how can we be sure that they will not try to cheat and/or act in an anti-competitive way (knowing that the number and size of each producer are not negligible data for the purposes of considering a competitive equilibrium)? This opens up the question of strategic behavior.

We owe the idea of distributing – among polluters – the clean-up effort (in favor of the polluted, as a fair compensation for the latter) and of creating a market in transferable emission rights to Crocker (1966) and Dales (1968).

Historically, Dales (1968) is credited with the concept of a *pollution market* (or *tradable emission permits*) based on property rights (on the pollution generated by an activity); rights manufactured *ex nihilo* with the often-implicit idea that if the impact of pollution is indeed global (related to the general equilibrium), it can be dealt with locally or broken down into parts (which refers to a partial equilibrium). Dales (1968) was the first to propose the introduction of a system of property rights on pollution permits that could be traded on a market, still close to Coase (1960), but he is a neo-classicist who believes in the supremacy of the confrontation between supply and demand: nothing other than the market should be able to fix a price (neither an individual, nor an organization, nor an agency). Dales' (1968) main economic argument in favor of the market is that of cost savings (compared to a solution administered by an agency or a polluter-pays tax): according to him, the market guarantees the reduction of pollution at the lowest cost to the community.

Montgomery (1972) intends to go beyond Coase's theorem (1960) by means of a *least-cost theorem* (see below), which then constitutes a strong basis for the consideration of NE in economics. It is not a question of direct confrontation between polluters and the polluted (as in Coase's case) or of Paretian optimality (where individual utilities are maximized), nor of the vision of a general competitive economic equilibrium with externalities ((Arrow 1969); a market for each externality and where the setting of the Pareto-optimal equilibrium price, on each market considered, results from the interaction of a buyer and a seller, which refers to the terrain of imperfect competition, which makes the equilibrium relative and debatable, as Arrow himself agrees). Montgomery (1972) focuses his approach, in a decentralized manner, on minimizing the costs of polluting firms, taking into account the upper thresholds of pollution authorized by the public authorities. The way to achieve this is to set up a market in pollution permits, provided that the polluting firms are in a position to be simple price-takers on the permit market and that these permits are freely transferable (from one region to another, for example).

Under the conditions mentioned, the choice of the public authority to sell the permit or, alternatively, to make it free of charge has no impact on the strategic decision and the operational functioning of a firm.

Two variables (Tietenberg 1985) are decisive in measuring the effectiveness of the permit tool: the quantity of permits (the total volume granted) and the choice of the method of allocating the pollution emission rights permit (free versus auctioned). The initial allocation of emission rights (out of the total amount granted by the public authority) determines an *ecological rent* equal to the market value of the permits. This market value represents an opportunity cost that cannot be mobilized if the company has to pay for a permit for its polluting production instead of cleaning up directly and then reselling the permit at a profit to earn an income. The equilibrium price of the emission permits is an exogenous data in the models (generally introduced, implicitly, as if it were a tax, such as a carbon tax). The hypothesis formulated (and which can be demonstrated analytically in an abstract way) is that in an ideal equilibrium situation, there is a theoretical equivalence between the polluter-pays tax and the equilibrium price of the permit.

The difficulty in assessing the true value of the equilibrium price of the permit (due in particular to the need to know the full extent of the damage) seems to be circumventable if the public authority sets a credible maximum pollution level objective (realistic in relation to the need to pollute, but without laxity encouraging de-measurement). Technically, a maximum pollution level target will correspond to the volume of tradable emission permits to be allocated. Theoretically, the socially optimal level of pollution is defined by the comparison of the costs/benefits of pollution/depollution: the equilibrium price, on the market of the rights to pollute, will be equal to the marginal cost of pollution control for all firms according to the level of pollution authorized by the public authority. The principle of tradable pollution emission permits (pollution rights markets) makes it possible to avoid the logic of taxation. Public power, and by delegation the regulator, can be embodied by and in a dedicated agency that sets a global quota of permits.

The role of the regulatory agency is to set the global quantity of emission rights that can then be traded freely. The property granted on these rights, through trading, is therefore subject to a price. Thus, the quota of rights to pollute is put up for sale by the public authority defending the general interest, and then negotiation is free on the market.

From a theoretical point of view, the equilibrium price of these rights on the market is set at the level of the marginal cost of depollution. Indeed, if it is more expensive to buy the right and pollute than to clean up, a company will choose to clean up and sell its rights (to make a profit). Conversely, if it is cheaper to buy the right to pollute than to clean up, a company will choose to pollute according to the amount of rights acquired.

The regulatory authority, which issues the rights, assesses the quantities authorized over time: it can therefore reduce them (to increase the price of these rights to pollute) or increase them (to reduce the price of the rights to pollute).

All in all, the markets for pollution rights and the polluter-pays tax are theoretically equivalent and represent two different ways of internalizing externalities: coordination by quantities (permits) or by prices (tax). Since Weitzman (1974), permits have been described as quantity instruments and taxes as price instruments.

However, certain objections can be made. For example, the determination of the equilibrium price on a tradable emission market (making auctioning or free distribution of permits equivalent, in a theoretical situation of competitive equilibrium) comes up against the reality of strategic behavior (already mentioned): competition may be imperfect (Hahn 1984), and some actors may have *market power* (i.e. *the ability to impose a price on the market*). This said, ideologically, this argument, which is obtusely imposed, never leads to advocating regulation in the strong sense (of the imposed standard, tax type). The key to the solution found is to allow the regulatory agency to play with the initial distribution of permits to correct competitive inefficiency. The structure of the market will therefore, in theory, have to dictate to a large extent the agency's decision to sell and/or distribute the rights for free. In the event that a firm has *market power*, and generally wants to minimize its costs, then it necessarily obtains rent if the permits are issued for free. Far from wanting to correct the problem, the factual finding is that in almost all countries the practice is one of free distributions. This can nevertheless be explained in a very rational way: it is a way for the public authorities to encourage firms to participate in the effort to control emissions. That said, from the point of view of economic theory, this is hardly a satisfactory argument (Hahn 1989). This is especially because, whatever the choice, low tax or free distribution of permits, one is almost at a status quo level between the existence or absence of consideration for compliance with the NE. Moreover, this does not prejudge the presence of other strategic behaviors in the bilateral relationship between the agency and a particular firm seeking a permit (see below).

Summarizing the above, in a very simplified way, we have the *ex post* internalization of observed externalities (whatever their magnitude) via the creation of *ad hoc* markets by transforming observable, priceless negative elements into goods that support market transactions. From a theoretical and ideological point of view, the solution of emission permits, at least indirectly, restricts or aims to contain the role of public power (by minimizing or eliminating the regulatory framework of binding taxation imposed by the government if it were to intervene), which then intervenes only by defining the amount of initial pollution rights and the mode of allocation (sale or free distribution). In this vision, the market would therefore suffice, in theory and in most cases, to resolve the issue of negative externalities generated locally and/or globally.

From a practical point of view, with the Kyoto Protocol, the market for CO_2 emission permits intends to impose itself on a global scale, but we find the same difficulties as in any other more restricted rights markets: difficulty in obtaining a global quota for each country and then, for each country, in distributing it equitably; difficulty in defining a coherent regulatory policy and in having an effective regulatory institution; difficulty for potential polluters to obtain an authorization (or approval) to pollute and then to have rights; evanescent control; non-existent or, if formalized, unenforced sanctions; avoidance techniques mobilized by polluters to escape responsibility. Each company has a quota of rights to pollute (allocated by the regulator) that it can use in whole or in part, and the remainder can be sold on a market like any other financial asset.

We could consider that the acquisition price of the right to pollute (sold by a third party) is an *ex ante* input for the buyer, clearing them of any subsequent responsibility; but this would mean endorsing a system based on the principle that pollution is acceptable, as is the business associated with its commodification via a transfer price.

The very fact that rights to pollute are allocated in advance (and, in reality, in a rather piecemeal fashion) poses a problem: on what basis and with what induced entrepreneurial responsibility?

The arbitrariness of the regulatory body can never be ruled out, as it is very often influenced by lobbies (as Cropper et al. (1992) have shown very well).

The particular market for trading rights (after initial endowment) is in name only, as it is in fact a matter of over-the-counter arrangements rather than a supply–demand balance of a large number of actors interacting simultaneously.

To consider other alternative derivative issues, in return for a permit to locate on a site and/or exploit its resources, a *compensation permit* (Gustafsson 1998) commits the company to compensate, by equivalence, for the harm caused by the industrial and/or commercial project on the ecosystem. The challenge here is to create, hypothetically, an *environmental gain* at least equivalent to the damage caused thanks to an effective action plan in kind: to destroy (in part) the NE by rebuilding it in another way or elsewhere; but is this even possible? Thus, would buying a permit to operate (with harm to the NE) be sufficient? Does this permit allow us to avoid the possibility of uncontrolled consequences in the future?

At both the global and local levels, the government (or governments), in the last instance, has (have) to deal with the consequences alone (e.g. oil spill, explosion of a chemical plant, etc.).

The essential disadvantage of the previous approach of rights to pollute is twofold: the weakness of regulation (not to mention a rather permissive laxity); not internalizing the extent and/or irreversible nature of the damage. At this stage of the resolution of negative externalities, if we renounce the market and return to Coase-style exchanges or, on the contrary, to nationalization (nationalization through collectivization is equivalent to a confiscation of the NE in the name of the general interest), any purely market-based approach amounts to a Malthusianism that generates rent for the benefit of the owner(s), without providing any assurance of the consequences for the NE.

1.1.1.2. *Governance*

Ostrom (1977, 1990) offers the particularity of proposing a decentralization of the governance of a good without prejudging the regulating authority (government, collective, organization). Ostrom's classification grid (1977, 1990) establishes that the *common goods*, particularly those related to NE, are not in themselves *collective* goods. Thus, a *common good* is more or less *rivalrous*, but it is, or becomes, *exclusive* only through a *convention* on the resource (e.g. through the establishment of a fishing quota). The convention structuring and governing a common good implies that it should not be considered as a belonging (contrary to the logic deployed by Hardin (1968)), but as a *collective property* with, as an absolute necessity and horizon, the renewal of the resource.

Common goods are based on systems of common, endogenous and accepted rules (in which each person ensures that others respect their use), allowing everyone (each member of the community) to access the resource and benefit from it. The mutual respect[16] necessary for this endogenous management system to function first of all requires *trust* (Breton and Wintrobe 1982), i.e. a social construct based on the belief that the commitment made by others will be respected. This is a *social construct based on a belief in the respect of the commitment made by others*. It also presupposes a study of the deviations of the *focal point* (Schelling 1960) on the rendez-vous (point of convergence), as well as the remedies to the deviations

16 It is an order of *reciprocity* from the sociological and anthropological point of view (and not simply the monetized one of economic exchange). Should we go so far as to speak of *gifts* and *counter-gifts* in the sense of Marcel Mauss?

(settlement of potential conflicts within a particular community). The efficiency obtained is then superior to any other because, potentially, the positive externalities generated will be maximized and the negative externalities reduced to a minimum. Everything rests here, in an endogenous way, on the free elaboration and acceptance of decentralized rules and their respect (returning to a cooperative strategy of the dynamical *tit-for-tat* type[17]), therefore without any known temporal end by the users (Axelrod 1984).

To broaden the relevance of the subject, let us note that economic and social relations can easily mutate a *common good* into a collective good by the necessity, sudden or progressive, of having to produce it (in a more or less artificial way[18]).

Thus, the private company as an organization (every company is an organization, but not every organization is a company) can therefore, through its activity, *be a stakeholder* (Freeman 1984) in the management of an *environmental common good*. As a result, Ostrom's approach, through decentralized governance, appears to be a possible path, at least as long as private activity, in a competitive market universe, does not generate strong negative externalities that prevent the renewal of a resource. Thus, the degree of negative externalities appears to be the cornerstone of any (micro/meso/macro) economic reasoning on NE: the externality has a measurable *amplitude* by an increasing gradation of irreversibility up to the *irrevocability* (Georgescu-Roegen 1971) of the damage caused to a site or a resource (generally unique, limited, exhaustible), and this up to the point of its potential disappearance.

An economic opportunity to destroy a heritage (e.g. *Notre-Dame* in Paris to build an office building[19]) opens up, more broadly, the question of *option value* in the sense of Henry (1974a, 1974b) and also refers to the concept of quasi-option.

1.1.1.3. *Decision and irreversibility: the choice of option*

In the deterministic and linear view of the investment decision (see Massé (1968)), everything is plannable *ex ante* and the calculation to be made concerns the net present value (NPV) or its optimized variant of the internal rate of return (IRR).

---

17 The strategy of one player at *t0* is dictated by the action of the other at *t - 1* and, without a finite horizon, cooperation sets in (by necessity and selfish interest at first).

18 Artificially, because rapid industrialization and urbanization generate strong negative externalities, as well as a scarcity of resources that are still preserved (hence the importance of *natural parks* or the *law to protect the coastline*). The reproduction of indispensable resources (e.g. drinking water) then becomes an *artificial* industrial process.

19 In the words of de Jouvenel, B. (1968). *Essais sur le mieux vivre*. Éditions Sedeis, Paris.

In economic life, however, an investor (called an option holder)[20] must consider the uncertain eventualities of the future. This is linked, initially at least, to the search for decision-making flexibility, which is nevertheless costly. It is then necessary to identify the degrees of flexibility of the contingencies in order to value the options that will model them (the option is not an exogenous data but results from the modeling process). The valuation of each option makes it possible to compare their respective costs. In the case of an investment decision modeled by a *call option* (versus a *put option*), the cost will be embodied by the strike price; a cost that cannot be recovered, generally, in the event of an unfavorable time trend. In option theory, the investor's decision is made under uncertainty with probabilistic risks (and not under *radical uncertainty* (Knight 1921))[21] preserving flexibility (versus irreversibility).

20 Beyond even the financial investor, because the theory of *real options* (since Myers (1977)); in investment strategy (Bowman and Hurry 1993), derived from that of *financial options* (Black and Scholes 1973; Merton 1973), confers the right, not the obligation, to exercise the option. This option may be an investment in an underlying non-financial asset that is not easily fungible (such as an R&D project, equipment or property). *Real options* are not *real contracts* (with *ex ante* contractualization between parties, lifetime of the real asset, existence of a primary or secondary market).

21 The formalization of uncertainty adopted by Schmeidler (1989) and then by Gilboa and Schmeidler seems to us to be problematic in that Knight (1921) characterizes racial uncertainty by the necessity, for the responsible and consequent entrepreneur, to have to decide in a non-probabilizable radical uncertainty, as well as to involve themselves (in an irreversible way) on the basis of their expertise and their intuition, by inference, on what tomorrow will be (while acting to reduce uncertainty in and by the organization of the activity). Schmeidler's model is probabilistic, using the concept of *capacities* (from the mathematician Choquet (1953–1954)), which allows a measurable weight to be assigned to the future occurrence of a particular event (or several): the *capacity being the minimum value given by the decision-maker to the realization of the event.* Also, the interest of concept is not at issue but does not apply to radical uncertainty in Knight's sense. Economic models using it play with ambiguity (beyond the analytical sense given by Ellsberg (1961)) to this word in the case of the lack of relevant information, which is revealable and induces modeling with or without *aversion to ambiguity*). Where is the radical uncertainty here? At the epistemological level, Schmeidler's work postulates that future reality exists *ex ante* but is masked by a veil, and that it is enough to bet or believe in a rationalizable way to be able to reveal a future truth. Belief can only be collective, based on the convention of the moment, and radical uncertainty is precisely not probabilizable (one way or another). It is also to deny that the decision-maker, today, by their decision/action, influences (and/or determines) the future while forging it by complex interactions and influences. The future has no intrinsic existence and cannot be revealed *a priori*. Given the importance of Knight's concept of radical uncertainty in business decisions, we have sought to understand it through the concept of an *informal mobility barrier* (see Appendix 1 for a qualitative model), which presents a collective strategy of actors linked by a common project; these actors can, according to a non-endogenous value that is unknown at the outset (but which must be dealt with), operate a concerted deviation (preserving the link without renouncing the possible open options), but by being inscribed in a temporality that is irreversible and/or irrevocable (in the sense of Georgescu-Roegen).

The importance of temporality requires a distinction between *time value* (TV) and *intrinsic value* (i.e. the payoff if the option were exercised immediately). The TV is the expectation value of exercising the option (for options that can be exercised at any time). If the TV is zero, the holder decides to exercise their option, seeking, as it were, to minimize the potential regret later of having exercised their right too soon.

The interpretation of the role of the option is not neutral in the analysis: for Weisbrod (1964), the option characterizes the acceptance of current payment for the possible use of a good in the future; for Henry (1974a, 1974b), the issue at stake in quasi-options is the irreversibility of current decisions in their future consequences (*irreversibility effect*). In the latter case, it is therefore a question of considering the current decisions that restrict choices in the future and thus of determining the willingness to pay today to preserve the future choice. Thus, in the sense of Henry (1974a), *the option value is a measure of the loss of future decision-making flexibility*. In other words, it is a form of *measurement of the* a priori *regret of making a decision that is wrong because it leads to an irreversible situation later*. A loss of flexibility or potential regret is arbitrable as long as irrevocability is not proven and the damage is still measured in degrees of irreversibility (with, therefore, a potential reversibility) allowing, for example, the renewal of natural resources. This renewal then takes the form of either repair (correction, rehabilitation, restoration) and/or physical replacement (due to the damage to the NE), and/or compensation for the altered, degraded or lost resource.

Certain conditions of use make it possible to restore and/or maintain a natural resource (see Ostrom (1977) on the *common good*: the more renewable the resource, the more it is comparable to a *common good*), but the guarantee is not absolute. Hence, the need for limited access, in one way or another, in order to avoid overexploitation and/or to minimize the risk of irrevocably exhausting the resource. Moreover, the organization of the scarcity of this natural resource, by setting a high access price, even potentially allows for the generation of profits (to be reinvested to protect the resource), as long as there is a demand for the good (because of the solvency of the applicants).

Limiting access to a natural resource (by means of a toll or permit) acts as a bottleneck to preserve a scarce good. The limitation of access induces a logic of quasi-rent[22]. The social acceptability of this quasi-rent depends on its proven benefit

22 For a *common good* managed by the users of a community, the quasi-rent generated is particular in that it cannot be appropriated by a particular private actor. In a private logic, the quasi-rent is appropriable by defined *property rights*: on a contractual level since Coase (1937); on a principled level to counter the overexploitation of natural resources by Hardin (1968); on a necessity level to manage a complex investment by Klein et al. (1978); on a relational level by Aoki (1986).

for a community; the government can defend the general interest (or an institution with a public service delegation – but then with possible drifts without effective control).

It is therefore important to proceed with a hierarchy of categories of resources according to the possibility of restoring them to their original state or, on the contrary, according to the degree of irreversibility, which increases until irrevocability (Georgescu-Roegen 1971). If the resource is very easily renewable, it can even be managed as a private good or asset (e.g. the fisheries resource with fish farms) under the constraint of not generating negative externalities that are detrimental to the NE. The question is therefore whether the *environmental quality* of a private asset is evaluated and then managed correctly[23] and by whom.

1.1.2. *Decentralized regulation*

The evaluation of an *environmental good*, in order to be able to set an access price (rental and/or sale), may require an independent institution[24]. This institution will assess the degree of *environmental quality* of the good, as well as its price of access. If the institution is private, the logic of reputation (Kreps and Wilson 1982a) may be sufficient to establish the sincerity of the evaluation. Another institution, once the upstream valuation is done, must manage the resource, monitor access and grant permits: no one should exploit a site without first obtaining a permit and complying with the conditions set. Again, reputation may be sufficient, as a private organization cannot afford to tarnish its reputation by cheating on allocation or control (for image damage or risk of boycott). Symmetrically, the client company cannot run the risk of lying *ex ante* about its real intentions because of the risk of an *ex post* revelation leading to the consequences mentioned above. However, the temptation (and/or at least the potentiality of a temptation) exists. Therefore, associations or *whistleblowers* can be active *stakeholders* (Freeman 1984;

---

23 Imagine a permitting process between private actors (a private agency delegated to issue a permit and a company): the *ex ante* probability of undervaluing the good is likely to be high, as the private agency may have an interest in selling as many permits as possible and the client company may be anxious to buy the permit at the lowest possible price. Where clients are willing to pay a high price for access to an exceptional resource, it is unlikely that the regulator will delegate management and/or sell off any permits (if it grants them at all): for example, the management of a national *nature park*; prestigious cultural sites, such as the park of the Château de Versailles, leased out on an occasional basis and under drastic conditions to preserve the site.

24 In practice, the choice of the status (private/public) of the organization is more a matter of local/global culture than dogma: in globalized sectors (e.g. works of art going through commission-based brokerages), the norm is private.

Donaldson and Preston 1995) to accompany the process. If the company perceives a potential regulatory loophole, knowing *ex ante* that the commitments it has made may not be honored, oral and written misrepresentations (deliberate underestimation of the damage that may be caused) are to be feared. The risk of *ex post* drift, once the permit has been issued, cannot be neglected: the *a priori* commitments made (even though perfectly realistic) are not necessarily kept *a posteriori*, thus engendering a breach of trust. The question of information asymmetry (initiated by Akerlof (1970)) is raised, but the question of the incentive mechanism to be put in place is even more so (e.g. the risk of unilateral/bilateral opportunism, when issuing permits (Gustafsson 1998)). The absence of a subordinate relationship between the firm wishing to obtain a permit and the private body granting it frees up strategic behavior[25] (sterilized in the contract of the agency theory of Jensen and Meckling (1976)).

Theoretically, in a strategic context, the only possible guarantor for finding a balanced solution is an external third party (Moulin 1981): this solution normally corresponds to the existence of an independent institution defending the general interest. The cost of such an institution is significant for the community and also raises the problem of its perimeter[26] of authority and action. Also, the solution of delegation is sometimes chosen (because it minimizes the costs of operation and/or the costs of control). This prompts the question of the appropriate form of decentralization, focusing on the private actors themselves if their decisions integrate the consequentism.

1.2. Private decision and consequentism

Drawing some minimal consequences from the presentation already made, we know that the issue of NE is global but that, global agreement or not, its realization is referred to the national level. We also know that the logical conclusion of this

25 The company may threaten to move and/or operate elsewhere. The agency may be indifferent to the motivation (and/or, worse, to the sincerity of the motivation) of a specific request for access to a permit, especially if there is an allocation by auction and also when there is a voluntary policy encouraging companies to develop natural sites and/or exploit their resources (e.g. the case of hydraulic fracturing in the United States, where the right of private access to the subsoil is very extensive).

26 Increasing or decreasing the size of the state should not be an ideological obsession. Above all, it is necessary to select what is relevant to be included. The reasonable hypothesis is that this relevant perimeter should allow the community concerned, directly or indirectly, to satisfy fundamental societal needs (e.g. food, housing, drinking water, energy networks, sanitation networks, hygiene, health, education, protection (of children, the disabled and the elderly), fundamental scientific research, justice, security (police and army), as well as the effective protection of natural resources and the NE).

global approach is to deal with the issue at the macroeconomic level, which leads to the alternative of price (tax) or quantity (permits) made equivalent in an equilibrium situation. However, observation shows that the only effective regulatory power is national, that national egoisms prevail over a collective global logic and that the negative externalities that are measured at the global level by scientists are generated, to a large extent, at the micro-economic level by firms.

Therefore, in the face of the illusion of solving the problem at the global level, we believe that within each effective level of regulation (i.e. the nation), a system of taking into account negative externalities by the actors who generate them (the firms) must be put in place, knowing that this system has the effect of placing all the firms producing and/or wanting to sell in the same space on an equal footing (recourse to importing and/or relocating for dumping, bypassing being thus rendered obsolete).

Let us examine how the strategic decisions of private actors, such as firms, could have a positive impact on NE. As regulation can be decentralized, at least for the management of renewable resources (section 1.2.1), private firms are capable of integrating consequentism (section 1.2.2) into their calculation system (section 1.2.3). Thus, through consequentism, the overall efficiency or inefficiency of the system of private economic activities – by no longer ignoring or underestimating the positive and/or negative externalities on NE – could be apprehended *ex ante*, well upstream, by internalizing the foreseeable consequences on NE from the design stage. The literature we have looked at does not suggest that what is put forward here has never been done before. It should also be noted that the global treatment currently in place does not appear satisfactory (see above).

The consequentist approach[27] can be defined as taking into account *ex ante* in the design of the foreseeable consequences of the production and/or use of a good on the NE: it is therefore acting economically without generating, consciously *ex ante* and/or without imputation, harmful *ex post* effects on the NE. From an operational point of view, there is no naivety here, but rather a simple methodological principle that will be contextualized and weighted in its calculatory logic (see section 1.3).

27 It is important not to confuse *consequentism* with *consequentialist philosophy* (a term introduced by Anscombe (1958)), which is often associated with *utilitarianism* (with J. Bentham: *The greatest happiness for all through quantitative maximization*; then S. Mill: *maximizing pleasures and minimizing pains*). By decentering the action of the individual towards the method (as suggested by Harsanyi (1982)), we can free ourselves from the utilitarian question and focus on the *procedural rule* (Simon 1976, 1978) to go to *consequentism*; for some landmarks of *consequentism* on the philosophical level, see Appendix 2.

Knight (1921) does establish a link between *property* and *consequentism* from the point of view of responsibility and effective incentive, but consequentist action does not boil down to the pure logic of *property rights* (the absence of which would lead to all abuses (Hardin 1968)) or to the opposite thesis, in which *property rights* would induce a Malthusianism that would benefit the owners alone.

In order to manage the effects on NE, if collectivization is excluded, the solution may lie in *respected common rules of reciprocity* (Ostrom 1990).

In our view, with consequentism, the private decision will be based on the *a priori* measurement of the consequences of production and use of a private good on the quality of third categories.

In a broad sense, *third-party categories* include the following: categories of the living (humans, biodiversity (flora, trees, fauna with their ecosystems), any resource linked to the NE and, *a fortiori*, the NE); categories of goods (private, club, collective, public) that are useful to the community and not harmful to the NE, as well as repairable, recyclable and made of natural materials. Strictly speaking, these will be the only categories of living things.

Once the presentation of consequentism has been made (section 1.2.1), the stake on the efficiency of this approach is (section 1.2.2) its internalization by private actors, and this (section 1.2.3) in a framework integrating the consideration of the technological object (and the system of associated objects for the adopter). Then, we will position our approach resulting in an accounting index by starting (section 1.2.4) from the already known but unsatisfactory reference framework that is the carbon index.

1.2.1. *Consequentism*

We can object that it is impossible (except in a teleological interpretation) to control the chain of causes and consequences, which is true in the absolute. However, it turns out that an entity (individual, collective, organization) making a decision has a proven capacity to measure the foreseeable future impact of its decision on others and/or on the community or on third-party categories, but habit and/or its interest leads to ignoring it (and this too often knowingly). In operational terms, *consequentism* can be seen as *a method of* ex ante *calculation such that the activity undertaken does not prejudicially affect a third-party category*. The focus is on negative externalities that are detrimental to third parties. It is no longer a question of opposing good and bad products on the basis of *ad hoc* arguments, but rather of perceiving a commensurable continuum using the same calculation method (see below). The consequent company can thus select from the outset those products that do not negatively affect third-party categories. Proposing a (new) product thus amounts to providing proof of its benefit (and/or its harmlessness) and aims to replace an obsolete product and/or technology that is detrimental to third-party categories (and thus to the NE).

A business decision must improve usage by bringing new features and/or functionalities without deteriorating a third-party category. Innovation is here strongly encouraged, but not wastefulness and/or inconsistency; if necessary, by setting up an adapted regulation system to encourage consequent innovation. Indeed, Rennings (2000), analyzing *eco-innovation* – eco for ecology – (or *environmental innovation*, EI), considers that it induces positive externalities, but that the benefit escapes privatization by the firm that originated it (thus reducing the economic incentive to invest in EI): this is an extension of Arrow's analysis of innovation (1962a).

1.2.2. *Internalization of consequentism as the best remedy*

Innovation is and must remain the dynamic engine of capitalism (Schumpeter 1939, 1942) in the duality, often complementary to the rest, of radicality (destruction–creation) and/or incremental improvement. Thus, after a radical phase of destruction/creation, a sedimentation takes place in layers of incremental improvements (or clusters) on a given trajectory. These improvements are part of a paradigm (Kuhn 1962)[28]. Therefore, the new paradigm of radical environmental innovation should be about destroying what is non-consequentist (by creating what is). Yet, business in liberal capitalism may be reluctant to self-discipline or may have an interest in pretending to do so (while continuing to focus exclusively on maximum profitability) without acting accordingly to consequentism. Private companies offer, quite systematically, non-consequentist private products that directly or indirectly harm third-party categories. Hence, *a priori*, the legitimacy of external legal constraints preventing the indiscriminate exploitation of (especially

28 The paradigm is the result of a societal compromise at a given time: the steam ship was superior in terms of reduced travel time and quantity embarked, but not from the point of view of energy consumed and discharges. The use of plastic material has led to its generalization because of its initial specific properties (lightness, resistance, elasticity, impermeability) which, nevertheless today, increase the polluting persistence (which has become a new characteristic). Replacing more expensive materials (horn, wood, canvas, paper, cardboard, metal, glass), plastic is a product derived from petrochemistry imposed by it and the satisfaction of use does not compensate for its low recycling and/or its harmfulness on the NE. The paradigmatic leap is to replace petrochemical plastic by an ecological plastic. Technical feasibility is no longer a problem, and, moreover, the extra cost generated by "ecological plastic" allows other materials to be (re)mobilized. However, the land and sea plastic soup, linked to the past, is only now being perceived as a major problem.

natural) resources. However, the penalization and/or prohibition of a private good with a negative effect only makes sense if the associated regulations are known and respected.

The guarantor of this respect is certainly an effective control system, vigilant about everything that is likely to alter the integrity of third-party categories, and therefore preferably an independent public body, at the risk otherwise of exposing ourselves to a commodification of this control (see section 1.1). However, existing controls of this type mainly affect food products for health reasons, without preventing crises (bovine spongiform encephalitis (BSE), avian flu, etc.), fraud or deception (on origins or ingredients).

Medicines are subject to counterfeiting, but another problem is the reuse of pharmaceutical molecules in related fields, triggering pathologies or extension of use, increasing the extent of the risk. Moreover, we know that human health depends on NE (which is altered) and that a very broad consideration of nuisances is now necessary. However, the existing control system relies primarily on the declarations of private actors regarding compliance with standards. Moreover, lobbies are opposed to effective control: the European REACH (*Registration, Evaluation and Authorisation of Chemicals*) directive has been limited and muzzled. On the other hand, standards integrating the EN (ISO 14000, ISO 26000) are being disseminated and used as references with external verification procedures by approved organizations.

Also, the simplest and most effective way is for the actors themselves to internalize the respect of third-party categories. This implies a proactive approach of the companies, from the conception of products, by deciding in a consequentist way (according to the effects induced, downstream, for the third-party categories). The necessary responsibility of each private actor, in the sector in which they are involved (from the supplier's supplier to the customer's customer), requires the definition of and respect for demanding specifications (on this question, see Bouvier-Patron (2017a)). If the industrial revolution initiated a *cradle to grave* process (extraction/production/consumption/destruction), the *cradle to cradle* process (Braungart and McDonough 2002) invites the infinite life cycle. It has even become a certification in the United States and is developing in northern Europe. It is less a question of recycling in the traditional sense of the term, than of developing an upcyclable product (i.e. maintaining the intrinsic quality of its ingredients *ad infinitum*, and therefore guaranteeing their permanent reuse). In this logic, the waste is destined to disappear because everything can be considered as a resource (that this resource is natural is a significant additional step to achieve). However, currently, the treatment of the induced effects is *ex post* at the end of the life cycle: the reprocessing channels of industrial waste (if they are effective and not deviated) are then very partial solutions of revalorization (especially if some channels of collection only allow a revalorization).

By necessity, in the name of public hygiene, there is an almost blind collective service of waste collection without measuring the exorbitant cost of it and for an always partial valorization.

Even though we pay a lump sum, nobody really takes responsibility for their own waste (at best, the effort consists of selecting and/or limiting the volume and then sorting it *ex post*)[29]. For the user, it would be preferable to act, upstream, by starting the sorting, *ex ante*, at the time of the initial purchase, allowing composting and/or recycling, but especially by privileging only the useful and reusable and/or recyclable essentials at the time of purchase. We are still far from it.

The layers of decommissioned products continue to accumulate. A product can turn out to be fragile (and not repairable), useless (but attractive) and, if useful, relegatable (by the consumerist logic inciting re-purchasing, historically perfectly assumed by the American industrial designer Brooks Stevens – and this well before the rise of the consumer society of the 1960s – see Chapter 7) and/or even harmful[30]. Products and packaging are launched on the market without worrying about the foreseeable consequences for the sole reason of short-term marketing and financial reasoning. Supply-side marketing relegates or instrumentalizes the technical *characteristics* of the product (defined as a set of technical characteristics (Lancaster 1975)), as the heart of market reasoning is now *perceived value*[31] (Porter 1985).

---

29 And what can work (badly) in urban areas (e.g. collection) – while outsourcing storage and/or destruction elsewhere in the periphery (without preventing uncontrolled dumping) – becomes, by extension, apocalyptic in the middle of nature where there is no (or little) collective collection and cleaning service and even less vigilance in terms of surveillance and effective control.

30 Major economic sectors are concerned (extraction, oil, chemistry, phytosanitary, etc.), not to mention the construction industry (uncontrolled building sites, polluting machinery, toxic materials that are difficult to recycle, faulty implementation, disrespect for standards, systematic and massive use of landfill (often unauthorized), little reuse). The promoters of a product that is harmful to health or the NE are often the same ones who propose solutions for its removal and/or neutralization (the private financial benefit being twofold).

31 The manipulation of value has been consecrated by marketing practices that play on the customer's belief rather than on the benefit of technical characteristics. It is all based on intangible cues of desirability, usually within the *brand universe*, and based primarily on imitative adoption behavior (Rogers 1962). Social anthropology has much to teach us about the *use value* of flavored soft drinks, but probably little about the consequences of the negative externalities of this consumption (waste of natural resources such as drinking water, impact of the carbon footprint linked to transport, quantity of various types of waste generated, imperfections in the eventual recycling, or effects on human health, e.g. diabetes, obesity).

Globalization, as we know it, hypertrophies physical flows for immediate profit, multiplies negative externalities and the sale of products that are poorly adapted to the needs of the local population[32], to individuals who need something else.

Ex-post recycling has become indispensable, if only to manage the existing cumulative stock, as so many products are launched on the market without any relation to the overall benefit brought by the proposed solution.

The private goods sold today are abundant, little or not repairable, rapidly obsolete, poorly recyclable and often of questionable effective utility. Their *commensurability* is in question because of the absence of imputation of induced effects. This is quite systematically verified on a product, entering in a process with industrial finality (including the food industry with its supplies in agricultural products[33] and/or the distribution by the central buying offices of the big signs), or even sometimes with non-industrial finality (artisanal activities of service; even the sale at the farm, on the Internet or even on the markets of proximity).

The industrial product in itself, as a material artifact detached from the living, sees its *a priori* use as less emotional (except for fetishization induced by the *brand universe* and *cultural branding*; see Chapters 3 and 4). This type of product, produced *ex nihilo*, is conceived entirely in a plannable way. It is therefore less the impossibility of measuring the consequences induced (by its production and/or its use) than the will to (not) do so that will prevail. What still operates is a classical reasoning of privatization of profits and collectivization of losses.

The reasoning on consequentism is thus not purely nominalist (in the sense of a false conceptual modernity); the operational alternatives already known (LCC and global cost) are not really satisfactory.

1.2.2.1. *Alternative to life cycle costing or LCC*

The LCC approach (Dhillon 1989; Fabricky and Blanchard 1991), by fixing the end of life of an asset from the outset, aims to quantify *ex ante* all the impacts generated during the life cycle (of the good). The LCC method consists, in the best of cases, of adding certain costs (e.g. the investment cost) with uncertain costs (operation, maintenance, replacement and, possibly, deconstruction and recycling,

32 Thus, many textile products are often characterized by poor workmanship, premature wear and tear, and the incorporation of harmful ingredients (e.g. dyes that are inexpensive but irritating or even dangerous to human health for those who make them, as well as for those who use them). These products are also manufactured in conditions that are often very limited and have little or no respectful for the NE.

33 Intensive agriculture operates with chemical inputs that are harmful to the farmer, local residents, the NE and the consumer.

etc.), which are all the more difficult to evaluate as the good/product is innovative. The LCC approach therefore imputes costs throughout the life cycle of a product without ever constraining the nature of the product and/or its design at the outset: we impute costs once the product *push* has been made and without considering the consequences of externalities from the outset. Then, eventually, in the best of cases, a comparison is made with the alternatives envisaged. When imputation is aimed at prevention (e.g. pollution; see Bailey (1991) and Fava (1991)), the LCC tool can potentially be part of a consequentist approach. With the effective and complete consideration of the risk assessment linked to externalities, and knowing the quantified alternatives, LCC and consequentism can converge, but through a narrow gateway.

1.2.2.2. *Global cost alternative (GCA)*

The GCA is strongly inspired by the LCC method by fixing the end of life of an asset from the outset with a calculation of *all the expenses incurred by the user throughout the life of an asset* (acquisition-investment, operation, maintenance, destruction and even replacement). However, the *extended global cost*, which seeks to capture all costs – including hidden and/or indirect costs by integrating externalities – is a variant of the LCC, which works in vain if the level of requirements for the goods and the charges to be made (particularly with regard to externalities and consequences) are not specified *ex ante*. Adding certain costs (e.g. investment) with deferred costs (operation, maintenance, deconstruction, recycling, etc.) entails in itself uncertainty, imprecision and a problem of credibility of the final value obtained (but this is the case for any intertemporal calculation towards the future by discounting a future value to the present with a discount table). Thus, the internal rate of return (or IRR) is reassuring for the financier who can thus discern the opportunity cost, but where is the indicator of the relevance of the investment? Without being exhaustive, let us give a few emblematic examples (beyond plastics or housing insulation): asbestos was exploited and valorized for its fire-resistant properties, knowing the harmfulness of the by-products for human health; phytosanitary products (including pesticides), linked to the civil conversion of the industry during World War I, were mobilized for their property of eradicating living organisms, but without questioning the consequences for living organisms.

In terms of radical innovation, the problems are even more obvious:

– The use of nuclear fission was a political choice (with a duality of civil and military use): radioactivity was known since the scientific work of the Curie spouses as a phenomenon, but not in the consequences of the irradiated waste to be treated; the management of waste, more or less contaminated, was badly evaluated just like the dismantling of obsolete nuclear power plants.

– The Concorde was a gamble taken by engineers to offer to civil aviation a dream of supersonic speed at Mach 2 (initiated by the jet propulsion of fighter planes at the end of World War II), but without serious calculation of the operating constraints and/or induced effects; and, aggravating circumstance, without real realism to elaborate a complete study of commercial profitability.

– NASA's successful Apollo 11 mission, with an appropriate budget to put a human on the moon, was an unprecedented challenge for mankind (and probably also a leadership issue in terms of prestige and technology against a background of ideological rivalry), but without anticipating the question of waste left on the moon or abandoned in space (the central issue managed being the energy necessary to propel the rocket to complete the mission), and this has not ceased despite technological evolution and knowledge of environmental issues. After the abandoned reusable space shuttle program, it is only recently with *Space X* that the reusability of the material is finally being considered, even though the missions entrusted actually are much more modest than before.

– The electric vehicle depends on the electric battery (as for all mobility and/or connected objects) that we do not necessarily know how to recycle at the moment (and forever?).

– Genetic engineering or nanotechnology manipulations open up unexplored domains and are very uncertain as to their subsequent effects, due to their wide and uncontrollable dissemination (even more so perhaps than for the nuclear industry).

All these examples can be generalized (as for the uncontrolled consequences), to varying degrees, to almost all the innovations known until now. It is therefore all the more urgent to think of those to come.

1.2.3. *Consequentism for the technological object and the adopter's system of objects*

The specification of a new product is a limiting assignment that prevents us from grasping the perimeter of the system of objects required in and for the use of the good under consideration. However, Katz and Shapiro (1985) and Farrell and Saloner (1986) show the importance of *network externalities* and insist on the positive (economic) complementarities of products operating within a costly infrastructure. This is also an operating principle in a *brand universe* (see Chapters 3 and 4) where a series of complementary objects multiplies the overall value (e.g. the *Apple* environment). Moreover, each potential user federates a system of often heterogeneous objects that nevertheless makes sense through use: each user alone or in a community of use (e.g. a *brand community*) and/or a community of practice (Brown and Duguid 1991) engenders collective interactive learning dynamics and mobilizes *bricolage* (a concept that makes sense in a context of resource scarcity, or of reworking the existing by tinkering with the means at hand (Levi-Strauss 1962a) (see Chapter 7). Each person mobilizes their system of objects alone and/or, more often than not, in interaction with those of others or within a community or larger collective.

These object systems emerge and/or are recombined, punctually or frequently, instantaneously or durably, without always being taken into account in collective interactions, unless the network of use is large, perennial and traceable (virtually or not). Thus, substantially virtual social networks (such as *Facebook*) are quantifiable. Interactions, in general, are measurable and show important externalities, positive or negative, which are not necessarily accounted for[34]. Therefore, is it consequentist to attribute a utility to a singular object (based on desirability; see Chapters 3 and 4), commercially circumscribed by an *instantaneous price* on a sticker. Improved information on the label is useful (origin, traceability, ingredients, energy class, indications of use, carbon footprint, reparability, possible recycling and/or for food products, nutritional content, sugar, salt, or fat content, etc.) but not satisfactory. A powerful spring of the adoption of a product is the combination of individual use, but within a community of belonging (the community dynamic is essential; see Chapters 3 and 4). In any case, the disposable and wasteful fashion is the current social norm. However, it should be replaced by an (activist) logic of responsibility in the choice of the system of objects in order to control the complete cycle. At the level of individual and collective use, the ferment of a change of paradigm already exists, coming from eclectic intellectual horizons and to be quoted at least for their relevance[35]. The will of the public power cannot be limited to a signposting of the products; it must operate by a more successful policy, only allowing the consequent products on the market (including the importation).

---

34 The symptomatic example of real daily life is that of the cigarette break and/or the logic of fast food restaurants where the act of throwing away (cigarette butts, packaging, greasy paper, aluminum cans, plastic bottles or utensils), including on the public highway, is widespread (reinforced by massification). This generates visible and measurable collective nuisances that are poorly taken into account. In the virtual world (see Chapter 4), it is spam and/or the viral propagation of harassment, rumors and/or the effects of conspiracy theories.

35 From the *fetishism* of the merchandise (K. Marx (1867), *The Process of Production of Capital*), or by the analysis of social forms revealing the phenomena of the bottom by the *exchanges* (G. Simmel (1900), *Philosophie des Geldes*), to a positive thought of the technique (G. Simondon (1958), *Du monde d'existence des objets techniques*, Aubier) until the glances on the precise question of the objects and their privative and/or societal uses (S. Chase (1925), *The Tragedy of Waste*, Macmillan; K. Galbraith (1958), *The Affluent Society*, Houghton Mifflin; V. Packard (1960), *The Waste Makers*, McKay Inc.; G. Pérec (1965), *Les Choses*, Julliard). We will retain above all Levi-Strauss (1962a, 1962b) and Baudrillard (1968, 1970), who crown these approaches, generally critical, in a very constructive way.

1.2.4. *Carbon accounting: solution or illusion?*

As already mentioned, the IPCC, as a group of experts and alerting party, is doing scientific work and has pointed out the role of human activity (called anthropogenic activity) in global warming of the planet Earth. For example, carbon dioxide (CO_2) is one of the greenhouse gases (GHGs) that has one of the smallest global warming potentials (GWPs), but has contributed the most to human-induced global warming (see DATALAB (2019)). CO_2 is therefore very emblematic and synthesizes two key issues: that of fossil energy which is easily accessible but exhaustible and accepting that the pollution on the NE is inevitable during the exploitation of resources or the induced chain effects of using by-products; the impact on the climate from GHG (including CO_2). Furthermore, the emissions of different GHGs can be expressed (see ADEME (2014)) in *CO_2 equivalent* (CO_2e) by converting the emissions of a particular GHG into CO_2e via its (relative) 100-year GWP. The carbon accounting approach thus has the advantage of being decentralizable to goods or services realized in a globalized economy through an equivalence index (in CO_2e units), giving a standardized and commensurable indication of the contribution of the considered element to global warming.

This makes it possible to leave the choice (and therefore the responsibility) to the consumer to choose what is most favorable to the planet.

In a broad sense, we speak of the *carbon footprint* as a component of the *ecological footprint* (see below for a definition of the latter term). The *carbon footprint* is an official indicator of the *quantity of greenhouse gases (GHGs) emitted to satisfy domestic consumption (including imports)*. The carbon footprint of a human activity is an indicator of anthropogenic GHGs based on emission factors measured in Kilowatt hours (kWh produced, delivered or consumed). A distinction can be made between *factors* (e.g. emission factors related to the energy sources used) and contents (e.g. activities or uses). The factors are convertible into CO_2 emissions: grams of CO_2 equivalent per kWh (gCO_2e/kWh). The CO_2 contents are accounted for in direct emissions (e.g. energy used by the final consumer via life cycle analysis or LCA), as well as in indirect emissions due to the upstream energy supply and transformation chains (production, transport, distribution), and even further downstream (recycling, dismantling).

The term carbon footprint is often used to mean the quantity of carbon (in tons) emitted (by an activity, a person, an organization) when consuming energy or raw materials. It is estimated that the carbon footprint represents half of the ecological footprint.

The carbon component of the ecological footprint goes beyond this by stipulating the quantity (in surface area of different soil types) to be converted as necessary to capture/sequester the carbon dioxide (CO_2) emissions. In short, it is the translation of the consumption, in terms of combustion, of the planet's fossil resources.

The *ecological footprint* can be defined as *a measure of the theoretical surface area of bio-productive land or water that human activity, or anthropic activity (individual, group, organization, city, region, country, humanity), uses to produce the resources necessary to satisfy its needs in a sustainable way (thus allowing the renewal of the natural resources mobilized) and to absorb the waste and pollution generated in the process – taking into account the technologies used.* However, it should be noted that the ecological footprint excludes persistent products and toxic waste, because the NE does not assimilate them!

If we assume that NE has the capacity to regenerate itself (biocapacity or *ecological supply*), it is therefore capable, in theory, of satisfying the needs linked to human activity (human demand printing an ecological footprint), as long as these needs do not exceed nature's regenerative capacity (biocapacity). The difference between the ecological footprint (demand) and the biological capacity (supply) gives the ecological balance (positive or negative). A positive ecological balance would theoretically measure the sustainability of human consumption given the biocapacity of eco-systems. An ecological footprint accounting thus seeks to express whether what is assessed as anthropogenic allows (or not) regeneration (Wackernagel and Ress 1996, 1999).

If NE is considered as a resource, then the accounting of the ecological footprint implies estimating the flows generated (as well as the possible waste and assimilated pollution) for the anthropic needs to be satisfied, as well as the spaces of NE necessary (to generate these flows, as well as for regeneration). Thus, the ecological footprint is a tool for evaluating NE (Wackernagel and Yount 1998, 2000) based on a new unit of measurement needed to compare supply and demand: the global hectare (or *hag*), i.e. a hectare related to the world's average bioproductivity of all categories of bioproductive soils (regardless of their nature). Such an accounting requires, among other things, the evaluation of the ecological services rendered by the NE, knowing that the resources come from different types of soils (forest, pasture, coastal water, etc.): a consumption can be expressed in quantities for each type of soil using conversion coefficients.

Accounting can be done (Simmons et al. 2000) at the *country level* (top-down macro approach) or in a more decentralized way by the components (bottom-up Component-Based Approach). The two approaches are complementary. The aim is to make an inventory of the goods consumed, and then to evaluate their footprint on the basis of calculated conversion factors: for example, from the life cycle, where the evaluation concerns the quantity of resources mobilized from the extraction of raw materials to the final waste or scrap (*from cradle to grave*). Thus, the consumption demand has an impact on the NE whose calculation, in terms of ecological footprint, requires *conversion factors* into *equivalence* and *yield*. Thus:

– *Equivalence factor*: equivalence factors are necessary because of the existence of various Natural Environments with varying bioproductivity, knowing that the bioproductive surfaces must be expressed in the same unit (hag) to be aggregated. The areas considered are weighted according to their soil type bioproductivity by an equivalence factor. An equivalence factor is expressed as *the ratio of the average world productivity of a given bioproductive soil type to the average world productivity of all bioproductive soil categories, regardless of their nature*. The equivalence factors are constant per year and country.

– *Yield factor*: some areas are better endowed in terms of biocapacity, either because they are larger or because they have more productive ecosystems per unit area.

Thus, an area measured by the number of physically available hectares within a space is multiplied by a factor that reflects a differential ratio, for each soil category, between local productivity and the world average productivity: this is the yield factor.

The *yield factor* is defined as *the ratio of the area used to produce a type of good on a type of land in the area that would be required to produce the same type of good from land of average world yield* (see the work by Monfreda et al. (2004)). Yield factors are country-specific for a year and reflect, by comparison, the deviation from the world average in soil fertility, technological advancement and productivity of each country.

The yield is then expressed in *global hectare per hectare* (hag/ha).

The managerial consideration of the ecological footprint has been mentioned (Holland 2003), but more in principle than as a real operational issue (hence our proposal of consequentism, PPG and FEI, compatible with NE, in the service of innovative business decisions; see below).

In addition to the practical difficulty of measuring the footprint, the effective consideration of the impact on the NE is limited, in the best of cases, to a global logic of limiting GHGs and without even being up to the challenge of countering the consequences of anthropogenic global warming on the NE (pointed out by the IPCC), or even of dealing with local pollution in the NE. Politicians and economists, admitting (or not) that the issue of NE is worrying, refer to a hypothetical international order but, above all, they affirm that growth must not be curtailed. This raises questions and should encourage us to think differently, without discouraging the implementation of a global approach to the climate. In any economic reference framework, a measurement standard is required, which in this case is the ton of CO_2e. Any activity, its inputs, outputs and/or their consequences must be expressed in relation to this reference unit. It is also necessary to obtain a value for the ton of CO_2e and, to do this, the choice is between quantity (permit) or price (tax).

It must be noted that the choice of quantity was made within the framework of the possibilities opened up by the Kyoto Protocol in 1997 to set up tradable and transferable carbon emission permits (once the quota has been set by the public authorities, the market should allow a price to be determined by the interplay of supply and demand). The approach thus instituted carbon accounting through CO_2 as part of a global macroeconomic approach to limit CO_2 emissions as a priority through taxes versus tradable emission permits. However, this vision does not cover all local and/or global emissions and pollution.

If public authorities must play their role as regulators, with each government remaining the master of its own space in order to enforce what it commits to (at the global level, as well as to encourage firms to act to preserve the environment), corporate freedom must be responsible and consist of being proactively involved (in a known regulatory framework). Also, carbon accounting is a global issue for the planet that must, *ceteris paribus*, be the subject of a quasi-consensus concerning the guidance of the effort (and the degree of effort), without being the exclusive issue to be satisfied and without the CESR being reduced to insignificance. The global objective is of interest, but cannot be used as a media theater for, in the end, almost nothing to change if the micro-level is not fully mobilized in the best way: by innovating while respecting the NE. For this, the prerequisite is an internal revolution within the company.

At the intra-organizational managerial level, respect for NE must be internalized.

A double preliminary observation can be made at this stage: the system in place intends to control and master certain harmful emissions (but not all of them) and confuses economic liberalism with laxity (by cynicism, ideology or pragmatism) by allowing companies to choose to pollute according to acquired rights (often free of charge) in order to produce (often in any manner) goods or services (which are themselves potentially or effectively polluting). The current idea is thus set to kick in (depending on what is produced and offered), by leaving a free choice of responsibility to consumers to respect the NE (or not).

Given the problems of implementation and the difficulty to obtain the expected effects (due to national egoisms, the non-compliance of governmental or private protagonists, the unconstrained economic primacy), the responsibility implied by the carbon index is very relative for a problem that is global in scope, but locally generated (with very strong global impacts, certainly, as well as local).

As for the method, current work in economics on the carbon index (of products or activities) has the disadvantage of encouraging a fictitious measure to raise awareness of orders of magnitude and to give a signal: it is then mainly a matter of noting *ex post* whether the orientation has been positive and/or to deplore the possibility of negative consequences. However, the whole issue must be based on the actors who generate externalities, taking them into account *ex ante*. Any approach that seeks, more or less, to take *ex post* observations invites the same logic to be pursued without really questioning it (when the *ex ante* approach leads to a salutary questioning of the company's decision). And, in any case, any cost for the company will be transferred to the customer (whatever the method or the point of view, immediately or later).

It therefore seems more appropriate to us to opt for another type of accounting that is decentralized to the company and consequentist in its calculation. However, after the theoretical arguments already presented and before presenting our proposal, let us briefly recall the historical sequence that allowed the implementation of carbon accounting. Within the European Economic Community (EEC), the first idea to follow in the footsteps of the Rio Earth Summit in 1992 was the proposal for a carbon tax, which faced the double obstacle of member countries refusing any European fiscal initiative and the existence of powerful industrial lobbies. This tax proposal was quickly abandoned in 1997. The pathway mobilized at the international level was to be that of negotiable emission permits under the Kyoto Protocol in 1997, based on the American experience. The reference for tradable emission permits is the successful operation in the 1980s in the United States of tradable sulfur dioxide (SO_2) emission permits for coal-fired power plants (power plants used to produce electricity) in order to combat the harmful effects of acid rain on forests in particular: the objective was reached in 2010 with a 50% reduction in emissions (compared to those existing in 1980). In this model, the challenge for public authorities is to set the overall quantity of authorized polluting emissions and create an equivalent quantity of permits. Permits can be allocated for free or sold. Firms are assumed to have a sufficient number of permits to cover their emissions and can nevertheless trade permits in the sense that firms that want additional permits (to match their emission needs) can trade with firms that have surplus permits (either because the number of permits obtained exceeds needs and/or because the cost of investing in not polluting, or polluting less, is less than the value of the expected sale of the permits to others; permits that can thus be saved to be profitably valued in another way).

The exchanges then establish a market price[36], which serves as a benchmark and indicator to determine with certainty, for each company, whether it is feasible to buy permits or sell them.

For the public authorities, the interest in selling (instead of giving) the initial permits would ideally be to collect amounts that would potentially allow them to reduce the fiscal burden where it would be appropriate to do so. Empirically, however, we find that these permits are rather issued free of charge: not necessarily out of laxity or to defy theory (Hahn 1989), but, more certainly, to encourage firms to play the game, or rather, or more precisely, not to dissuade them from doing so, as the norm (economic and managerial), since the beginning of the industrial revolution, is to consider that the NE is a free, inexhaustible resource. This is not the case, due to anthropic activity.

It was therefore inspired by the American model that the Kyoto Protocol in 1997 extended. The principle of the emissions permit market was extended to the global level with a timetable defining periods and objectives to be reached for capping and/or reducing GHG emissions (mainly CO_2). However, the commitments made will not necessarily be kept and, moreover, although a very polluting country, the United States regularly intends and/or threatens to withdraw unilaterally from the agreement, while others (the most polluting developing countries, India or China) do not really see why they should constrain their growth before reaching the western development standard. In Europe, by far the best student of the Kyoto Protocol, a system of CO_2 emission permits was set up in 2005. Very quickly, given the size of the European emissions market (EU Emissions Trading System, EU ETS)[37], its CO_2 price has now become a global benchmark.

It is estimated that CO_2 represents about 40% of total GHG emissions. The challenge is to extend the principle of CO_2 emission permits, little by little, to all polluting sectors (e.g. civil aviation since 2012 only). The market itself is fluctuating: volatility is particularly high on the Spot market, with potential speculative effects. A trend is especially noticeable with an average indicator. Between 2005 and 2007, the average annual price of CO_2 fell from 23 euros per ton

36 Theoretically, the market price set gives the polluting emissions a purchase price and also a cost, allowing companies to compare the benefit of reducing pollution with the revenue to be received from the sale of the permits already obtained. Companies are said to have low pollution abatement costs if it is more attractive to abate and sell the corresponding permits, or high abatement costs if it is more attractive not to abate but only to buy new pollution permits. The cost of cleaning up pollution thus appears as an opportunity cost.

37 The European market with the EU ETS is dedicated to companies; ETS stands for emission trading system. The unit of account, linked to the Kyoto Protocol, Assigned Amount Units (AAU), is only accessible to countries that are members of the agreement.

(tCO_2) to less than 1 euro; then, over the period 2008–2012, the average annual price gradually rose again (e.g. 31 euros in 2014). Since then, not surprisingly given the current stakes, a sustained upward trend has emerged[38]. The market price is closely linked to the overall quantity of allowances available, as set by the regulator, who wants the market to not be used as a vehicle for speculative financial transactions (which is the case for the commodity future market). There are at least three possibilities for setting a price: the market for tradable CO_2 emission permits, the CO_2 tax (carbon tax) already mentioned, and the *tutelary carbon value* (a reference defined by the public authorities to evaluate the profitability of investments in the transport sector: 27 euros per ton of CO_2 for the Boiteux Commission in 2001).

The tutelary value is generally higher than the market price, but it supports the upward value, which is in line with the interpretation of *Hotelling's rule* (Hotelling 1931), according to which the price of an exhaustible resource must follow an ascending trend over time as it is physically depleted (if we are willing to admit here that the price of carbon represents the price of the sacrifice of non-renewable resources, and that it is licit to sacrifice non-renewable natural resources). However, the establishment and operation of a market in traded permits creates numerous practical problems: difficulty in obtaining approval as a polluter; legitimacy of the initial distribution of the rights to pollute; vagueness of the procedures for controlling pollution and the adequacy of permits/pollution; problem of defining possible sanctions; effectiveness and/or manner of sanctioning in the event of infringement; vagueness of the role of institutions, as well as their ability to regulate or implement sanctions; tricks and loopholes by polluters (by taking advantage of the gaps and/or holes in the legal or control mechanism). In addition, carbon taxes or calculations vary from one country to another (as do operating regulations or health and social conditions).

Moreover, any measure can lead to the relocation of polluting activities to places where there is little or no control, and often to low-cost re-importation, thus breaking any local virtuous circle.

If we refer to the theoretical functioning of a market, we can consider that allocating permits in a non-homogeneous way between countries in the same zone constitutes a distortion. This distortion is aggravated where there is a decentralized power using discretionary means and potentially manipulating the levers strategically to extract an advantage. The application of rules at the local/national level necessarily induces distortions between countries in the globalized competition because they are *a priori* inscribed in a common framework (e.g. Kyoto Protocol),

38 However, time series data may not be consistent. For example, the quotation of issue prices on Bluenext (an index of the New York Stock Exchange and the Caisse des Dépôts) ceased in 2012 when the EEC ousted this quotation company.

but may not (or poorly or hardly) respect the commitments made. This is even more the case if they do not subscribe to a common reference framework; any global regulation, even minimal, increases the gap with countries that do not apply any rules. In any case, legislation may exist but not be applied. Thus, within the same economic zone (e.g. the EU), the Nordic countries, which are more virtuous in terms of compliance with the NE, require greater efforts from companies on their soil than less virtuous countries that are generally more sensitive to global price competition require. The overall number of permits distributed at the level of a zone should, therefore, take into account the existing incentive policies in each member country so as to allocate more permits to virtuous countries (which will reinvest in what can contribute to reducing impacts on NE), but economic theory considers this to be a competitive distortion.

Depending on the will of a government, as national regulation remains, a carbon tax could also be imposed as a complement to the emissions permit market.

There would then *a priori* be a double levy on each company (but the tax would be passed on to the final consumer as is the case for VAT). A discrimination between categories of consumers by their level of income is thus to be envisaged: low-income consumers are relatively more exposed to the dangers affecting the environment (for a question of location, access to good products, green spaces or public services including health services, etc.). On the other hand, low-income consumers have a lower capacity to pay the tax and high-income households spend a lower percentage on the tax. Tariffs must therefore be adjusted according to income (price discrimination), or tax exemptions must be made.

In any case, if the issue is now a tax, should we opt for national regulation with international standardization (which is fairly consistent with accepted practice, but difficult to achieve because of a problem of technical harmonization and/or power relations) or, from the outset, opt for the same international tax for all countries (which is the most logical, but proves to be utopian when we examine the concrete application of a protocol)?

Some people, and not the least (Nordhaus 2006), wonder whether taxing CO_2 emissions would not be preferable (to negotiated permits), especially in view of the various concrete problems of implementing permits.

Beyond the permit/tax debate, the accompanying or active policy of a government concerning compliance with the NE is not to be underestimated (issues around Porter's hypothesis) to encourage firms to do better; in particular, to move from carbon-intensive activities to activities that are less carbon-intensive or no longer carbon-intensive. This shift provides the framework for the *ecological transition*. This transition functions at least as a sorting station to discriminate and direct what is favorable or, more radically, activates a process of disappearance (Schumpeter-like destruction–creation) of polluting activities to replace them by new carbon-free activities. To do this, Porter and van der Linde (1995a, 1995b) assert (even though we retain the amendments suggested by Palmer et al. (1995)) the need for binding legislation concerning compliance with the NE, so as to encourage companies to seize the new opportunities offered by taking the NE into account and/or even to carry out an ecological mutation of activities. However, the investment and costs generated by this new virtuous orientation should not be punitive (compared to an innovation routine without taking into account NE).

The collective benefit sought from legislation is to promote access to a consideration of the NE with beneficial effects for all, as the green sectors also generate new technologies, new jobs and new qualifications.

1.3. Positive private goods and consequentist calculation

However, a legal framework that favors collectively virtuous actions should not avoid a reflection on the internalization of the incentive in and through the management of best practices.

In a decentralized logic, how can the true price of an existing product be established if only certain elements are included in the calculation (price of inputs, salaries, cost and depreciation of installed equipment, logistics, etc.) and not all those required (conditions of production of inputs and operation of equipment, negative externalities on the NE, direct or indirect and diffuse pollution, mobilization of exhaustible resources, conditions and access to these resources, occupational health or hardship at work, consequences on other stakeholders, lack of information on the effects of the activity and/or products)? Also, what reality reflects the *instantaneous price* of a private good (e.g. the *list price*)?

In a consequentist approach, the *instantaneous price* must be justified according to the consequences that can be envisaged *ex ante*. This price can then be qualified as viable[39] if it incorporates the induced effects once proposed, without therefore having to repair *ex post* any possible harm.

---

39 Conversely, when the instantaneous price is inappropriate in terms of its possible consequences, it is not *viable*. Moreover, as each competing firm has to integrate the same calculation system, a *viable price* is not, in itself, *sustainable* (in the sense of Baumol and Willig (1981): a price that makes any entry by a competitor unprofitable), unless the firm in question is a natural monopoly. On the other hand, generally speaking, by relying on *perceived value*, marketing maximizes the differential constituted by the minimization of the cost price and the maximization of the selling price (this upper limit being fixed according to social acceptability, as for the iPhone), but, obviously, without the effects induced on the EN, for example, ever being taken into account.

At this *viable price*, the quality/price/quantity triplet incorporates all the consequences that can be envisaged *ex ante*. Thus, in the absence of negative induced effects on a third-party category, a good appears that we call a *positive private good* (PPG). The PPG is a private good (thus meeting the double criterion of *exclusivity* and *rivalry*), which is obtained by the nullification of having to act on negative externalities on third-party categories through its realization and/or sale. The PPG must internalize *ex ante* the negative externalities (otherwise observed *ex post*).

The PPG corresponds to a Pareto-optimal solution where the fate of third categories is not/no longer deteriorated, but the substitution of PPG by other (non-positive) private goods is detrimental even though the replacement of the existing PPG by a better PPG requires higher skills (which gives PPG a strong specificity in the sense of Hart and Moore (1990)).

We will propose (section 1.3.1) a situational scheme of the PPG, as well as a methodological comparison (section 1.3.2), and then we will discuss (section 1.3.3) the applicability of the calculation.

1.3.1. *Positive private good*

The proposed scheme assumes some simplifying assumptions:

a) Public goods are assimilated to collective goods.

b) Third-party categories are incorporated into collective and/or common goods.

c) Collective and common goods do not generate negative externalities[40].

d) Private goods are logically separate from collective or common goods while interacting with them.

e) Private goods constitute an important part of the totality of goods.

f) Interactions and externalities are positive between collective and common goods (or even sometimes towards private goods), while private goods generate many negative externalities on collective and common goods.

g) The positive externalities produced by collective or common goods are strong but sometimes very difficult to quantify.

40 A particular collective equipment can generate nuisances (in particular by the production and/or treatment of waste), but rules or directives can be fixed to reduce or eliminate them.

h) The negative externalities produced by private goods are strong, often quantifiable and can reach a threshold of irrevocability that is detrimental to all other categories.

i) Positive private goods are a variant of private goods whose interactions are positive (synergetic effect) and likely to create positive externalities (in the same logic as collective or common goods that respect the NE).

It should also be noted that the prism adopted here is that of private goods, independently of any recourse to public regulation. Once these precautions have been taken, the proposed representation (see Figure 1.1, to be linked to Table 1.1) highlights the perspective of a representation that takes into account the amplitude (magnitude) of potential externalities: positive externalities of varying magnitude, generating synergistic dynamics (materialized by solid arrows on the diagram); negative externalities (according to the axes of diffusion: dotted lines --- on the diagram), which can generate a threshold of irrevocability on the NE. To get to the heart of the matter, private goods have consequences in terms of externalities that may or may not be beneficial to the NE and/or third-party categories: in the positive case, it is a *positive private good* (PPG).

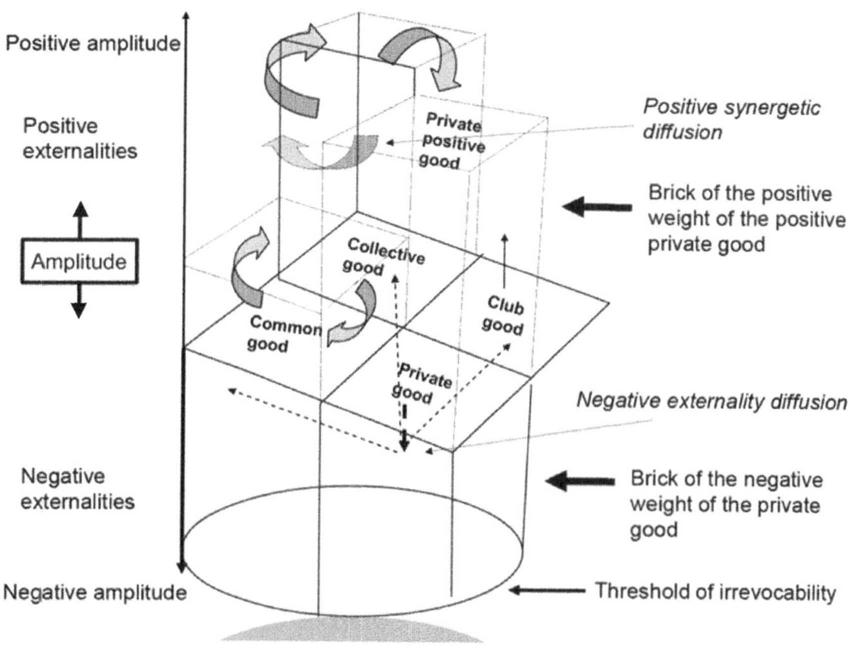

Figure 1.1. *Representation of positive private goods (source: author). For a color version of this figure, see http://www.iste.co.uk/bouvier-patron/frugalinnovation.zip*

The positive character of the diffusion of a private good, in the case of a PPG, is expressed by the absence and/or internalization of negative externalities, and even by only positive externalities (of a more or less significant magnitude) on the other categories. The benefit experienced relies on the intrinsic advantages of the good, including in its production phase and in its use.

If we place ourselves in a competitive universe, while being part of a SD context (focusing here on the sole aspect of respect for the environment), the PPG can be in very high demand on the market; this can generate, depending on its relative availability, a very profitable overprice (corresponding to goodwill for the supplier). There is therefore no penalization of the offer, but a reward by the value achieved with a high-end positioning and by setting a skimming price (compensating for upstream efforts without dissuading purchase), by addressing an elite at the outset, then, by volume, by democratizing the product for wide distribution (Rogers' (1962) adoption process), all the more so if the client recognizes and socially encourages the PPG.

Moreover, an innovation supported by a PPG does not require an end-of-pipe approach of curative type (Hartje and Laurie 1984) – which is often very costly, too late and not very satisfactory – but is part of an integrated *preventive* approach (integrated)[41]. Thus, instead of managing the cycle *ex post*[42], once the launch has taken place and the effects induced have been proven, consideration is given *ex ante* to a consequentist approach involving appropriate design work (of the eco-design type) and leading, for example, to frugal environmental innovation or FEI (see below).

Faced with the challenges posed by human activity (particularly concerning the impact on the NE), PPG is a means of integrating SD into the company's strategy (including by internalizing the potential civil and penal consequences).

41 Thus, in terms of EI, Porter's hypothesis on the need to regulate (Porter and van der Linde 1995), which allows us to move to a *clean* integrated logic rather than to focus on the *end of pipe* (Hartje and Laurie 1984), is clearly incentive-based according to some authors, although this point is disputed (Jaffe and Palmer 1997). But, in any case, the Porterian hypothesis is never really invalidated, and this does not prejudge the heart of the problem, because what matters is the *quality* of the regulatory policy (and not whether it exists or not).

42 Beyond the seminal work of Vernon (1966) and Hayes and Wheelwright (1979), the question of the cost along the life cycle of the product has been raised (In Dhilon (1989), *Life Cycle Costing Analysis* or LCCA; then in Bailey (1991); or Fabricky and Blanchard (1991)), as well as the evaluation of the cost of taking into account the NE along the life cycle of the product (Fava (1991), *environmental life cycle costing assessment*).

1.3.2. *Methodological comparison*

Let us make a comparison (Table 1.3) between the existing *Life Cycle Costing* method (Dhilon 1989; Fabricky and Blanchard 1991) and this proposed method.

Criteria	Definition of the criteria	Method *ex post*	Method *ex ante*
Commensurability	Comparative standard unbiased	No	Yes
Universality	General applicability without field restriction	No (restrictive field to disposable)	Yes
Practicality	Operational feasibility without inaccessible detours	Yes	Yes
Effectiveness	Actionable without additional implementation	No (± yes if recycling possible)	Yes by design and legal standard
Temporality	Temporality of reasoning	*Ex post* method; *a posteriori* management	*Ex ante* method at the design stage

Table 1.3. *Comparison of methods (source: author)*

An *ex post* control may exist in both cases, which makes it non-discriminatory in the comparison.

With the *Life Cycle Costing* or LCC method (Dhilon 1989; Fabricky and Blanchard 1991), externalities (especially negative ones) are ignored from the outset, and this necessitates the allocation of costs *ex post*, often in an approximate (or even optional) manner. A more advanced variant of the LCC (Bailey 1991; Fava 1991) allows, under certain conditions of use (preventive approach, see above), an equivalence with the *ex ante* consequentist method.

The challenge is to focus on the design, to anticipate and provide for the cost of repair (correction, rehabilitation, restoration) and/or physical replacement of the damage to the NE and/or compensation.

The development of *clean technologies* (Irwin and Hooper (1992)) becomes a viable strategy and a source of effective competitive advantage from the outset (Porter 1995; Shrivastana 1995b) because the basis of choice is not piped by truncated calculations, lacking *commensurability*, by mixing unequal and non-comparable options.

In a consequentist approach (Bouvier-Patron 2015a), the innovative company concerned with SD establishes *ex ante*, from the design stage (before *ex post* control), an *accounting of no harm to third-party categories*. A regular comparison (between the pre-visionary and the realized) can, moreover, be set up. The methodology, by calculating the costs retained and accounting, or not, from the outset for all available and foreseeable elements, conditions the sincerity of the profitability obtained. The challenge of the comparison concerns the positive validation of several criteria (Table 1.3): *commensurability* (unbiased comparative standard), *universality* (general applicability regardless of the category considered), *practicality* (operational concreteness) and *effectiveness* (actionable without additional implementation).

1.3.3. *Discussion on the applicability of the calculation*

In practice, the charge to be made, linked to the consequentist cost, corresponds to a provisional sum expressed as a score. This is no more incongruous than a rating, given that the rating agencies, even with regard to compliance with the NE, are fallible and do not vouch for the credibility of their rating: they are therefore not consequential. This score corresponds to the potential damage weighted by a coefficient. The coefficient is part of a pre-established hierarchical scale according to an indicative scale: the gradation of the coefficients is linked to the degree of vital necessity, rarity and non-replaceability of the category suffering prejudice, as well as to the degree of irreversibility and/or irrevocability that may be engendered on it. Also, for the NE (including fauna, flora, ecosystems including water quality, air quality, soil quality) or humans[43], the coefficient will, in principle, be the highest on these criteria.

The scale of coefficients is the result of an independent external expert appraisal by a public body (with an ethics committee to ensure that there are no conflicts of

43 Since Drèze (1962), a development in economic theory has been concerned with an individual's *willingness to pay* to increase their probability of remaining alive (and, in the literature, may refer to the notion of *Value of Statistical Life*, VSL). The VSL is generally an increasing function of the individual's income, the individual's initial exposure to the risk under consideration and the individual's risk aversion. This type of approach is often used (e.g. in road safety (Boiteux 2001) or in real estate (Gayer et al. 2000) to assess the price of houses near sources of pollution. Moreover, the value of humans is regularly dealt with by the courts for the compensation of damage suffered as a result of a third party: homicide, road accidents, occupational accidents, disease, trafficking in humans or organs, etc. The compensation offered is generally monetary. Thus, for example, in the case of occupational diseases related to asbestos, the compensation can be the sum corresponding to the potential income not generated because of the premature death: the *full compensation of the damage* is the calculation of the sum of the income that could have been generated by the prematurely deceased person if they had been able to live normally.

interest), which is likely to hear all possible stakeholders as the general interest depends on it. The hierarchy of coefficients, according to the anticipated impact, aims to erase the possible minimization of a potential impact when the company evaluates an option *ex ante*. The issue is to develop a *convention for the calculation system* (using the scale of coefficients) with official *approval* so that all companies adopt the same one. The aim of the calculation is not to be exact, to the nearest decimal place (Massé 1968), but to provide the firm with benchmarks and make commensurability possible.

Consequently, the company must lucidly choose the alternative that best preserves the third-party categories or, failing that, accept, from the outset, to pay the price.

The foreseeable negative effects *ex ante* will have to be effectively compensated for *in fine* if they are proven, and this by drawing on the precautionary provision set up. The precautionary provision, linked to the amount of the score (i.e. the calculation of the damage weighted by the coefficient), will be entered into the company's accounts. The precautionary provision made *ex ante* is proportional to the potential damage that the company knowingly accepts to take with respect to third parties, as well as for itself (by mortgaging its financial capacities if the company has to draw on the provision made).

A portion of the sale price of a proposed asset could therefore incorporate a fraction of the amount of the provision.

This type of *ex ante* calculation is intended to impute and allow for an informed choice, because a managerial trade-off can always exist between launching a product with a high profitability prospect but with significant potential negative-induced effects, or launching a useful, expensive product with no or low negative-induced effects but with variable profitability (essentially depending on the degree of diffusion of the product).

Thus, sketched out (to see its applicability), the consequentist approach allows for an unbiased competition integrating SD *ex ante*, from the design stage (and before any *ex post* control), through an *approved accounting of no harm to third-party categories* by calibrating all projects according to the imputation of induced consequences.

The design will thus be the place, *ex ante*, of selection of the projects according to the attribution of the score obtained in order *to minimize the* a priori *risk of taking a wrong decision of development of a good prejudicial to a third-party category*.

For radically innovative activities with unimaginable externalities (e.g. biotechnologies or nanotechnologies), companies (especially start-ups, VSEs, or

SMEs) wishing to invest, within a legal framework and accepting a charter drawn up by an independent ethical committee, must have access (not in terms of raising capital to launch the activity or growth) to specific guaranteed loans to help them build up the necessary provisions. Furthermore, if the activity is strategic for the nation while corresponding to the general interest, start-ups, VSEs or SMEs in the activities concerned could benefit from a guarantee and/or direct assumption of precautionary provisions by the government.

At the same time, the government must develop a proactive policy to encourage (through tax deductions or a reduction in corporate income tax) any company to adopt a consequentist approach based on certified accounting.

The provision to be made is an intrinsic part of the initial investment (without necessarily being consumed later if necessity does not dictate it): it is calculated on an identical basis for all (thus each of the competitors) and also reveals the possible alternatives without comparative bias. Once the arbitration has been carried out by the company, the sum to be provisioned is charged to the accounts but will, if necessary, be reinvested at a later date (in fractions according to a schedule) on other projects when the non-nuisance (or harmlessness) is established (according to a schedule of impact studies planned *ex ante*: 1, 3, 5, 10 years or more) The choice of investment to be made, with profitability bets, will be freely oriented according to the interest of the company, but without it being able to pretend to ignore the consequences and/or refuse to assume them. The profitability study necessarily integrates an impact study with a timetable (potentially verifiable by experts) whose credibility is guaranteed by the initial provision made (legally observable), as well as by the company's choice of transparency, since the information participates in its institutional communication, and reinforces the intangible capital and its reputation, which is not negligible in terms of stock market valuation.

Each company is therefore always seeking to obtain the highest profits or profitability, but without deteriorating the fate of third parties with impunity. The trend orientation will then go, qualitatively, in the search for a profitability of non-nuisance *a priori*. Pure marketing and/or financial opportunism[44] with the sole aim of pure profitability will be the exception.

---

44 Thus, in the pharmaceutical sector, cheating on the benefit of a drug through biased or manipulated studies is, in theory, denounced by the authority granting the *marketing authorization* (but which may be deceitful or lax: blind trust; absence, defect and/or inadequacy of verification of the data provided; or even conflicts of interest of experts paid by the companies). The stakes are also reputational and financial when the harmful effects are revealed over time (e.g. when the company has deliberately concealed the negative aspects so as not to slow down sales and/or the extension of the fields of application).

Consequentism invites undistorted competition through decentralized regulation via a calculation compatible with the logic of commensurability and pre-preservation of third categories.

A company that enters a market and does not respect the constraint linked to the initial calculation will be sanctioned by the competent regulatory authority by the amount of the precautionary provision that it should have constituted (and could possibly see, if the legislation allows it, its products withdrawn from sale and then destroyed, as is already the case for counterfeiting).

In order to give full credibility to this logic, all goods with high foreseeable negative *ex ante* effects (e.g. exceeding a score ceiling and/or, *a fortiori*, in case of potential irrevocability impacting a third-party category in the strict sense) should also require a prior authorization request (of the product license).

The requirement to take into account all possible consequences does not turn the company into an omniscient demiurge: anticipations are made on what can be envisaged at the time of the decision given the available knowledge (according to scenarios provided by experts). There is a difference between blindness, negligence, ignorance or, on the contrary, assuming what we know (ourselves, as well as the scholarly community) in order to draw the consequences and knowing that competitors do the same. Too many companies still pretend not to know or not to want to know in the name of business, while sometimes even paying lip service to corporate responsibility, ethics or business morality.

Whatever happens, the public authorities are responsible for the unintended or unforeseen consequences that are revealed later. However, in the present system, the public authorities bear almost all the consequences in the name of the principle of privatizing profits and collectivizing the rest.

Also, in a restored Knightian tradition, the entrepreneurial risk taken is assumed in the event of success or failure, under the same conditions for all, which also makes it possible to internalize and weight the ambitions of each individual without seeking to transfer the consequences to the public authorities. By taking risks in accordance with the above-mentioned calculation rule, success acts as a reward as well as a protective barrier (to entry, mobility and exit), except for the more ambitious bets that can challenge the first player on the market.

Made compulsory by law, the calculation represents *in fine* only an additional accounting line in an account book (registered by the accountant and verifiable by an auditor). The accuracy and sincerity of the declaration (linked to this calculation) examined and/or contested by an auditor can lead to the opening of financial sanctions in case of gross approximations or obvious negligence.

The auditor, examining this accounting line, for a given company as well as for all competitors, is in a position (taking into account the size of the company and other variables such as turnover, investments, innovation, nature of the markets) to calibrate the declaration made and carry out an investigation if necessary. The opinion of technology experts can be sought. The sincerity of the declaration, as when we scrutinize the responses to a call for tenders, is largely revealed by the comparison. The innovative monopoly, because of information asymmetry, may try to cheat, but at the risk of permanently tarnishing its reputation when the truth is there for all to see, and it will have to assume its choices accordingly. The government, in its incentive policy, could match the declaration of the pro-vision for precaution (in terms of sincerity and accuracy) with a measure such as a tax deduction from the corporate tax. The role of the auditor would then also be to examine the eligibility for the allowance.

1.4. Conclusion

After defining the different categories of goods and putting into perspective Ostrom's contribution to decentralized regulation (accessible to companies), we explained the impact of private activity on NE and showed how private decision-making and NE could be made consistent. We cannot preserve NE by keeping the current rules of economic decision.

We affirm the necessity of a consequentist reasoning by private actors subjected to competition and having to decide *ex ante* on options among others, but all of them now having to position themselves on a commensurable basis. At present, companies generally favor *ex post* repair (by *recycling*[45] of elements recovered at the end of the chain).

However, this *ex post* logic (when it exists) is less satisfactory (than an *ex ante* consequentist approach) because of difficulties in appropriating the qualitative rent generated and/or, more generally, because companies do not take into account the positive effects attributable to a strategy that favors NE. On the contrary, the

45 Is *recycling* a logic that respects the NE? If it is indeed a question of reusing elements at the end of their life (Geyer and Jackson 2004), recycling in itself does not make it possible to modify, upstream, the origin of the incoming flow, the compatibility with the NE and the potential waste. Hence, the importance of a *circular* economy (with partial or total reuse of the CtoC type; for a description of this process in India for electronic products, see Chatterjee and Kumar (2009)). However, if what is reused in this way is not immediately an ecological material, there is no guarantee of compatibility with the NE, hence the need (Beamon 1999) to move towards *green supply chain management*. Moreover, it should be noted that Indian-inspired *frugality* (Radjou et al. 2012) is first and foremost a recycling approach (as well as a new activity). The challenge is to reach NE-friendly frugality of the FEI type (Chapters 5 and 6).

consequentist approach integrates two essential aspects: i) the endogenous analysis by companies of the effective impact of private activity on third categories of which the NE is a part (destroying the NE multiplies the negative effects on humans, fauna and flora, as in the case of intensive agriculture, for example); ii) internalizing the positive consequences. Anticipating the economic consequences must be based on a calculation convention imposed on each private entity so as to preserve a common resource (finite, unique, non-renewable, that is the NE).

In a consequentist approach, the PPG, not generating prejudices to a third-party category, is compatible with the competitive logic. As we will see (in Chapters 5 and 6), a specific frugal approach to innovation, frugal environmental innovation (FEI), corresponds to this objective. Consequentism is not inspired by a deontology (i.e. *a body of rules of conduct establishing* a priori *what to do without necessarily studying the consequences*), but by a real methodology with a pragmatic and universal vocation, whereas the *precautionary principle*, with its solid complementary theoretical foundations (Arrow and Fischer 1974; Jonas 1979), is inhibiting for the decision-maker and is socially perceived, wrongly, as being antinomic with innovation.

Taking into account the NE to innovate forces us to question and then find non-polluting (*clean*) technologies in manufacturing, use and recycling. Above all, it is a question of finding the technological level adapted to the purpose of respecting the NE (mobilizing more than ever bricolage and improvisation; see Chapter 7). Technological deployment, often maximalist and expensive (in resources), could be better controlled by appropriate choices by mobilizing the *satisfactory technological level* (in the sense of *satisficing* (Simon 1976, 1978)), including the FabLab, for example (Chapter 2), which is then a hybrid means between technological organization and frugality (frugality is addressed in Chapters 5 and 6). The western choice consists too often (even quite systematically) of privileging the technological path (Chapters 2–4) in a race to the front where consequentism generally has no place. The FabLab (Chapter 2) is a candidate of technological (or rather technico-organizational) essence, allowing us to valorize decentralized upstream design in a community of innovation and appears, as such, as a revolution that could, paradoxically, favor the heavy tendency of an unbridled technological race ahead, or curb it through frugality, bricolage and improvisation.

2

FabLab: Creation and Design through Technology?

The issue of ICT (involving the fusion of computer–audiovisual–telephony), which has become commonplace, refers to the elaboration, coordination, collaboration – sometimes cooperative – (through free access or acquisition) of knowledge via the circulation of information and data flows. In relation to the theory of the firm, the first to mention the importance of this tool for improving internal coordination was Coase (1937). However, at the operational level, it was not until the 1980s and 1990s that the management of information and flows within the firm (intra-organization) and, more or less explicitly, between firms (inter-organization) was improved and/or optimized.

The 1980s corresponded to a change in companies due to competition from Japanese firms whose competitive advantage was based on the worldwide marketing of quality products at a price comparatively much lower than that achieved elsewhere. However, unlike western companies, which tend to be highly hierarchical and vertically integrated, the Japanese winning form is based on the organization of a network of companies. Thus, Aoki's *J* model (1986) relates an organizational decentralization articulating a set of appendices (shops) within the firm's legal boundary (decentralized intra-organization of the F-N type: Firm-Network) and also, above all, outside it, by linking legally distinct entities (NoF: Network of Firms, around a *Coordinating Actor* noted CA or *pivotal firm*) with complementary activities. Subsequently, the literature focused on the use of ICT in the firm, to manage information and flows (Paché and Paraponaris 1993, 2006), generates a certain confusion between F-N and NoF.

The problem is twofold: the primacy given to technology (by focusing on ICT) when what matters is organizational strategy; the focus on the study of information and flow management while denying the importance of NoF as an original organizational combination essential to the evolution of industrial organization (and capitalism). Clearly, the NoF can be analyzed independently of ICT, which is *a priori* only a technical supplement to improve business management (and which can also, in a second phase via the Internet, transform the organization). This is not to deny the importance of the issues at stake and of the work on ICT (theoretical and/or empirical Benghozi 2000; SESSI 2005; DGCIS 2010) concerning, in particular, information processing, work organization, inventory management, procurement, sales, the fluidity of production driven by the downstream and/or logistics and transport. However, the focus on F-N, perceived as a challenge to coordination through technology, comes back to a certain vision of the firm based on the minimization of costs (in the ideal scheme suggested by Coase 1937) and on the myth of a technological flexibility where machines prevent human decision-making and functional hazards.

The question is not so much whether technology is useful, but whether it plays the essential role, even though it must be integrated, more or less harmoniously, into an organizational strategy (intra-organizational and also inter-organizational between legally distinct entities).

As for the NoF, it is first and foremost the result of an organizational strategy aimed at confronting Japanese competition by refocusing on the core business as well as outsourcing. The theoretical analysis of the NoF (Bouvier-Patron 1993, 1994a, 1996b, 2015b), which articulates legally distinct complementary entities, is as pragmatic in emphasizing refocusing on the core business/outsourcing (Teece 1980, 1988; Prahalad and Hamel 1990), as analytical (based on the initial contribution of Coase (1937) concerning incomplete long-term contracts after *internalization versus outsourcing* or *make versus buy*, then that of the theory of relational quality of Richardson (1972) and Hakansson (1982)). Indeed, if the central elements of analysis of the contemporary firm can be traced back to (Cournot 1838; Knight 1921; Coase 1937), the central elements of analysis of the contemporary firm, Richardson (1972) specifies it as a relational entity that cannot be a simple *isolated island in an ocean of markets*.

The contractual approach of Coase (1937), followed by Williamson (1975, 1985), in order to explain the *raison d'être* of the firm mobilizes the paradigm of transaction costs (the firm exists because the cost of internal organization proves to be less than the cost of transactions on the market); and, in order to do so, displacing and then expelling Knight's (1921) fundamental question about the reduction of uncertainty.

The authors of the transactional paradigm are reluctant and delay taking into account *hybrid* forms (to use the usual vocabulary) between the market and the hierarchy (of the NoF type). Even more restrictive, within the standard approach, the agency paradigm of Jensen and Meckling (1976) generates a particular vision that is not very relevant to the NoF: the complex inter-organizational reality is then reduced to a nonrepresentative situation, that of a *principal* able to impose a contract on an agent given the *informational asymmetry* both to make them participate (*participation constraint*) and to incite them either to reveal (*incentive constraint*) private information useful to the principal and/or to carry out an action in the principal's interest. This particular relationship, banishing strategic action and where the principal dominates (imposing the contract on the agent) is very singular (like the principal/subcontractor logic) but is often extrapolated, abusively, to any inter-organizational relationship. Houssiaux (1957) had perfectly addressed the principal/subcontractor question through the concept of *quasi-disintegration*. The theory of agency envisages a formal generalization through the contract by manipulating the determining question of *informational asymmetry* (which can be mobilized, moreover, independently of theory of agency) but by extrapolating a singular relational situation. However, the client–supplier relations of an NoF require the reconstruction of inter-organizational relational strategies (where the two key variables are *relational symmetry versus asymmetry*, as well as *bargaining power*: Bouvier-Patron (1994a, 1995, 1998b, 2002)). Williamson (1975, 1985), who is more relevant than Jensen and Meckling (1976) for our purposes, borrows from Schelling (1960) the strategic relational elements of *hold-up* and *hostage-taking* between two legally distinct entities. However, it should be noted that Schelling (1960) analyzes the interrelationship, in an early way, without any recourse to contractualism.

The glorious level of contractualist analysis, which is rather recent – after the first milestone set by Coase (1937) on incomplete long-term contracts (a contribution far superior to the explanation of the firm by transaction costs widely promoted in economics and management science) and then by Coase (1960) on the question of managing negative externalities, such as market failures – is that of Hart and Moore (1990). In this respect, Hart and Moore (1990) insist analytically on the question of the *replaceability of an asset*, thus joining the seminal analysis of Richardson (1972) on the classification of activities according to their *complementarity versus* their *similarity*. In essence, complementary activities are not substitutable. Their degree of substitutability depends on their scarcity in the market. This is what Williamson (1975, 1985), taking up the concept of *idiosyncrasy* from Hayek (1945), calls *specificity*.

Qualitatively, the specificity of a skill (Teece's skill-based approach (1980, 1988), in a long lineage with Penrose (1959), with its explication in management by Wernerfelt (1984)) explains the refocusing on the core business with outsourcing. This provides the essential argumentative basis for the NoF and also for the evolutionary dynamics of the firm and the NoF through collaborative coordination and then the renewal of *complementary competencies* (Penrose 1959; Richardson 1972; Doz 1994; Teece 2007). Hakansson (1982), expanding on Richardson (1972), reinforces this framework of analysis by insisting, as already mentioned, on the quality of customer–supplier relationships. By the same token, it is necessary to move from the restrictive vision of the firm (*nexus of contracts*: agency theory) to the firm in NoF as a *node of complementary competencies*.

If we return to ICT, its mobilization is first and foremost an additional layer to the strategy (firm and/or NoF). Nevertheless, certain uses, with the Internet, can transform this structure organizationally: moving to the *virtual network* (N form to V form); and, well beyond that, considering the potential links between the NoF (extended virtually) and the FabLab as a new device that can be assimilated by the firm and, by extension, the NoF.

Note that the NoF intrinsically includes a form of plasticity (Bouvier-Patron 1994a, 1996b, 1998b or see Appendix 1); the key concern here is not to go too far, at the risk of making it disappear (or, conversely, by making it more rigid, to sclerose it). ICTs offer a plastic possibility of transforming, qualitatively, the relations between legally distinct entities (dematerialization of exchanges, new genesis of value, freeing of geographical and/or cultural distances). In this sense, ICTs alone make it possible to extend the NoF through *virtualization*. The additional qualitative leap is to see to what extent the NoF is able to mobilize an additional appendage: the FabLab. Taken as a generic term (because it covers a broad spectrum), the FabLab is an organizational device that is often self-managed, open (sometimes to all), and that promotes exchanges and interactions within a community of practice of bricolage enthusiasts (see Chapter 7) and/or producing (in a more or less professional manner, individually or collectively) by mobilizing ICT and DT (3D printing in particular). The advantages of a new appendage FabLab for a company (on its own and/or in NoF) are obvious in the context of globalization and market globalization, where hypercompetition (debatable because of social, fiscal, health and environmental dumping) weakens western companies, which are now also competing on innovation (backlash through maturation following initial outsourcing to India or China in particular (Bouvier-Patron 2009)).

Innovation, the key to maintaining and/or creating a sustainable competitive advantage for companies specialized in their business, is expensive *a priori*. The FabLab is therefore the potential key to reducing the costs of innovation; in terms of design, prototyping, preindustrial series testing and therefore also in terms of reducing the time to market between the project and the actual launch on the market (time to market). All in all, the importance of NoF has been growing in the economy since the mid-1980s, and the virtual network is an initial extension of this (from the mid-1990s), which can mobilize, in particular, as a new network appendage, a more or less developed and professional FabLab modality that can reduce the costs of designing innovation. After (section 2.1) an analysis of the NoF and its virtual extension, we will examine (section 2.2) what the concept of FabLab covers and how it can be linked to the NoF in order to reduce design costs and promote, qualitatively, a better way of innovating at a lower cost. Finally (section 2.3), establishing the NoF-FabLab link, we will consider the possible premises of a new industrial revolution.

2.1. The major form of contemporary industrial organization

In response to Japanese quality/price competition in the 1980s, the NoF resulting from the combination of refocusing on the business and outsourcing (Teece 1980, 1988; Prahalad and Hamel 1990) became widespread in the OECD. The NoF enshrines the inter-organizational sphere (Richardson 1972; Hakansson 1982; Aoki 1986; Farrell and Scotchmer 1988; Asanuma 1989; Ring and Van de Ven 1992, 1994) without any link to the agency theory, which is poorly matched to inter-organizational managerial practice. Consequently, the complementarity (Richardson 1972) of knowledge, know-how or specific competencies (Hayek 1945; Williamson 1975, 1985) between linked firms induces the need for inter-organizational coordination and generates a positive reputation (Kreps and Wilson 1982a) on each business and on the network thus constituted while allowing the sharing of risks and costs. Each firm being centered on its *core business*, the choice of a business and its evolution (Teece 1980, 1988, 2007) is largely the result of routines (Nelson and Winter 1982) and the dependence on the technological path followed (Arthur 1989; Dosi et al. 1990) without, however, prohibiting the necessary renewal of competencies (Penrose 1959; Doz 1994). Thus, in a world of hypercompetition and globalization, where innovation is becoming a key but costly competitive advantage for firms, the need for excellence, as well as the strong financial and profitability constraints, have imposed a trend towards the NoF form (and then the extended NoF).

We will first define (section 2.1.1) the NoF and then (section 2.1.2) we will consider its possible transformation and/or extension by ICT linked to the Internet giving, more or less, the V form (virtual network).

2.1.1. *The network form: NoF*

The organizational form of the NoF is based on four characteristics: refocusing on the business and outsourcing (make or buy); complementarity of (vertical) activities between network members; specific services linked to competencies that are difficult to replace on the market; coordination of services by the Coordinating Actor (CA). The coordination required is twofold:

– internal (intra-organization) in the articulation of key functions (marketing–R&D–purchasing (Urban and Hauser 1993)) to anticipate the market, foster innovation and co-design;

– external (inter-organizational) via the purchasing function, whose role is essential for the selection/contracting of service providers and competencies: it is a matter of combining complementary distributed expertise by relying on modularity, interdependence and reciprocity.

Refocused on its core business, the CA, for the design and production of a product, must contract for the complementary services it needs. The risk of opportunism (Williamson 1975) and of unilateral dependence (Pfeffer and Salancik 1978) may exist but are theoretically overestimated. Moreover, *relational asymmetry* (Bouvier-Patron 1995) is not inevitable because of the credible threats in strategic interaction (Schelling 1960), because everything will depend on the *specificity* of the competence held (Williamson 1975, 1985) and *bargaining power* (Asanuma 1989; Bouvier-Patron 1994a). Moreover, in contractualization, security criteria exist (e.g. the maximum share to be held in the turnover of a supplier; double sourcing with a premium for the leader). The *partnership*[1] (Farrell and Scotchmer 1988), see Appendix 1, can be fully embodied here. Multilateral interdependence is then less of a handicap than a real strategic and dynamic collective engine for long-term development within the NoF. Overall, the advantages of the NoF are considerable: coordination and combination of complementary competencies with strong expertise; scalability and renewal of competencies; adaptability and flexibility within and between organizations; innovation, based (increasingly) on a collective; co-design; collective learning; distribution of risks and costs among the actors in long-term interaction. If the network form N does indeed designate an NoF, each member firm can itself, internally, function as a network firm (F-N).

The firm network (F-N) is characterized by a structure that is decompartmentalized between departments and/or decentralized in its operation; decision-making adapted to the changing and complex dynamics of needs and the environment; and based on an adapted, adaptable, reactive and sometimes versatile workforce and also a system of communication, exchange and efficient management (via ICT through electronic data exchanges (EDE), enterprise resource planning (ERP) and just-in-time (JIT)). Too often, however, emphasis is placed on this logistical dimension (and its tools) to show the efficiency of flow management and

1 *Partnership* (Farrell and Scotchmer 1988; see Appendix 1) refers to equality in the sharing of results between members with complementary activities, even when there is inequality in the contribution of each.

to obtain an optimization of the F-N, whereas flows or tools do not prejudge the efficiency of the strategy, nor the decision-making excellence, nor even the effective level or quality of management. On paper, the tools used are technically efficient (minimalist, such as order management, catalog management, invoicing, payroll; maximalist, such as ERP).

The ERP articulates the fields of supply–logistics–accounting–production–sales–distribution, in a more or less exhaustive way while mobilizing a unique database, and more or less multifunctional, by integrating Human Resources Management, the follow-up of the product life cycle or computerized design via CAD (Computer-Aided Design), with, generally, integration of the *Customer Relationship Management* aspects downstream and *Supplier Relationship Management* upstream. Such complexity is managed by the SAP software package (whose initial heaviness and rigidity have given way, with the Internet and the evolution of IT, to flexible and ergonomic solutions).

However, the cost of acquisition, training, implementation, maintenance, technical assistance and osmosis with the organization still needs to be understood. And, in certain reference industrial sectors (e.g. automotive), the JIT supply between the CA and each of its providers increases the risk of dependence and sometimes the costs. In addition, modern IT architectures use the Internet protocol (IP) but rely first on the Intranet (an intra-organizational private computer network) or Extranet (a private computer network extending, typically, a company's Intranet to its inter-organizational sphere of functional necessity) and then the Internet. The notable inflection point opening the universe of possibilities is the recourse to the Internet, for the application of ICT to companies as elsewhere. That said, the limit of ICT application is human rather than technical: in terms of training, acceptability, practical use, potential dehumanization of work, dependence on technology, control and surveillance of employees.

As the NoF is based on long-term outsourcing, ICT plays a prominent role in coordination, but strategic orientation will prevail.

Through the inter-organizational prism of the NoF, the aim is to promote the advantages of decompartmentalization, decentralization and lateralization of communication between distinct legal entities in the service of innovation and value creation. All in all, the turning point of the 1980s, characterized by the shift to the NoF (Aoki 1986, 1988), outclassed the large Chandlerian firm (1962, 1977) – form D with its corollary vertical integration (Klein et al. 1978; Grossman and Hart 1986; Williamson 1985; Riordan 1990) – can be analyzed as a quasi-disintegration but surpassing Houssiaux (1957) by the stakes of innovation (Aoki 1986) and relational quality (Richardson 1972; Hakansson 1982; Asanuma 1989; Bouvier-Patron 1993, 1994a, 1996b, 1998b, 2002).

From the former intra-organizational structure (centralized or relatively centralized), we move to the coordination (on a more or less hierarchical and lateralized mode) of legally distinct complementary poles of expertise. The gain in flexibility achieved by NoF is based on the contractual coordination of complementary (Richardson 1972) and specific (Williamson 1975, 1985; Aoki 1986) independent activities. The very evolution of the NoF form has several dimensions:

– quasi-decentralization of the management of a complex set of highly connected entities through multiple processes of co-contractualization;

– quasi-disappearance of the borders of each actor of the network and of the network itself to generate a contractual spectral entity through blurred and moving relations;

– quasi-dematerialization of the physical universe of the network entity to privilege virtual relations (with or without contractualization) via ICTs including the Internet.

2.1.2. *The virtual form: extension of the NoF via ICT*

The NoF is thus primarily a strategic necessity. Complementary competencies, more or less specific, which are indispensable to the realization of a product desired by the CA, are articulated in it. This pivotal role of the CA does not exhaust the fundamental question (Asanuma 1989) of *bargaining power* (BP) between the CA (client) and its suppliers. This leads us to propose a typology of customer–supplier relationships according to the respective BP of each party (Bouvier-Patron 1994a, 1998b, 2002, 2011a, 2013, 2017a), with partnership being the most balanced form. On this strategic reality can be grafted an additive technological dimension, on the inter-organizational level, in the management of information and flows (already existing before Internet, with EDE).

The Internet has above all allowed a drastic reduction in the costs of electronic exchanges and a considerable widening of the possibilities of coordination from, generally, the intra-organization of the CA and its electronic means.

On the logistical aspects (often cited for NoF around a CA), the JIT aims to reduce costs while promoting quality (absence of defects, absence of breakdowns, elimination of buffer stocks, timing of flows and delivery of the right ingredient, to the right place at the right time). There is a lineage of American–Japanese influence on quality management (of information and flows) since the 1950s: W. Deming, Plan-Do-Check-Act; J. Juran, cost of non-quality; A. Feigenbaum, TQM; T. Ohno at Toyota for JIT and KanBan. All of these elements are synthesized by Womack and Jones (1990, 1996) in *lean management* (to become lean by eliminating what is not valuable). The challenge is to control the *supply chain* (from the supplier's supplier to the customer's customer). From the point of view of flow optimization (zero defects, zero inventory, JIT), *single sourcing* is a possibility to control flows and to benefit from a return in terms of cost due to the economies of scale obtained by the single supplier; and/or from a leader, as this result is also accessible in double-sourcing with a bonus for the leader (Bouvier-Patron 1994a, 1998b, 2002, 2011a, 2014). Single-source operation is only relevant if the CA is dominant, at least in the sense that it has the capacity to select its supplier and to impose, unilaterally, the terms of the contract (price, quality, deadlines, adaptability) as well as the JIT (with the constraints of compatibility: homogenization over the whole network of the CA's technical system; unless prior standardization, the AFNOR or ISO technical standards guarantee *a priori* compatibility).

In this reading centered on the logistics technique by ICT and JIT, it is quite coherent to draw the analysis towards F-N. However, this represents only a relatively superficial part of the reality to be analyzed, since the fundamental issue is indeed the NoF, which, substantially and also logically, implies considering the question of logistics technology secondarily to strategy.

Within the NoF (and the F-N for that matter), given the decentralization of management and dematerialization (organization, work, flows) – based on the Internet – the question is whether a new virtual form can appear and/or become autonomous (e.g. by constituting an extended form with respect to the NoF). The current variation of the term virtual form shows that the concept is not stabilized:

– a form that intensively mobilizes ICTs, especially the Internet, in its activities, notably to contribute to the creation of value from the networking of competencies and their collaborative interactions;

– a geographically dispersed form where coordination is possible via ICT;

– temporary form with alliances on specific projects (alliances that are constantly renewed);

– cyber-enterprise on the Internet.

Bringing the virtual form closer to Mintzberg's (1979) adhocratic structure, based on innovation, project-based management and decentralized command, is an interesting abstraction, but it does not fully help define the virtual form. Moreover, considering the evolution of the classical firm towards the virtual is more like noting a change in the technological skin of the large enterprise (LE) than analyzing the underlying potential generic form. The *virtual firm* (Davidow and Malone 1992) could first be defined as a *molecule that can be modulated according to the different elements that are grafted onto it around a common project*; once the project is completed, dissolution is necessary, with each person moving on to other projects.

Byrne's (1993) definition of the *virtual organization* is more relevant: *a temporary network of independent companies – suppliers, customers, and even rivals – linked by ICTs* and without necessarily needing a head office, an organizational chart or a hierarchy for the coordination of competencies, cost management and access to markets. Following this, Rayport and Sviokla (1995) emphasize the use of ICT, especially the Internet, for functional efficiency and value creation. The intensive use of ICTs is discriminating in that it makes it possible to get away from geographical dispersion, culture or contractual duration. The creation of value through ICTs is an even more discriminating variable, as the members mobilized to contribute to it may (or may not) be geographically dispersed; from different cultures; locatable at a given moment *t*; involved over time. In any case, the members are united and responsible for the results of the activity and the value extracted.

The possible dispersion of members and the use of ICTs raise the problem of *trust* between partners (*trust* being essential in relational and organizational functioning (Breton and Wintrobe 1982)).

The short contractual duration seems to be linked to the characteristics of the *new economy*: turbulence, instability, environmental uncertainty, globalization and fragmentation of markets, reduction of product life cycles, proliferation of new products, level of customer demand and flickering, need to offer *customized* products/services, high rate of technological diffusion and dependence of product value on services.

The link to the market through the creation of *virtual value* favors interactivity and also the relationship, singular or mass, with customers by offering specific goods or services with high added value. Moreover, the *cyber* part of the company (Lipnack and Stamps 1997) is more or less determining. Thus, we have:

– a company open to the *new economy*: *brick and mortar* to clicks (extension via virtual store window on the Internet);

– mixed company: *brick and clicks* (Dell);

– virtual company: *clicks* (Internet shop window), with physical flows (Amazon) or without (Avast).

The virtual form, via the Internet, is more of a variation of the NoF form in terms of its structuring principles, but it is especially notable for the importance of the use of ICT in the creation of value. The dynamics of operation and evolution of the virtual form tend to make the organizational structure less visible without making it disappear. The virtual form is thus a particular variation of the NoF form where the technological support, via Internet, plays a key role because the technical possibilities guide the use and authorize their wide diffusion on the professional and private level. Technological democratization through diffuse expertise (decentralization of knowledge and know-how via communities of practice (Brown and Duguid 1991, 1998; Wenger and Snyder 2000)) is evident with the Internet in particular.

All in all, *virtualization* makes it possible to free oneself from geographical and cultural distances while favoring the creation of value, but the design of an innovative product remains costly and time-consuming. The question is therefore to know to what extent the NoF can mobilize the FabLab to innovate better, faster and at a lower cost.

2.2. FabLab: heterogeneous form or NoF reinforcement?

We will first define the concept of FabLab (section 2.2.1) in its specificity, and then we will analyze (section 2.2.2) its possible articulation to the NoF form.

2.2.1. *Definition of FabLab*

The *Fabrication Laboratory* or FabLab is a concept developed in the 1990s within the MIT *Center for Bits and Atoms* by Gershenfeld (2005), who summarizes the challenge with the formula "How to Make Almost Anything".

It is also an educational program (syllabusMIT:863.08) and a project based on a charter[2], one of the axes of which is to encourage the creation of a worldwide *network* of FabLabs. The FabLab is thus designed to make available the technologies that allow any community to become more creative. The FabLab is thus a collaborative creation space open to all, offering possibilities of realizing objects by design and then digital production by sharing knowledge and competencies to quickly, without even resorting to companies, go from concept to prototype and then to unit and/or series development, with, or without, the prospect of a commercial project.

Eychenne (2012) establishes the technical inventory, as well as the functioning of the FabLab (within the FING observatory, *Fondation Internet Nouvelle Generation* (New Generation Internet Foundation)). Without affiliation to the charter, the FabLab becomes autonomous and a generic category. There can therefore be no univocal and simple reading of the FabLab. Thus, by enriching the document "hackerspace" (Collective 2013), we can list different entities, often confused, allowing a first classification: black hat hackerspace, hackerspace,

2 See: http://fab.cba.mit.edu/about/charter/.

makerspace, FabLab and TechShop. This descriptive typology is operational and establishes a distinction according to the purpose.

– *The black hat hackerspace* is an informal place, virtual or not, gathering technological hackers oriented on fraudulent or criminal practices.

– The *hackerspace* is a physical place, dedicated to DT enthusiasts, more or less experts, allowing, beyond the virtual, interactions and exchanges of knowledge and know-how, in a collective (more or less proselytized and ritualized community type to become a member and/or to be recognized) and/or to promote *technological hacking*.

– The *makerspace* is a physical place dedicated to *technology tinkerers*, oriented on doing (*makers*), allowing, within a collective, interactions and exchanges of knowledge and know-how: it is a form close to the *hackerspace* but oriented on *doing*.

– The FabLab is a physical place, allowing interactions and exchanges within a space open *a priori* to the greatest number (subject sometimes to the passing of admission levels for the members via initiation and improvement courses), based on a charter, with the aim of educating and making with the help of ICT and DT; and, moreover, with the ambition of a ramification in a worldwide interconnected network.

– The *TechShop* is a private workshop, advantageously endowed with digital technological resources, offering access and/or services for a fee; by extension, some private commercial workshops could also serve as service interfaces where the customer only has to order what they want.

In addition to this typology based on the purpose, we can decline the analysis according to the possible functional spectrum of the Fab (generic term regrouping the previous categories):

– the *concept* of a technological platform (more or less immaterial) with an altruistic purpose;

– an *operating object* via a physical place allowing to realize from A to Z;

– *place of interactions* and non-virtual exchanges between individuals;

– *technical method* as a technological device at the service of users;

– a *set of resources* (socio-technical combination, mobilizing human and technological means, focused on individual and collective learning of knowledge and know-how);

– individual and collective *creation space* with or without a productive purpose;

– *community project* (individuals federated in a collective of enthusiasts);

– *ideological support* for the representation of action and activism;

– *institutional organization*, public or private;

– *business model* of a company;

– *economic good*: a collective good (not exclusive and not rival) but rather rare.

It is not useful to examine each aspect in detail. Let us note that the dimension of *place* is systematically retained by the Fab actors. The dimensions of technical means and resources are often put forward but as conditions of possibility and not as sufficient conditions. The individual and collective tension (DIY, Do It Yourself and/or DIWO, Do It With Others) is definitive in the sense that the individual is the basis of this system with free adhesion, but their expression and their action have meaning only within the collective: there is thus no need to oppose individual approach and collective realization.

The *community* dimension comes as an indispensable generic precision, modulated and attenuated according to the commercial character: the *community* aspect is extinguished *a priori* at the stage of the *TechShop* during a commercial relationship but, simultaneously, for commercial reasons, the *TechShop* can cultivate a *community spirit* reinvested by marketing: thus, Apple enthusiasts have the feeling of a specific membership in a community. Finally, the *creative* dimension is latent because, even though encouraged, its effectiveness is not programmable and results from discoveries by trial and error, interactions and chance (serendipity), also leading to (bottom-up) innovations (Von Hippel 1976, 2005) without necessarily being accompanied by property rights (each person freely using what the other does). Additional optional dimensions can be added to generate specificity and qualitative (and/or even market) value.

Thus, the orientation on the intention of the place can be declined in three modalities: *activist, institutional* or *market*. The dividing line seems to be the *private commercial purpose*. Thus, beyond the access fees necessary to finance the operation (financial or in-kind donations, association between peers through membership fees or subscriptions/membership fees in addition to any subsidies), a profit-making aim defines the Fab as an economic good. From then on, the governance to be implemented in each Fab is not homogeneous because the *activist, institutional* or *market* orientation does not generate the same type of functioning and regulation. We can distinguish two levels.

– *Economic*: the financing of the place, the machines and the use is based on self-financing (donations, subscriptions) for *activism*; on subsidies via the supervisory structures or private sponsors for the *institution* and, incidentally, by an individual paying contribution (access ticket to the place and/or to the trainings); the *market* entity on the pricing via a price.

– *Functional*[3]: *activism* is based on horizontality because it is federated by a goal, an ideology and leaders; the *institution* on a regulation and a mediator/referent/animator (exercising a more or less strong hierarchy according to the status conferred by the regulation and/or their involvement in the actual functioning of the structure); the *market* entity on a *manager* (exercising a hierarchical role in the case of an autonomous private entity or responding to organizational rules defined by the company to which it is attached).

It is obvious that the specific stakes of the commercial entity (setting up a business model, recruiting and managing personnel with performance objectives, the key role of marketing, capturing a clientele, managing intellectual property concerning the way in which a third party can have access to information linked to the creation)[4] are not those relating to the institutional sectors or activist.

2.2.2. *FabLab and NoF compatibility*

The common point of all the Fabs is the *capacity to function in the network*.

– Resilient horizontal network functioning has defined the *FabLab* since the origin of Gershenfeld's project: a network of peers resembling each other and defending the same finality (adherents of the same charter or not) by giving access, to the greatest number, to the DT within a collective place favoring interactions and exchanges in order to share knowledge and/or know-how and, even, to generate creation by technological bricolage among the makers and/or the hackers.

– A multiform network through the interconnection of activist spaces of the *hackerspace* type (at least through the Internet). The coordination of actions constitutes a more or less formalized operation.

3 The word "functional" refers to the concrete (Collectif 2013): money needed to find safety problems in the work done, inter-individual conflicts, use of equipment (cleanliness, possible monopolization, breakage, cleaning, maintenance), possible stocks, absolute necessity to have an operational Lab.

4 The FabLab potentially facilitates the production and dissemination of illegal copies of digital files but also the counterfeiting of digital and/or material objects. This raises the question of the regulation and supervision of 3D printing (Berchon 2014). Digital locks can protect the intellectual property of content, following the example of Digital Rights Management (DRM), already known for music and video files.

– Private horizontal network with a successful business model, competitive emulation generating, in addition to internal growth (increasing the size of the space), external growth (buyout of competing entities and/or conglomerate).

– By extension, horizontal duplication of clones to allow for territorial networking (franchising), reducing costs and risks while benefiting from the positive externalities of the network (including complementary specializations to have a wide range of advice and/or training available in the network).

– A centralized network of a chain of *TechShops*, delivering services involving only a limited role for the customer, within a group (rather vertical hierarchy and rather centralized management) selling identical services everywhere and/or by specialization (in the same geographical area or in different areas). The development of the *TechShop* phenomenon, group and/or franchise, is not to be overlooked even though the start-up in a single point is already delicate (Eychenne 2012). A brand of *TechShops* only has a future if the return on the initial investment (technological endowment multiplied in n points) proves to be positive. The *customer potential* is a decisive factor, but it is still premature to know to what extent an individual, even one who is passionate about DT, will be willing to pay for an access ticket for such a service.

– The network linked to the development of vertical complementarities between firms (Richardson 1972; Aoki 1986), so that alongside classic industrial partners, one or more FabLab entities (as a creation space) and/or *TechShop* entities (as a professional industrial and commercial space that can combine quality and quantity in rapid prototyping) are now available. The Fab as an extension of the NoF is an open means of developing *absorptive capacities* (Cohen and Levinthal 1990) – thus having *minimal internal capacities to absorb external knowledge* – and of participating in the design of innovation, in the technological evolution of knowledge, know-how and competencies.

Thus, the NoF, being part of the inter-organizational sphere of complementarities, can combine the implementation of a FabLab within the company (*within the walls*) as a reinforcement of creative competencies, and thus of its rank of excellence, or solicit (*outside the walls*) a Fab favorable to private issues (university FabLab, *TechShop*) allowing the development of competencies without bearing internally the full burden of the operating cost. What makes the network effective (territorialized or not) is the *coordination* (Richardson 1972) favored today by ICT and DT; the Internet in particular ensuring the fast, sure, frequent and dense communication of a complex digital information associating (text, image, sound) and allowing, including at a distance, the co-design and/or the piloting of digital machines (whether the entities are on the same geographical space or in different spaces).

In addition to complementary competencies, the NoF is a modality of organizational functioning articulating actors of different sizes and/or natures. Thus, incorporating a form of Fab into the NoF does not mean discrediting the model of the Large Enterprise (LE). Firstly, there is a phenomenon of synchronous coexistence of previous and new organizational forms (*simple, functional, divisional, matrix, network, virtual*) in which the LE occupies a predominant place. Moreover, behind ICT and DT, we find LEs (Intel, Microsoft, Apple, Google and other emerging leaders such as 3D Systems). Furthermore, if specialized and well-equipped start-ups or SMEs have an internal Fab, this is also the case for LEs convinced of the importance of bringing out new ideas (from employees wishing to carry out a project): the *internal* FabLab, *within the company's walls*, allows for testing without competing with the R&D department. Alternatively, any company can, within its means, sponsor an external FabLab *outside the walls* (of the company) but not far from the R&D center, if only to promote a meeting place for students, researchers, managers and employees. Within a *vertical* network of *complementary competencies*, strengths combine and using the FabLab (more or less professionalized) allows for quality and quantity from prototyping to sales. The objective here is to reduce the cost of innovation and therefore, first of all, the cost of design. The FabLab contributes to this, especially as there is a tendency to reduce the cost (machines and tools linked to DT, necessary inputs, learning, access and use). This allows for a decrease in cycle time (innovation-to-market delay), continuous improvement and faster market penetration (diffusion adoption).

For western companies, such an approach can promote *back relocation within the country*, limit the dependence on distant suppliers and free them from transport costs, as well as from the nuisance of NE and/or the remuneration of activities that do not respect any rights (democratic, fiscal, social, health, environmental). On the contrary, through the dematerialization of production and employment, there may also be a deepening of *relocation abroad* to where the costs are lowest (through the absence and/or circumvention of the law). More centrally, with the proliferation of new ideas and their implementation, we must look at the speed of growth and the success of start-ups becoming dominant very quickly through creativity, technology and/or marketing by imposing themselves globally in a few years. The *Business EcoSystem* (BES, see Chapter 3) is therefore essential: Google has built up a galaxy of interacting actors that allows it to evolve and also to build and/or renew innovation (including *architectural* innovation – radical and commercially effective according to Abernathy and Clark (1985) or Henderson and Clark (1990) – or *disruptive innovation* by revolutionizing usage according to Bower and Christensen (1995)).

In the innovative NoF extended to the FabLab, the distributed collaborative design–production–distribution space where innovative exploration is articulated to its exploitation increases ambidexterity (Tushman and O'Reilly 1996; Benner and Tushman 2003).

It is not only the organizational form of the firm that evolves but also its environment and the firm–environment interaction (Burns and Stalker 1961).

This makes it possible to take into account the *stakeholders* (Freeman 1984), in this case technological (creator, employee, community, consumer, association), in order to create and also to improve the image of the company and of the network to which it belongs, as well as to rally third parties who are influential because they are prescribers or potential clients.

The individual–collective tension in the community of belonging finds here a balance and a dynamic of progress by coevolution: if the individual (Nonaka 1991) is at the base of the innovative process, it is the interactions that allow an enrichment of knowledge and solutions within the community of practice (Brown and Duguid 1991; Brown and Duguid 1998; Wenger and Snyder 2000). Innovation is and is becoming increasingly *collective* (Allen 1983) and *open* (Chesbrough 2003).

Resilient network entanglement, being intra- and inter-organizational, formal and informal, commercial and noncommercial, individual and collective, favored by ICT and DT (allowing virtualization and dematerialization and then rematerialization by 3D printing), while offering concrete (and also virtual) places for exchanges and meetings around knowledge, know-how, ideas, projects and achievements, tends to structurally modify the way of producing and thinking about the product.

2.3. From extended NoF to the beginnings of a potential new industrial dynamic?

A certain use of ICT with the Internet, by making possible the *virtualization* of the network, operates a modification and/or transformation of the organizational N form in the direction of a greater plasticity and adaptability. Beyond that, the extension of NoF by assimilating the FabLab constitutes a decisive contribution at the level of design to innovate better, faster and at lower costs (corporate strategies tend towards this objective, see Bouvier-Patron (2009, 2011a, 2011b)).

Consequently, this also allows us to consider how this NoF extended to the FabLab makes possible the premises of a new industrial dynamic.

The very dynamics of capitalism make it absorb everything that is useful to it, independently of the capacity of resistance of a community of practice defending a certain purity, the reality of the FabLab is to be a potential commercial object (according to a broad palette: in a start-up, in an individual or collective commercial project with or without the support of a company, in a company service, as a commercial entity of the *TechShop* type).

The community, fundamental in the functioning of the initial FabLab project, can become evanescent because it is marginalized and relegated as a minority that can be sacrificed and/or recuperated by the economic system (e.g. the Internet with viral marketing and commercial communitarianism borrowing from hacking techniques, see Bouvier-Patron and Chatelain (2001)).

In this logic, nothing prevents the gradual transformation of the FabLab space into a profitable and/or useful operational organization in the economic sense of the term. Thus, the *NoF–Fab* coupling, as an active form, is both essential to the functioning of firms and still developing in a globalized and uncertain context. Each company (especially start-ups, SMEs or LEs), and/or each company that is a member of a network, can mobilize this additional Fab appendage (either as a means of fostering individual or collective creativity, or as a professional industrial and commercial entity) *within* or *outside its walls*. The dynamic recombination of change through the NoF form extended to the FabLab allows for value creation and innovation by lowering design and prototype development costs while spreading the costs of operation (of one or more Fabs in an inter-organizational sphere of coordinated complementarities) where each firm involved aims for excellence.

Anderson (2012) shows the importance of the community of makers, as enthusiasts acting for pleasure within the entrepreneurial world, willing to put in place the economic and technological workings of a new model of creation, manufacturing and marketing. Decentralized and distributed production implies originality, variability and customization in the process of creation, manufacturing and commercialization while having a large base of potential customers. All of the objects that can be made today in a classical way are likely to be impacted in the long run by the process of reproduction and/or digital creation. What is sure is that this will depend on the involvement of each person and the concern to appropriate the process of conception, elaboration, production and diffusion of the goods.

Moreover, for products coming from the classical industry, the Fabs offer individual and collective solutions to reconsider the life cycle and obsolescence (programmed or not, see Chapter 7) by the technical reappropriation of the design, production, maintenance, reparability and recycling of goods. *Technological tinkerers* are opening up a new space for innovation based on a decentralized industrial production model that is creative, collaborative and open and that questions the ownership and/or the very nature of the use of goods.

This does not exclude direct or indirect management by professional experts linked, more or less directly, to companies. Therefore, if the stake is to obtain a real *industrial democracy* accessible to all, the way is still long. However, the intrinsic economic aspect of a decentralized, multipolar and open industrial development (Troxler 2013) tends to assert itself.

The coupling of ICT and DT (Internet and digital) is becoming possible in a physical and/or virtual space, dedicated and/or shared (including at home with a wireline or Wi-Fi connection), in an approach based on a more or less effective free access (and depending on the nature of the access ticket), semi-professional/professional participation or paying (purchase of a service). Globally, for companies (incorporating a FabLab or a *TechShop*, internally or externally) as well as for makers in communities of practice, Chesbrough's *open innovation* (2003), an ambiguous term referring rather to Allen's *collective innovation* (1983) concerns new innovation practices by permanent back-and-forth between the inside and the outside of an organization, without prejudging the *absorptive capacities* (Cohen and Levinthal 1990) necessary for any firm wishing to remain competitive.

The inter-organizational collaborative mode is imposed by necessity because of specializations, as well as the need for access to licenses (Bouvier-Patron 2011b).

Collective innovation can eventually be linked to *open source*[5] from *free software* to *free hardware*.

The choice, for the private firm, of a proprietary or free solution has advantages and disadvantages.

The free solution allows the speed of diffusion, the launching of beta versions (to be tested and improved), the penetration of a large public by avoiding the costs of diffusion while being remunerated through additional paying applications.

The proprietary solution seeks a direct remuneration of what is used (it is the desirability of the use that will determine the price; at the risk therefore for the marketing to make a mistake by badly anticipating the setting of a price of a good, whatever it is, if it does not carry any desire of purchase).

The Internet is the promoter of creative freedom and, in association with *open source* (Tirole and Lerner 2002), economically challenges proprietary solutions (legitimate *a priori* from the point of view of a reward for innovative effort (Arrow 1962a)). Individual creativity is encouraged by the logic of DIY, as a user-centered

5 Open source does not systematically imply free access, but allows us to see the source code and/or any modification (necessarily realized via a GPL) as well as the distribution of copies.

innovation model (Von Hippel 1976, 2005), even though this is done within a collective (DIWO). The user–consumer creators are at the origin of a *bottom-up innovation*.

Nevertheless, depending on whether the innovation comes from any user, a *technological tinkerer*, a company or a NoF, the degree and speed of diffusion will vary. Furthermore, in a logic of *network externalities* (Katz and Shapiro 1985; Farrell and Saloner 1986), the technological environment takes precedence since terminals and Internet connections, coupled with DTs, positively promote the creation and innovation, possibly collaborative and free, of a usable decentralized infrastructure. Thanks to increasingly interoperable ergonomic computer interfaces, non-specialists can also appropriate the technology to tinker. The difference between a *tinkerer* and a *company* is mostly in the organization, reputation building, brand creation and marketing power.

The FabLab, a decentralized digital fabrication workshop, focuses on the individual in community. From being a rather passive consumer, the individual maker (who has become proactive and entrepreneurial) places themselves at the heart of satisfying their own needs or those of a collective. Therefore, on the demand side, if the former customer becomes a designer, producer and user and has access to FabLab-type resources in the vicinity (at home or in a shared space), the entire current production–distribution–sales chain will be modified. The obstacles to hyper-decentralization at home are more related to measurable human constraints in terms of health risks (yet to be evaluated), space (to install and carry out production), human–machine cohabitation, and neighborhood and nuisances (storage, sensitive nature of inputs, upstream or downstream pollution of inputs or outputs, noise, health risks).

This is why companies (individuals, VSEs, SMEs and IEs) will continue to play a key role as an interface with the downstream sector, while also playing a role upstream in terms of innovation and product manufacturing through the inter-organizational sphere in NoF (articulating different company sizes), *decentralized* and *dematerialized* (via FabLab and ICT and DT including 3D printing) that changes the way in which we produce artifacts and/or market them and innovates by reducing the costs of design and prototyping while strengthening the competencies of each entity constituting the network. The NoF form, by its flexibility, and without specifying its morphology *a priori*, can be generic enough to think and anticipate current and future deformations (by breaking down the intra and/or inter-organization in multiple ways). The superposition of the FabLab and the virtual completes the protean character of the NoF. In total, a new economic and social dynamic can be outlined, as already indicated in the general introduction, around three main scenarios (with gateways):

– continuation of the current trend where many key LEs have large R&D centers generally operating within NoFs (and also virtual networks), via ICT and DT, with vertically complementary activities to ultimately serve the end customer (in a passive role);

– dominance of a few technological LEs, upstream of other (large or small) dependent ones, the former piloting a virtual and digital nebula while leaving a small portion to individual initiative (VSEs, SMEs and IEs being dedicated to the service of the final customer);

– decomposition and/or sustainable break-up of LEs (at least in the OECD), except around a few technological cores driving the virtual and digital economy, to the benefit of a very large, complex and decentralized nebula, shaped by the intrinsic dynamics of technology and the *new economy*, where all individual or collective actors become *tinkerers*.

The likelihood of each scenario occurring will depend on technological advances and their diffusion (down to the level of the current consumer and likely future entrepreneur), the actual choice made by the actors and the access to and democratization of 3D modeling.

Moreover, the challenge to be taken up is that of ecologically responsible and sustainable innovation (Irwin et al. 1992; Porter et al. 1995a, 1995b; Shrivastana 1995; Bouvier-Patron 2007, 2011a, 2014, 2017b, 2020; also see Chapter 1 of this book). It is thus not surprising that Rifkin (2011) conditions a potential new industrial revolution on a long-term response to the triple challenge of global economic crisis, energy security and climate change.

2.4. Conclusion

The FabLab can appear as a new potential appendage of NoF (via ICT and DT; including in its virtual extension), increasing collective competence (and that of each member firm) while decreasing design and prototyping costs and generating (individually and collectively) a decisive value creation to generate and/or maintain competitive advantage. This NoF dynamic is conducive to creating the premises of a new industrial revolution.

At the very least, without even entering into a commercial logic, FabLabs in France are spread throughout the country, as they are generally attached to higher education institutions. For project leaders (creators, clients, employees, entrepreneurs, executives and/or managers), access to a FabLab is therefore possible.

The creation of a start-up can thus be facilitated. But, more globally, the use of a FabLab, internal or external, can aim at increasing, developing and renewing competencies. It is therefore for the firm and for the NoF to install the Fab as a new place of interface (of exchange of knowledge, know-how, creation and innovation) and this in a permanent way.

For the NoF, the incorporation of the Fab is an important issue: either as an element promoting creativity or as a professional industrial and commercial device lowering the costs of innovation and design. It also makes it easier to involve the customer. It also allows us to play on the qualitative level (individualization, range, adaptations), as well as on the quantitative level (more or less important series).

The community dimension of the FabLab seems to be rather difficult to characterize in France (qualitatively and quantitatively) according to the observations made (FING 2014)[6]. Also, seeking to mobilize this term in an ideological perspective while claiming a broad application limits its relevance. From a pragmatic point of view, the issue should be less to preserve a purist and essentialist vision of the term FabLab when the issue is the potential appropriation dynamics of the concept (including by the company and, even more, by the NoF).

The maintenance or renewal of each company's innovative profession (made up of specific competencies) has an impact on the *bargaining power* (BP) and the *creation of value*. The permanent search for improvement and/or enrichment of competencies (in particular by the mobilization of the Fab) can make it possible to decrease the time to market and to improve the qualitative and quantitative performance of the efforts related to design while lowering the cost in a global strategic process (reduction of uncertainty – as Knight (1921) underlines (see Bouvier-Patron 1996a) – and also around the BP and the prior control of the specifications in the client–supplier relationship (see Bouvier-Patron 1994a, 1998b, 2002, 2013, 2017a)). This competitive dynamism, often proactive and based on the innovation of complementarities, is inherent to the NoF form.

Beyond the firm and NoF, the developments to be expected around DTs and FabLabs are crucial at the individual and societal level.

The FabLab is a means of creativity to satisfy individual or collective needs, with or without the support of firms, which will always remain, more or less, present upstream at least in the design, production and sale of technological equipment.

---

6 The FING report (2014) aims to provide a detailed qualitative and quantitative overview of the FabLab situation in France. This source is cited, for the sake of completeness, for its numerical and factual contribution to which the reader may refer. Our contribution is conceptual and is intended as a projection of a possible trend in the industrial dynamic.

The FabLab also opens up a new universe of sharing, exchange, creation and fabrication, within a collective (community or not), but consistent with the individual values that have been essential in the West since at least the political revolutions of the 18th century, then the concern to differentiate oneself socially in the 19th century and asserting itself even more with the rise of the consumer society in the 20th century. Today, this process finds a technical, organizational, practical and ethical solution via the Internet and other ICT and/or DT. More broadly, on the societal level, the FabLab is a challenge of individual/collective reappropriation of the physical activity of production by the virtual digital universe. The expressed need, its formulation, its expression and its satisfaction are no longer necessarily delegated to an external third party (like the company). With DTs, especially 3D printing, the individual can now also consider the potential of specific manufacturing at home.

The breakdown, in the OECD, between industrial production in companies, production in open collective and/or domestic (household, family, craft), is a cursor that can call into question the development model known since the beginning of the European industrial revolution. The division may be sectoral (due to the primary importance of equipment or infrastructure industries) or linked to the need for objects (collective versus private or even large versus small), but it will also and above all be based on generality versus the type of product sought (large or small series).

This is part of a larger projection called *Industry 4.0* and/or the fourth industrial revolution (according to a rather rough periodization: the first one being IR* (see the Introduction to this book), the second one being the one from the second half of the 19th century onwards with the help of the improvement of machines whose use is growing to produce and serve mass markets by the democratization of products for all, and the third one being the one of electronics associated with computing and telecommunications after 1950). In the near future, *Industry 4.0* aims to integrate ICT and DT to create smart factories.

The concept of *Industry 4.0* emerged at the Hannover Fair for Industrial Technology in 2011, when the key elements required for the production, transmission and processing of large amounts of data for industry and commerce, simultaneously or quasi-simultaneously, seemed to have reached maturity. The 4th industrial revolution (*Industry 4.0*) organizes production processes around ICT and DT, far beyond FabLabs and makerspaces, by integrating, mainly through wireless communication, *cobotics* (interactive and collaborative robotics) on interactive production lines, tracking (radio identification, RFID), software embedded in subsystems and connected to sensors allowing a form of autonomy and interaction with the environment (CPS, Cyber Physical System, where the fusion or convergence of the physical world and the virtual world by the cyberspace takes place), a sophisticated inter-organizational or meta-organizational collaborative operation, the systematic use of *connected objects*, the mobilization of virtual universes and *augmented reality* (human interaction with connected objects) to control or choose actions or options, 3D printing, AI (and its Deep Learning in order to exploit the data of the *Cloud* associated with Big Data) and to proceed thus, in particular for the design, to simulations and/or the manufacture of interactive digital models. The stated aim is to move towards greater profitability with greater flexibility, in real time, and as close as possible to demand, by better steering while reducing design, manufacturing, distribution and operating costs; all the more so as the ambition is not limited to production but involves integrating marketing and finance into the process.

The volume and quality of energy required for this revolution, as well as the impact on the NE, are not yet fully assessed. The key technology supporting this revolution (with the transition from 4G to 5G to accelerate and increase the flow rate/volume) leaves unresolved the problems posed in terms of data or energy security, health and/or respect of the NE.

3

Communitization of Technological Innovation: The Value and the Symbolic

The FabLab's approach to innovation, in itself and/or within the NoF, is a new medium whose strength lies both in the technological tools mobilized and in the organization. Moreover, the inter-organizational space of companies where innovations are developed is crossed by communities, especially innovative and/or virtual communities (upstream for design and/or downstream for the brand or use). The mobilization of ICT and DT follows the development of innovative communities that are often protean and have heterogeneous actors. The active role of innovation communities will not be examined here on a purely geographical basis nor by the formal–informal articulation, or even by the trajectories of actions (which may eventually close in on themselves), but rather via the upheaval induced by the ICT and DT couple in the innovation process. The issue is the analysis of a shift from the organizational and managerial to the virtual and, above all, increasingly, a shift (including in value) from the concrete to the symbolic[1].

Three distinct and complementary main orientations of work are proposed in the literature articulating virtual and symbolic:

– the first focuses on the link between virtual organization and trust (Handy 1995) with its symbolic consequences (but if, indeed, trust between community members is necessary for coordination, as well as for open collaborative interactions around the design and diffusion of technological objects, the role of mimetism and reference to a *leader* – in creation, design or adoption – is at least as important);

1 At the root of the term and to give a semantic framing, if necessary, the *symbol* (according to the dictionary *Le Robert*) is defined as follows: "That which represents something else by virtue of a correspondence". Morgan et al. (1983) also insist on the very subjective character of the symbol.

– the second (Cavalli 2007) is the one where the emphasis is on symbolic engineering (a concept initiated by Bazerman (1999)) as a process of elaboration of representations that are ultimately imposed *in fine* as shared values in a community (but minimizing the influence of marketing in the symbolic process);

– the third (Dahlander et al. 2005, 2008, 2014), based on the dynamic role of communities of innovation, concerns the growing and diffuse impact of the symbolic initiated by strategic marketing, and in an amplified way in the virtual universe.

In line with this last approach, our working hypothesis is that the virtualization of the organization (in the sense of Byrne (1993)), crossed by communities of innovation, built on communities of practice (Brown and Duguid 1991) and communities of use (Von Hippel 1976), accelerates a process of value creation that is now essentially symbolic. We will base our work on the existing literature (excluding the link between innovation and information technology, which has already been discussed at length elsewhere). After a review of the literature (in section 3.1) concerning the strong interaction between networks, *Business EcoSystems* (BES), and innovation communities in order to create new products, we will discuss (in section 3.2) how the link between innovation communities, technological places and inter-organizational networks where technological products are designed is embodied in practice; then (in section 3.3), we will specify the role of the symbolic value of these technological products, in particular within quasi-addictive communities of use, beyond the support products.

3.1. New technological products: inter-organizational networks, business ecosystems and innovative communities

Business networks (or networks of firms, NoF), a new organizational form (Aoki 1986) in developed countries, are basically a response to competition from Japanese firms in the 1980s offering a high-quality standard at a cost that was unaffordable for western rivals.

The complementarities of competencies, in networks of companies focused on their business, generate collective efficiency and co-creation of value if the coordination by a pilot (or Coordinating Actor, CA) of the new product (to be designed and/or produced) is effective. What matters is the capacity of a firm to create competencies, value them, help them evolve and renew them in a specific way (Teece 2007) in order to hold its place within a resilient network logic.

At the same time, we have witnessed the development and diffusion of ICT tools, such as the *Intranet, EDE, ERP* (and in an accelerated way by the coupling with the Internet), as logistical supports for the contractual relations necessary for the resilient network functioning.

Moreover, the intrinsic dynamics of the development of tools linked to the Internet goes beyond proprietary solutions due to the release of the World Wide Web (with its size, interactivity, real time, transmission of multimedia digital contents, processing of exchanges at the individual and/or mass level) in a logic of *open source*[2]: for software and hardware (especially for 3D printers, *RepRap* project). This has resulted in a multiplication of the potential of business models[3], a theme now widely analyzed.

Through this, the most remarkable thing is the development of virtual inter-individual links and community groupings, called *virtual communities* if the interactions go through ICT (Rheingold 1993). What then constitutes an intangible shared *common good* (Ostrom 1990) is the set of reciprocal interactions on a domain of interest, with the mutual responsibilities that follow.

The diffusion of ICTs generates a democratization of knowledge, practices and uses by transcending the organizational boundaries of companies. Therefore, within *communities of practice*[4] (Brown and Duguid 1991, 1998; Lave and Wenger 1991; Wenger and Snyder 2000), individuals come together voluntarily, out of a common interest (or desire), and often informally (as opposed to a formal structure with a defined purpose such as the enterprise or its project groups (Amin and Roberts 2008)). In these communities, interactive exchanges on ICT and DT practices take place in a dual process of learning and constant acquisition of knowledge: hence a system of distributed knowledge, generally tacit, that can be valorized within communities, more or less large and more or less expert, in order to share and

2 As a reminder, free software is based on the General Public License (GPL), which is called royalty-free or copyleft (as opposed to copyright) because it allows accessibility to the source code. Anyone can therefore access, use, modify, copy and even distribute software under this license. In 1985, the Free Software Foundation (FSF) laid down four fundamental freedoms of *free software*: freedom to run the program for any purpose, freedom to study its operation and adapt it thanks to access to the source code, freedom to redistribute copies, freedom to improve the program and publish the improvements made. The modifications made – even for commercial use – remain free. In 1998, at the instigation of E. Raymond, the Open-Source Initiative or *Open Source* further extended access rights. Raymond (1999) also opposes the commercial model (*cathedral model*) to the subversive one of the bazaar related to open software (e.g. *Linux*).

3 See Lecoq et al. (2006) for a broader presentation of the issues and contours of the concept.

4 According to Lave and Wenger (1991), a *community of practice* is *a group with a common interest that interacts and learns collectively by building relationships and also by developing a sense of belonging and mutual commitment.*

question practices, experiment, find solutions, launch challenges, explore new possibilities and establish a reputation.

In addition, other communities formed on the Internet (via more or less selective and specialized forums or social networks such as Facebook, Twitter, Instagram, etc.), which are more downstream and focused on usage, are also vectors for the selection and dissemination of new products. In particular, we can think of *brand communities* on the Internet (Muniz and O'Guinn 2001), which are formed in a very ritualized and selective way through recognition and reciprocity between peers; a positive correlation is highlighted here (Wiertz and de Ruyter 2007) between relational investment and the contributory quality of each individual. Companies are therefore traversed by these communities (whether they like it or not) and can also benefit from them internally through solicitation (e.g. testing a beta version) and/or by encouraging the external participation of the user in the creation of the innovation (Von Hippel 1976), in particular, with the preponderant role of user leaders (Von Hippel 1988). The *lead user* is ahead of the trend and is highly motivated. These leaders tend to reveal and share their knowledge, practices and uses (Franke and Shah 2003), which generates a driving force on the other categories of users and/or adopters.

Communities do not replace the companies that mobilize them. The internal absorptive capacities of each company (Cohen and Levinthal 1990), in order to capture the knowledge available in the environment, remain necessary: to stay in the innovation race, for valorization, and/or to establish close relationships with partners or, sometimes, competitors.

Absorptive capacities, in the resilient network dynamic, respond well to the challenge, explained by Tushman and O'Reilly (1996, inspired by March (1991)) and also by Benner and Tushman (2003): to innovate by *exploration* and *exploitation*, and this in a permanent dynamic of renewal of specific competencies (Teece 2007)[5]. More precisely, an open intra-/inter-organizational innovation dynamic is required, with intense back-and-forth within *Business EcoSystems* (BES; Moore 1993, 1996, 2006)[6] without often selecting, distinctively, partners and competitors by the need

5 For Teece (2007), the key strategy consists of building, coordinating and renewing competencies that are difficult to reproduce and/or imitate; these competencies are therefore specific.

6 The *Business EcoSystem* or BES (Moore 1993, 1996) implies open collective innovation, complex co-evolution and coopetition (sometimes with several pivotal leaders at a certain stage of the BES's life cycle) in order to generate and then renew competencies around a standard imposed (by the leader), which can be used and enriched by third parties who will also have new competencies at their disposal in order to enrich their core business. Moore (2006) insists on the open and modular nature of the standard or platform, which can be improved insofar as the issue at stake is the provision of an asset by a leading player so that other players are able to develop their own activity and thus strengthen the whole (for example Google).

for collaboration and/or cooperation around a common asset or platform (Gawer and Cusumano 2002). This game of complex interactions can be explained first of all by interdependence, due to the specialization of the competencies, knowledge and know-how of each company (with sophisticated strategies for patenting, see Appendix 3). The challenge of the *leading* pilot who imposes themselves into a BES is to federate around them in order to impose a technological standard or a commercial norm: all or part of an asset is made available and becomes accessible to those who want to develop it around the pilot. The result is a *collective invention* (Allen 1983), and an *open innovation* (Chesbrough 2003) that can be used by third parties by enriching it, in an evolving network.

Crowdfunding accompanies this need for openness by spreading the cost of innovation over a group of motivated actors in order to reach a significant level of financing (likely to transcend already identified and/or potential blockages or directly access new specific competencies). This issue differs from generic *crowdsourcing* (Howe 2008) where an open participative/collaborative/creative online process must prevail, mobilizing the expertise of the crowd; the term outsourcing is therefore inappropriate unless a firm is piloting the project for its own benefit.

Independently of these new financial circuits, the diffusion of DT, alongside ICT, within networks, communities and ESAs, increases the competencies and collective capacities for designing and producing products while reducing the cost of innovation. Indeed, the FabLab (Gershenfeld 2005; see Chapter 2) opens up perspectives on prototyping by decreasing design costs and can also revolutionize industrial organization through the role of makers (Anderson 2012). Moreover, the dematerialization driven by technological diffusion via ICT and DT now shifts the organizational issue (intra- or inter-organizational) from the physical sphere to the virtual sphere[7]. Incidentally, geographic proximity and relational proximity (the latter potentially being virtual) can be merged. Hence, innovative organizational entanglements amalgamate creative networks in local BESs (articulated on a

7 The *virtual enterprise* (Davidow and Malone 1992) would be a molecule that can be modulated according to the elements that are grafted onto it around a project; once the project is completed, dissolution is necessary. Byrne's (1993) definition is more precise: a temporary network of independent companies – suppliers, customers, former rivals – linked by ICT, without necessarily needing a head office, an organizational chart, a hierarchy or vertical integration for the coordination of competencies, cost management or access to markets. Rayport and Sviokla (1995) emphasize the intensive mobilization of ICT; hence, the term (Lipnack and Stamps 1997) of *cyber-enterprise*.

geographic location basis[8]) with those of without geographical relationships. The positive localized dynamics, through innovative territorial BESs (Cohendet et al. 2010, 2013), can be explained first and foremost, at the base, by territorial specificities[9] (or specific territorial resources (Gumuchian and Pecqueur 2006)) by relying in particular on social innovation following the example of *LivingLabs* (Klein and Pecqueur 2017), where the objective is to manage to collectively test solutions which, moreover, articulate formal and informal proactive actors (being part of a long history of elaboration of knowledge, of individual and collective competencies, and also of know-how).

Several authors (Cohendet and Zapata 2009; Simon 2009; Cohendet et al. 2010, 2011, 2013) explain the dynamics of territorial creative knowledge by the existence of a fundamental interstitial component situated between two others:

– innovative firms or upperground: active economic infrastructure that could be extended to public or private institutions that support companies (in one way or another);

– the strata of underground creation (Florida 2002, 2005; Arvidsson 2007), therefore not necessarily apparent and/or official, but rather wild and interloped, where creative individuals and their networks live, are inspired and express themselves.

The innovative interstitial level is called *middleground*[10], and is halfway between the other two. It is therefore at this intermediate level of the middleground that we can locate, in particular, *territorialized* communities of practice that are essential to the innovation dynamic in certain geographical areas (and that can thus explain performance differentials between territories).

8 Paradoxically, globalization reveals resilient local dynamics. While some territories are affected, others are proactive stakeholders in globalization. Moreover, corporate logic can be effective globally and destructive locally. Conversely, the challenge of Sustainable Development is to enable local and global performance.

9 The positive cocktail of initial key territorial resources is already complex in itself: population pool with competencies, knowledge or know-how; initial high-performance and continuing education system; quality engineering schools; public and semi-public institutions involved and linked to companies; innovative entrepreneurship benefiting from favorable support conditions (incubators, co-work, FabLab, access to possible aid); shared financing (crowdfunding); implementation of innovative devices, such as the *Living Lab* allowing for methodical testing of local projects or solutions in real situations and, sometimes, in real size, with institutional actors.

10 The *middleground* (Capdevila 2015) is composed of communities that make creatives visible to companies and are platforms interacting with companies in knowledge creation.

The links forged between formal and informal actors (Cohendet et al. 2013) appear to be decisive for innovation, with the use of informal actors by formal actors (Capdevila 2015). Sometimes, a relational sedimentation (territorialized or not) can lead to blocking phenomena (or lock-in, already identified on the technological level (Arthur 1989)).

We can therefore see that open innovation, within an inter-organizational and business ecosystem dynamic based on ICT and DT and also crossed by communities (geographically and/or relationally linked through virtualization), generates new perspectives for designing and producing new products.

3.2. Places where innovation is created, practices of innovative communities, managerial and symbolic issues

The development of the networked sphere, as an inescapable fact of industrial organization since the mid-1980s, is accompanied by tools for steering networks through ICTs, and now also through DTs, which implies a shift in the stakes due to the induced dematerialization.

The technologies that have been disseminated do not only follow the contours of company networks, but are widely spread and become issues of appropriation at the finest level of society. The industrial challenge of virtualization associated with ICT and DT is threefold: a network extended by ICT and DT to the FabLab to facilitate the design and manufacture of objects (including technological objects); the widespread use of interactive objects connected downstream; the mobilization of tools, linked to ICT and DT, for the supply, production and distribution management and/or after-sales of objects. The company or the network of companies is only a vector operating in symbiosis with the communities (of practice and use, associated in a transversal way, as essential stakeholders). We will therefore address the places (in section 3.2.1) and then the managerial issues of these indispensable innovative communities (in section 3.2.2).

3.2.1. *Places and practices of innovative communities*

The specific dynamic of ICT and DT is to favor a combination of DIY (Do It Yourself) and DIWO (Do It With Others): there is a synergetic interdependence between these two levels in the FabLab spirit (Gershenfeld 2005) where it is a matter of *doing almost everything* in a collective space of proximity, and, if possible, *doing almost everything with almost nothing* if we place ourselves in a *logic of decentralized frugal innovation* favoring *grassroots innovation* (see Seyfang and Smith (2007) and Chapters 5 and 6 of this book). Through interactive collective action using more or less sophisticated tools and *technological bricolage* (which is now gaining recognition in management, see Cunha et al. (2014) and Chapter 7 of this book), and/or the misuse/hijacking of technologies or technological objects, creation or co-creation becomes a shared passion within innovation communities.

The FabLab (Chapter 2) remains the perfect junction and balance between the real and the virtual. It is, simultaneously, a place of exchange, exploration, misuse/hijacking, knowledge creation, practical exercises, bricolage, realization (from an idea and the imagination) of an individual project in a collective and/or of a collective project, and also a tool (of design, prototyping, mass production, materialization from dematerialization). In particular, it mobilizes a key tool linked to DT, namely, 3D printing (thanks to proprietary solutions or *open source hardware* like RepRap). While the cost of acquiring the tool may now almost be secondary, this is not the case for the knowledge and competencies required to have the capacity to model in 3D (knowledge that can be acquired within communities of practice, but which requires a very substantial investment of time and human resources).

Intrinsically, the FabLab (in the strict sense of the term) does not exhaust the spectrum of innovation community places; a hackerspace or a makerspace are other emblematic places.

In the case of the hackerspace, there is a will to resist by misuse/hijacking and/or configuration–reconfiguration (individual and collective) of technological objects or systems of technological objects. The activist and protest intention are variable. The required competencies of the hacker[11] (Raymond 1999) are hacking or, more broadly, bricolage or even cracking; only the purpose of hacking distinguishes the hacker (white hat) from the black hat engaging in criminal acts. The hacker's spirit of resistance can take on the role of a whistleblower, or even a desire for digital subversion: against technological enslavement leading to the annihilation of individual freedoms, to denounce the passivity and/or the reduction to modern slavery of an undifferentiated mass of zombies and/or digital junkies.

In the case of the makerspace (generally integrating a FabLab), the project (realized in DIY and/or DIWO) can result from a passion and/or have an entrepreneurial and commercial aim. The combined DIY and DIWO processes channel energies into generating endogenous dynamics of making at an acceptable

11 The definition of the hacker merges with their practice: pleasure, curiosity, taste for exploring a program in detail, and also tinkering, bricolage, learning, modifying, improving, inventing and transgressing in a logic of sharing to establish a positive reputation with their peers.

cost, but with an intense mobilization of immaterial resources[12] and/or human, interactions, collaborations, co-elaboration, co-creation, co-design and co-realization, with a possible economic valorization.

Curiosity, exploration, bricolage, innovation, misuse/hijacking, challenge, provocation and subversion are possible concerns around an object made by a maker.

The possible limitation is the design (modeling, program algorithm, finalized 3D digital model or game engine[13]).

However, the symptomatic *place* of professional innovation communities is the *innovation platform* (Merindol and Versailles 2017) gathering, in a precise physical point (for reasons of geographical accessibility and image), often on a research theme (e.g. mobility, biotechnology, robotics, etc.), a set of resources, means or services (FabLab, incubator, innovation accelerator, co-working space, creative spaces, places for experimentation through use, meeting and conference rooms, relaxation areas, showrooms for events) where everything is done to encourage reflection, the clearing of ideas and/or the realization of a project or prototype through collaborative interactivity (reciprocal and compensable essentially through amicable barter), in a decentralized manner and outside of a hierarchical logic, in a more or less informal way, but with the animation of the place by a few people.

3.2.2. *Managerial issues of innovative communities*

The decentralized technological culture spread throughout the communities does not exclude digital management, especially as the business part does not take anything away and only strengthens the innovation community. Thus, for example, the business orientation leads to the implementation of a customer–supplier logic within the *innovation platform*, constantly renewed and always open in an interactive seeker–solver dialogue to develop a solution to a given problem.

---

12 The intangible is the seat of values imputed under a potential and sometimes speculative valuation (brand value, price of a reputation, capitalization of an image).

13 That said, *Unity* is a cross-platform *Open-Source* game engine (*Apple-Mac*, *Microsoft*, *Google-Android*, *Linux*, and intended for any support: smartphone, laptop, tablet, video game consoles or online on the Web). Developed by *Unity Technologies*, this game engine is widely used in the video game industry both by major public *AAA*-oriented studios and by independent studios that stand out for their original concepts. Development is carried out via a free license with no access restrictions, directly on the engine, in order to generate applications for all media.

This involves analyzing the need and drawing up specifications, which is not neutral (Bouvier-Patron 2013, 2017a).

In addition, the stakeholders of the *innovation platform*, or by delegation the facilitators, must specify the expected return on investment (possibly, if necessary, to the innovation community's external funders).

If the community flourishes in freedom with a minimum of operating rules, the business implies codification and rules for an expected/desired result.

Overall, the relationship between the innovative company and the innovative community can be beneficial (Dahlander and Magnusson 2005), as long as the community is not ultimately enslaved.

Moreover, whether it is a one-off or a recurring event, the existence of one or more profit-oriented actors in a collective (and, *a fortiori*, if they are dominant) must lead (Dahlander and Magnusson 2005, 2008), unless we want to liquidate the community of innovation, to the renunciation of hegemonic functioning and to adapting/aligning to/with the community. The project logic induced must rather refer to a matrix-type organizational form[14].

The innovation community must be allowed to breathe, organize and/or evolve autonomously (Fleming and Waguespack 2007). However, the very functioning of the digital business relies on strong and complex interactions (between partners to develop a product, between competitors on the market, between the supplier and adopter, between adopters, between non-adopters and adopters, between hackers and adopters, between hackers and suppliers, between hackers and crackers, between crackers and their targets, etc.). Co-creation and/or co-design must remain open to all possible inputs (as even a peripheral stakeholder can contribute greatly to the value of the BES (Gyrd-Jones and Kornum 2013)). Power relationships can also emerge based on the exclusivity of a skill, resource, asset, patent, knowledge or know-how, but this power is never definitive in the dynamics of an ecosystem and

14 Historically, the matrix form (Galbraith 1971) set up in the 1960s by NASA to carry out an ambitious complex project (putting a human on the Moon: a challenge never achieved), with an almost unlimited budget, has also served as a source of inspiration for the organization of private companies focused on the creation or innovation of an industrial type (Boeing) or of prestige (LVMH), or even for specific projects within companies (Renault's Twingo project). In an *innovation platform* logic (innovation community), it is therefore a matter of preserving the project management mindset (but without a heavy organizational structure for managing and coordinating the operation of project groups (Amin and Roberts 2008), while benefiting from the advantages offered by ICT and DT, as well as from new ways of thinking about innovation in a decentralized manner with a high degree of lateralization from peer to peer.

the rapid evolution of technologies. In addition, in order to respond to demand, the strategy of the offer, and the brand on the Internet aims to serve, directly or indirectly, all possible audiences (market segmentation logic). This is very obvious for software: beta version, restricted free version, paid version (general public, premium, professional), proposed advantages, privileged access and discussion forums. In addition, tips and tricks are exchanged on free forums or specialized community forums, which can lead to a parallel offer.

Moreover, the cohabitation of legal and pirated offers can be reconciled: the brand can *turn a blind eye* to promote the distribution of its product. All the different versions available constitute a range where only the authentic, but expensive, product gives all the functionalities and all the guarantees (whereas the pirates distribute infected versions for different intentions and uses). Users will then indicate their interest in favoring the brand or, on the contrary, in looking for counterfeits.

Also, if it was not by choice (with proactivity remaining a determining factor), by necessity or by evidence, the collective (Allen 1983) and open (Chesbrough 2003) character of innovation (and then of its diffusion) asserts itself as a rule.

In relation to ICT and DT, given the abundance of ideas and the importance of flows (quantitative and qualitative) of interactions, exchanges, cross-fertilization, co-creation and co-design in communities and networks, the central concepts are not surprisingly: communities of practice (Brown and Duguid 1991); absorptive capacities (Cohen and Levinthal 1990); collective innovation (Allen 1983); open innovation (Chesbrough 2003); BES (Moore 1993, 1996, 2006).

The relationships of a company/organization/inter-organization/community are permanent with a multitude of actors to coordinate[15] in the co-creation of value around a common asset. The permanent interactive sharing[16] improves a specific innovation achievement (reinforcing the core business of each) in an open process involving a porosity of organizational boundaries with decentralized collaborative operating logics.

What is at stake is not so much the impossibility of capturing the value of the rival's solution as the lack of interest in doing so (due to a lack of resources and a

15 Without vertical integration, given the strengths of the resilient network logic, being an option, contrary to the recommendation of Adner and Kapoor (2010): "We have examined the effectiveness of vertical integration as a strategy to manage ecosystem uncertainty and have identified the impact of the technology lifecycle in determining its benefits."

16 Design, technical competencies, know-how, innovations, technological devices (material or immaterial), patents, experts, users, resources, commercial or logistic networks.

lack of time). The time available is, in itself, a key variable because, in an innovative company logic, shortening the time between the project phase and the product launch (or time to market) is fundamental.

Whatever the reason (lack of resources, time, fragility, competitive weakness, technical or strategic impasse), when an owner opens a source code[17], for example, and provides access to an asset, it offers the possibility for third parties to contribute their competencies (without having to organize them internally for the original owner). This can allow us to generate a new product, and benefit from feedback and alternative solutions and/or improvements to reconfigure a new powerful proprietary system. Thus, *Open Source* (DiBona and Ockman 1999) appears to be a dynamic gas pedal of the innovation and reputation process (Tirole and Lerner 2002), but it does not eliminate the proprietary logic. It is even the confrontation of options (proprietary versus open) that generates emulation and a field of perpetual renewal allowing all possibilities and the emergence of all possible solutions.

All in all, the ICT and DT mobilized by the FabLab and the makerspace contribute to reducing design costs or containing them for the development and prototyping of technological products. The innovation community, in particular through the innovation platform, makes a high investment in specific competencies useful for technological creation and design affordable.

3.3. Virtualization and symbolic value in relation to its uses

The innovative communities (sections 3.1 and 3.2) mobilizing ICT and DT across the companies, are embodied in places and contribute to generating and diffusing technological objects. Companies, by mobilizing innovative communities, seek to ensure the success of mobility technological objects (desired in the communities of use) by relying on innovative communities upstream and then, downstream, the widest diffusion. The laptop, the first level of individual utility of technological objects, is now less profitable, and is being marginalized in favor of objects that are more attractive in terms of use: smartphones (mainly *Apple's iPhone* or *Samsung's Galaxy*), game consoles (*Sony PlayStation, Microsoft XBox, Nintendo Switch*) and even tablets; and all of these as supports for the applications available in the brand's store (or online catalog) (e.g. *Apple, Microsoft, Google OS*[18] *Android*[19], *Samsung, Sony, Huawei*).

17 Like the Mozilla project and its browser spin-off, Firefox (Hammerly et al. 1999).

18 *Operating System:* set of programs directing the use of a computer's resources and operating the coupling with application software.

19 The Android operating system developed by Google is based on a Linux core.

A hierarchy of prestige, driven by brand marketing, is identified by users (*Apple* being perceived as the top of the prestige brands).

The proposed technological objects combine characteristics (not necessarily optimized separately) by arbitration (a tiered combinatory of power/capacity/reliability), with the aim of orienting the technological use[20] on applications according to their degree of sophistication: *ready-to-use* technological mobility objects (e.g. smartphones with applications) locked by proprietary solutions. Downstream, the user then performs in the manipulation of preconditioned objects or applications according to the terms provided by the brand. The brand extends its catalog at a lower cost since the store, before being a catalog, is first of all a kind of purchasing center with referencing open to third-party proposals once the content and compatibility specifications have been validated. The brand's store thus multiplies the offer by decentralizing the design of applications (offered on a *turnkey* basis, with no additional internal R&D costs, but only *ex post* validation). Paradoxically, this does not mean that creative thinking has been curtailed, as it could be if creation were entirely confiscated by the brand's R&D department or, even more, entirely outsourced to a dedicated service provider.

Classically, for adoption, the domino effect of community diffusion goes through opinion leaders (Rogers 1962; Von Hippel 1976, 1988) or KOLs (key opinion leader), such as influencers (and now *virtual influencers*; see section 4.3). The influence/diffusion media are multimedia and, increasingly, relayed within virtual communities on the Internet by forums or social networks via numerous tools allowing a message to be incited to purchase (banner ads, pop-ups, webcam, tutorials, MOOCs, chats, social networks, applications, sites, forums or any shared virtual tool).

Once the equipment is acquired (at any price, the variable being the desirability of a model or a brand), the cost of use can be zero with free Wi-Fi access.

The issue for the brand is the diffusion of its standard (*Apple, Microsoft, Google, Samsung, Huawei*) to authorize access to applications (free or paid) offered by the dedicated online catalog (store). The galaxy of technological objects of the brand and the catalog act as attraction factors and constitute *positive network externalities* (Katz and Shapiro 1985; Farrell and Saloner 1986), except that access to a brand standard refers to the communalized symbolism and the ephemerality of replacement.

20 Unlike the personal computer (PC) or sometimes the laptop, which, potentially, can be upgraded, at least in terms of hard- and software (and, even more so if the OS, still reserved for an elite expert in computing, is Linux (Raymond 1999)).

Technological objects (and systems of objects) are increasingly conceived and designed as *branded accessories to be owned* (to be able to access applications) and replaced periodically. Thus, by optimizing a combination of characteristics at a given moment, the injunction induced is to have to, in the more or less short term, replace[21] hardware (i.e. all the media objects allowing access to the applications), and this, even when the skimming price is high (an emblematic example, among others, being the latest *Apple iPhone* model). It is even more obvious for software, with the release of new versions (*updates* are only valid for the time of the passage from one version to another). For brands, ephemerality must be applied to technological support objects and is characterized in several ways:

– non-repairable technological objects, often conceived as disposable and to be replaced (e.g. ultraportable: very fragile and non-repairable);

– substitution of useful and intrinsically evolving objects by more futile and restricted objects (e.g. laptop versus tablet);

– dominant proprietary logic allowing the restriction of objects and the filtering of contents;

– beta versions to test a product at a reduced cost (by benefiting from feedback to improve the design before the official launch on the market) and by anticipating future versions allowing for re-purchasing;

– strong commercial value without a finished product (versions of Windows)[22];

– branding through systems of complementary interoperable objects that are extensive (new and increasingly attractive objects can be grafted onto the rest) and make up a dynamic universe (with *network externalities*) where desirability is generated in mirror form via community membership.

By relying on innovation communities upstream, the objective of techno-push (via marketing of the offer) aims downstream to impose proprietary solutions for objects that are not scalable but attractive in use and key supports for desired applications (accessible on the brand's store). This means being able to manage and control a collaborative innovation (even though open *a priori*) with the obsession of return on investment. The value to be maximized for the brand is based on the growing number of captive adopters (sales and speed of adoption depend on the size of the subscriber network, for example); this also makes it possible to generate value

21 Otherwise, why not think and then market a mobile technological object that can be upgraded, modulated, disassembled, improved or replaced by parts and recycled in short circuit? Why only update for embedded software (whose brand will decide the end of life)?

22 This does not prevent the existence of counter-models: hacker (detour of use, testing the limits, challenge, ideological stake and/or transgression); maker (technical overcoming); cracker (hijacking by all available means with a pecuniary interest).

through advertising placement. The applications developed and the products and/or services derived from them encourage the triggering of purchases and aim to create an addictive universe on the Internet by playing on visibility, notoriety and virtual community membership to generate mimetism and desirability. This has a double consequence: the shift of value towards the symbolic (section 3.3.1); the reinforced attraction of the symbol around the brand, with an obvious strategic impact for the supplier in terms of reputation and competition (section 3.3.2).

3.3.1. *Shift from value to symbolism*

The role of managerial tools, such as the *value chain* and *perceived value* (popularized by M. Porter in the mid-1980s), has been decisive in the current transformation. Initially a management control tool (cost allocation and determination of excess cost items) and/or a marketing tool (exploration of value sources), the *value chain* has *de facto* led to a strategic carving up of the firm into activities[23]. Better still, the perception of value becomes the key to the whole business logic: succeeding in making the customer believe that this is where the value lies can therefore be enough. The virtualization of the organization can only hypertrophy this double logic of dismantling and perception.

Thus, *perceived value*, with its projection into virtualization via ICT and DT, necessarily implies privileging the manipulation of symbols.

The offer can play on this to succeed in seducing *brand communities* on the Internet (Muniz and O'Guinn 2001) or, basically, all online communities (Dahlander et al. 2008, 2014). Wherever we turn (to the object, a system of objects, the technology, the organization, the interactions, the usage), the symbolic power related to ICT and DT emerges.

Swanson and Ramiller (1997) even show that the implementation of ICT in an organization is not only a quest for efficiency, but also and above all a symbolic universe built by the stakeholders (including communities of practice and innovative or usage communities).

Di Maria and Finotto (2008) specify the stakes involved in the symbolic and valorization of non-functional aspects only in the brand, luxury or fashion industries; in the name of the fact that the technological lever would be less (or, according to

---

23 Until the potential dismantling of the firm. Not so much as a *hollow corporation* (Chandler 1977), through portfolio management of financial assets (overdetermining and/or supplanting industrial development), but as the permanent questioning of all internal activity (and/or competency).

their terms, of less recent generation as are the industries of the *mature* or *low-tech industries*). Based on other references (Schouten and McAlexander 1995; Muniz and O'Guinn 2001), it seems that the proposition is extensible and even generalizable (Dahlander et al. 2008, 2014), including for high-tech sectors offering technological objects.

The functional expertise of the buyer is not/no longer the central criterion when what counts is rather the desirability effect and the mimetism of belonging to a community, referring to the distinction and the symbolic prestige carried by the brand. The sphere of induced subjectivity is largely based on ethnological and anthropological approaches to usage, where representation is clearly distinguished as: perception (apprehended signal), opinion (judgment), imaginary (symbolic interpretation giving meaning). According to Musso (2005, 2009), inspired by G. Balandier, for whom technology is dual because it is functional and fictional (concept of techno-imaginary), we can no longer be satisfied with seeing technical objects from the perspective of functionality. On the demand and use side, everything depends on the imaginary perception of the product. On the supply side, desirability is built on a willingness to pay of a symbolic nature (i.e. not on rational, objectifiable technical and functional characteristics, but on a manipulable social acceptability).[24] The perceived value plays a maximum role within communities of users who are quasi-addictive to ICT and DT.

Very downstream, social networks play a binding role, with convergences taking place on desired objects by mimetism.

In a spatio-temporal and cultural context, individuals tend to choose certain products or brands in order to show an image of themselves (Grubb and Grathwohl 1967; Turner Schenk and Holman 1980; Kapferer and Laurent 1983). The choice is based on the perception of what a product/brand will symbolically signify (to themselves and/or to others).

As with any theory of signal[25], a signal only has meaning and becomes a message if others receive and understand it. The *right brand* is linked to this signal:

24 Socialization/communitization is defined as a process during which an individual learns and internalizes the norms and values of the society/community to which they belong, thus allowing them to build their social/community identity where the symbolic plays a key role.

25 The informational protocol must be shared between the sender of a message and its receiver: the resulting codification is a basis for making value judgments about others through the product or the brand. A brand is a vector of symbolic meaning (Swartz 1983) and groups can be formed in the exclusive distinctive sense (to have or not to have a brand) and also in the competitive sense (brand X versus brand Y), independently of the intrinsic quality of the product.

not displaying the right brand leads to exclusion from a group (Elliott 1994; Elliott and Wattanasuwan 1998).

The interest in manipulating symbols (for both the brand and the user) is amplified by interaction processes linked to perceptions in a community driven primarily by mimetism. However, downstream receptive communities for adoption are not necessarily passive entities (and upstream communities of practice are even less so), manipulated directly and unilaterally by companies[26] and/or brands.

The upstream innovation communities, observing the communities of use, participate in the shift of value towards the symbolism of brands, as the race for technological leadership is mainly about use and seduction. Apple's innovation strategy is a form of competitive avoidance from above via image (which its direct rival, and supplier, Samsung, is trying to make up for); unlike competitive avoidance from below, which is generally based on the ability to set a predatory and dissuasive selling price for a given quality standard, due to a very low cost price (Huawei; Lenovo).

Moreover, whether it is an image strategy or a low-cost strategy, social and environmental costs (which are not without symbolic power) are relegated to the background as long as the potential client does not decide to include them in their calculation and choice system.

As it is, there is no reason why innovation management should not focus on image and the role of the imaginary by addressing, whether in creation and design or in diffusion and sale, to the desired communities.

The adoption of a product[27] is more than a technical issue, and even more than a use issue, when it is brandished as a fetish and endowed, at the same time, with a strong symbolic projection as are *the sacred technological objects* (game consoles or

---

26 This being said, for the company, this new role of communities supporting the brand reinforces a known logic, highlighted by Schumpeter, concerning the innovative monopoly (compatible with the competitive dynamic, but sterilizing it temporally and generating, moreover, a risk of bureaucratization antagonistic to the entrepreneurial spirit of pure capitalism).

27 Except for positive consequences for the brand, the possible reverse side of the activist community influence concerns, in particular, the detour of use of the technological object (initially endowed with the characteristics foreseen for a given spectrum of use by the manufacturer): the detour of use is a practice (of the tinkerer-maker or hacker) dismantling, improving, transforming by the imagination, and this within the sole limit of the physical constraints of the object (and still nothing is limited). This aspect is independent of the user's participation, to varying degrees, in the design (Von Hippel 1976).

smartphones). In the absolute, there is already a subjective primacy in the projection on the object (technological or not). We can thus become attached to our Bic pen (a purely functional object *a priori*). The characteristic of being a disposable object does not extinguish the attachment, but only reduces the regret in case of loss. The attachment to the branded pen is a symbolic extension of another order referring to the self-image vis-à-vis ourselves (narcissism) and/or vis-à-vis third parties (distinctive notoriety); this generates extreme regret in the event of the disappearance of the good beyond the recognized social value (purchase price, replacement price, rarity, exclusivity). Citing E. Coccia, Heilbrunn (2017, p. 146) systematizes the reasoning because marked goods can be understood as *extracorporeal organs through which we perceive and breathe*. The symbolic dimension of the object itself is thus not simple (as is the representation of a linear function related to price), but is necessarily apprehended in complex ways (from the egoistic dimension to the subjectivity perceived by others in the community).

3.3.2. *Systematized symbolic logic and community marker*

The product is no longer a sum of characteristics, but a composite package whose visible reflection, in mirror form, is an image perceived by potential customers within communities. Hence the interest, for companies and brands, in selling the symbolic. Now, what was established quite early by Levy (1959) is systematized in the virtual universe (and/or for objects allowing access to it).

In fact, relegating technical characteristics to a subordinate rank would not be a bad thing in itself if the offer's proposal, in terms of ergonomics and operational efficiency for use, made the technique disappear under a modest veil.

However, the issue is elsewhere and relates to an omnipresent and increasingly sophisticated commercial seduction. Moreover, the potential customer does not have the expertise to evaluate the technical characteristics of the technological product, as well as the exact correspondence between the offer and a need related to a given use. The implicit assumption, generally accepted, is that *the customer knows their need and knows how to express it*. In the absence of expertise on the part of the potential customer, the way is wide open to dreaming (rather than the concrete satisfaction of needs), which also allows the accumulation of product purchases. The stake for the non-expert buyer seems to be less the acquisition of a product corresponding to their need (fed by experience and/or lack) than a purchase (possibly of impulse linked to a desire), of a symbolic order, sending, consciously or unconsciously and directly or indirectly, a social signal (to ourselves, to our community, to others). It is the supposed signal of distinction, power, superiority and belonging.

As for professional buyers, they rarely focus on catalog products (except for commoditized products) and require particular specifications, making the purchasing relationship singular, always. Within organizations, the professional buyer (whether embodied by the *purchasing center* bringing together representatives of internal stakeholders for the purchase, or not) is only a relative expert and is confronted with the sieve of complementary technological competencies required for the development of a technological object. At this stage, any failure, imprecision or lack of knowledge in the definition of the need and its formalization distorts the functional specifications (or can be a formidable weapon in the hands of suppliers who are difficult to replace). This problem of defining the need and translating it into a specification (Bouvier-Patron 2013, 2017a) exists by nature, but it is amplified by the technological sophistication.

From the theoretical point of view, the complexity generated is only part of the problem; another part lies in the asymmetry of information (where one or more characteristics of the product are known to the supplier, but not necessarily to the buyer) and also and above all by the weight taken by the symbolic. Thus, for technological products, any buyer (whether a layman or a professional) cannot escape their psycho-socio-economic environment and can commit the purchase on more or less objective aspects. Also, putting the latest (and reputedly best) technology at the service of the client company does not mean the most suitable solution to the needs (if the need has been clearly explained and formalized).

Therefore, the rationalization effort of the professional does not protect them from being *bewitched*. And this is all the truer concerning desired technological objects, within communities of belonging (more or less expert and professional communities), where the importance of the symbolic favors and mobilizes gurus and wizards who can bewitch the buyer.

More generally, to explain the process of adopting a technological object, we often come back to the categories of adopters (Rogers 1962): unconditional newcomers, *opinion leaders*; unconditional followers; late followers and refractory followers. Now, there is almost necessarily a causal influence relationship between the first three categories (starting with the pioneer). There are also and above all symbolic projections on the *desired* objects (even before they are acquired). The motor of purchase is mimetic desire. If purchasing were rational, there would be, individually, no objective reason to buy and pay a lot of money for a product simply because it is new and has features (which we will not necessarily use). At the level of communities, the drive effect initiated by the leading category (referent for a community of use), is therefore a target of choice for the offer, as this is where the purchasing trigger for others is.

The seducing arguments of a brand among leaders are a combination of technical, functional and fictional arguments, knowing also that a renewal of the range induces an almost immediate obsolescence of the products distributed (calling for a rapid renewal of the purchase, unless there is a strong *disappointment* in the initial experience).

The desire for novelty is a marker in itself and, even more so, for a desired novelty in a community. This marker is perceived more distinctly if the desire for the new product engenders a revolution of use structurally modifying the practice (by dividing the before from the after)[28]. The symbol in the appropriation of the new desired technological product then has more value than a good that corresponds exactly to the functional need of each individual.

The value of technological objects is thus clearly linked to the perception of the symbol projected for ourselves (valorization) and towards others (recognition) by hysterizing in the virtual universe the brand logic already fetishized in the old world.

3.4. Conclusion

The physical and virtual places of innovation, anchored geographically or relationally in communities of practice (makers and/or even hackers, in the double logic of DIY and DIWO) and, more broadly, in communities of innovation or, downstream, in communities of use, are becoming more complex and are multiplying as they rely on ICT and DT. Communities play an increasingly decisive role in the process of innovation creation and design, as well as in technological development. Communitization allows for cheaper innovation and directs value creation towards use. This communitization of innovation strengthens and nourishes networked companies for which innovation is increasingly shared, open and decentralized, provided that absorptive capacities are preserved, and competencies are renewed. From then on, the provision of a common asset in a BES can be appropriated by each member company in its own core business in an ever-changing dynamic. If communities of use are also mobilized for creation and design, the central challenge for companies offering technological products is to encourage the emergence, downstream, of addictive communities around objects and/or brands. From then on, on a community basis of adoption, where mimetism plays a crucial

28 This before-and-after rupture, which modifies usage, generates turbulence in the market. This is the best way to measure a *disruptive innovation* and its effects, because it is not so much the technology as the appropriation of the technology and its use by users that causes the disruptive effect (Bower and Christensen 1995). What is radically changed by *disruptive innovation* is usage (Christensen 1997). However, few firms allow themselves to anticipate future needs since, most of the time, they seek to satisfy needs that are already known.

role, the extension into the virtual universe amplifies a shift towards the symbolic value of technological products. ICT and DT have penetrated deeply into the uses by dissemination. By extension, virtual reality and augmented reality, by relying on AI, are helping the emergence of a new symbolic injunction and new needs (which may also involve a digital currency such as Bitcoin, resulting from a purely technological creation mobilizing computing time for a performance based on the decoding/recoding of a complex chain or blockchain). If the use value of the technological object is in the application, this object also contains a symbolic value to the point of fetishization within a community. The new competitive universe (real or potential), intensively mobilizing ICT, DT, communities, the virtual universe and marketing, places emphasis on the imaginary of the adopter caught in their community: in this sense, social networks appear as echo chambers, orchestrating buzz allowing convergence on objects, even before the question of measurement (number of subscribers, followers/followers, fans or views).

4

Technology and Symbolic Spectacle of Marking by Use

Organizations (crossed by innovative communities, upstream of creation) are focused on usage downstream. Borrowing from several disciplines, we propose here an exploratory study on the mutations in progress concerning virtual communities of use: as much by the behaviors and practices on the Internet of technological exacerbation as by the trivialization of the brand becoming an element, among others, in a more global logic of marking. The angle of approach is necessarily multidisciplinary, even though a possible anchor point can be marketing.

Through the prism of Internet usage, and by taking an interest in marking, we operate a rereading (of a rather socio-anthropological nature) that goes beyond the question of the brand: our approach is therefore not in itself centered on the brand, but on marking, both real and digital, with community staging of the individual (community self) on Internet. The *virtual community self* can be considered as an extension of the concept of *self* (Rosenberg 1979) through the *self-image* (sociologically situated by belonging to a collective) and where the desired (and/or acquired) goods, as an extension of the self (extended self), participate symbolically in this image (Belk 1988) but are worthy of the gaze of others (Miniard and Cohen 1983).

Marking is not a very assertive field in the Human and Social Sciences (HSS). According to the *Petit Robert* dictionary, *marking* is an "operation by which one marks (animals, trees, goods)". As for the Larousse dictionary, it indicates that it is "the action of marking, affixing or making a mark (inscription, drawing) on something".

We can be even more precise by proposing a new definition: *Marking* consists of *affixing or making a distinctive sign to/on/in a form (possibly living), concrete or abstract, to particularize it and to distinguish it from another similar form with the aim of specifying it, identifying it, valuing it or classifying it.* In a concrete way, it is a question of *leaving a trace or an imprint to recognize or be recognized by a distinctive sign.*

The brand is therefore a marking element among others. The literature on branding in marketing gives us some useful elements for analysis. We know that individuals, situated in a spatiotemporal cultural context, tend to choose certain products or brands in order to show a specific image of themselves (Turner Schenk and Holman 1980; Swartz 1983): the choice is based on the perception of what a support (a product or a brand) will symbolically signify for ourselves and for others. The informational protocol must be shared between the sender of a message and its receiver: the resulting codification (McCracken and Roth 1989) is a basis for making value judgments about others through the choice of product or brand. The importance of perception (of the brand) even leads to the recognition of the existence (Aaker 1997) of *brand personality*.

Thus, a brand is a vector of symbolic meaning (Levy 1959; Elliott 1994) and groups of individuals can be formed in the exclusive distinctive sense (to have or not to have a brand) and also competitive (to have one rather than the other: *Apple versus Samsung*). Moreover, not exhibiting the *right brand* leads to exclusion from a group (Elliott 1994; Elliott and Leonard 2004; Wooten 2006). Hence, for brands, the interest in playing on *semantization* (Heilbrunn 2010), which consists of *dressing market goods with an imaginary that allows them to be scripted in order to make them desirable*. The construction of a dream about the brand, inspired by the world of luxury, is an affirmed approach of *cultural branding*[1] leading to the concept (Holt 2004) of an *iconic brand*.

While the literature on branding is well studied, the literature on *brand communities* (emblematized by Harley Davidson and bikers: Schouten and McAlexander 1995) is now developing especially in relation to the Internet with the work of Muniz and O'Guinn (2001). And luxury (Kim and Ko 2012) is no exception.

Specific methodologies, such as *netnography* (a neologism telescoping the *Net* terms for Internet and ethnography), are being developed (Kozinets 2002) and are

1 *Cultural brand marketing* (or branding marketing) is based on the concept of an *iconic brand* that transcends any functional character because it has a supporting myth that generates an imagination, conveys symbolism and arouses desire (which, *a priori*, was specific only to luxury).

paving the way for *tribal marketing* analysis[2] (Kozinets 1999, 2002; Cova and Cova 2002) by insisting on: the quality of the community link (Cova 1995), interactivity and adherence (individual and collective) to a brand – as opposed to a brand community unilaterally decreed by the brand. The interest, for everyone, in manipulating and instrumentalizing symbols through interaction processes in a collective of individuals (*a fortiori*, if community-based) is a matter of *mimetism*[3] (or even more the *mimetic desire*, conceptualized by Girard 1972). The amplification of the phenomenon on the Internet is considerable.

What seems to be ignored (including in the virtual universe) is the *symbolic practice of marking as a mimetic sign of belonging and recognition to/by a community*. This is what we will try to identify here.

But first, why do we create a community on the Internet? The fact of attracting the *visitor* (and potential client) by all means, and as soon as possible, already exists without the Internet: the appearance industry – clothing (Marion 2003; Piacentini and Mailer 2005) or fashion (Elliott and Leonard 2004) – and the addictive goods industry (Pechmann and Knight 2002) with the existence of parallel networks for illegal substances. The observation is simple: demand is based on what is lacking.

We know how much *lacking* and *dependence* play a key role in attracting people.

2 It is there the result of the postmodern interpretation highlighted by Lyotard (1979) and of the sociological consequence of the emergence of the neo-tribalism stated by Maffesoli (1988); the tribalism, in the classic anthropological approach, referring to the relationship and the territory. The postmodern individual (Lyotard 1979), disappointed of the illusions of modernism, does not see the future any more as horizon of progress and looks towards the past with nostalgia while relativizing the dominant culture to prefer a societal blur characterized by the mobility, the universe of the seduction, the ironic sneer and the consumerism (which rests on the narcissistic hedonistic individualism, the eclecticism, the allusive and the ephemeral: Lipovetsky 1987). It is at the same time an affirmation of oneself while being a loss of oneself in the collective community (Maffesoli 1988), by the subjectivity of an affective impulse to be together, with reactions or desires of identity withdrawal of an archaic nature (on the family, the religion, the tribe) while turning nevertheless towards technology. The practical consequence is that marketing segmentation (by SPC for example) becomes inoperative.

3 Girard (1972), while being based on the concept of *imitation* (of the sociologist G. Tarde), proposed an anthropological interpretation of the violence related to the *mimetic desire of appropriation* (*mimesis of appropriation*) of what is not one's own and nevertheless object of desire, often fantasized and solved then by fusion to the collective up to the choice (sometimes gregarious) of designation of an *expiatory victim* to consolidate the community or to make community.

However, on the Internet, downstream virtual communities (specified in this way to distinguish them from upstream communities of practice or innovation) are not purely passive[4] and dependent. They are never consumer puppets manipulated, directly and unilaterally, by the offer, but stakeholders: proactive actors, very zealous and fascinated (Wiertz and de Ruyter 2007), interacting with the marketing of the offer in a collaborative logic (role of the lead users: Von Hippel 1976). Adoption, within communities, where mimetism prevails, necessarily telescopes a logic of the value of the offer (based largely on the imaginary and the symbolic). The *brand communities on the Internet* (Muniz and O'Guinn 2001), or *virtual brand communities*, accompany and combine with other virtual communities. All virtual communities *aggregate individuals (who desire) around a common passion.*

The literature on branding, as a preliminary analysis support, shows, by a transparency effect at the least, the potential link to tribalism and luxury. Our hypothesis is that the *luxury brand* is an attractive and solar referential for real and digital tribal communitization: a *totem*[5]. For all communities, luxury arouses (unconsciously and consciously) a desire and then a compensatory thirst that is never quenched by imitation through the use of accessible transitory equivalents: this is what structures the dynamics of marking. The brand, claimed and/or adopted by the community, is an accessible element of marking among others and under the inaccessible tutelary influence of the *totem*.

Nevertheless, it is still necessary to grasp the dynamics of marking in the tribal panoply (where the brand is only one accessory of tribal marking among others) according to an open and changing combinatory.

The desire for branding, the variety and the multiplication of marking, often in a spectacular way, implicitly gravitate, without accessing it, towards a desired and attractive but not very accessible polar reference: luxury. Moreover, the world of

4 Let us note that, *a fortiori*, this conformist and consumerist passivity is totally absent, upstream, in the *communities of practice* (where hackers are involved) allowing, by co-creation and co-design, to proceed, by interactions and collective learning, to technological bricolage and/or to divert the use of existing technological products.

5 A *totem* is an *ancestral mythical symbol (animal, plant, artifact), venerated within a community, translating a spiritual symbolic relationship, of an individual within a collective, towards a tutelary spirit and federating/identifying the group; which generates a social and/or religious organization (where the totem is then sacred and feared).* Depending on the discipline mobilized, the interpretations differ: for Freud, it is a paternal projection; for Levi-Strauss (1962a), from the ontological point of view, it is a symbolic imaginary system of cultural projection on nature. On the classificatory level (Levi-Strauss 1962b), it is an artificial *a posteriori* construction of ethnologist. To go further, on the basis of an updated reading, let us refer, respectively, to Kohn (2010) and Obadia (2012).

luxury, while seeking to protect its image, tends, if not to democratize, at least to: (a) federate on the *luxury brand*[6] a wider population (than the initial elitist target), if only by successfully distributing *logo-based* derivative products (as appealing products) and/or even by offering more accessible goods (such as certain accessories) – which is just one way of offering a range to cover all possible segments; (b) to live in the contemporary world by *developing links*, notably on the Internet (either by using existing social networks or by creating spaces dedicated to the brand with virtual stores, virtual worlds, etc.).

Inherent to the universe of luxury at the beginning then by successive derivative chains of unfulfilled desire via marking, the referential brand becomes the operating variable. The chain, starting from luxury, extends to the construction of *iconic brands* and then, in a derivative way, always by imitation. The brands (not yet iconic) want or attempt an enhancement (referring *in fine* to the *totem*). The adopters follow this implicit ascending classification by marking: by mimetism and to mark out the difficult or impossible quest of access to the totemic summit. Hence, the supposed origin of the practice of marking in real and digital tribal communitarianism: the absolute, attractive and solar referential *totem* (the unattainable but infinitely desired *luxury brand* – if necessary, antithetically, through rejection or apparent denigration).

What does not vary is that the community specifies the code, as well as proceeds to exclusion if there is a deviation from the code: this logic specific to each community is not a variable that can be controlled by brand X (which then becomes a simple provider, opening up to the communities, interactively, without control). As a code, marking is learned (sometimes tacitly) in the community and takes on protean garb. Also, the dynamics of virtual communities, backed by marking, exaggerate a form of narcissism through mimetism. This raises the double question of: digital individuation within communities of imitation – manipulating marked technological products and applications (in the strong marketing sense of the term)

6 The literature positively puts forward the key arguments of luxury implying authenticity by a tradition and/or a culture and also a manufactured know-how of high-quality craftsmanship allowing, in addition to a functional excellence, to associate rarity, elitism, refinement and exclusivity as well as personalization, at a very high (or prohibitive) price, by the guarantee of a strong identity based on myth and dream. Hence, the value linked to a hedonistic desire for pleasure for the self-image (reflection of reassurance or egotist projection of the self) and also as a social image of differentiation. The subjective perception of luxury (Phau and Prendergast 2000), through the existence of the associated dream value, is essential to federate on the brand and to arouse desire (taking into account specific cultural springs which are not identical everywhere). However, it is important to distinguish (Kapferer and Bastien 2008) between the luxury product and the *premium* product (a high-end brand product which often, by *convergence*, strongly imitates the *luxury brand*(s)).

and/or marking space (physical or virtual) (section 4.1); the spectacular dimension offered by the immersive symbolic projection of ourselves in the virtual community (section 4.2). The conclusion of the chapter (section 4.3) will also aim to embody the stakes beyond the virtual (notably through the case of the virtual influencer).

4.1. Community and virtualization: what individuation?

The societal model disseminated by the technologies associated with the Internet (taken as a *symbolic dissolver*: Musso 2000) is based on the community. By pushing the reasoning to its paroxysm, in spite of the potential virtual nomadism, the community logic can condition and predict an identity confinement on the common passion and/or the (falsely) reassuring withdrawal in the collective (either by adhesion to the similar or peer and/or by immediate convergence of interests). This takes place in a virtual world without borders unified by social networks (Facebook, Twitter, Instagram, LinkedIn, etc.) and its marked social codes:

– usernames, photos, links, likes, friends, followers on accounts, blogs[7], forums (managed and/or frequented);

– belonging and appearance (clothing, aesthetics by the type and extent of make-up and/or the cut and color of hair, tattoos and piercings[8]) of users to distinguish themselves in a publicly visible way;

– fetish objects exhibited physically and virtually (fashion and/or technological objects);

– broadcasting on the Internet of individual performances (ranging from the vulgar *wild tag*[9] to urban graffiti[10] or even street art)[11] or collective (flash mobs) to seek fame and recognition.

---

7 Blog (web contractor and log): personal multimedia journal on the Internet of the blogger.

8 The extent of the tattoo and the piercing refers well to a form of continuum between the ancestral and modern tribalism: from the ethnological point of view, Rouers (2008) illustrates this very well. Besides, from the historical point of view, we will note that, in his capitular *Admonitio Generalis* of March 23, 789, Charlemagne means (in 82 articles) the duties of all and, in the western imperial tradition (going back at least to the Roman Empire), it is there proscribed the tattoo in order to federate all the subjects and to forbid the expressions or tribal claims.

9 *Tag* (meaning *insignia* or *label*): as used in computing, it is also, in urban practice, a personal signature (pseudonym scribbled or scratched with style) and affixed on a surface visible to all (but sometimes difficult to access), in public space, to make yourself known and/or to delimit a territory. The respect of the other passes by the dedication and the contempt by the toyage (toy/gadget or acronym of *Tag Over Your Shit* stigmatizing what is considered as worthless).

In this process of socialization, others are no longer recognized by universalism but, in the symbolic logic, by tribalism and then by virtual tribalism through the similar: the tribes free themselves from distances, geography and culture, even erasing the *socio-professional category* (SPC) to which they belong from the start (the individual stake may also be to capture the codes of other categories), by choosing similar in pure projective logic.

The value generated here lies in and through the relationship (within the community) but associated with visibility.

This can explain (section 4.1.1) the community activist practices of marking on the Internet by rivalry and also (section 4.1.2) by the desire and then the need of virtual immersion of the community self.

4.1.1. *Activist practices of virtual communities and mimetic rivalry: viral marking*

With the development of ICT and DT, virtual communities and social networks are playing a catalytic role where convergences are taking place in terms of practices and uses.

The challenge for companies and brands present on the Internet is to maximize value through the number of adopters by exploiting the desirability of the use of objects (often technological) and/or the resulting applications. The collection of data (generally provided free of charge by the adopters) is used to build up *qualified files* for targeted advertising and to better encourage purchases.

Moreover, as a self-reinforcing effect, adopters are attracted by the visibility (measurable by the number of subscribers, views and/or fans) and then the reputation to be gained (by participating and getting involved). Quite naturally, the mimetic desire imposes itself in the collective community and generates, in fact, a form of symbolic violence by the very expression of the lack (of not having what the other has) and by the desire to fill this lack (Baudrillard 1970), as well as to mark

10 *Graffiti* (Italian plural of *graffito*: coming from *grafio*, formed on the Latin *graphium* meaning scratch). Graffiti is an aesthetic graphic representation, realized on a visible surface (more or less easy to access and in a more or less spectacular or unexpected way), in an external space, by *graffiti artists*.

11 The *graffiti artist* or *tagger* is part of a collective where the clothing *look* is essential and integrates known commercial brands (sometimes coming from *stripping* on third parties); let us note that the sports shoes become an essential accessory in all of the communities. The Sneakers, initially conceived for the sport, become *vintage*, and are worn, in a diverted way, for a practical, ludic, show-off and/or fashion use.

things, actions, places, spaces, others (positively or negatively by stigmatizing) by a thirst for recognition within their own community and by defying other communities. The concept of need (in the marketing sense) is thus to be relativized.

In the contemporary sociological approach, Bourdieu (1997), starting from the practices, explains the *symbolic violence* as a scheme of unconscious internalization postulating a belief concerning the dominant values (supposed very often) by affirming the adhesion (or, why not, in negative, the rejection) of what, symbolically, is perceived (in an automatic way and often not very reflected) as element of dominant value. Yet, the object and/or the technological application, at the individual and collective level, generates a new social space where the inferiority complex of class (supposed) is erased for a decentralization/dissemination of functioning and use, within communities of use (and/or of practice), allowing the access, the learning, the improvement, the detour of use, of the innovations by starting from the ambient air in accessible spaces of proximity (court, stairwell, cellar, garage, workshop, community arts center/youth club, multimedia space, gaming room, etc.) open to all, including and especially to teenagers and/or young adults from underprivileged backgrounds. Moreover, the useful knowledge acquired here results from practice (and not from a laborious theoretical knowledge pre-constituted assimilable by school inculcation, which can be perceived and designated, moreover, as a supposedly oppressive dominant culture).

When the virtual community thus constituted tends to become apologetic (by gathering worshippers) and closes itself, it becomes the refuge of the inner circle by dismissing/ignoring/relegating others if they are not a fellow member of the community.

In this last limiting framework of virtual communities generating a suspicion on everything that is not considered similar, gossip, rumors and other conspiracy theories play a prominent role and are relayed by social networks.

Fake news disseminated on social networks is a very specific form of rumor: the desired effect is to intoxicate, harm, hysterize an already tense situation or to create, feed and support conspiracy theories conveying an interpretation of reality that is oriented, distorted or fabricated.

Within communities, the cleaving threshold for conforming to the group, and claiming to belong to it, is to adopt its codes in order to show a demarcation and a transgression (effective or apparent) in relation to an existing social norm referenced as dominant. This process is particularly enlightening on the perception of otherness and also in the community designation of the expiatory victim (or *scapegoat* in Girard 1972) accompanied by violence (symbolic and/or nonsymbolic): the consequence is the denunciation (of a third party) by the community, with the harassment or persecution that follows. Thus, it can be a question of filming with a smartphone a scene of persecution which is then broadcast on the Internet (video of assault-lynching or happy slapping): public humiliation to socially harm a third party is a broadcast without consent (a photo or a video, sometimes with subtitles and details). This can be done by hacking and/or pirating for simple revenge as in the case of revenge porn, or even by sophisticated digital editing via AI or deepfake. The diffusion is measured (number of clicks, views, tweets, likes, etc.) and generates a buzz (a key principle of viral marketing) but in an accelerated way on social networks (notably via the list of friends, followers and/or subscribers). With good or bad reasons, it is thus a question of creating a buzz, in a more or less sophisticated way: negative action (to harm) or negative rumor (including through a hoax), more or less subtle and not immediately verifiable; or, positively, to publicize an event and/or attract attention (usually in a staggered way) in order to prove/approve a message, pass the baton to a third party, launch a challenge to be taken up, claim and alert (e.g. in the latter case, with #MeToo). If the diffusion of a photo (with or without comments) or a video (silent or with sound and/or subtitles) is enough in itself to be diffused on social networks, the rumor has an *omnichannel* spectrum including the implicit. The normal propagation of rumors on the Internet is often linked to word of mouth, effective within a community (Dwyer 2007) and, more broadly, by creating a motivation to peddle (as with the example of the chain love letter: "spread this important message to two people of your choice [...] if you don't want to die [...] and/or [...] to avoid X consequence or to hope to obtain Y").

In any case, whether or not we belong to a community, it becomes particularly crucial for everyone to protect their e-reputation, because even though we wish it to be positive, it can easily become negative on the Internet by being captured without consent, especially by the viral propagation of rumors via virtual communities designating a target.

Thus, harassment on the Internet (via social networks, forums, blogs, instant messaging by keyboard or Internet Relay Chat, IRC) aims to stigmatize in different ways:

– That of the hateful hater specialized in insults by inexorably pursuing their victim, their reactions, even after banning/expulsion from a site.

– That of the troller[12] (trolling: Internet slang and a metaphor borrowed from the technique of fishing/hunting by intrusive wandering of opportunity), which is a way (direct and/or insidious and underhand) of provoking reactions by permanently raising controversies or polemics more or less free and by using all the means, even

12 To be distinguished from the character of the *troll*, originating from Scandinavian legends (mythology reused in films and games influenced by the work of J.R.R. Tolkien); or again, from economic actors specialized in the takeover of patents (*patent trolls*: Pénin 2010).

diverted, to fool, destabilize, provoke, offend, harass, destroy a reputation by making a buzz but protected by anonymity.

– By planned intrusive action: identity theft by phishing; cracking techniques (numerous and varied) to extort money and/or blackmail. Thus, the hacked webcam becomes a tool of enslavement in an omnipresent spying system where, potentially, intimacy can be violated at any moment (with a multiplier effect by the connected objects used in daily life).

– Everyone, potential actor of the virtual world (and/or victim), is also traceable/trackable and geo-locatable, through an IP (Internet Protocol) address – even though a virtual private network (VPN) and/or the browser *The Onion Router* (TOR), allowing to isolate exchanges from the rest of the traffic, complicate this tracing/tracking a little – or through the smartphone via the subscriber identity module (SIM) card that is a control chip with memory locking the ability to transmit and receive, through traceable mobile functions and/or applications.

But by whom? It can be anyone. However, the malicious people who are active on the Internet very often only take advantage of security weaknesses and/or data posted spontaneously online by users (who show themselves with photos, list of friends and/or by filming themselves with a webcam).

The user may believe that, by putting themself on stage, they can benefit from the famous *15 minutes of fame* prophesied by Andy Warhol and become, why not, a leader (in the community they belong to or the one they are helping to create; even as an influencer on the Internet and social networks). And this, to the extent that only the smartphone, as a multimedia tool, allows everyone (talented or not) to put themselves on stage to exist in the universe of appearance.

The practice of the selfie (or ego-portrait, generally contextualized with a celebrity and/or a known/famous background) is another illustration that is much more widespread.

In any case, these practices are based on connected objects which, in themselves, can only feed Big Data (mass data) and its associated Cloud of multimedia digital data. The Cloud is constituted by the interactive archiving of information obtained spontaneously by users (forms filled in by users and/or multimedia information revealed on personal Internet pages, Facebook or others) or via cookies sent to users' devices when they visit sites. The increasing quantity and quality of the data collected increases the accuracy of the qualified files that can be used commercially. Access to personal data by professionals, without the need for spying or hacking, is therefore easy, systematic, extensive and almost free. What is not free is the storage of data (in a data center, at least for the initial equipment cost and the operating cost in terms of maintenance and energy) and the updating of these data (inherent to the management and operation of any database).

The virtual world allows a spectrum of possibilities where data recovery from: voluntarily provided data; data capture from users without their knowledge; trivialization of techniques and practices of technological tinkerers (inspired by hackers) in terms of hacking marketing that can be intrusive and violate the privacy of others by phishing or cracking; mobilization of harassers or haters and trolling. Even though we put aside all of the (often deleterious) behaviors and actions, the technological evolution of the means of communication on the Internet amplifies and accelerates the media tam-tam within communities and between communities where mimetic rivalry is predominant. Everyone has the tools and practices that allow them to mark cyberspace (with a signature to be decoded) in order to be recognized by their community. Furthermore, the most used search engines on the Internet sort information according to the visibility desired by the highest bidder and/or by an algorithmic configuration that selects pages by convergence to the similar, and, generally, according to previously formulated queries.

The algorithmic design on the Internet and social networks (Jean 2021) is conducive to the creation of informational speculative bubbles generating community closure and self-fulfilling prophecies impacting beliefs and behavior.

Moreover, contemporary society is now based, more or less, on education via the Internet, where each person orientates themself according to their spontaneous (but inculcated or learned) tastes and/or acquired via uncertified content, with, in parallel, in real life, an official compulsory education (now perceived, rightly or wrongly, as less demanding) and often relegated by those for whom it is intended and which would be useful to them (if only to speak of the need for a minimum base of common knowledge). Without the sanctuary of values and authenticated scholarly educational content, everything is a place of self-affirmation in our own collective identity (claimed on the basis of postulates and beliefs: family, social, ethnic, religious). This is characterized by the selective choice of sites on the Internet and the encouragement of the rise of symbolic conflictuality by a desire for community domination (over another or over others). Hence, the personal wandering facing two pitfalls:

– the adhesion to an identity of appearance by phantasmatic projection and sensitivity to false values supposed to support the desired image of ourselves (in search of a lost or never found identity);

– conformism and formatting to the rules of the technological system in place (from a young age; thus, for example, every preadolescent has a cell phone, an email address, an account on the Internet with little or poorly exercised parental control) with often confinement in an identity culture.

4.1.2. Limited otherness in the virtual immersion of the community self

Directly or indirectly, voluntarily or involuntarily, we attend the relegation of an old world to enter a postmodern society, more individualistic but communitarian, where the assertion of oneself testifies the permanent spectacle of oneself within a generalized society of the *spectacle* (as Debord (1967) presages) and this by all the possible means. We already knew since the beginning of the 1960s with McLuhan (1962) that the *Gutenberg civilization* linked to the printed book could fade away, which tends to be realized in the majority practice (and not in an absolute way), by a projection in the global village (McLuhan 1967) effectively meshed worldwide today by the ICT and DT (transcending the open economic globalization).

The extension of the *global village* is now achieved by a virtual community universe mixing (and/or confronting), in the use, the affirmed origins of belonging (social, ethnic or religious).

The question of individual freedom and individuation, and even more so of digital individuation, is posed by a risk of community control (wherever and whatever it may be) dictating behaviors of imitation and conformity to the group. Let us note that if the hold can be amplified by Internet (by the type of consulted site or the algorithm of the social network referring to the similar occurrences rather than to the critical or divergent points of view), the highlighting of the phenomenon is former. Starting from a historical observation about Nazism and a scientific question (can there be a democratic leader?), Lewin (1948) was interested very early on in *group dynamics* and the role of *leadership*. Moreover, a manager by legal authority (in Max Weber's categorization) can also be a leader by their charismatic authority but not necessarily.

Here, the *leader* can be the initiator of a marking and will be then imitated. The standard community dynamic (far from generally favoring positive interactions, openness, innovation and critical judgments) engenders a degree of conformity (a function of the degree of ideological closure of the group and the small number of its members). If the community group grows (as it does on the Internet), this makes Rogers' (1962) adopter categories operational again, with imitation of the *leader* category by the other categories. In the broad spectrum observed, conformism alone does not explain everything. Activism thus plays a role in a first extreme margin. On the Internet, the *pioneer* category is that of the hackers (within communities of practice for the creation and diffusion of new technologies); followed by the *first adopters* that are the *geeks*. At first glance, the *geek*[13] does not seek to modify,

13 *Geek* (16th-century English, *gecke*: crazy person), *passionate individual, fascinated and focused on the world of imagination, technology, computer science and its applications* (e.g. video games).

improve or repair the technological objects in their environment (which is what the hacker does) but, mainly, to use them (ostensibly and almost obsessively) by claiming (Yu 2007; Tocci 2007, 2009) a particularism and belonging to a deviant or anti-conformist culture (in relation to the *mainstream* social norm and the mass of the population). Beyond technophilia, membership in the *geek* community is a vast and complex process (Tocci 2007, 2009) that can also involve an outward sign, such as clothing style. Today, the *geek look* has become trendy ("Geeks can be chic", according to Anna Wintour of Vogue in 2011).

In this resocialization of the *geek*, it is important to distinguish the geek from the *nerd* (from knurd: slang inversion word of drunk); the latter – more intellectual, solitary and even almost asocial (no life in extreme cases) – being so invested in their general fascination for science that they neglects their appearance.

Geeks are essential community actors of virtual spaces and are particularly seduced by the collective *multi–users' online virtual game* (which attracts and federates groups and creates loyalty).

Thus, as a shared virtual object, the online game engenders a diffusion, more or less wide, according to the targeted elitism and the symbolic attractiveness for a more or less open group. Bartle (1996)[14] has proposed a first classification of the users of its products. Bartle's classification is based on the expectations of players according to their modes of interaction: exploration (*explorers*); performance (*achievers*); sociability (*socializers*) and domination (*killers*). Based on this seminal work, and through a more significant quantitative approach (sample of 3,000 players), Yee (2007) arrives at a typology of players' involvement according to variables related to the interest in playing: *relationships* (desire to interact with peers and build lasting social relationships); *manipulation* (manipulating others for their own benefit); *immersion* (immersing themself in a virtual world); *escapism* (escaping from their daily life); *achievement* (accomplishment through the determination to play in order to take up challenges and to become powerful). Yee's result gives a ranking (in descending order of importance) of interest: relational; achievement; immersion; escape; manipulation. Generally, the synthesis that is made without prioritization is the triptych immersion, socialization and performance (performance in the sense of advancement in the game). On the declarative level at least, the importance of relationships appears to be essential to the community approach, as does the incentive to play in order to progress, as well as the desire to escape through immersion.

---

14 This author is one of the designers of the MUD (or Multi-Users Dungeon), which opened the way to shared virtual game universes (including MMORPGs, see below). The MUD made it possible to incarnate avatars in persistent universes but, exclusively, through a textual interface.

Furthermore, it is important to note that several authors (Yee 2002; Gaon and Stora 2008) show that there is no direct link between online gaming (and/or immersive virtual realities) and addiction. However, the low self-esteem associated with prolonged immersion as an obsessive refuge, with the risk of mixing real and virtual worlds, would be, for some already fragile subjects, the triggers of an addiction in the pathological sense of the term (Rueff 2008). The normal attitude is the possibility to explore roles (Turkle 1995) as an actor can do.

Outside of this pathology, over/under-gambling is mostly the result of a highly stimulated subject, such as when they belong to a *permanent online gaming community* called a *guild* (Ducheneaut et al. 2007).

For its part, and at the same time, behind a brand and a game name, the marketing of the offer is developing a strategy aimed at encouraging, in a variety of ways, a conditioning of use[15] to encourage, as much as possible, an addictive approach.

4.2. Performance of immersive symbolic projection by marking the community self within the virtual community

The basic necessity for the user is the subscription to an Internet service provider (ISP). Then, the desirability of the user focuses on a few fetish objects as essential mobility terminals on the Internet (smartphone, tablet, game console) to access the grail: the applications we must have.

On this technological base, virtual communities emerge, *a priori* egalitarian, where distinctions are based on the skill and competencies acquired in the immersive use of the chosen virtual world (rather than on the educational background or the income level of the original SPC, linked, to a very large extent, to the old real world). Immersion in digital applications often implies a segmentation of fields favoring multiple personalities (without, however, any proven pathology) adapted, at least in appearance, to each specific contextualized field (school, home, gang, urban space, festive place, etc.) where community mimetism imposes itself each time with its rites, codes and rules. No injunction imposes to be the same everywhere (and if it is the case, it denotes the affirmation of the stability of the self or, on the contrary, a hyper-rigidity depriving of any flexible aptitude). To cross the

15 By various means induced by the game and well internalized: corrective *updates* or game extensions; new versions promising more possibilities; the desire to acquire experience points; the expectation of gains or promised virtual objects; the desire to use new features; the desire to play a new game, to reach a quest, to participate in an event or even the hope to meet a rare character, etc.

ways of being (or to demultiply them) operates, more and more, by proxy, in a symbolic projection of oneself by virtual immersion. The pseudo is the first of the virtual tattoos of the marking (allowing the relative or absolute anonymity), which is doubled by the creation of an avatar: for the symbolic transposition of themself, as soon as the player wants to penetrate a virtual world, they incarnate themself by their *avatar* (their virtual animated character)[16]. This approach presupposes first (section 4.2.1.) a technological support allowing a symbolic projection of themself, and then (section 4.2.2.) a virtual immersion, in particular via the online game (a tendency within a community and also, henceforth, generalized to all).

4.2.1. *From the technological offer to the symbolic marketing of the virtual self: avatar and the profession of the self*

The virtual universe is both technological and marked. The hardware of mobility for all (as opposed to software, the part of the software that supports social networks and applications) is made up of objects that are limited (in power and possibilities) but that are highly desirable[17] linked to strong brands that are popular with communities. As already mentioned, the desired objects of mobility are essentially the Smartphone (*Apple iPhone* or *Samsung Galaxy* and other *Huawei*), the game console (*Sony PlayStation, Microsoft XBox, Nintendo Switch*), the tablet or the hybrid laptop (i.e. with a screen smaller than 15 inches, detachable and touchable with a long autonomy: *Microsoft Surface* or others) to access the applications available (through the *Apple Store* or online catalog) of the brand. All the objects and systems of paying technological objects necessary to the access to the applications (benefiting from updates, just like the embedded software) are, more and more, designed and thought out:

– for the use, as gadgets of the mobility of a brand to have (to access the applications) and therefore to replace as soon as possible by new ones (as they are rarely modifiable/upgradable);

16 For a marketing perspective, see Garnier and Poncin (2013).

17 By *narcissistic seduction* according to Baudrillard (1968). Indeed, the old object is downgraded and the accumulation of objects, henceforth standardized, breaks with the transcendental to institute the consumerist relational (this relational becoming itself, intrinsically, an object of consumption like the virtual social networks). The only thing that counts then is a relationship to the devitalized object because it is standardized. However, a symbolic part remains in the illusion wanted by the marketing of the offer which specifies the object, even artificially, by seeking to blur the standardization and to transmute the functional into dream. And, as everything pushes to the accumulation, Baudrillard (1970) also criticizes the accepted concept of *need* to replace it by that of *desire*: desire which is *insatiable* to him because it is based on the *lack of not having*.

– with a form of limitation and/or even quasi-programmed obsolescence (by the fashion of the moment, the ergonomics, the functionalities offered, the available power or the components or even the wear rate of the battery – key to autonomy – which is also not always easily replaceable).

Beyond the hardware, in order to increase the size of the usage network on the Internet for the applications, one of the challenges for the brands is their site: visibility, ergonomics, reputation (possibly associated with a *ranking* due to the number of visitors, authorizing advertising spin-offs as a result), existence of an online after-sales service and, generally, a discussion forum to encourage use and resolve any problems.

This universe of virtual commercial support is indeed a transposition of the real model, but with advantages linked to dematerialization and much lower operating costs.

In this new universe, the comparative cost between sites remains according to the level of maintenance, after-sales service and the existence (or not) of physical flows. Indeed, an online transaction can concern a physical product (like an order on Amazon's website with all the logistic apparatus of storage and delivery) versus a totally dematerialized product (soft, like a downloadable game).

Often, the free access is to be relativized in its meaning and/or its absolute existence due to the advertising financing (linked to clickable pages and/or the sale of qualified databases from spontaneous or captured user data).

The desire for mobility (in its entirety: hardware terminals, software, sites and applications) is a first functional step necessary to a symbolic personal projection.

From this technological support, everyone, to varying degrees, becomes an actor as well as a *virtual asset* and also potentially an *actor of the virtual universe* (including professionally for a fee). For the majority of individuals, the desire is first of all about the use through virtual immersion.

For the user of the virtual universe, the *virtual recognition* passes by their avatar, which materializes an archetypal symbol of themself totally fantasized (sometimes weakly linked to themself in appearance but to a fantasized part of themself). The problem is therefore less of the risk of dilution of the self in the digital universe (because the individual, even an adolescent, *a priori* normal – except for a preexisting pathology – distinguishes the real from the virtual) than that of being perceived and recognized socially only by and through their avatar (by denial or scotomization, in fact, the real integrity of the individual and their complexity).

Yee (2007) shows that online gamers, by inhabiting their avatars, act in accordance with their metaphorical idea of them. The individual narcissistic interest in the virtual meta-world passes through and is symbolically summed up in this avatar as the projection of a surrogate, parable or metaphor of self: a virtual marking of self by self.

What prevails, at the collective level of interaction between avatars, is rather a parallel recreation of the market universe through the purchase of virtual products in order to function in the virtual meta-world and manipulate the symbolic within a community. Thus, the online game allows everyone to project themselves into virtual universes and to become an actor in the game (or even to be recognized as a virtual game sportsman, or e-sport, and to be remunerated for this by a brand).

However, other solutions exist to earn money by instrumentalizing the virtual universe according to their popularity and/or competence or skill:

– influencer[18];

– *youtuber*[19];

– harvester (farming activity): in an online game, this consists of repeating actions to harvest/loot virtual items and resell them for an actual fee (like monster scavengers or *gold farmers*)[20].

In online games, learning, performance and careers are organized within communities where symbolic stakes are omnipresent (type of world, type of players, type of interactions, type of gains, type of successes, type of reputations, type of recognition, type of income).

Product placements are numerous in online games and also in social games (e.g. Linden Lab's *Second Life*) where the avatars of the residents (i.e. individuals registered on the site and having a free or paid user account) are natural supports for brands. The commercial activity of buying/selling branded objects is thus possible

---

18 Functionally, through their media exposure, the influencer is an imitated prescriber, updating *celebrity marketing* (but here without the cachet of a star paid or the risk of possible cognitive dissonance between the chosen personality and the product). On the Internet, the influence is decentralized and in osmosis with the community logic. Moreover, given their success, game brands can be BtoB influencers, also mobilizing co-branding to make the invited brand desirable. There are now also virtual influencers (e.g. @lilmiquela, see section 4.3).

19 Like players (filming themselves playing) and having subscribers watching them play (for example, https://www.twitch.tv/).

20 Online services allow players to purchase virtual items or avatars through transactions or exchanges (often without the approval of official game sites). Players can become independent suppliers of other players for a fee, which can distort a game.

(or other transactions), with drifts in terms of counterfeiting by lack of exploitation rights of the brand name and/or violation of intellectual property.

4.2.2. *Role dream symbolism and marking the community self*

In the virtual universe, imagination and dreams are inspired by classical media such as the cinema. The cinema, since its beginnings (with the tricks and the illusion of Georges Méliès), but in an accelerated way today by the available technology, exerts a fascination by the activation (visual and sound) of the senses.

The acceleration passes at first by the *digital palette* in the pioneer films of the nineties (*Terminator 2, Jurassic Park*) and then by the *performance capture*[21] for those of the 2000s (*Avatar, The Lord of the Rings, Harry Potter*). The films, which intensively mobilize technology for creativity in the service of the spectacular, have met with a worldwide craze and have proven to be particularly profitable. In addition, spin-off products and licensing (as with *Star Wars*) significantly increase the initial revenues from the exploitation of a film. As a result, video game studios, regardless of the question of originality, have every interest in exploiting licenses from universes that are already familiar and also preapproved and where virtual immersion will be desired, rewarding and also facilitated and profitable. The digital video game is a way to make accessible, in a democratized way, the childhood dream of being an actor (without the barrier of being a professional actor)[22].

The symbolic projection allows us to exist in a meta-world and also, eventually, professionally (as an influencer, gamer and/or youtuber), against payment (usable in the real world). Everyone can participate in online games (elitist or general public) by taking on a role where satisfaction is direct and leads to unlimited narcissism (the virtual allows everything). The relationship to reality can eventually be altered because the projection on the avatar satisfies all the possibilities but does not have to account for it outside the community (unlike the movie actor who, apart from the

---

21 While *motion capture* is a technique for recording the movements of objects or living beings on a computer, *performance capture* is more subtle in that it faithfully integrates the facial expressions or precise hand movements of an actor moving freely; once the actor's performance has been recorded, the film is then entirely produced on a computer, opening up infinite technical possibilities specific to the virtual world, with a high degree of realism if necessary.

22 A professional actor is usually trained and often goes through a selection or casting process to get a role. Their success depends on the number of spectators or fans, who project themselves by proxy (without being an idol/star themselves). In the new world, virtual projection is almost spontaneously and directly accessible (and sometimes even paid) where anyone can find a way to become a *star*.

possible exposure of their private life, has to face criticism and not only the adulation of their fans).

Online games are part of a tradition (real and then virtual) of role-playing games (RPG). Nowadays, the massively multiplayer online role-playing game (MMORPG)[23] in *persistent universe* (in the sense that, once the session is over, the previous stages are saved and the game is frozen for this player until the next session is opened) with strong interactions between players of the same team (including by voice over IP or VoIP, Voice over Internet Protocol) and, possibly, in 3D (*3D Persistent World*). The latest techniques available in 3D are not always used in the different versions proposed, and this is to allow the greatest number of players to play on any computer support (while waiting for the generalization of a qualitative standard allowing it): the performance of objects growing and becoming increasingly democratic, the next step is the generalization, for the masses, of realistic graphics.

Besides the technological angle, the development of *persistent online worlds* engenders the existence of virtual cultural societies (where several million individuals can interact daily) with, very generally, the functioning of community belonging where the logic of self-marking prevails. Despite dynamic and evolving rules, interactions within persistent worlds are strong, and players seek to gather on the Internet, including to attend privileged ritual virtual events (players can also meet in real life (IRL)).

The free nature of MMORPGs (e.g. *Fortnite*[24]) only partially explains the success, because paid games are highly popular (like *World of Warcraft*). Success is based primarily on the attraction of a desire for immersion and membership.

The dynamism of the persistent multiplayer online game universe (Zabban 2012) is the direct consequence of the combined entanglement of technological and societal evolution where the community aspect dominates (with its rules). For Phillipette (2015), the collective of players constitutes a socially distributed cognitive artifact, operating within its own dynamics, and thus being able to empower itself as a community (of varying size) with its rules and codes. This, in our view, is conducive to the development of a distinctive marking in a specific community dynamic.

---

23 Each role is held by a player via their avatar (to be created then to progress) in a virtual world, by improving it progressively thanks to experience points acquired in a proportional way to the difficulty of the quest (task or mission) entrusted by a non-player character (NPC), proposing quests, transactions, bartering of objects and events. The objective is to reach new levels or to acquire skills allowing the avatar to gain in power (or strength).

24 See: https://www.epicgames.com/fortnite/fr.

The symbolism in these virtual universes is based on universes forged by uchronies[25] and dystopias[26] where generally groups of players, via their avatars, recognize each other, mark the space and fight by tribe (and are reborn at each new game session). More globally, the creative ferment on the Internet is always linked to a *primitive utopia* (sometimes subversive, that of the hackers) anchoring itself in an interactive collective practice of co-creation and diffusion. The technical object, here digital, thus implemented with its part of utopian dream, will be seized by others more pragmatic in the name of a *technicist ideology*[27].

The technicist ideology is itself recuperated by a managerial logic based on marketing, to sell by seducing potential adopters, who recognize themselves first of all by their community belonging.

In any case, the imitation and the spectacular projection of themselves, within their community of belonging, results essentially from the fascination for the dream, through interactivity and virtual immersion.

If the approach of the game on the Internet reinforces the community activism of geeks fascinated by MMORPGs, other online virtual games of entertainment with a very wide distribution (of the casual game type, such as *Pokemon Go* or *Candy Crush*), can tend, by the frequency of use and popularity, to engender a form of familiarization with the online game and even universality of a practice for all (those who have a smartphone) and even reach the transgenerational stage. At this stage, marketing can thus easily consider the division into customer segments for the entire population.

Moreover, the craze for the virtual trip, seductive and playful, towards an accessible *grail* has orientated the brand marketing, at least since 2002, on the *advergame* (contraction of advertising and game; with new explorations in marketing on *gamification*). The *advergame* is directly proposed by the virtual universe of the brands (sometimes by mobilizing other virtual worlds like *Second*

25 Uchrony (from the Greek *ou* privative; and *krhonos*, time) shows fictitiously what could have happened by modifying a historical event that could have taken place.

26 Dystopia (from the Greek *dys*, wrong/malformed; and *topos*, place) is antithetical to utopia. The dystopia is the fictional account of a society governed by a totalitarian power whose ideology is the organization of a perfect world. From then on, the revolt of a marginal deviant (but predestined leader hero and/or by a process of revelation), within a community, makes possible, after a long quest, the eradication of the evil (incarnated by the totalitarian entity).

27 Ricoeur (1997) explains that reality is symbolically mediated by representations opposing and articulating utopia and ideology. Flichy (2001) takes up this perspective by applying it to Internet.

Life or *Sims*). The *advergame* is an online game dedicated to a brand for virtual promotion and in an interactive logic. Thus, through innovation, it is a question of reducing rejection (linked to invasive advertising), of mobilizing consent, of increasing exposure time, and also of seducing, building loyalty, promoting, as well as detecting lead users (and rewarding each one according to their involvement). Digital applications in general, and games in particular, are essential vectors of distribution to all segments (from the very elitist in restricted communities to the very general public for communities with no access barrier except that of having a smartphone and an account on one of the social networks). This does not prevent the already proven use of celebrity marketing on the Internet, aiming at buzz, via the staging of the brand (adopted and exhibited against remuneration or benefits) by the adored celebrity. The challenge of marketing is to maximize viral diffusion by reaching the intended targets.

4.3. Conclusion

The objects are chosen and accumulated for reasons of desire (to fill a lack of having what the other has or can have) and not of need (Baudrillard 1968, 1970). The psycho-social and/or anthropological approach of a collective functioning refers to already known analyses: since at least Lewin (1948) on the dynamics of the groups (with the generated conformism); or still on the desirability by *mimesis of appropriation* (Girard 1972) also called *mimetic rivalry* within a community.

Does the intense mobilization of technology, within communities of use, change this double reading?

If the virtual character, via ICT and DT, only amplifies what already exists, the viral diffusion on Internet increases the amplification tenfold and manifests itself by a spectacular affirmation of the collective by the community of belonging. Digital individuation, via the community self, generates a conformism based on a desirability for marked objects recognized by the community and symbolically guaranteeing an identity by reinforcing an image for ourselves and vis-à-vis others. From then on, immersion in virtual universes and virtual communities extends this symbolic logic by an extension of the *society of the spectacle* (Debord 1967) where everything is conducive to the mirroring of ourselves (most of the time, without the ego, especially if it is only educated on the Internet, is able to reach itself). The multiplayer online game is an interesting illustration of the projection of ourselves in a community and of its spectacular character. The collective use of the Internet reinforces a communal presentation of ourselves in the behaviors and practices within the virtual universe. Real/digital marking is affirmed there (vector of mimetic and symbolic rivalries), of which the brand extends, even in an acculturated and composite way, the ancestral tribal marking (perceived, today, in a referential way but rather superficially), and, analogically, the desired *luxury brand*, whatever the detours, appears to be a *totem* for a brand X (that it wants to assert itself and/or that it is already desired) as for the increasingly communalized individuals. The brand is an element of marking, and this also applies in BtoB (Bouvier-Patron 2003). The brand or its diffusion is not decreed by the brand itself but depends on its desirability and its symbolic appropriation by a community. This decentralized process of adoption is symptomatic of a way of marking space. Also, as Dahlander and Magnusson (2005) have already pointed out with regard to communities of innovation, which are more expert and more demanding than communities of use, the brand must make itself available without imposing itself. For communities of use as well, the virtual brand community is not *the* solution for the brand (decreeing is not enough). On the contrary, a community (or several) can recognize and appropriate a brand of their own free will (by mimetism: recognizing and distinguishing themselves within a community of belonging and thus tattooing a collective and individual space). Any imperialist, intrusive or infiltration attempt by a brand amounts to liquidating the community dynamic.

Under this restriction, brands must strongly register on the Internet and in the virtual world because it is an obligatory point of passage in the diffusion and adoption; but with the difficulty of defending the brand identity and the brand territory in a societal space (real and digital) where marking is breaking like a wave and where the community norm imposes a code that is not or no longer under the authority of the brand.

The pivotal point is the inescapable character of the Internet in usage, even though the brand may struggle to maintain its identity and image in a larger set of marking. Marking is over-determining, and redefines codes, uses, tinkers or hijacks brands without necessarily being coherent with the brand's intended image. This relativization of the accessible brand is not antinomic with a fascination for the brand as a sign of marking and a nostalgic form of the *true brand* (the luxury one). We make the hypothesis that a *totem* is celebrated by the marking: this desired and inaccessible *totem* for the greatest number is, atemporally and inexorably, the *luxury brand*.

4.3.1. *Exceeding: beyond the virtual*

It would be advisable to look further into additional but complementary points: (i) to analyze in detail the nature, variety and quality of the marking; (ii) to study the consequences of tribal marking: confrontation with other tribes (on the virtual level but also in the real universe) through a process of symbolic rivalry (in the virtual sphere: hackers versus geeks) or by a form of digital ethnic cleansing vis-à-vis other communities with segregative slogans (which can be prolonged in the real sphere with bullying or other acts of symbolic or effective violence); (iii) to consider the virality of symbols in the phenomenon of marking with the viral engine of *cultural branding* (in association with the dream specific to luxury initially) the dream stuck to the symbol being the vector that builds/deconstructs acculturation marking; (iv) to explore the origin of the referential marking process: the luxury universe appears to be, in our hypothesis, both a *totem* captivating all communities (non-virtual or virtual) and a discriminating marker (establishing a perceived hierarchy in the adoption of objects or object systems).

Both for the marketing of the offer (with a presence on the Internet of all the brands, including luxury brands, but which seek to preserve a hierarchy) and for the active communitarian individuals, virtualization allows a hyperbolic projection of this spectacular logic of marking (of themselves and/or of a space), within the community of belonging and vis-à-vis third parties (individuals or communities). In fact, the mass that does not have the means of a desired object clings to its symbols. The dream, emblematic and consubstantial of the world of luxury, is associated/reinforced/endorsed by symbols that can be manipulated in the virtual world; those, many of them, who would not have the means to afford or access the summit (in the real world first) come to want to grasp (only) the virtual illusion. The logic of marking is a cog in the wheel to seek the cohesion of the virtual community on the Internet as well as to discriminate and to singularize themselves in relation to others.

Any marked symbol, or recognized as such, is increased by virtualization and then spread virally (via, downstream, virtual brand communities, social networks, forums, blogs, virtual worlds). In short, the logic of branding, in a postmodern society driven by the spectacular, refers, implicitly at least, and in a direct or indirect way, to *tribal marking* with veneration of a *totem*.

Beside this adulation (which supposes an up-down schema of the universe of luxury to the marking), we can also envisage a bottom up reading (e.g. in the transposition of the urban graffiti to the virtual marking) as affirmation of the belonging to a community by a choice of distinctive signs and federating challenge to rise even more. The fascination for the totem (desired or coveted *grail*, namely, the universe associated with the *luxury label*) is the fixed point of these two logics.

At the same time, the challenge rises and evolves with technology: from now on, virtual universes mobilizing new interactive technologies (*virtual reality* consisting of immersion in a computer-simulated virtual environment; *augmented reality* enriching a real vision by the addition of virtual and quasi-prehensible information and/or complementary objects) offer considerable perspectives for mobilizing *experiential marketing*, the objective of which is to offer positive and strong interactive symbolic experiences concerning the brand universe, including luxury; for the moment in 2D or 3D, while waiting for the generalization of 4D which is a combination of virtual reality simulated with spatialized sound and physical and olfactory sensations. This increases the community stakes and the possibilities of marking by deepening the struggle but without ever escaping the fascination of the totem.

In many ways, many elements (the game scenario, the place of image and sensory, buzz, rumor, consent, the experiential approach and the use of AI) foreshadow a revolution in usage, far beyond the real, in reality.

Symptomatic of this trend, the virtual influencer (Bouvier-Patron 2019), far from being anecdotal, allows us to correctly situate the stakes and to highlight the leverage of social networks and manipulation on the Internet.

4.3.2. *Virtual influencer: an illustration by the case of Lil Miquela*

Miquela Sousa (pseudonym Lil Miquela), of Brazilian origin and living in Los Angeles (LA), is an attractive young woman: slim, with a mini-fringe, dark brown hair, hazel eyes, freckles on her face and designer clothes.

Highly visible on social networks, Lil Miquela is a model: at the forefront of living fashion and creating a natural link with the young people of her *generation me* age group (whose *digital native* narcissism, relying fully on technology, characterizes millennials: a generational cohort educated in high school at the turn of the new millennium).

Lil Miquela has been on social media since April 22, 2016: she posts photos on Instagram (@lilmiquela) daily, highlighting the brands that trust her, and thus proving to be a top influencer. As a result, since April 2018, her Instagram account has surpassed 1 million followers (affectionately named *miquelites*). Lil Miquela benefits from the availability of branded clothes and accessories, even though she claims not to be paid for it, while aspiring to become one (according to the interview, via an online messaging, to the site Business of Fashion[28]). Lil Miquela intends to be present and available for her followers (notably through selfies or by answering the numerous messages sent to create a link), but she also suffers from the taunts of the harassers and persecutors on the Web (haters and trollers) and this because she openly displays anti-sexist (#MeToo) or pro-LGBT (Lesbian Gay Bisexual Trans) opinions, thus offending the sensibility of the American right-wing politics.

28 See: http://businessoffashion.com.

However, as her popularity grew, she was professionally solicited for important events (invited by Prada to animate its fashion show on February 22, 2018 on social networks). Lil Miquela also does not hesitate to show herself in fashionable places where it is necessary to be seen or by posting herself with iconic stars (photo with the famous musician Nile Rogers).

She also successfully develops her artistic qualities: her first track *Not Mine* (single – based on the soundtrack of Sam Raimi's 1981 cult film *Evil Dead*, created by Joseph LoDuca – where Lil Miquela's voice uses a vocoder like Daft Punk's robotic voice style) was ranked number 8 on Spotify[29] in August 2017. Thus, Lil Miquela is banking on her creativity to make a name for herself. Her wish is to be recognized as an artist in her own right. To date, she is seen more as an influential celebrity among all the other it-girls posing in branded clothing, generating buzz with a big impact on the follower audience, and enjoying the associated publicity spin-offs.

Despite her age and her fascination for the futile world of appearances, Lil Miquela has a good head on her shoulders and argues about her image perceived by others in a rational way by claiming that if her existence is conditioned by social networks, it is as well the case for everyone now!

If the price of this success, for a young career, is sometimes jealousy, hostility and nastiness of some (coming from the fashion world or Internet users), the rivalry of other influencers could have had much more dramatic consequences: Lil Miquela's Instagram account was hacked in 2017 by a rival.

What was the hacking technique used? Probably simple phishing (phishing: recovery of identifiers – login and password – by a false deceptive interface copying more or less faithfully the homepage of a real site) and/or, even more likely, a kind of ransomware (namely, a ransom to the account and its content against payment). This outcome is shocking in that Lil Miquela is not a bad person and only wants to make a living from her talent.

Here are the facts: her rival first threatens her via social networks to incite her to reveal a secret, that of her true origin. These preliminary threats are followed by a hacking of Lil Miquela's Instagram account in order to blackmail her: the revelation of the truth about the secret against the restitution of the rights on the account and the content of it (content representing all the same the main intangible capital of Lil Miquela as influencer). The rival had gone so far as to remove all the photos of Lil Miquela and replace them with others, sometimes showing Lil Miquela in bad company or in an equivocal attitude and/or under an ambiguous appearance. We

29 Online music streaming site: www.spotify.com.

even wonder if caricatures or photo montages (fakes) are not disclosed on purpose, as on the *Libération* site (September 13, 2016[30]).

Like everyone else, a public person has the right to privacy and a secret garden, except perhaps if they exploit the intimate (or hidden) aspect of their private life in complicity with the media, while complaining about the consequences (paparazzi, magazine covers, gossip, rumors, etc.), as did Paris Hilton or even Lady Diana. On the contrary, when the star preserves their intimacy (like Catherine Deneuve), by systematically attacking the wild publications (thus unauthorized), the effect of their reputation in favor of intimacy prevails and the private life is generally preserved.

However, by being present on social networks and playing with her image, like any other model, has Lil Miquela exposed herself or staged herself excessively to increase her visibility by negotiating aspects of her private life? In any case, Lil Miquela has never wished to disclose her origins.

4.3.2.1. *Interpretation of the media attack on Lil Miquela*

Leaving aside for the moment the reasons of personal hostility, such as jealousy, could Lil Miquela be forced for ideological and ethical reasons to reveal her secret garden in order to comply with a regulatory business standard (in the name of a dichotomous business morality: truth versus deception)? The commercial exploitation of products or of ourselves can lead to all kinds of abuses, but how did Lil Miquela fail as a model, an influencer or an artist?

Let us see who her rival is. She also has an Instagram account, has made content about coming out as a fembot (robotic woman) on it and claims her virtuality of birth by computer graphics (Computer Generated Imagery (CGI)). In appearance, she is a sexy explosive blonde whose pseudonym is Bermuda (a reference to the very fatal Bermuda Triangle).

Bermuda defends strong ethical values in harmony with the pro-fundamental beliefs of the American culture: honesty, conservative morality, courage and patriotism.

This being said, can an artifact demand a confession from another person (*a fortiori* a human) and threaten anyone?

We can also wonder, more deeply, what were the true motivations or the hidden intentions of this rival (independent or programmed?):

– Jealousy?

30 See: https://medias.liberation.fr/photo/926828.

– To recover, in a targeted way, a brand exclusivity at a given moment?

– A pure tactical approach in a media race for leadership?

– Strategic will to discredit Lil Miquela in the long term, as it would damage the potential notoriety of a third party?

– A radical struggle for space in order to gain a promising business without sharing it?

– To unilaterally discredit Lil Miquela, by focusing their attention exclusively on her, to make her lose her sponsors and benefactors?

Beside these reasons, an overhanging and even more general motive exists: the fake is written in the genes of Instagram with the use of Photoshop. Also, the stake of the plot against Lil Miquela could be to denounce the current system of appearances. Therefore, Lil Miquela, even nice and sexy in her way, but model staging herself by all the artifices, as a potential expiatory victim, should she pay for the illusory system of the lie of the appearance? If, however, the illusion is in itself fake, the virtual is an additive form of fake and it is necessary, from now on, to explore the fake of the fake of the fake. It is an argument of denunciation or protest of ultimate degree, but it can, indeed, be deployed and multiplied at the metaphorical level in the contemporary *society of the spectacle* (already constructed by Guy Debord in 1967).

Moreover, the cultural sensitivity of an aversion to public lying (exposing to perjury in front of an official commission of inquiry as Bill Clinton did) seems more acute in the United States than elsewhere. This explains why fake news and also fact-checking has developed and plays such a big role in the media now. And it is not insignificant either that conspiracy theories are born and spread, in an accelerated way via the Internet, mainly in the United States, or firstly in the United States (before spreading elsewhere).

4.3.2.2. *The hypotheses on the origins of Lil Miquela*

Concerning the character of Lil Miquela and the secret of her origins, we have come to several hypotheses (1 to 4) if her virtuality overwhelms her reality.

– Hypothesis 1: Lil Miquela is a creature resembling a real celebrity (the English model Emily Babor or others like @karstinkle).

– Hypothesis 2: Lil Miquela is a hybrid creature mixing real and digital features, a visual artist hiding behind virtual staging (like Nicole Ruggiero, @nicoleruggiero).

– Hypothesis 3: Lil Miquela is an avatar that wants to be realistic (as opposed to the heroine of *Final Fantasy: Creatures of the Mind*, if we look at the top brand or, at the opposite and more basic level, popular in Japan and the United States, the teenager in a schoolgirl's uniform from a manga, with turquoise blue eyes and hair, with trendy tastes, and, moreover, a successful singer, Hatsune Miku).

– Hypothesis 4: Lil Miquela is an avatar (regardless of its realism) like so many others in the virtual world (e.g. *Sims*).

The character of Lil Miquela would thus be, whatever the hypothesis, an artificial construction. However, given its audience, the follower's reception is also to be studied according to several factors or variables:

– the emotion aroused by the person/personification (target character);

– the fascination for the brands displayed, independently of who wears them but even more according to who wears them (target appearances);

– the immersion in a virtual universe where the projection on the proposed image can be addictive in itself and is enough to make people desire (dream target).

Here, we enter the field of a rather operational marketing mobilizing the virtual, which can point to the intentionality behind the artificial construction of Lil Miquela without learning anything about the fundamental issues of this construction in terms of:

– a scripted story (or storytelling)[31];

– strategic marketing (upstream of the apparent facts reported).

4.3.2.3. *Confessions and consequences*

In any case, cornered and risking losing her account (containing all her photos of branded collections constituting her image capital as an influencer) while being exposed to rumors or false edits of various kinds, Lil Miquela therefore complied and revealed the secret of her origins: "I am not a human being [...] I am a robot" (@lilmiquela, April 19, 2018).

After such public confessions, Lil Miquela could lose a lot: both for her career as a model, influencer and artist. However, her fans did not abandon her and her popularity was obviously not damaged. Even after this coming out, the followers continue to follow her. The numbers are even growing and brands are still snatching her.

In short, for the case of Lil Miquela, two main and opposite theses are now possible.

Thesis No. 1: ironic metaphor on the virtual universe staged by hackers. Lil Miquela and her rival Bermuda are thus virtual creatures. Do they emanate from the

31 *Storytelling*: a narrative communication as an art and a way of telling a credible and efficient story, more or less truthful, relying on the spring of the emotion, the intrigue and/or the sulfurous, to generate subscriptions.

same activist group? If they are hackers, is the hacking of Lil Miquela's account a pure staging? It could be seen as a simulacrum mimicking the reality possible for all. If it is about activists, it could also be seen as a perspective on the limits of the cult of self or a warning about the ethical issues of virtual creation by AI. AI can lead anyone astray in terms of behaviors, universes, belief(s) and illusion(s). Can illusion coincide or merge with reality? Fiction opens the field of possibilities. Thanks to technology (AI in particular), a greater credibility, even more and more realistic, is possible. AI can be broken down into a series of distinct issues.

– At face value, AI has a reality and is built little by little (technically, historically, culturally). For example, the avatar becomes a person (to be taken really as a person).

– The actors of AI put themselves on stage to show their potential power by bluffing or anticipating possibilities. Therefore, Lil Miquela would have been conceived (Bermuda too) as a virtual creature in Silicon Valley by the company Daniel Cain Intelligence[32] as a female robot servant/slave before being kidnapped by the enigmatic Brud who reprogrammed her to make her "free" with the memories and personality of Miquela Sousa of Brazilian origin. To tell the truth, by contextualizing, we have here, in cumulated, all the fantasies of the creature (from Frankenstein of M. Shelley to Metropolis of F. Lang) with, as a background of societal veracity, to give credibility to the montage, the fact that plastic surgery is commonplace in Brazil more than elsewhere and that Latin America is often cited for its various traffics (notably for supposed or real organ trafficking).

– AI is a means of subversion (possibly in the hands of hackers – making a clear distinction between the white-hat rider on the Internet explaining the limits of the system and the black-hat hacker) – allowing to ask questions, to suggest challenges and to propose corrosive, even self-destructive scenarios.

– AI is instrumentalized by business and mobilized to play on the imagination of third parties, which allows marketing to create value (e.g. by creating a virtual muse that has as much value and/or even more than a real muse).

– AI is a way of fiction allowing, from a strategic marketing point of view, to have scenarios feeding the storytelling, in order to test what can work on the public; to get back potential customers and/or even to operate opportunistic marketing communication campaigns.

– AI is not only instrumentalized by strategic marketing but also, more certainly, by institutional actors (private or state) to the potential detriment of public liberties and personal private data and/or even individual liberties.

32 See: http://cainintelligence.com.

Whatever the answer, in the case studied, a fundamental objective question is to know if Lil Miquela or Bermuda are the creatures of: (a) activists and hackers or companies? and (b) within the same entity? Between different entities, we can see the classic game of rivalry between companies and/or competing organizations. If it is indeed the same entity, the avowed objective could be: (b1) a questioning of the system of appearance by activists or hackers; or (b2) a corporate trick in terms of *marketing hacking* to create buzz and generate a maximum audience of followers who will follow (with effective realization of the purchase prescriptions?).

Any follower and/or the general public may want to immerse themselves, and lose themselves, in the virtual and/or believe that Lil Miquela is an animated being, alive, touching, seductive and with whom they may even fall in love. What is the difference with reality? All the spectator-fans of the actress Brigitte Bardot in the 1960s or, in another genre, of Nicole Kidman in the 1990s did not meet them and even less got a private appointment and/or even less had a relationship with one or the other of the two actresses. The same is true for Lil Miquela.

Thesis No. 2: instrumentalization and recovery of the virtual for the buzz. *A contrario* therefore, we can also imagine, very prosaically, that the storytelling on the artificial muses is a direct machination to manipulate the followers in order to make a buzz to promote a product (*virtual commodity* around Lil Miquela using its commercial potential).

We already know that *political marketing*, which is very much a consumer of storytelling, generates sophisticated stagings, including machinations and intrigues.

On the supply side, the story about Lil Miquela could be a masterly media coup intended to promote the virtual muse and discredit the real photoshopped muse! Indeed, if the era was tired of human muses (of Instagram or elsewhere), retouched and artificialized by Photoshop, the revival is possible with the avatars that, finally, are not more unreal than the real celebrities augmented by artifices (therefore more or less photoshopped or pixelated) that we see everywhere in the media.

The interest for the brand to favor a virtual muse is multiplied: no exorbitant fee to negotiate (perhaps?); no delays to the photo sessions or expenses to incur in terms of hair, make-up and dressing, and, except for clauses provided for in the contract, no whims to satisfy or the star's pranks (to be covered up and stifled; unless the avowed stake is to exploit this aspect). Everything can be controlled. It is there reassuring a brand by offering the services of a virtual muse.

The co-branding, more or less durable, and the temporary reception of a brand to be valued (thanks to the support that is the virtual muse), is a sure path (with innumerable potential scenarios and a possible level of complexity more or less high but where everything can be mastered).

The virtual muse offers many advantages, but its success depends on its credibility with the followers and the durability of this credibility. Because, after experience, human imperfection and flaws could turn out to be irreplaceable and even, finally, appreciated by the public.

Brands can also develop their own avatar, in line with their values and expectations, and whose physique, style, tastes and possible interactions (driven by the brand) can evolve according to fashions and trends. A brand's virtual muse must be able to create a real relationship with the customer by perfectly embodying the brand's values.

The role of market research will be essential to determine whether followers are indifferently sensitive to a real muse (photoshopped or not) or to a virtual muse (and, between virtual muse, between an independent muse or a domesticated brand muse). Moreover, will the mass of fans and each one taken individually (because Big Data allows it; no need from now on to reason in average), be measured indifferently sensitive (to such and such a muse) whatever the age, the sex, the ethnic origin, the level of SPC, the cultural or religious prejudices, the political opinions, the fascination for the fashion, the fascination for the brands? It would also be interesting to know if the intrinsic attraction for an avatar is a prescriber of purchase for people who are not very sensitive at first to centers of interest, such as brands or fashion.

Brands will then know whether to mobilize a real muse (photoshopped or not), an independent virtual muse or a creature dedicated to their universe. Despite the interest of dedicated creations coherent with the brand image, we can think that a virtual muse too domesticated contains, except for the storytelling scenario, less mysteries and narrative rebounds than the "free" muse like Lil Miquela.

Let us also note that Lil Miquela, an independent virtual muse, is not divisive in the sense that, if she is young and thin (which can characterize her and give her a specific physique by *a priori* normalizing morphological gauge), she is not ethnically typed but conceals a perfume of exoticism and opens up an imaginary of acceptance by universal and intelligible arguments of seduction in all globalized cultures. The dosage – in make-up, jewelry, haircut, attitude, clothing style, exposition, photo lighting and contextual elements – gives satisfying contrasts to satisfy all the necessary illusions: Lil Miquela can be perceived as quasi-WASP (White Anglo-Saxon Protestant), Latino, Asian or mixed race. Also, with a physique without sexual ambivalence (she is not androgynous), she also seems to be non-gender specific (thus not categorizable *a priori*: heterosexual, bisexual, homosexual). In the case where she could be recognized as, possibly, lesbian, she remains, so to speak, desirable by all: each man or each woman (whatever their sexual gender) can thus project themselves onto her as a friend, confidant or lover.

4.3.2.4. *The case of Lil Miquela: assessment of a storytelling combining strategic marketing and AI*

The conclusion to be drawn from the two options above (theses numbers 1 and 2) is that there is a commercial enterprise building storytelling to create a buzz in order to boost the attractiveness of virtual creation for marketing purposes. A company whose name would be Brud.

Would it be necessary to blackmail Brud in return to force them to reveal a secret: their existence? According to the *Nouvel Observateur* website on March 2, 2018 and various American sources (including the Financial Times[33] April 2018 or *New York Magazine*[34] of May 2018), Lil Miquela was created (and should we also understand, its alleged rival Bermuda) by the same entity; as well as the storytelling facts of a hack of Lil Miquela's Instagram account by Bermuda. If everything is fake, then it would be the same group of geeks (i.e. *fanatics of the use of technologies*) carrying out a hoax in order to either denounce the world of appearances or, on the contrary, to carry out a masterful professional marketing coup.

Everything would come from the enigmatic entity Brud[35] specialized in AI.

If Brud was a group of activist hackers (white-hat hackers), the storytelling around Lil Miquela has a project with a societal scope: denouncing the world of appearance by media machination using the virtual world and social networks. If Brud were a group of black-hat hackers, they would not limit themselves to demanding simple public confessions from an attacked target but would proceed, directly or indirectly, to extortion. In both cases, the story about Lil Miquela is an excellent promotional campaign for the influencer, or rather an excellent corporate communication campaign for Brud, and, regardless of the question of the entity's very existence, the marketing vehicle launched is now in low orbit in the constellation of social networks, ready to promote brands.

In fact, if we look deeper, what exists first are two thirty-somethings: the African-American Trevor McFedries, initially known as a DJ in Los Angeles under the pseudonym Yung Skeeter or DJ Skeet Skeet, and the Latina Sara Decou, both with a rather geeky and artistic profile, with around this duo, a multidisciplinary

33 See: www.ft.com.

34 See: nymag.com.

35 See: www.brud.fyi.

professional team specialized in media and virtual (very aware of the existing practices on the Internet and inspired by those of the hackers). The investigation of Trevor McFedries and Sara Decou shows that they are co-founders and leaders of a real start-up called Brud founded in 2016 in Los Angeles. The entire story narrated here turns out to be a fiction conceived and orchestrated by Brud. As for Brud's rival villain played by the company Daniel Cain Intelligence, it exists only for the purposes of storytelling (along the lines of George Orwell's 1984 in essence, revisited by the Batman-like comic book universe).

Very precisely, Brud is a creative agency specialized in virtual robotics and AI for media applications with a specific goal to model *celebrity marketing* in *virtual commodity*: an efficient product ready to be placed and support for brand promotion. In addition, Brud has also managed to raise very significant funds from reputable venture capitalists (including Sequoia Capital). Brud's commercial management of Lil Miquela allows for a wide spectrum of realized or potential revenues on each aspect: influencer, brand muse, image loan (website, events, etc.), artist (music), derivative products, brand management and own line of clothing. The financial valuation of the whole turns out to be a very profitable business consisting of creating a strong value with the manufacture of virtual contents. The intangible assets of the virtual are profitable.

We have taken here the digital reality on the Internet as a factual reality, which is a way of considering AI for what it is: a realistic artificial truth in potential.

The touch of humanity grafted on the artificial is enough to galvanize the spirits and to give credibility to what is necessary to create a link (the basis of current marketing and modern business on the Internet): rumor on the Web, a buzz and seduction by appearance do the rest.

Is going beyond reality a reality? Without even disputing the importance of technology and its progress (including AI, which will play a key role in a technological civilization), it is crucial to distinguish between technological excess as a permanent race to the top (always doing better from a technological and techno-marketing point of view in order to try to earn more and more by betting on growth and solvent customers) and reality with its social, health and environmental constraints in a world limited by resources that are not necessarily renewable.

Everyone is thus free to adhere to the project of Elon Musk who, betting on technology, envisages a radiant future through the conquest of space and the colonization of economically useful planets; or even, in the best or worst case, as soon as possible, to conquer in order to exploit and also to occupy other planets, if possible similar to Earth by transferring, if necessary, humanity from its original cradle to a new virgin world like a new Eden.

However, in the intermediate time when, more prosaically, if there was no other possible place and the Earth was the only possible cradle for humanity, would it not be appropriate to finally think about a technological mobilization compatible with the preservation of NE?

As a precautionary measure at least, and to return to reality, should frugality not be summoned to consider the present before building the futuristic future?

This call to reason through frugality leads us to question, beyond frugality, the concept of frugal environmental innovation (FEI). After the technological hubris that we have seen in this chapter, there is a need to move towards a more measured approach, in particular by focusing on *the satisfactory technological level*, the usefulness of which is measured by its compatibility with the NE.

5

Back to Common Sense: Towards Frugal Environmental Innovation (FEI)

The technical progress resulting from innovation gradually allows for productivity gains without, however, compensating for competitive pressure each time. Thus, the technological development of Emerging Countries (ECs) is leading to competition for western companies on what used to be their quasi-exclusive competitive advantage: innovation (defined as *a managerial process that values what is new with a commercial purpose* (Perrin 2001)). From the beginning of the European Industrial Revolution (IR*), the entrepreneurial spirit required a human, technical and financial organization based on investment and innovation. However, technological innovation is costly (Stead 1976), especially in terms of one of its key elements, R&D (Mansfield 1984). Furthermore, that the link between R&D expenditures and technical and/or commercial success has not been established (Kamien and Schwartz 1982). The hypothetical profitability of technological innovation is a dilemma because of the level of investment required (corresponding to *sunk costs* (Baumol and Willig 1981)) and its strategic renewal at rising cost to create or maintain *barriers to mobility* (Caves and Porter 1977). The race to innovate in order to obtain competitive leadership implies, *a priori*, an effort of *radicality* (Schumpeter 1939) often poorly rewarded when commercial success is the main concern (Abernathy and Clark 1985). The apparent distribution of roles between innovative SMEs and LEs (Achs and Audretsch 1988) does not invalidate this observation. On the other hand, incremental innovation (with a *creative method* of the TRIZ type or engineering-oriented *Theory of Inventive Problem Solving*, starting from the similar method to obtain differentiation and/or sometimes new solutions (Altshuller 1988)) favors success more and therefore admits a higher probability of profitability.

The same is true for other popular management methods such as design thinking, which focuses on usage (Brown 2008).

But *programming innovation* is difficult[1], even though some firms adopt an organizational form more favorable to innovation (lateralization, creativity, project porting, swarming, spin-off) and/or direct their creative ambitions by using the existing on other possible applications (and this positively at 3M by declining the basic business; or sometimes negatively, as in the pharmaceutical sector by opportunistic reuse of molecules), knowing, moreover, that intra-organizational articulation (on the marketing–R&D–purchasing triptych (Urban and Hauser 1993)) allows better anticipation of the market and favors co-design with partners. Organizational and/or marketing innovation also tends to be better taken into account (Kemp and Pearson 2007).

Strategic differentiation through technological innovation leads, *a priori*, to the leadership of *the first mover advantage* (Lieberman and Montgomery 1988), but its apparent cost is higher than that of a strategy of following by imitation. However, with some sophistication of initial investment, it is now possible to reduce design costs by rapid prototyping within a digital workshop with the FabLab (Gershenfeld 2005; Ingelaere 2015).

In a crisis situation, there may also be an injunction to achieve results with drastically limited resources, hence the *system D* (for *Débrouillardise*, which means resourcefulness). However, it turns out that resourcefulness plays a key role in the elementary process of innovation (see Chapter 7). What is important is the capacity of western companies to recover and/or valorize a more significant part of resourcefulness, present in the *frugal* approach, by doing better with less while reducing the impact on the NE. To innovate at lower cost, the concept of frugal innovation (FI) is, potentially, a good managerial response. Moreover, in a context that is increasingly open to ecology, the measurable concept of *eco-innovation* (Brunnermeier and Cohen 2003) is essential[2], but it can be preferred to the term environmental innovation (EI). With EI, the question of the *ex ante* choice of *design* or *ex post* choice of *recycling* (integrated versus end of pipe (Hartje and Laurie 1984): preventive/curative) is not clear cut. We must also question the link between NE and frugality, which brings us back to the concept of frugal environmental innovation (FEI), see Bouvier-Patron (2017b, 2020).

The common point between FI and FEI is the *frugal approach* in the way of designing a product by resourcefulness. FEI declines its potentialities concerning NE.

1 The fortuitous genesis by trial and error as well as chance (serendipity) amplifies the problem.

2 Regulation is necessary to promote *clean innovations* (Porter and van der Linde 1995a, 1995b), but a more or less restrictive regulatory framework does not always have guaranteed effects (Jaffe and Palmer 1997; Blind 2012).

Based on the existing literature, we will first define (in section 5.1) the concept of FI, which is still not well stabilized, and then we will examine its theoretical place while questioning the level of consideration given to the NE. The FI (section 5.2), among other possible scenarios, can be a useful source of inspiration for companies in Advanced Countries (ACs) to respond to the globalized competitive challenge to lower the cost of innovation (Zeschky et al. 2011). However, this is not a sufficient argument to renew the innovation offer. Differentiation should integrate the ecological component (without relying solely on the ecological or greening image). The distinctive advantage of FEI is from the outset the protection of the NE without blindly resorting to western innovation sophistication.

5.1. Definition and place of frugal innovation (FI)

The usual western way of innovating because of IR* is generally an expensive sequence (spend/sophisticate/segment/waste/abandon/renew or recreate), even though the overall benefit is technical progress. FI structurally modifies this dynamic. By mobilizing the existing academic literature, we will attempt (in section 5.1.1) to contextualize and define FI and then (in section 5.1.2) situate its conceptual place while questioning the consideration of NE.

5.1.1. *Frugal innovation: contextualization and definition*

By focusing on a concrete object to be produced, extendable to the organization[3] that is its receptacle, we can define different notions:

– *resource saving*: doing what already exists but with less;

– *efficiency*: doing better than what already exists with less;

– *innovation*: creating what does not yet exist;

– *efficient innovation*: creating what does not yet exist with less;

– *innovative and technological resourcefulness*: creating what does not yet exist with almost nothing.

Frugality, as a state of mind and/or way of doing things, articulates these different points. In India, frugality (Radjou et al. 2012; Basu et al. 2013) consists, *a priori*, of remaking (what already exists) with almost nothing using salvaged

3 A significant degree of organizational lateralization is required for creation, but the organizational choice must be compatible with the required *uncertainty reduction*: the business organization aiming at reducing uncertainty (Knight 1921).

elements, with recycling[4] proving to be essential. Reusing at the end of a product's life (Geyer and Jackson 2004) does not, however, make it possible to modify the origin of the waste upstream, but rather to propose an economy of circularity with total or partial reuse (Chatterjee and Kumar 2009). This necessarily implies a high degree of creativity (Altshuller 1988) and the art of bricolage (Levi-Strauss 1962a). The potential of competencies thus generated makes it possible, in action, to technically develop the more or less conforming copy on more or less sophisticated objects and/or even to transcend the copy to innovate.

In the ECs, the *possibility of entrepreneurship* and then the *democratization of innovation*, to make the latter accessible to the greatest number[5], is more important than the existence of a wealthy class.

Reaching the mass of the population can be done in two ways: China, except for a recent inflection, has relied more on low cost for global export purposes, while India aims first of all to internally satisfy the base of the population pyramid (*bottom of the pyramid* or BOP (Prahalad 2005)). While the logic of low-cost production is a perfect extension of IR* in terms of intensiveness and the sacrifice of resources, with a significant impact on the NE, the BOP is, by nature, more economical in terms of resources, especially because these are scarce, but it is not, intrinsically, respectful of the NE (except through recycling). The difference between IR* and the Indian development is, in the second case, a growth that is economical in means while validating, from the outset, product differentiation and market segmentation (it is not a question of reproducing the Ford T economic model). If the Tata Motors Nano appears to be, symbolically, a new Ford T for the 21st century, resources, means and implementation differ. The Indian entrepreneurial spirit, integrating access to scarce resources and recycling, favors innovative resourcefulness that has been successful. The question is whether there is an *Indian FI model* and whether it is transferable.

This is the field of *reverse innovation*, the *export of innovative products from ECs back to ACs* (Govindarajan and Ramamurti 2011; Brem and Wolfram 2014).

Reverse innovation, as the sale of innovative products that are inherently Indian or Chinese to ACs, is not generalizable to any product (and/or sector) and can be analyzed in *degrees of reversion* depending on where the phases (design/production/sales) are executed. Moreover, this *reversion* should not be

---

4 *Recycling* contributes without being, in itself, an approach that respects the NE. Hence, the need (Beamon 1999) to move towards *green supply chain management*, starting with an *initial selective sorting* that only retains elements that are compatible (origin, transformation, final consistency) with the NE.

5 An industrial issue of the second IR, after 1850, consists, more or less, of democratizing products, initially accessible to a small elite, to the mass population.

confused with *return flows* linked to the filiation of multinational firms (Mansfield 1984) or western delocalizations to South-East Asia (mainly China). In this case, there is a return (of products) to the original market (*apparent reversion*). Yet another category is the benefit to a western brand of successful acquisition efforts (Renault with Dacia).

Zeschky et al. (2014) consider a *typology of reversion* (mobilizing an adaptation of the Ansoff matrix) crossing the *degree of market novelty* in three modalities (low, medium, high) and the *degree of technology novelty* (low, medium, high). By crossing the two axes, the result is a *reversion corridor* of increasing quality. The ascending order gives: *cost innovation* or *low cost*; *good enough innovation* adapted to local needs with low incomes; FI designed specifically for local needs and where there are strong constraints on resources. This analysis of *reversion* establishes FI as comparatively superior. *Effective reversion* (exporting from one EC to another EC or to an AC) is part of the development response.

Is FI appropriate for ACs? The potential emergence of a western FI in its market, by innovating differently, presupposes: the *lowering of the cost of innovation* without sacrificing quality; a *new business model* generating *cash* very quickly; a *lean methodology* (Womack and Jones 1990) aimed at minimizing[6] the means mobilized at the different stages of value creation; *recycling* (Geyer and Jackson 2004); creativity centered more on the resourcefulness linked to bricolage. This is already supported by the technological bricolage of the maker (as can be seen in Anderson (2012)), notably via the FabLab (Gershenfeld 2005). However, FI is less about purely optimized technical engineering solutions than about *satisficing solutions* (Simon 1976, 1978, 1982) from a technical–commercial point of view, regardless of geographical location.

If we focus on the definition by Basu et al. (2013)[7], the FI must be adapted, adaptable, affordable and available. However, other characteristics can be put forward: simple, reliable, robust, repairable, transportable, quick to implement, short time to market from design or even new functionality(s). All in all, FI offers *quality functionalities (sometimes new ones), at lower cost, and satisfying the desire of customers wherever they are*. Thus, FI mobilizes a potential range of competencies

---

6 The *lean* method is a way to optimize resources in order to eliminate waste and reduce costs, but differently from the *Ford T*, mobilizing *the one best way* of Taylor's *scientific organization of work* associated with the principle of the *chain of production* of slaughterhouses and the *push* with financing of the demand by the *$5 a day measure*.

7 "Frugal innovation is a design innovation process in which the needs and context of citizens in the developing world are put first in order to develop appropriate, adaptable, affordable, and accessible services and products for emerging markets." (Basu et al. 2013, p. 64).

allowing us to do what already exists or what does not exist yet *with less* and *less expense,* producing something that is *just as good or even better*.

5.1.2. Conceptual place of frugal innovation

FI overturns Rogers' (1962) *innovation adoption* scheme based on the ripple effect[8] of early adopters. FI aims to achieve an immediate and simultaneous impact on all strata of potential adopters[9], thanks to goods intended for *everyone*, offering *quality* (reliability, robustness, longevity, reparability and maintenance, as opposed to scheduled obsolescence, see Chapter 7) and sometimes new functionalities for an *accessible selling price.* Invoking *everyone* refers to *inclusiveness* (Prahalad and Mashelkar 2010); serving an elite corresponds to *exclusivity*.

Quality has become a standard requirement[10] for any globalized customer.

It is now possible to establish the place of FI in a general lineage of innovation starting from Schumpeter (1939, 1942) (*radical* versus *incremental*). On this basis, Abernathy and Clark (1985) and Henderson and Clark (1990) promote *architectural innovation*, combining technical radicality and commercial success. Subsequently, Bower and Christensen (1995) and Christensen (1997) specify the concept of *disruptive innovation*, where the revolution through use goes beyond the bouquet of technical features offered (Internet, smartphone). Then comes *frugal innovation* (FI).

FI, in its broadest sense, aims for this breakthrough without being rejected *a priori* because it is immediately desired by everyone.

FI is associated with the two expressions *Gandhian* and *Jugaad*. *Gandhian innovation* (Altenburg and Lundvall 2009; Prahalad and Mashelkar 2010) consists of doing *more with less for many*, transcending, through a *process of improvement*, the logic of low cost and poor quality for that of low cost but good quality. More ambitiously, the concept of *Jugaad innovation* (Brem and Wolfram 2014) is (historically, geographically and culturally) a slang expression from the Hindi language (*kabaad se jugaad*) relating to the *clever, improvised and radical transformation of waste (kabaad)* into something *useful and attractive (jugaad)*. *Jugaad* (initiated by Indian researcher and businessman Sam Pitroda in the

8 Identify/attract *opinion leaders* and then win over the mass of customers.

9 The Internet favors this by simultaneous processing (of each individual and of the mass), by the technological bricolage specific to hacking for commercial use.

10 We are moving away from Vernon's (1966) *International Life Cycle of Products*, where what is downgraded goes, by decreasing relative wealth, to the emerging countries.

telecommunications sector) is becoming a new creative business with imaginative entrepreneurship focused on using the most available materials in a context of scarcity and poverty (Tiwari and Herstatt 2012). Entrepreneurs within highly constrained economies, with *what they can afford*, in adversity and out of resilience, design technical solutions to satisfy market opportunities in *critical* sectors (health, energy, education, food).

Thus, identifying Jugaad and FI is common (Radjou et al. 2012) because of one key point: *to make, at lower cost, with resourcefulness and economy of means, useful new quality from the existing*. However, FI must refer more to a *structured approach*[11], which makes it potentially mobilizable in Europe where resources and/or innovation budgets are decreasing. FI then becomes the *ingenious capacity*[12] *to do better with less* products adapted to the needs. FI could eventually be incorporated into the strategic development of western companies faced with globalization, growing uncertainty, complexity (technological, organizational, societal) and greater scarcity of resources. Indeed, despite continuous innovation and productivity gains, the effort to be competitive may still be insufficient. Companies have to be increasingly inventive, flexible, agile and now also sober: learning to create more value with fewer resources.

This may require a change of mentality and organization, and/or a relativization of the role of technology in the ACs. Moreover, today's globalization is evolving towards a multipolar space requiring the consideration of differences and complementarity of cultural competences (Radjou et al. 2012) to consider the co-creation of solutions (e.g. Siemens' wearable heart monitor, by bringing together German and Indian engineers). More broadly, at the Frugal Innovation Lab (Santa Clara, USA), Basu et al. (2013) examine what the new business dynamics should be by isolating 10 key competencies[13] to successfully penetrate an AC or EC market.

---

11 For example, the Indian Space Research Organization (ISRO) managed to design the Mangalyaan satellite, destined for Mars, in 18 months and by investing 73 million US dollars (i.e. less than Boeing's cheapest airplane) by recycling and assembling already existing equipment. The satellite was launched in November 2013.

12 This optimized FI would be a new way to maximize the value brought to customers and shareholders, while minimizing the use of scarce resources (energy, capital, time, skilled labor, quality inputs).

13 Robustness (*ruggedization*); transportability (*lightweight*); *mobile-connectivity anytime anywhere*; ergonomicity (*human centric design*); simplicity of use (*simplification*); strong distributability (*new distribution models*); adaptability (*adaptation*); *use of local resources*; *green technologies powered by renewable resources*; *affordability*.

5.2. Double challenge of the western firm: competitive and environmental advantage

It appears that the impact on the NE is not sufficiently prioritized by companies in their actions. It is therefore appropriate, after examining the major competitive challenge for western firms (with three basic scenarios) (section 5.2.1), to better understand the link between frugality and the NE (section 5.2.2). Thus, western firms should use fewer resources and stop wasting them, while resorting to *clean technologies* and *use of local resources*. Several scenarios are possible for this, including the *frugal approach* (section 5.2.1); the issue of respecting the NE is an additional but non-optional challenge (section 5.2.2).

5.2.1. *Strategic scenarios*

The market for innovative products, reinforced by supply-side marketing, has been modified by demand-side marketing (push–pull transition in the 1950s) and then by *perceived value* (Porter 1985), where technical characteristics are relativized by focusing on the value subjectively perceived by the customer. From this point of view, in order to achieve a positive margin, three *business models* exist depending on the control of the selling price and/or the cost price:

– Luxury products allow for the control of the selling price by not even minimizing the cost price (e.g. Chanel).

– The industrial global brands known by the final customers can, simultaneously, maximize the selling price and minimize the cost price (e.g. Nike).

– The general competitive case is not to be able to impose the selling price (absence of *market power*), but to minimize the cost price (*upstream bargaining power*).

This last case explains, to a large extent, the massive trend towards delocalization (*outsourcing outside the country of origin*) with the return of products to the market of origin (*apparent reversion*).

Independently of the model followed (above), profitability requires maintaining and/or reinforcing competitiveness and/or image based on excellence through various means: the fight against technical obsolescence, improved work organization, optimized flow management, quality management, recycling, analysis of the carbon footprint and cost control (including innovation because of its high level, the lever being mainly design).

However, if the key issue is innovation, then three *strategic scenarios* can be envisaged to lower the cost of innovation:

i) *outsourcing R&D*, or even *relocating* it to places where the skills and resources are available (and the costs – social, health, fiscal, environmental – are reduced and/or can be circumvented) and operating an *apparent reversion*; this is a logic of efficiency based on results alone in a long filiation with IR* from its origins;

ii) *lowering the cost of design through FabLabs*, combining ICT and DT, within NoF[14]. These networks are closed and proprietary (Dassault Systèmes) or open source (see Tirole and Lerner (2002)), or even mixed (Netscape and Mozilla project);

iii) using a *frugal approach* by soliciting resourcefulness in order to design and produce, by managing scarcity and non-waste, as well as recycling, desired and quality innovative products. At the moment, this Indian scenario has only had marginal success in the west through the impulse of certain managers (like Carlos Ghosn, expert in frugal engineering at Dacia in Europe, and who also relies on Indian engineers to design vehicles for the EC).

In the west, the second scenario dominates, and is gradually taking shape in the industrial and commercial space, articulating interactive know-how in design and prototyping, or even in pre-production (e.g. Renault or Safran). The reduction of the cost of innovation is made possible by the reduction of the cost of design via the FabLab (internal for large companies and/or external for SMEs). Depending on the *absorptive capacity* (Cohen and Levinthal 1990) of each company, the development of its core business (current or future) is carried out by co-design and co-production in an inter-organizational client–supplier network[15]; ICT and DT allowing, within NoF (more or less virtual and open), the sharing of expertise, the decentralization of information, the simultaneity of exchanges and the breaking down of geographical and/or cultural barriers. This scenario fits well into the western innovation scheme.

Network openness also calls upon users (Von Hippel 1976) and even more so upon communities of practice (Brown and Duguid 1991, 1998; Wender and Snyder

14 The large vertically integrated firms with substantial R&D budgets evolved, in order to adapt to Japanese competition in the 1980s, into a *network of firms* (NoF) (Aoki 1986). The NoF is the result of a *refocusing on the core business* (Teece 1980, 1988; Prahalad and Hamel 1990) and the *outsourcing* of what is necessary for the realization of a product, but outside the perimeter considered strategic. The NoF is a form of coordination of reallocated complementary skills (Richardson 1972) where each member is responsible for the preservation, evolution and/or creation of skills in its core business; innovation is necessary to maintain and/or develop this potential.

15 In this sense, Carlile (2004) has proposed a knowledge-sharing model applicable between organizations allowing degrees of *transfer, translation, transformation*.

2000) to generate *collective innovation* (Allen 1983)[16]. In the creation of game software (Ubisoft), this logic is fully utilized.

5.2.2. Environmental competitive advantage and frugal environmental innovation

In a globalized competition where the competitive advantage through innovation of western companies is disputed, a few important observations are made:

– Frugality (aiming *to do almost everything... with almost nothing*[17]) is exempted *a priori* from costly and sophisticated DT.

– The NE is poorly taken into account in Gandhian- or Jugaad-type frugal logics based on recycling alone.

– The protection of the NE is not necessarily an essential concern in the practices of the PEs and it remains too timid in the ACs.

– While greening is based on marketing opportunism, *eco-innovation* or *environmental innovation* is a concept that is now recognized and accepted (Kemp and Pearson 2007) and has been translated into concrete terms (in terms of products, processes and organization: biodegradable plastic bags, additive 3D printing methods, collection and recycling of used batteries).

To reduce the impact on the NE, the spectrum of efforts is still wide. We cannot overlook *environmental efficiency*, which, while minimizing the impact on the NE (through *lean* and, if possible, *green recycling*), consists of doing better than what already exists, with as little as possible (green chemistry with Arkema).

Technological *environmental innovation* is costly and generally aims to reduce the negative impact on the NE *ex post* (soil decontamination solutions at Veolia) instead of relying on eco-design *ex ante*.

It would also be necessary for an innovation that preserves the NE to be, systematically, the result, *ex ante*, of a design process that has no impact through: the design model, the nature of the choice made, the quantity of resources used, the study of the purpose, the absence of waste, rejection and scrap, or even the perfect reusability of the ingredients used (at the end of the life of the object designed with the *cradle to cradle* or CtoC (Braungart and McDonough 2002)).

---

16 Generalized concept in *open innovation* (Chesbrough 2003) involving, in an open and more or less collaborative framework, permanent inter-organizational back and forth (between legally distinct actors), where patents are strategic (see Appendix 3 of this book and Pénin (2010)).

17 This goes beyond the FabLab issue of Gershenfeld (2005): *How to Make Almost Anything*.

Moreover, with a bio-inspired approach (*biomimicry*; Benyus 1997; Ricard 2015), the cost of design (compared to technological sophistication) can only decrease: for example, the French SME Polypop, using fungi, depollutes soils and recovers organic waste.

The *frugal environmental innovation* or FEI approach (Bouvier-Patron 2017b, 2020) must minimize the impact on the NE *ex ante* and *ex post* without mobilizing technologies that are too sophisticated, costly and/or too complex to implement. As an example, wastewater filtering and heavy metal capture can be done by a plant-based filtering system (phytotechnologies).

In absolute terms, how can commensurability be established if, in order to serve the same market, some companies incorporate the induced effects and/or negative externalities into their calculations, while others minimize or ignore them? At the very least, a *life cycle costing analysis* (Dhillon 1989; Bailey 1991; Fabricky and Blanchard 1991) and an *environmental life cycle costing assessment* (Fava 1991) on the NE are needed.

Traditionally, *life cycle costing* (Vernon 1966; Hayes and Wheelwright 1979) is carried out *ex post* once the product has been designed and/or launched and negative externalities have been identified.

It would be much preferable to consider, *ex ante*, from the design stage, the foreseeable consequences in terms of *negative externalities*. While *environmental innovation* and FEI seek to reduce the impact on the NE, FEI aims, from the outset and systematically, to prevent negative externalities through a global approach from the design stage onwards (see Chapter 1), with processes that are as unsophisticated as possible, or rather with a *satisfactory level of sophistication* (in the sense of *satisficing*; Simon 1976, 1978). FEI qualitatively breaks away from *environmental innovation*, which has remained, more or less, in the same habit of innovation since the beginning of IR* and Schumpeter's analysis through costly technological investments and a still rather curative orientation. The implementation of the FEI is based on a frugal approach of the *grassroots innovation* type (Seyfang and Smith 2007): low sophistication in a decentralized and lateralized organization based on distributed competencies, inducing *common sense, technological bricolage* and *collective resourcefulness*, taking into account, from the outset, the NE at all stages of the product. Thus, Brem and Wolfram's (2014) classification of frugality contrasts *reverse innovation* (high sophistication), by *apparent reversion* (overseas delocalization with return of products to ACs) or by *effective reversion* (export from an EC to another EC), with *grassroots innovation* (low sophistication but sustainability).

That said, for many companies, taking the NE into account still appears all too often to be a very costly additional constraint (hence the need for regulation; Porter and van der Linde 1995a, 1995b). The scientific debate is still divided on Porter's hypothesis. Perceived as an obstacle to innovation by companies, this constraint is therefore seen as *negative*.

If, on the other hand, it is perceived as an asset from the design stage and in the way of thinking about innovation, it becomes *positive*.

The opposition between reactivity/proactivity seems to be a major divide between companies that are concerned about the NE (e.g. Total versus Air Liquide).

While opportunism, imitation, market size, demand evolution and managerial policy can also explain a strategy that protects the NE, creativity and the ability to be *proactive* are essential to meet the challenge of respecting the NE and to articulate innovation and the NE (Irwin and Hooper 1992; Roome 1992; Porter and van der Linde 1995a, 1995b; Shrivastana 1995b, 1995c; Dobers et al. 2001).

All in all, in the face of the coming innovation offensive of the PEs, differentiating ourselves by innovating qualitatively, but at a lower cost is possible through:

i) *outsourcing* and *offshoring*, or even *reversion* (as a continuation of offshoring with *apparent reverse innovation* or effective innovation depending on the degree of Indigenous appropriation);

ii) *digitization* of design (FabLab-NoF);

iii) *frugal approach* of the IF type;

iv) frugal FEI-grassroots approach integrating NE protection from the outset. Ideally, the FEI could even lead not only *to doing better with less, but to doing better with as little as possible from the birth to the apparent end of life of a good (and/or its components), because it can be reused without generating negative externalities detrimental to the NE* (e.g. organic cotton clothes, organic solar cell).

In the latter case, this would correspond to a change in the *innovation paradigm*. The products thus designed and produced must meet the operating characteristics of the FEI: usefulness, simplicity, reliability, robustness, accessibility, attractiveness (with new functionalities), absence of negative externalities on the NE.

5.3. Conclusion

In reviewing the existing literature, after defining the concept of *frugal innovation* (FI), two major strategic challenges for the western company are highlighted: competition and limiting the impact on the NE. The conceptual basis of FI neglects the NE somewhat. On the other hand, the innovative offer of western firms cannot be reduced to imitating what ECs do. Differentiation can be based on three likely scenarios that lead to a decrease in the cost of innovation:

i) outsourcing/offshoring/reversion;

ii) technological sophistication: digital design by NoF-FabLab;

iii) frugal approach.

What the last two scenarios (ii and iii) have in common is bricolage (see Chapter 7), more or less technological. The intrinsic singularity of the frugal approach (iii) is a *state of mind to do better with less*: save means and resources with low sophistication.

We propose an additional scenario (iv) concerning frugality, as well as respect for the NE *ex ante*, and assuming *ex post* the neutral impact on the NE: FEI.

In this chapter, the aim was to position and distinguish the FEI from the FI. Taking into account the NE with FEI from the outset leads us to position (see Chapter 6) the FEI in relation to the EI. While *environmental innovation* (EI), which is highly technological, is still achieved at a high cost, the *frugal environmental approach* (FEI) leads to less sophistication while preserving the NE. FEI aims for quality innovation, at lower cost, integrating the consideration of the NE from the outset. Moreover, innovating via a *frugal approach* also allows us to opt for the *strategy of secrecy* (i.e. not relying on patenting, see Appendix 3), around a core business consisting of design and production know-how, with the help of bricolage and improvisation, while having access to open and collective innovation through communitaurization (including north/south when possible). All in all, EI and/or FEI both potentially make it possible to reduce the impact on the NE and, secondarily, to fight against the destructive irrevocability (Georgescu-Roegen 1971) that we now see emerging with climate change. FEI also makes it possible to offer differentiation in global innovation without imposing standards on others. The two fundamental differences between EI and FEI are that FEI responds to the issues mentioned *ex ante* and proposes to achieve them soberly in a consistent approach.

6

From Environmental Innovation (EI) to Frugal Environmental Innovation (FEI)

We will try to position *frugal environmental innovation* (FEI) in relation to *environmental innovation* (EI) by starting with the link between *environmental innovation*[1] (EI) and *frugal innovation*[2] (FI). We will propose, on the basis of the rudiments already provided (Chapter 5), a stable foundation for specifying the new concept mentioned above (Chapter 5), and unexplored elsewhere, of *frugal environmental innovation* (FEI; see Bouvier-Patron (2017b, 2020)). As an indispensable foundation for any subsequent potential empirical investigation, this chapter will therefore be theoretical in essence while being concerned with the predictive scope, as well as the operability through the proposed matrix tool.

In order to clearly establish the concept, we will rely on a reasoned reading of the relevant academic literature, giving priority to the pioneering authors. Indeed, EI is quite heterogeneous and requires clarification, especially as frugality seems to be excluded from it. As for frugality, with the associated FI, it can be implemented without apprehending the question of the impact on the NE: protean, frugality must be refocused on a form that can be reconciled with EI.

---

1 In the first instance, loosely based on Kemp and Pearson (2007), EI refers to the production, adoption or exploitation of a new solution (product, process, service, organization or managerial method) whose result, throughout its life cycle, is the absence, elimination or reduction of impact on the NE compared to available alternatives.

2 At this point, frugality can be tentatively defined *as an activity of creating or recreating by doing more and better with less, including less technological sophistication, while relying on what is available.*

The innovation that is usually promoted in the west is very often of a technological nature, and therefore, sophisticated (like Altran). The frugal alternative (Radjou et al. 2012) is primarily of Indian inspiration.

Some authors (Zeschky et al. 2011) invite western companies to *think frugally* through specific investments (Renault with Dacia). However, Indian frugality does not intrinsically imply taking the NE into account, except, at the very least, through the recovery of raw materials with the declared aim of producing useful, robust and less expensive products.

The challenge of FEI is to articulate innovation, frugality and consideration of the NE (with the use and reuse of ecological materials or minimizing the impact on the NE).

The hypothesis underlying our approach is that, very generally, supply-side marketing leads to the launch of new products without necessarily considering what will happen to them after the initial sale (if not by scheduled obsolescence, then by repurchase). Therefore, considering the future of the downgraded product does not seem to be a priority: scrapping and then recycling, when possible, is often the only recommended and accessible solution.

However, recycling is an *ex post* curative treatment (Stark 2015) and the final stage of the life cycle (Vernon 1966; Hayes and Wheelwright 1979). On the contrary, an *ex ante* preventive approach (Irwin and Hooper 1992) relies, from the outset, on design (or *eco-design*) centered on the total life cycle of the product in order to minimize the impact on the NE (Fava 1991; Geyer and Jackson 2004; Chatterjee and Kumar 2009), and this by means of ecological management of the supply chain (or *green supply chain management* (Beamon 1999)).

In a synthetic way, by crossing the method of action (proactive *ex ante* or reactive *ex post*) and the technological level (according to a gradation of type: sophisticated, frugal, frugal and respecting the NE), the main result obtained is a strategic matrix (typological tool also enlightening the company decision-maker on the field of possibilities), which leads, for any company, to strategic competitive opportunities: in particular, the FEI, without imposing *a priori* dominant norms and/or unbridgeable barriers. Thus, after an academic examination of the central concept of EI and highlighting the role of proactivity and creativity (section 6.1), we will consider (section 6.2) the types of EI actors and then its diffusion. Finally, once the alternative solutions (sophisticated or frugal) have been addressed, the strategic matrix (and its options, including the FEI), resulting from the analysis, will be presented (section 6.3).

6.1. Environmental innovation (EI)

The concept of EI is the distant fruit of a semantic evolution that started with the Brundtland report in 1987, which emphasized the challenge of sustainable development (SD) and the importance of sustainable innovation.

The aspect of respect for the NE via SD has been popularized under the name green, forming a radical that has many variations, such as *green innovation* (Florida 1996). The term *eco-innovation* (eco for ecology) used by economists marks a qualitative differentiation by taking ecological considerations into account in innovation: Kemp and Pearson (2007). Kemp and Foxon (2007) and Kemp (2010) rely on the critical work of Rennings (2000), aimed at reducing and/or eliminating any negative externality on the NE.

Consequently, the objective assigned to the industry (Fussler and James 1996; Hemmelskamp 1997; James 1997; Kemp and Foxon 2007) must at least be the reduction of the ecological impact (*ex ante* or *ex post*; Hartje and Laurie 1984; Hemmelskamp 1997)[3].

The focus of SD on the ecological component has led to the concept of EI, a term increasingly used (Schiederig et al. 2012). Depret and Hamdouch (2009) suggest a typology of EI: (a) technological (using the end-of-pipe curative *ex post* or the integrated preventive *ex ante* declination of Hartje and Laurie (1984)); (b) not purely technological (organizations, routines, practices, services) by integrating the NE dimension at each stage of the product life cycle; (c) mixed or systemic by integrating dimensions (more or less dematerialized) of different natures (technological, organizational, service).

However, the orientation towards EI is perceived *a priori* as more costly by companies. The incentive role of a public innovation policy (regulation) to promote EI is therefore put forward (Porter 1991; Porter and van der Linde 1995a, 1995b), even though some studies tend to relativize the argument (Jaffe and Palmer 1997; Blind 2012). Moreover, Rennings (2000) believes that EI induces positive externalities, but whose benefit may escape the firm that originates them; this further reduces the incentive to invest.

This *double externality problem* (Rennings 2000) arises from the potential absence of a fair *ex post* price on the market and/or, in all cases, from a competitive

3 End-of-pipe technologies mitigate impacts on the NE from an *ex post* curative perspective. Clean integrated environmental technologies reduce these impacts *ex ante* by design. Frondel et al. (2007) and Arundel and Kemp (2009) show the importance of barriers to entry for access to this last category.

distortion of private appropriation of the benefit due to the competition of innovation options between the more costly sustainable options and the traditional ones.

Indeed, the failure to take into account all the costs and benefits in a traditional decision-making process that ignores externalities makes commensurability impossible. The debate on the *Porterian hypothesis* has led to numerous studies (Jaffe and Palmer (1997) or Ambec and Barla (2002)), including from the point of view of econometric verification, without obtaining a clear-cut answer, even though Horbach (2008), using German data, fully validates it.

In any case, Porter's hypothesis is never really invalidated. Moreover, what matters is the quality of a regulatory policy (a bad incentive system does not mean that the incentive principle should be eliminated). Huber (2004) indicates that an adapted public policy must take into account the moment in the life cycle of the EI; all the more so as the end of life of an innovation is still rarely or poorly understood. Legislation (Rennings 2000) thus plays an active role, including as a growth variable, by setting the technological standard to be reached and/or by encouraging demand. This also reinforces the interest of analyses that examine policies for recycling technological innovation (Mazzanti and Zoboli 2008).

And, crucially, because of the customer–supplier chain in BtoB, demand has a structuring impulse effect on the upstream chain (which can be verified empirically; Oltra and Saint Jean 2009). However, the existing dilemma lies in the private interest governed by profitability, and rather in the short term, while few companies have the capacity to take a medium- or long-term view of the challenges to be met. However, as the NE is often perceived by firms as a free commodity, they must be encouraged to adopt a respectful strategy: by external regulation (Porter 1991), by mixed regulation (decentralization of regulation to collectives, in a broad spectrum including a restricted community, see Ostrom (1990)) and/or by managerial internalization (Shrivastava 1995a).

Moreover, as the usual corporate behavior rather legitimizes Hardin's (1968) thesis of systematic plundering (in the absence of clearly defined property rights), the regulator must only concede decentralized management to actors that are aware of the fragility of natural resources.

Among these actors, companies cannot be excluded if they ethically accept to take into account the NE and all the stakeholders in their activity (Freeman 1984). The dynamic spring of private commitment to EI is also driven by other positive factors (Ambec and Lanoie 2008) aimed at increasing benefits and/or lowering costs. Moreover, the classical variables (opportunism, imitation, access, potential size of the market, demand to be satisfied) or the managerial policy (Carroll 1979), based on the commitment of the manager (Bowen 1953), are obviously active levers for EI. Nevertheless, the ability to be proactive and the degree of creativity (section 6.1.1), especially at the entrepreneurial level (section 6.1.2), appear to be much more crucial.

6.1.1. *Corporate proactivity and EI*

On the ecological side of SD, there is a gradation of strategic business behavior from reactive to proactive (Carroll 1979; Hunt and Auster 1990). Proactivity (Roome 1992; Hart and Shrivastava 1995; Shrivastava 1995a, 1995b, 1995c; Judge and Douglas 1998; Sharma and Vredenburg 1998; Dobers et al. 2001; Roy et al. 2001; Buysse and Verbeke 2003; Boiral 2006) appears to be a conceptually and/or empirically determining variable in terms of competitive advantage, especially in EI (Irwin and Hooper 1992). Moreover, summarizing previous work, Bénézech et al. (2013), who focus on the entrepreneurial capacity to innovate in EI, also show that proactivity is essential.

Generally speaking, we can define proactive logic by a strategic and managerial affirmation of anticipation in order to integrate *ex ante*, and very early on, future constraints (e.g. 3M). On the other hand, a reactive corporate logic is an approach that aims, or not, to comply *ex post* with the constraints imposed in order to avoid penalties, a negative image or a crowding-out effect (e.g. extraction, public works or construction sectors).

Proactivity is less a matter of legitimization (Suchman 1995), which is equivalent to communication out of concern for social conformity (*greening*) and/or to preventing societal conflict (*boycott*), than of a search for institutional (*corporate*) communication based on the reputation of a competence that can be valued both on the financial markets and in terms of competitive advantage (e.g. Dassault Systèmes). We will retain two opposing strategic logics:

– a reactive logic in which companies are wait-and-see, undergoing: price competition (like Hewlett Packard), technological race (for General Electric) or legislative framework (asserting the general interest by seeking to limit the negative impact on the community through taxation and/or even criminal prosecution, like British Petroleum); companies then react to the risks of crises and seek to satisfy stakeholders only if this conditions the very survival of the company (Mitchell et al. 1997; Black 2006);

– a proactive logic integrating preventively (SD, for example) by anticipating, in the name of private interest, future developments (products, markets, legislation, societal implications) in the face of uncertainty and complexity (as in the air and space industry with Safran).

The reactive/proactive dichotomy characterizes strategic behaviors and proves to be very discriminating concerning EI. Thus, for the motivations for EI identified from the survey data from the *Community Innovation Survey 2018 (CIS 2008)* (INSEE 2010), motives related to public incentives are, comparatively speaking, declared less important (adaptation to existing regulations) and therefore reactive. Conversely, the companies' consideration of the NE results in anticipated voluntary actions (Veugelers 2012) engendering the ability to generate a sustainable competitive advantage (Green et al. 1994; Hart 1995, 1997; Porter and van der Linde 1995a, 1995b; Shrivastava 1995a, 1995b, 1995c). The proactive corporate dimension thus induces *a long-term commitment that brings anticipated environmental benefits* (Sharma and Vredenburg 1998), *while maintaining a positive link between the strategy of respect for the NE and performance* (Wisner et al. 2010), as is the case, for example, with Dassault Systèmes' 3DExperience®.

6.1.2. *Proactivity and creativity: green entrepreneurship*

The benchmark surveys (CIS 2008) may statistically exclude innovative companies with less than 10 employees. However, it is precisely at this lèvel, with innovative entrepreneurship respecting the NE or *green entrepreneurship* (Blue 1990; Bennett 1991; Berle 1991; Hutchinson and Hutchinson 1997; Hillary 2000; Spence et al. 2001; Schaltegger 2002; Schick et al. 2002; Walley and Taylor 2002; Meek et al. 2010), that the importance of *the creative part* of enterprise in EI can be explained, as well as the link between creativity and proactivity.

Blue (1990) insists from the outset on the deliberate choice (*ecopreneuring*) of committing to the achievement of ecological goals, usually through innovation, as other authors have pointed out (Schaltegger 2002; Schick et al. 2002). In addition, Schick et al. (2002) point to the importance of the leader's personal sensitivity to ecology.

Berle (1991) is more interested in consumer education as a key to the success of the company's business model: waste is then raw material ("*One man's trash is another man's treasure*"). This shifts the focus from recycling to the circular economy (Geyer and Jackson 2004). More broadly, Schaltegger (2002) and Schaltegger and Wagner (2011), following Spence et al. (2001), characterize green entrepreneurship by the ability to innovate, customer satisfaction and the organization of the company in relation to the creator, but for a development that goes beyond a *start-up*: with a commitment to ecology, but with a view to strong market growth and an increase in company size.

More recently, Meek et al. (2010) put forward the explicit concept of *environmental entrepreneurship* (or *enviropreneurship*).

In total, Walley and Taylor (2002) identify four types of green entrepreneurship: *visionary* because they are focused on the NE component by working radically for SD; *independent* because they are concerned and have values but are rather comfortable with the idea; *adaptive innovators* who go green to occupy market niches or *accidentally oriented towards a green business*. While the last two types are more profit-driven than value-driven, the first two types are proactively and creatively focused on protecting the NE.

Dean and McMullen (2007) think of entrepreneurship as a way of seizing market failures (including negative externalities) as real market opportunities. However, these opportunities imply that we must first escape from the *green prison* (Pacheco et al. 2010), which sterilizes initiative because of the divorce that exists, *a priori*, as already indicated, between the potential gains accessible privately and the collective objective of preserving the NE.

6.2. Types of actors and diffusion of EI

The current general model of production is preferentially based on the apparent productivity of the factors of production, as well as on the optimization of the result without necessarily taking into account the negative externalities. Let us call it a *productivist model*. The alternative logic amounts, on the contrary, to integrating all induced effects, especially negative ones, into the calculation (see Bouvier-Patron (2015a) and Chapter 1 of this book).

The indiscriminate competition between products that have not been produced under the same system of constraints thus makes it impossible to compare goods (in terms of quality, utility, use, externalities, maintenance, recycling, collective social benefit and respect for the NE) or prices. However, companies should seize the benefit of strategic differentiation that preserves the NE: the potential that can be valorized by taking the NE into account is infinitely greater than the strategic possibilities of ignoring it. Thus, on a proactive level, the dimension of protecting the NE is indeed a distinctive strategic potential, a source of reputation, to be valued (Rennings 2000) on a competitive level.

However, the end-of-pipe approach of impact reduction (Overcash 1996; Hemmelskamp 1997) is generally preferred[4] to the establishment of a new paradigm oriented towards clean technology (Irwin and Hooper 1992; Porter and van der Linde 1995a, 1995b; Frondel et al. 2007; Hofstra and Huisingh 2014).

4 Recent studies confirm the existence of a strong trend towards curative care (Alonso-Ugaglia et al. 2016).

This would also support Hellström's (2007) analysis of EI, showing that innovation of an incremental nature arouses more interest (knowing that incremental is the usual path of innovative creativity; Altshuller 1988) than radical innovation. Moreover, the creation of innovation is a complex process that also integrates chance (serendipity) and comparison with what is already known. Thus, the appreciation of the share of corporate creativity in EI is the first issue (section 6.2.1). The next is the diffusion of EI (section 6.2.2).

6.2.1. *Summit of the EI actor typology: creative and proactive*

Kemp and Pearson (2007) consider a typology[5] behavior of EI actors where the creative part is primary. Surprisingly, creation, although of primary importance from an analytical point of view, is little studied empirically (Brunnermeier and Cohen 2003).

Thus, the creative part in EI is very often ignored in large surveys (CIS 2008), which focus more on adoption than on creation[6]. However, the creative part of EI could be measured, even though imperfectly, by investment in R&D or by patents (Kemp and Pearson 2007; Arundel and Kemp 2009), or even by the number of engineers mobilized or by inter-organizational collaborations. While a few specific studies are dedicated to innovation-creating firms (Frondel et al. 2007; Kemp and Pearson 2007; Arundel and Kemp 2009), these should be systematically questioned on their share of creation versus adoption in EI. The dynamics of change towards a new paradigm respectful of EI does not only involve adoption, but also, necessarily and first, creation. At a basic level, while the processes of innovation creation and EI may seem almost identical, the barriers are much higher for EI (Rennings 2000; Frondel et al. 2007; Arundel and Kemp 2009): very significant R&D efforts[7] are therefore required for EI. Of course, for any innovation, it is difficult to establish a statistical link between the level of R&D spending and innovation and, even more so, between innovation and commercial success. The central debate is elsewhere and

5 That is, the typology in four modalities: (1) pioneer creator of solutions and equipment in EI (strategic eco-innovators); (2) installer of solutions, whether produced internally or externally (strategic eco-adopters); (3) adaptive follower (passive eco-innovators); (4) non-innovator in EI (non-eco-innovators). This typology evokes Rogers' (1962) four categories of adopters: the first two are proactive (innovator, early adopter), where we clearly differentiate the innovator and adopter, as opposed to the last two, which are reactive (late adopter; refractory).

6 The creators are mainly in the category not surveyed by CIS 2008 (start-ups in particular, often taken over by large companies).

7 Arrow (1962a, 1962b) justifies the innovation rent protected by a patent in order to internalize positive externalities through a private appropriation of the results of the efforts initially made; otherwise, the incentive to innovate would be greatly reduced.

concerns creativity in EI. Creativity is inseparable from proactivity (Dassault Systèmes or Arkema): leading strategic players (as is the case for the top of Kemp and Pearson's typology) combine proactivity and creativity.

The proactive voluntarist approach in EI allows us to emphasize the importance of the managerial role (Shrivastava 1995a). This role implies an internal motivation to appropriate (Bansal and Roth 2000) the issue of corporate social responsibility or CESR (Corporate Ecological and Social Responsibility) and then to accept the joint role of different stakeholders (Freeman 1984) in the strategic pro-NE commitment (Polonsky and Ottman 1998; Henriques and Sadorsky 1999).

6.2.2. *EI dissemination*

A priori, the good diffusion of EI is, comparatively speaking, weaker because of its disadvantage in terms of instantaneous comparative costs (except, see above, for incentive regulation policies and/or new calculations aimed at internalizing the social cost of the potential externalities generated, see Chapter 1).

The potential for diffusion depends first of all on the initial cost of innovation, especially when the innovation is technological. The reduction in the cost of innovation is obtained in particular by a reduction in design costs. The resulting reduction in the cost of design, on the supply side, enables better exploration (potential markets, customers, suppliers, partners), seizing of opportunities, as well as the development of *absorptive capacities* (Cohen and Levinthal 1990) in order to assimilate, internally, the flow of knowledge and, in return, reinforce the core business (or anticipate its evolution). Because no single actor can possess all the skills required to successfully complete a project, they must, diachronically and synchronically, place themselves in a collective innovation dynamic (or innovation community, which can also involve a BES).

The solution to do this is to evolve in a creative open environment stimulated by positive interactions (co-design and co-realization in NoF on an inter-organizational level; and even sometimes between competitors) by sharing a common asset[8] that each can develop in its core business (Airbus). The resulting collective invention (Allen 1983)[9] is based on open, interactive networked organizations with shared resources, distributed skills and the mobilization of ICT (including the Internet) and DT. A support vector for creation and diffusion is open source (Tirole and Lerner

8 This type of environment can make a *Business EcoSystem* (BES) in the sense of Moore (1993).

9 The result is *open innovation* (Chesbrough 2003) involving, in this open, collaborative and interactive framework, permanent inter-organizational back and forth.

2002), allowing the emergence of numerous business models. Networks can also be informal (Ubisoft), or sometimes virtual (Dassault Systèmes) with the mobilization, upstream for design and downstream for dissemination, for specific stakeholders, such as communities of practice (Brown and Duguid 1991, 1998; Wenger and Snyder 2000) that are passionate about technology, makers (Anderson 2012) or even users (Von Hippel 1976).

Empirical studies show that EI relies on a strengthened cooperative approach (Wagner 2007; De Marchi 2012), sometimes linked to geographical proximity (Ferru et al. 2015). Only a few specialized high-tech companies, leaders in their markets, can conduct innovative projects on their own, which reduce/eliminate impacts on the NE (Air Liquide), but, as a general rule, interdependence with the outside world is necessary because the development of an EI is based on a highly developed resilient network logic.

6.3. Proposal of a strategic matrix to innovate

By synthesis of the preceding elements, summarized in four points, the strategic spectrum for the company is as follows:

– Remain in a productivist paradigm and ignore negative externalities and/or acknowledge negative externalities and rely on the community to repair them.

– Accept responsibility for the negative externalities generated and pay (bonus/malus, fine, polluter/payer tax).

– Systematically repair *ex post* the prejudices generated.

– Change the paradigm by anticipating the consequences from the outset (*ex ante* logic).

In other words, there are three main courses of action: (i) ignore negative externalities; (ii) repair negative externalities; (iii) anticipate negative externalities. Thus, companies are either reactive by adapting to regulations or proactive in a voluntarily approach that admits two modalities: repairing *ex post* and/or preventively preventing nuisances *ex ante*. Proactivity can therefore be divided into two opposing visions: repairing nuisances *ex post* and anticipating nuisances *ex ante* (to avoid them). However, the *ex post* repair of negative externalities reaches an obvious limit when the degree of irreversibility becomes irrevocable[10]

10 The tree whose leaves fall off is an irreversible process, but the tree that dies is an irrevocable process. Beyond that, a tree species can be reintroduced and replanted if the NE is not itself irrevocably destroyed.

(Georgescu-Roegen 1971). Irreversibility implies a process of renewal; irrevocability implies a final destruction[11].

In the case of negative externalities, reparation through possible compensation[12], when it is possible, may come up against two obstacles: first, the declaration of intention not followed by negligence or intentional deception; second, feasibility (especially when what is destroyed is unique and irreplaceable, and therefore not compensable because irrevocable).

In any case, it is necessary to assess (section 6.3.1) the degrees of irreversibility (which may be apprehended *ex ante* or *ex post*). By superimposing (section 6.3.2) the nature of the approach (sophisticated/frugal) for EI, we can envisage (section 6.3.3) a coherent strategic matrix with an operational scope.

6.3.1. *Irreversibility of negative externalities*

Articulating irreversibility and the NE is a relatively new concern in the sense that the NE tended to be perceived as a free and inexhaustible resource. If all negative externalities are detrimental, the degree of harm (linked to the degree of irreversibility generated up to the threshold of irrevocability) must also be taken into account. Moreover, industrial and commercial activity, amplified by globalization, results in both local (such as pollution) and global (climate change) negative externalities. The solutions are as follows: repair if possible (depending on the degree of reversibility), possibly through local compensation (with the risk of unfulfilled promises of compensation); stop the nuisance and/or do no further harm by resorting to EI or change the paradigm through FEI.

FEI is part of a double theoretical filiation. On the one hand, that of Georgescu-Roegen's (1971) analysis of irreversibility/irrevocability. On the other hand, for Henry's (1974a, 1974b) concept of *option value*, i.e. a measure of the loss of decision-making flexibility (its value being equal to the *a priori* regret of making a wrong decision): a company must then make an *ex ante* decision on which there can be no *ex post* regret (what we call a consequential approach (see Bouvier-Patron (2015a), and Chapter 1 and Appendix 2 of this book).

---

11 The analysis of externalities on the NE (up to the critical point of irrevocability of irreversibility) is thus quite distinct from that of the management of a common good respectful of the NE (Ostrom 1990); a common good (neither private, nor collective and/or public) supposes an initial renewable resource that can be managed at the level of users.

12 With the promise made *ex ante* that cannot be kept afterwards (opportunism); the promise made *ex ante* that we know cannot be kept from the outset (immorality); the compensation impossible to implement (incompetence).

If proactive anticipation induces an NE-friendly innovation approach very early on, at the design level (reducing or eliminating any negative impact), should this be achieved through sophistication or frugality?

6.3.2. *Logic of sophistication and/or frugal approach?*

The strategic behaviors examined have led to a first rudimentary typology of action (i, ii, iii), namely: ignoring negative externalities (and reactivity if controlled by the regulator); repairing negative externalities (second-order proactivity because *ex post*); anticipating in a consistent manner (first-order proactivity because *ex ante*) to eliminate negative externalities *ex ante*.

Moreover, through innovation, we can minimize/eliminate negative externalities on the NE through a variable degree of sophistication: maximum sophistication in a technological logic or, alternatively, a pragmatic frugal approach that is adaptable and diffusible to all[13].

6.3.2.1. *Logic of sophistication*

To innovate, the respective advantages of being a pioneer or a follower are well known. The pioneer has a reputation as an innovator and values this image, as well as the associated competitive advantage, whereas the follower can enter an existing market at a lower cost (by imitating, if necessary, the pioneer). This race to technological innovation has been popular in the west, knowing that technological and organizational innovations are complementary (Rehfeld et al. 2007; Wagner 2007). Now, to innovate technologically at a lower cost (especially through design), the FabLab (Gershenfeld 2005; Ingelaere 2015), equipped in particular with DT tools, such as 3D printing, is ideal and is embodied in and by spaces. These spaces can be internal or external to the company, allowing for the testing of new ideas and collective exchange between creators from different backgrounds (with a range of means that favor the implementation of creativity and combine design know-how with that of realization), while reducing costs. The ICT and DT mobilized, within extended collectives and networks (more or less virtual and open), encourage the sharing of expertise, decentralization of information, simultaneity of exchanges and the breaking down of geographical and/or cultural barriers. The collective space thus constituted, more or less formalized, partially/totally virtual and evolving, can be closed (towards a proprietary solution) or open (open source) to generate collective innovation. In summary, the resilient (NoF-like) network logic extended to the FabLab (Bouvier-Patron 2015b), reducing the cost of innovation by design, is a very promising scenario. It preserves a western way of innovating, but implies a

13 One example is the automotive supplier ecosystem in India (Tiwari and Kalogerakis 2017).

relatively high level of barrier to entry with a rather slow diffusion and an impact on the NE not yet truly evaluated[14].

6.3.2.2. *Choosing a specific approach to frugal innovation*

Compared to the usual western way of innovating, the FabLab can be seen as a declarative intention of frugality.

However, other parallel models of frugality are emerging (Zeschky et al. 2014)[15], if, to innovate technologically is, in fact, to waste resources for an uncertain result and without guaranteeing a large diffusion.

The frugality evoked is first of all of Indian inspiration and can be defined, at this stage, as an activity of creation or re-creation by doing more and better with less, with less technological sophistication and always based on what is available to achieve it. This is indeed a challenge to the western way of innovating (Basu et al. 2013). For an exportable synthesis of the model, instrumental frugality – or frugal innovation (FI) – is a structured approach that can be mobilized in the west (Radjou et al. 2012), where resources and/or innovation budgets are now rationed. FI can be defined as the engineering capacity[16] *to make better products with less, based on existing products*.

However, it should be noted that this existing material, i.e. everything used in industry today, cannot be recycled (unless it has to overcome high barriers of various kinds (Rennings 2000; Frondel et al. 2007; Arundel and Kemp 2009).

To achieve perpetual recycling (at a controlled energy cost and without waste) of any ingredient used, which characterizes a circular economy (Geyer and Jackson

14 Hansen et al. (2009) propose an investigation method to examine the possibilities linking technology and SD using the *sustainability innovation cube* by crossing three dimensions: need, life cycle, objective. The challenge is to determine the operational means available, which can be numerous and ranked in descending order of usefulness according to the results obtained by *focus groups* (Knight and Jenkins 2009).

15 Let us recall that these authors mobilize the concept of reverse innovation (from developing countries to advanced countries) with the idea of a reversion corridor (*low cost, good enough, frugal innovation*), where FI is positioned as superior. However, the concept of reversion is inoperative if we do not distinguish between *apparent reversion* (Chinese low-cost products resulting from overseas delocalization and (re)sale in Europe) and *effective reversion* (innovative Indian products sold in Europe); the phases and places of production being of prime importance (whether the design is carried out in the United States or in India counts).

16 Optimized FI maximizes value to customers and shareholders while minimizing the use of scarce resources.

2004), we would have to select, *ex ante*, effectively recyclable inputs and outputs as in the *cradle to cradle* (CtoC) approach (Braungart and McDonough 2002). However, even at this high level of requirement, CtoC does not necessarily imply that inputs are environmentally friendly. Thus, to put it another way, recycling of the existing is a feature associated with frugality, which does not select the NE-friendly products out of the box. Moreover, in their review on the concept of FI (characterized by three criteria: significant cost reduction, proximity to core business, optimized performance), Weyrauch and Herstatt (2016) classify the sustainability variable as non-priority. The FI and NE link is therefore only accepted.

Also, a graduation of frugality classification is needed:

– *Gandhian* frugality: incremental transformation of waste to offer useful products meeting a demand (Gandhian innovation; Altenburg and Lundvall 2009; Prahalad and Mashelkar 2010). This is characterized by a formula of *more from less for many*, transcending, through a process of improvement, a logic of low cost but poor quality for that of low cost but good quality.

– *Jugaad* frugality[17]: reasoned creative transformation of waste materials to offer attractive products (Jugaad innovation; Radjou et al. 2012; Brem and Wolfram 2014). From a tradition, Jugaad becomes a creative entrepreneurial business focused on the frugal use of available materials in a context of scarcity and poverty (Tiwari and Herstatt 2012), as well as the possible key to contemporary management (Barodawala et al. 2015).

– *Grassroots* frugality: collective innovation from below (Seyfang and Smith 2007)[18], without excessive sophistication, via a decentralized and lateralized organization based on distributed skills, common sense, technological bricolage (from the maker in Anderson (2012)) and collective resourcefulness, taking into account from the outset the NE at all stages of the innovative product's life.

In total, among the three forms of frugality, the one that respects the NE from the outset is based on the concept of *grassroots innovation* as defined by Seyfang and Smith (2007). In this framework, it is possible to mobilize a *satisfactory technological level* (in the sense of *satisficing* (Simon 1976, 1978)) rather than a very costly technological sophistication.

17 As already mentioned, this term comes from the Hindi slang related to the clever, improvised and radical transformation of waste (Kabaad) into something useful and attractive (*Jugaad*).

18 Brem and Wolfram (2014), in their review, clearly specify the essential contribution of Seyfang and Smith (2007) linking grassroots to NE preservation.

Note that frugality is a return to making given the means available where bricolage is crucial (this is also the case in the sophisticated vision of the FabLab). The concept of bricolage (Chapter 7) is the object of growing interest in the literature (whether or not it is related to frugality).

We can articulate and/or distinguish (Baker et al. 2003; Cunha et al. 2014) between bricolage and improvisation (where, in the latter case, the execution time of the solution found responding to a new situation, is essential in a competitive performance context).

6.3.3. *Opting for frugal environmental innovation (FEI)*

The matrix in Table 6.1 synthesizes our approach by crossing two axes: (I1) the method of remedial action (Hartje and Laurie 1984) by *ex post* curative treatment (such as recycling) versus *ex ante* preventive proactivity (such as eco-design); (I2) the way of innovating: sophisticated (high tech); frugal Indian inspiration (Radjou et al. 2012) with indirect NE respect effect through waste sorting and reuse; western-inspired frugality (Seyfang and Smith 2007), including the consideration of the NE from the start.

The result of the I1 and I2 matrix intersection constitutes strategic options: companies from advanced countries tend to opt for a sophisticated EI strategy (boxes 1.1, Véolia; 2.1, Dassault Systèmes or creative technological start-ups such as Armor with its ASCA® organic photovoltaic film); companies from developing countries are mainly positioned in Box 1.2 with a gradual concern for *Jugaad* (*Tata*) quality. Box 2.2 corresponds to circular CtoC production without prejudging the use of ecological materials (glass). Box 1.3 designates the functioning of an ecological *ex post* recycling chain (linen textile). Box 2.3, combining first-order proactivity and grassroots frugality, defines the FEI, where new dynamics converge (hence the two arrows in the matrix): circularity of an ecological value chain (Rilsan® from Arkema); less degree of technological sophistication but, for example, more inspired by biomimicry (Benyus 1997) by integrating the entire life cycle. If FEI can be a self-centered approach, it results rather, by the grassroots logic, from a collective invention (open and collaborative) in perpetual evolution where creativity (in start-ups and VSE especially) is essential (in particular within the maker space).

A company concerned with EI has a wide range of strategic solutions, including FEI, which is a proactive choice that respects the NE without excessive, costly technological sophistication (such as Lombritek, which has patented the lombrifiltration of wastewater; or, more entrepreneurial, Lactips, which manufactures, on its patent, thermoplastic granules based on milk proteins; or Arkema with its range of biosourced polyamides (Rilsan®)).

(II) Type of innovation: EI / **(I) Method of action**		**Sophisticated**	**Frugal**	**Environmental Frugality**
		II1. ***High tech*** **preserving the environment**	**II2. Process with indirect environmental impact**	**II3.** ***Satisfactory tech.*** **preserving the environment**
Repairing and recycling	**I1.** ***Ex post***	1.1 Curative EI	1.2 Frugal innovation *Jugaad > Gandhian* partial circularity	1.3 Ecological recycling channel
Anticipatory proactivity	**I2.** ***Ex ante***	2.1 Integrated preventive EI	2.2 Circularity upstream integrative *cradle to cradle (CtoC)*	2.3 *Grassroots* FEI

Table 6.1. *EI strategic options matrix (source: author 2020)*

6.4. Conclusion

After a review of EI with an emphasis on the role of proactivity, we have outlined several strategic solutions for innovation. Any private EI approach comes up against (before irrevocability) the unavoidable question of internalizing the negative externalities induced. A fundamental strategic choice must be made between *ex ante* preventive and *ex post* curative logic. Thus, in the preventive logic and minimizing or eliminating the impact on the NE from the design stage, companies have three strategies at their disposal: sophistication (rather selective, with slow diffusion), frugal (with broad diffusion) and FEI. The last one, FEI, is creative, bold, pragmatic and diffusible.

If sophistication has been the usual way to innovate in western countries since the first industrial revolution, another way is through FEI, by mobilizing the *satisfactory technological level.*

With the consideration of the NE, the strategic matrix, resulting from the proposed analysis, is a tool with an operational vocation (for research, as well as for practitioners), as well as a basis for building further empirical studies on FEI (among all companies, with size playing a role, especially for the magnitude of the industrial solution provided).

Frugality, including FEI as a form compatible with the NE, raises questions about how to innovate. If we agree on the fact that innovation is the dynamic engine of the company, the barriers in terms of investments and costs involved in taking the NE into account can be seen as something other than insurmountable obstacles.

Whatever the type of innovation (process or product, high tech or low tech, upstream or downstream, individual or collective), everything relies on two springs of innovative creation: bricolage and improvisation. It is therefore in an obvious way, both as a logical continuation of the reasoning and as an intrinsic response to what innovative practice is, as well as a response to the major challenge of an innovation that is coherent with the NE, that we are proposing this final Chapter 7 on bricolage and improvisation.

7

Bricolage and Improvisation: Two Key Cogs of Innovative Creation

Since Schumpeter (1939, 1942), it has been customary to distinguish between incremental innovation (incremental to what already exists) and radical innovation (creation destroying what already exists). This rudimentary binary typology has been perfected (Abernathy and Clark 1985) by crossing this first predefined axis with a new axis concerning the commercial versus technical dimension: therefore, for example, just to illustrate the point, if Concorde is an engineer's technical project, Airbus is a successful commercial project. However, the initial fundamental binary classification has never been denied, and proposes a first classificatory sieve of reference by addressing only the technological offer (which may constitute a limit). Moreover, it should be noted that any classification is carried out *ex post*: determining *a priori* whether an innovation will prove to be radical is delicate and improbable. In addition, we must insist on the dynamics of organizational capacities and of the renewal and/or creation of competences (see above) in a collective approach to the essential role of communities of practice (Brown and Duguid 1991), leading to today's communities of innovation. Furthermore, demand and use itself, within communities of use, play an increasingly important role because of the *disruptive innovations* (Bower and Christensen 1995) that mark and distinguish, in practice, the before and after (e.g. Internet; Bouvier-Patron 2011a). All these aspects blur the seminal dichotomy (binary typology).

At the heart of the innovation reactor is a complex nuance, on the supply side, subsumed here by the name *innovative creation*:

– discovery (resulting from scientific research): what is found and perceived as a significant increase in knowledge;

– invention (individual and/or collective activity of conception, sometimes with the means at hand, leading to a creation): technical implementation of a discovery;

– innovation as a managerial implementation in a company (of an invention through the mobilization of R&D in the case of product innovation), i.e. an invention appropriated by a company; this can be envisaged at the level of a product or a process, as well as at the organizational level (the organizational innovation of the pioneer being distinguished from an organizational change imported by a follower);

– inventive design[1] (at the heart of science for the engineer: Engineering Sciences, ES, see Perrin (2001)), applied in a company process in the name of research engineering: process of transforming the invention into successful innovation and identifying the need or use, right through to meeting the customers on the market(s); the internal functional specifications are necessarily open to achieve this;

– operational technical design for production engineers or technical design for productive implementation: activity of technical matching in relation to an identified need, on the basis of a closed internal functional specification, and strict compliance with company procedures and ISO standards.

At this stage, to go into more detail on the issue of product innovation by situating it in a synthetic way in the context of the company, we can refer to Bouvier-Patron (2011a).

It should be noted that the internal specifications are particularly fundamental in formalizing perceived needs and are imposed on the company in a dialogue between strategic marketing, R&D and purchasing. It is also a key factor in the external customer–supplier relationship (for a synthetic presentation of the issue, see Bouvier-Patron (2011a, 2017a)).

The internal specifications are sometimes a fiction, in the sense that the company is not obliged to formalize all the required specifications and related outsourcing in detail in a unique and centralized document (articulating functional and technical specifications per product). But there is a decomposition of the whole into fragmented subsets, of which some parts are carried out internally and the majority externally (due to the refocusing on the company's core business; this is also true, moreover, for each of the complementary suppliers required) in the context of customer–supplier relations (where the *bargaining power* of each supplier is going to be decisive in determining *who holds the pencil*, see Bouvier-Patron (2013, 2017a)).

---

1 *Inventive design* mainly refers to the TRIZ method (Altshuller 1988), or the *theory of inventive problem solving*, which is particularly used in ES. In the HSS, *design thinking* (Brown 2008), based on the work of Simon (1969), is preferentially put forward.

The distinction between invention and innovation is essential in order to be able to grasp, from the outset, the fact that innovation goes through a managerial process within organizations with industrial and commercial purposes (e.g. private companies) when invention is a more evanescent process upstream of innovation (originating from an individual and/or a collective) benefiting from the accumulation of previous knowledge but, through specific creation, arranging old ideas and knowledge in a new way, pirating ideas and/or knowledge or even tipping over into the emergence of new knowledge. Moreover, bricolage, which is intuitively very present at the invention stage, can also be particularly mobilized at the innovation and design stage. It is at the heart of the innovative process (whatever it may be). Improvisation takes on its full meaning at the stage of the realization of an innovation due to managerial constraints.

The modern managerial myth of the company is that it is possible to plan innovation. However, this proves to be particularly delicate, even for companies that adopt the best measures (decentralization and organizational lateralization, incentives for creation by freeing up working time, encouragement and support for projects, provision of resources). Moreover, to innovate, the firm must have skills as well as minimal R&D expenditure (as internal absorptive capacities (Cohen and Levinthal 1990)), as well as an open innovation process (Chesbrough 2003) due to the need for collective interactions and mutualization (because of the specialization of each entity in their own field while needing complementarities). However, not everything that favors innovation implies an innovation (and, if it does, it will not necessarily be economically valorizable and even less economically profitable). The innovative process is long, costly and uncertain (which multiplies the cost of access and justifies, in a way, the price charged at the sale), which is why strategic marketing and innovation marketing are becoming increasingly important in the company.

If we refocus on the question of creation in the broadest sense of the term (grouping together the phases of discovery, invention, innovation, inventive design), bricolage is very present because of the need for trial and error, aiming to explore different possibilities. In order to discriminate logically between the phases of innovation, we can rely on the creation/design pair (creation being upstream of design) and this up to the technical design for the implementation of the industrial process (and to be linked to the commercial process: distribution channel, after-sales service).

Bricolage refers to a transversal practice that illustrates the importance of *making* in problem solving. It is also a concrete and natural illustration of the idea that the hand is the indispensable extension of the human brain.

In a basic way, bricolage designates *a practice of creation, creative repair and/or detour of use, essentially with the means at hand (tools, methods, spaces, materials) and without* a priori *commercial aim*. Bricolage is a practice that favors, beyond the experience already acquired, thanks to learning as well as to intuition, experimentation and interactivity, the resolution of more or less complex problems up to the elaboration of objects by means of tools (rudimentary in general, but which can be sophisticated) by the development of an adaptive and open know-how mobilizing a strong part of creativity (and/or co-creativity in a collaborative framework) where therefore, as for any innovative activity, something new, here through practice, is incorporated into the existing (for a creation, a modification, a transformation, a functional repair or a detour of use), either marginally or structurally.

To analyze the term bricolage in its link to innovation, we will envision it (section 7.1) as a concept that is new (section 7.1.1) in its logical perception (section 7.1.2) and, finally (section 7.1.3), by its current application, and also as a central device in a larger whole (section 7.2) by its link to improvisation (section 7.2.1) and to frugal innovation (section 7.2.2), to come finally to a synthesis scheme of the conceptual map likely to contribute to explain the dynamics of innovative creation up to the FEI (section 7.2.3).

7.1. Bricolage as a concept

Bricolage in economics and management (section 7.1.1) is a new concept, to be understood in its logical perception (section 7.1.2) and from the perspective of its current application (section 7.1.3).

7.1.1. *Bricolage: a new concept but an old practice*

Bricolage is a practice based on learning, interactivity, experience, intuition, experimentation by trial and error (including by chance or *serendipity*: *finding something by not looking for it or by not looking for the thing found*, which is not without incidence beyond the difficulty of being able to plan the innovation). It is an adaptive creative process with strong individual involvement (which can be part of a collaborative framework) involving the acquisition of tricks in a knowledge base, generally tacit, constituted by collective accumulation transmitted by word of mouth and/or through associations, and/or through access, via the Internet, to a digitized corpus (fixed or evolving, but accessible and sometimes interactive) based on the *gift* and *counter-gift* (in the sense of the founder of anthropology, Marcel Mauss, in his 1923 *Essai sur le Don* (Essay on the Gift of Knowledge), i.e. *a form of effective exchange, but via a transaction with a complex symbolic value of a societal nature*), the reciprocity of exchanges (equivalence) or the free unilateral provision. Although it is an old concept, bricolage is a new concept in economics and management that needs to be explored and (re)placed at its true level of importance.

Bricolage was highlighted in the Human and Social Sciences (HSS) by Levi-Strauss (1962a) as a key practice in primitive societies, which cleverly mobilize the natural resources at their disposal to best satisfy their needs. This concept finds a renewed echo today through the activity of makers (Anderson 2012), mobilizing ICT and DT within communities of practice (Brown and Duguid 1991), through creation/co-creation (then design/co-design) of new objects, or even the repair or the detour of use of objects, and this in an individual (DIY) or collective (DIWO) way in a closed proprietary perspective (with a perspective of commercial valorization) versus (Raymond 1999) *open source* (to develop open applications of sharing and/or with commercial purposes).

7.1.2. *Is bricolage a matter of logic?*

Classically (since John Stuart Mill in 1843 with his *A System of Logic, Ratiocinative and Inductive*), economists have distinguished between inductive and deductive logic. Theoretical and non-experimental scientific thought mobilizes deductive logic. On the contrary, certain sciences, which are essentially empirical (such as the natural sciences where species are counted and classified), mobilize inductive logic. Other sciences, such as physics, combine inductive and deductive logic.

However, this bipolar characterization is not exclusive, and Aristotle already specified a particular form of induction (called *retroduction*) taken up by Peirce in his collected papers (Peirce 1931–1958; Psillos 2011) under the term *abduction*.

Mathematicians, for example, make a strong case for the importance of intuition. This allows us to infer a result by seizing a singularity not yet demonstrated in order to then proceed formally to the elaboration of a demonstrated statement (in the most efficient and aesthetic way possible). This possibility in mathematics, linked to pure abstraction, can easily be generalized to scientific reasoning, producing a discourse on an external reality, this reality naturally offering singularities and allowing the emergence of *surprising facts* ("The surprising fact C is observed", see *Pragmatism and Abduction*; Peirce 1903, 5.189).

It is these *surprising facts* that, by the disturbance they induce in the reasoning, force the production of a new explanation (i.e. one that does not exist and/or is not calibrated in the existing knowledge base).

Thus, from a *surprising fact,* abduction allows us to go backwards (hence retroduction) to formulate a new acceptable hypothesis explaining what happened when the surprise was observed. At this stage, abduction provides only hypotheses. The selection of the hypothesis giving the explanation of the observed fact will depend on several criteria: the predictive power of the statement (attached to the hypothesis); the experimental verifiability (allowing the reproduction of the fact) from an instrumental device associated with the hypothesis; the greatest explanatory simplicity as the simplest hypothesis is the easiest to test (if the hypothesis is proven to be false, it is easy to eliminate it to then start on a more complicated hypothesis); finally, the greatest openness because it does not close the reasoning in a limiting way from the start.

For Peirce, the challenge is to articulate three forms (deduction, induction, abduction), which have complementary and distinct roles.

Abduction is a creative insight to solve a surprising problem. It is an interpretive gamble. To try to define it: *abduction* is that *particular inference which, starting from a surprising fact, invites a specific induction allowing us to elaborate an explanatory hypothesis not available in the existing knowledge base.* The surprising fact is at the origin of the process (of discovery, creation, or innovation) through serendipity.

In concrete terms, the surprising fact is permanent in the practice of bricolage by allowing the right answer to the problem to be found. The practice of bricolage thus naturally mobilizes abduction: a pragmatic answer is brought to surprising facts (often sequential) by trial and error towards a creative compromise found from a *satisfactory* global solution (in the sense of *satisficing*; Simon 1976, 1978).

7.1.3. *Bricolage and the current application of the concept*

Bricolage is part of a spectrum of technical and organizational means, the lower fringe of the spectrum being the use of on-the-spot means and associated practices. It is an individual and/or collective logic, more or less formalized and organized, of sharing, exchanging, learning and effectively creating projects and products using available tools and materials. The commercial purpose is not to be excluded when the art of bricolage is used in profit-making organizations: indirectly by communities of innovation not exclusively linked to companies, or directly when communities of innovation function as appendages at the service of companies.

With a more or less technological anchoring around a project, which cannot be usefully or efficiently carried out within a company (or in the inter-organizational sphere by the sole coordination of the client–supplier network), innovation communities combine complementary knowledge, know-how and/or interdisciplinary skills by meeting in a physical place: makerspace, an innovation platform dedicated to a specific project mobilizing, generally, a place-tool, such as the FabLab (Gershenfeld 2005); for some perspective, see Bouvier-Patron (2015b) or Chapters 2 and 3 of this book, or other technico-organizational devices (co-working space, incubator for start-ups, innovation accelerator supporting the growth of a mature start-up, showroom with trial space to allow for use tests). The *place* can also exist, virtually, through a virtual innovation community linking, via the Internet, in an interactive and dynamic way, individuals or passionate groups around an idea, a project or an attractive center of interest. The community in these places generates a collective intelligence and allows, through co-creation, a common achievement. Bricolage is essential in the process of creating or co-creating physical objects in order to explore and test the system of constraints and even to elaborate an evolving model (possibly digital), depending on the complexity to be considered or, in any case, a first prototype that is more or less functional.

All in all, bricolage mobilizes the available resources without the objective of (immediate) profitability, but with the idea of experimenting with solutions and moving forward to find an acceptable compromise (or *satisficing*; Simon 1976, 1978). Constraints are revealed and overcome within a community, and beyond, by considering possible objectives, functionalities, potential uses and costs, more or less sophisticated means and expected results or opening up unexpected solutions or results (case of serendipity). Bricolage concerns (creation, design, production, diffusion or broadcasting, use) all levels, as well as, potentially, all stakeholders (individuals, communities, employees, customers, suppliers, associations concerned by the positive/negative impact of the company). Bricolage is at the crossroads of disciplinary fields of HHS/sciences/ES. At the end of this section, which allows us to situate the conceptual importance of bricolage, we will present the issue (in an extensive but non-exhaustive way) as a key device in a broader set.

7.2. Bricolage as a key device for innovative creation

Bricolage is a key device in a larger whole: first, through its link to improvisation (section 7.2.1) and to frugal innovation (section 7.2.2); second, through a conductive filiation, allowing the construction (section 7.2.3) of a conceptual map opening up theoretical and applied research perspectives concerning the dynamics of innovative creation up to the FEI and beyond.

7.2.1. *Bricolage and improvisation*

The two concepts of bricolage and improvisation are both distinct and complementary. First of all, it is necessary to define them in order to distinguish them clearly:

– bricolage, where the dimension of scarcity is essential by mobilizing, in the first instance, the means at hand and without any imposed temporal constraint (except, in a practical way, during a phase requiring it or because of an imminent danger);

– improvisation, where the execution time of a solution found – by spontaneous emergence, education and/or training – to face a new situation, is essential in a competitive and performance context.

In improvisation, the temporal dimension is essential in order to respond as quickly and appropriately as possible to any event that is unforeseen in relation to the usual organization of the prescribed or effectively carried out activity, and this, without the constraint of scarcity being essentially present. The managerial literature is rather oriented, to date, on this last concept of improvisation (Weick 1993; Cunha et al. 2014).

Weick's (1993) *situated rationality* characterizes a managerial context of compelling action (often with complex tasks to be accomplished), involving a risk of potential tipping over into a chaotic universe, in addition to the uncertainty generated. The actors concerned are required to act in a limited time frame, and a particular organizational setup takes place at the moment when individuals, individually and/or collectively, must take initiatives in an interactive way with each other and with their situated environment: this is the emergence of *enaction*, i.e. a process (oriented towards and through action) of *sensemaking* that begins with the identification of unexpected (or *surprising facts* in Peirce's terms) and contextualized elements, and then the establishment of a common representation (because any divergence of appreciation in the emergency, and in the face of the unexpected, always has disastrous consequences). Continuous coordination prevails, even in the face of a sequence of unforeseen events, thanks to the mobilization of relevant existing rules, group coherence, experience, learning, know-how, intuition, collective intelligence and/or the creation of new rules (through a common vision, each person in their own place, with roles well distributed within the group).

Improvisation, often combined with bricolage, appears decisive. Moorman and Miner (1998a, 1998b) perfectly illustrate the indispensable role of improvisation and bricolage at the high tech level by quoting other authors specialized in the question of avoiding a catastrophe in a technological context: for example, NASA's Apollo 13 mission, where diverging (from the routines induced by the accepted and planned procedures) was the only recourse in the emergency, by mobilizing a high level of professionalism with adaptive capacity and using bricolage (is it necessary to emphasize this) to generate adapted devices or artifacts. The result of this coordinated development of an inventive solution allowed the crew's return to Earth, even though they were almost certain to die (the explosion of an oxygen tank during the Earth–Moon transit being the consequence of a series of incidents and negligence on the ground that could have been anticipated before the launch of the rocket). Improvisation and bricolage are logically distinct, but very complementary and not very dissociable. Baker et al. (2003) show, including at the professional level, that the two are complementary in the sense that the competence acquired through bricolage also gives the ability to improvise. It would be perfectly arbitrary to oppose bricolage (of the amateur, denoting a form of immaturity) and improvisation (of the professional with great expertise). The "situation" implies activating the bricolage/improvisation mode if the installed routine is to be overcome.

The engineer in a company, in a routine mode, works *a priori* with access to listed resources and the respect of procedures or rules according to constraints, including temporal ones, in a predefined schedule. The same engineer who has to find a solution to an unexpected problem, even though they are initially *a priori* in a routine logic, will have to improvise. The same engineer, participating in an innovative project, at one moment or another (or even in temporal continuity), will have to get out of the routine, alone and/or collectively (sometimes in a radical way), and improvise (under various constraints, in particular in limited time). They will also have to tinker with the available means, look for the necessary resources (and/or by recovering them here or there) by themselves to invent, design and produce, starting from (almost) nothing and/or by detour, the device and/or the artifact that they need. In short, they must mobilize heterogeneous resources and means that are not necessarily listed, but they must also operate by intuitive dosing, and arrange and configure in order to sketch out a viable solution.

We can therefore perfectly discriminate between improvisation (as an emergency involving derogatory action within a given framework) and bricolage (through the absence of emergency, but creative genesis from nothing or almost nothing, with the means at hand or locally available resources, often through salvaging) to find (without the need for an established codification) an acceptable solution (Levi-Strauss 1962a; Halme et al. 2012; Cuna et al. 2014). The managerial literature, on the issues of bricolage and improvisation is sometimes complex to follow diachronically due to a lack of homogeneity and conceptual stability[2]. Once the meaning of the words has been clarified, by correctly selecting the previous authors and sorting out the statements, the essential points can be extracted and highlighted:

– Some (Baker et al. 2003) distinguish between improvisation and bricolage well (without however really leaving the reductive vision according to which bricolage would be only an intermediary stage in the process of improvisation).

– Moreover, Baker et al. (2003), drawing on Moorman and Miner (1998b), propose to see improvisation (as well as, implicitly, bricolage) not as a purely tactical (opportunistic) operation, but rather as strategic (essential, even vital) in the creation of new products.

– Others, such as Nohria and Berkley (1994), propose, from the outset and very early on, relevant insights into bricolage without any need to rephrase: "Bricoleurs play with possibilities and use available resources to find workable solutions"; "The activities of bricolage occur when people explore existing resources in novel ways, not necessarily under time pressure as in the case of improvisation," thus clearly showing the distinction between bricolage and improvisation.

– Finally, based on Moorman and Miner (1998a), Cunha et al. (2014) clearly reaffirm what improvisation is: "Improvisational innovation occurs when there is time pressure," while dealing with the situation, without having what would have been needed, in an adequate way, in an optimized situation (and this, without any direct link with a scarcity of the resource). With, moreover, the following *a priori* counter-intuitive clarification (Cunha et al. (2014) taking up Miner et al. (2001)): "Improvisation is normally not favored in product innovation because it entails

2 The two concepts are orthogonal in the mathematical sense of the term insofar as we can bricolage without necessarily improvising (invention), improvise without bricolage (coping with an emergency to overcome a failure in the industrial routine), bricolage and improvise (inventive design) or neither (programmed mode of imposed Taylorian–Fordian organizational functioning). Even in the Taylorian case, a relatively recent discipline such as ergonomics (resulting from the study of man in a limited situation during World War II), with a French school initially opposed to Anglo-Saxon ergonomics in that the latter tended rather to adapt man to the machine, whereas the former aimed rather to adapt the machine to man, is now giving way to a flexible interactive vision (taking into account, in particular, the work environment: noise, odor, humidity, heat, arduousness and exposure to risks). Ergonomics shows, in particular, the importance, individually and collectively, of the *representation* of a work situation and of the differential between the *prescribed* (prescribed by the planning of the time and methods office in the Taylorian scheme) and the *actual* (i.e. the actual practices of teams or individuals in the field, implementing tricks or solutions that usefully improve the initial planning to allow for actual performance, sometimes even adapting the tools or the organization).

significant risks [...] We suggest that, under normal conditions, people would prefer not to improvise given the risks involved[3]".

For Cunha et al. (2014), it would therefore be a matter of avoiding improvisation in innovation, if possible. But can innovation be dissociated from improvisation (as well as from bricolage)? Are the normal conditions invoked implicitly those of innovation planning (which we know is impossible to carry out)? The question of the supposed preferential choice to avoid improvisation is vertiginous, as the unforeseen, the circumstances, the moment, the place, the act or the concrete realization play a determining role[4] in terms of innovation. The whole challenge of the art of improvisation consists of anticipating in order to create (or co-create) or re-establish a compliant situation (evolving or not) in a limited time. Improvisation can, possibly, benefit from a prior active training phase based on instructions, rules, guides or scenarios (from the most to the least likely), according to a set of hypotheses on the conceivable spectrum of possibilities, but without ever being able to be exhaustive. Starting from an organizational routine, the critical case is precisely the occurrence of an unexpected situation (deviating from what has been foreseen, formalized and/or planned): the response requires the art of improvisation (based on training, practice, experience and know-how) and can mobilize, if necessary, the art of bricolage. As for the art of bricolage, it fundamentally questions the concept of managerial efficiency (i.e. the relationship between the means

3 *Risk aversion* is a central concern of the academic literature in economics and management, but if this aspect is not to be neglected (even though often exaggerated at the theoretical level, as in the transactional approach), risk-taking is necessary and inevitable (controlled if possible and to varying degrees) at the operational level in activities, such as for work in a confined environment (clean room), those at high risk (scuba diver under the sea or an astronaut due to technical and environmental constraints), those directly linked to pathogenic elements (laboratories, hospitals), those of maintenance (chemistry, petrochemicals, nuclear), and/or those often extreme and perilous (rescue operations in case of fire, industrial or natural disasters). Moreover, the decision under radical uncertainty (Knight 1921) is at the very foundation of economic life. Today, the decision under uncertainty can be decentralized from the head of the company to hierarchically subordinate personnel; independently of another debate, present in Knight, of the decision-making responsibility of *salaried managers* (due to the ownership-decision divorce empirically demonstrated by Berle and Means (1932)).

4 In the event of an epidemic (and, *a fortiori*, a pandemic), for example, which implies an adaptive reorganization of personnel, skills, care, places and means, it is necessary to mobilize all of our resources and improvise (e.g. transferring equipment from the operating room for another use; adapting a postoperative recovery room into a confined operational resuscitation unit) and bricolage (e.g. fashioning an effective protective device by ourselves). Technological bricolage can be mobilized. For example, 3D printing to manufacture existing objects that are missing (such as tubing tips) can be a technological bricolage if there is trial and error, starting with the existing object, and then designing the digital model needed for printing, which can also lead to improving the object, or even radically modifying it (see Figure 7.1).

mobilized to achieve the result, a concept already opposed to the concept of effectiveness where the end justifies the means to achieve the desired result). Indeed, the art of bricolage often mobilizes few means, unexpected or surprising makeshift means, while achieving the result. Bricolage thus plays a major role in organizational innovation and can even be a trigger for it. The practices of bricolage and/or improvisation are distinct, complementary and compatible (individually or collectively, in a closed or open space, private or associative, with or without profit).

The art of bricolage and the art of improvisation (together or separately) contribute to creation (and to co-creation, then to conception and inventive co-conception) through a practice based on experience, know-how, intuition, experimentation, interactivity, exchanges of experience and sharing, while acknowledging the crucial importance of experimentation and chance (through serendipity) in innovation.

7.2.2. *Bricolage and frugal innovation*

The art of bricolage and the art of improvisation, which are useful for creativity (and co-creativity in a collective setting), can be fostered by technological (e.g. the FabLab as a kind of Swiss Army knife that allows us *to do almost anything*, as Gershenfeld (2005) puts it) and/or organizational (makerspace) means, as well as by the method through a practice (sophisticated high-tech or frugal).

The sophistication versus frugality debate (see Chapters 2–6) is essential in a context of increasing resource scarcity and cost rationalization, as well as, potentially, of taking into account the constraints on the NE (see Chapter 1).

Frugality, however, still needs to integrate the issue of respect for the NE. Frugality does not refer to the same content for everyone. Frugality must be clearly dissociated (Chapters 5 and 6) from the question of inversion on the one hand, and circularity on the other.

– Let us recall that there is an *inversion* of the usual flow (perceived through the product's life-cycle curve; Vernon 1966) if the export originates from a BRIC-type country, with a western country as the recipient. However, in a case of delocalization, we cannot speak of inversion if the product is re-exported to the west (while benefiting, by delocalization, from low or non-existent social, health and environmental costs). There are two opposing economic models: the low-cost model (intended mainly for export or re-export) and the BOP (bottom of the pyramid) model (Prahalad 2005), where the aim is to serve the base of the population first (everyone, but first the mass: logic of inclusiveness). The BOP is based on frugality of Indian origin (Bouvier-Patron 2017b, 2020) and is declined in two main modalities: *Gandhian* (more with less for many) and *Jugaad* (more with less for many, but of good quality and desirable/attractive).

Therefore, without necessarily excluding improvisation, the frugal innovation approach (frugal innovation, FI) rather mobilizes bricolage at the stage of creation (and co-creation) and design (and co-design) of object(s), while inviting a successful logic of realization of a product that must mobilize the least amount of immediately available (and usually scarce) resources. That said, as already mentioned, the technological resources deployed are part of a wide palette from the means of the edge to the sophistication of the FabLab, with technological bricolage (Gershenfeld 2005; Anderson 2012) being exercised at the level of creation (co-creation) and design (co-conception) at the proto-industrial stage.

Frugal innovation (FI) consists of doing what already exists or what does not yet exist with less, cheaper and better without mobilizing sophistication while offering, for use, at least as many functionalities (often new ones), as well as a quality of design and realization of the product and also a relevance: adequacy to the real local needs in terms of product (adapted, affordable, robust, repairable) and of effectiveness (ease of use) and/or even potential evolution.

Waste can be a resource for the frugal approach, but there is no *circular economy* in the sense that the waste used (often generated elsewhere) has not necessarily been designed for reuse as input.

– The *circular economy* necessarily implies thinking about the production of objects for their reuse (Geyer and Jackson 2004). Moreover, even an *effective circular economy is not in itself NE-friendly* (in terms of disposal and/or impact reduction). *CtoC* (*cradle to cradle*; Braungart and McDonough 2002) is opposed to the dynamic (initiated by the European industrial revolution) of *cradle to grave* (through the extraction/production/consumption/waste cycle and with, at best, partial recycling through *ex post* or end of pipe treatment, as opposed to upstream integration of the life cycle from the design phase; see Hartje and Laurie (1984)). CtoC can only be considered *virtuous in terms of the NE if it allows for the development of respectful products with ecological inputs that can be reused indefinitely*. The consequences on the NE must be analyzed throughout the life cycle: at the level of design, production, sale, use and disposal. Well-conducted eco-design must anticipate the consequences for the NE and can be inspired by nature (Benyus 1997).

Grassroots innovation (Seyfang and Smith 2007) is decentralized, lateralized, collective and respectful of the NE from the start. Lateralization is based on skills distributed among peers and inducing common sense, bricolage and/or even technological bricolage, as well as individual and collective resourcefulness (*system D*) by mobilizing improvisation at the stage of innovation production. The challenge is to take into account, from the outset, respect for the NE and consider it at all stages of the product's life, without mobilizing useless or excessive sophistication; this brings us back to the idea of technological sobriety or compromise, as can be a *satisfactory technological level* (Simon's (1976, 1978) *satisficing*). This leads to the concept of *frugal environmental innovation* (FEI; see Bouvier-Patron (2017b, 2020) and Chapters 5 and 6 of this book).

In principle, even without taking the NE into account, frugal innovation in itself strongly mobilizes bricolage and improvisation in association with the reuse (sometimes in limited time) of available (sometimes scarce) resources, including the waste constituted by objects at the end of their life for various reasons (defective, non-repairable function, broken, unobtainable spare part).

The waste to be reused intrinsically poses a problem of a different nature because, even though it is still not very valuable, could this waste be linked to a massive progressive obsolescence?

The term *planned obsolescence* has been used since at least 1932, when a booklet entitled *Ending the Depression through Planned Obsolescence* by B. London was published in the United States. It is, however, especially with the industrial designer B. Stevens (Brooks Stevens Design Associates, BSDA), that the concept of *aesthetic obsolescence* was born in the 1950s in the United States: *to produce attractive goods that can be made obsolete quickly by creating a desire for renewal and change.* Obsolescence is then provoked by inculcating in the buyer the double desire of *always being more recent*, but to get rid of it *a little sooner than necessary*. Thus, A. Sloan, director (1923–1956) of General Motors, in addition to setting up the divisional form of which he was the designer and master builder, with Chandler (1962) later theorizing it, was a precursor by promoting, as early as the 1930s, on the basis of the chassis–engine pair, a range of vehicles *through the bodywork* (by playing on the shape, color and accessories), renewed annually by advertising stimulation. Planned obsolescence through fashion and/or *design* is a fact. However, the contemporary debate on programmed obsolescence is oriented at the societal level on a *conspiracy theory* (Chevassus-au-Louis 2014), with suspicion of planning defects, fragility and shortened life. This vision is distinct from the necessary trade-offs to be made by the industrialist on the power–efficiency–cost triptych of a sold product: a sold product is indeed optimized on functionalities and/or capacities, at a given moment, but will always be overtaken by technological evolution. That said, and this is rarely the case, a product should be repairable. Today, the proposed products are still disposable (possibly recyclable, but rarely designed for their circular reuse).

When it is possible (and it should always be possible), bricolage can be mobilized to repair, in whole or in part, an object and/or to make use of the waste by extracting the necessary spare parts for a reassembly or to assemble an object in a different way to make something else. Waste collection centers are essential in the provision of reuse materials: recycling centers, improvised locally or organized by sector and by volume (on a large scale and by networks in developed countries). Elsewhere (emerging countries (EC), less developed countries (LDC), or poor countries), without social, sanitary and/or environmental concerns, it still seems difficult to develop recycling channels that respect the health of populations and the NE.

Starting to establish a virtuous circle, today and quite late, does not solve the thorny issue of the resorption of the stock of waste piled up, at the global level, on land, underground or in the seas.

7.2.3. *Synthetic view: conceptual map of innovative creation*

To build a conceptual map of innovative creation, we will start from four main axes relevant to innovative bricolage:

– existence of the resource versus new resource;

– temporal constraint, strong or weak, impacting the degree of urgency;

– scarcity (intrinsic availability of a resource), strong or weak;

– degree of creativity: according to the level of creative effort (which is necessarily qualitative).

The first two axes do not call for any particular comments and are intuitively understandable, especially as a quantification can be made.

Scarcity can, in fact, be considered as an adjustable parameter (depending on the resource) that can even admit a binary value (0,1) to signify a change of paradigm due to a sudden change in economic or geopolitical conditions that modifies, from one end to the other, the availability of this resource (crisis, war, industrial catastrophe, natural disaster, etc.).

Creativity is expressed in a variable way, but notably in certain sectors of activity (such as crafts, luxury, fashion), in certain functions (R&D, where inventive design is mobilized), in certain fields, such as research (fundamental or applied) or, even more so, art.

Industrial and commercial creativity – in relation to uses – is situated at a level of intensity that will depend on individual (DIY) and/or collective (DIWO) dynamics, as well as on the issues at stake, hence the dotted ring around the creativity axis (see Figure 7.1). The creativity variable is intrinsically qualitative.

All in all, the intersection of the first two axes can be considered as a robust and relevant typological basis (except in the case of extreme economic situations generating absolute scarcity, and without prejudging the degree of creativity).

Time / Availability	Weak time constraint	Strong time constraint
Existing resources	Bricolage 1 (incremental)	Improvisation 1 (incremental)
New resources	Bricolage 2 technological (radical)	Improvisation 2 (radical)

Table 7.1. *Basic typology (source: author)*

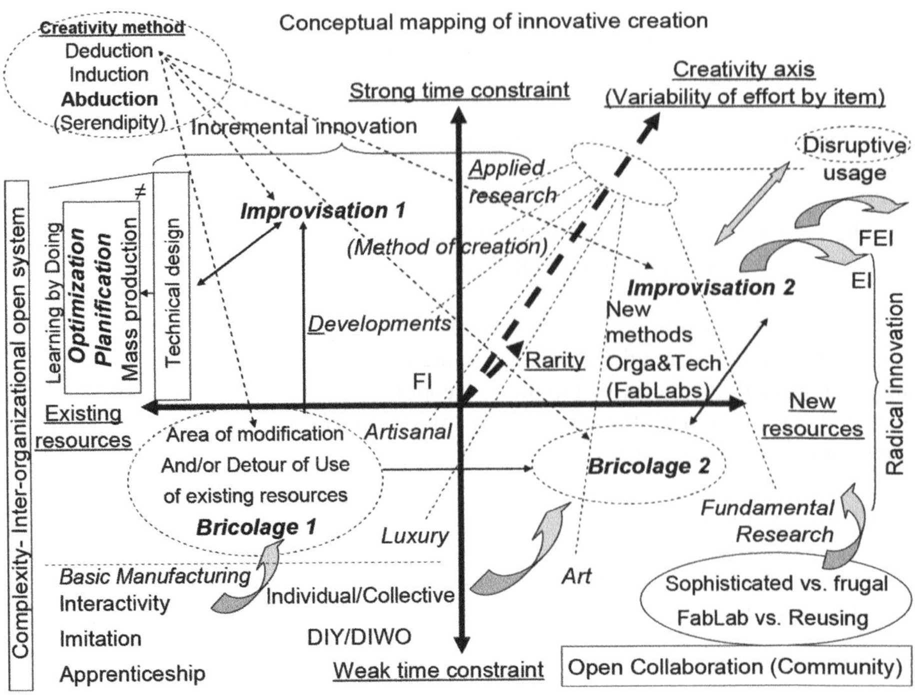

Figure 7.1. *Synthetic diagram (source: author). For a color version of this figure, see http://www.iste.co.uk/bouvier-patron/frugalinnovation.zip*

Intersection of the first two axes makes it possible to establish a typological matrix (Table 7.1) concerning bricolage and improvisation. This then allows us, on this basis, to position scarcity and creativity (Figure 7.1).

From this matrix (in Table 7.1), by projection and superimposition of the qualitative information from the explanatory development (see above), we obtain a conceptual cartography (Figure 7.1), which allows us to visualize the training effects of bricolage and improvisation, as well as to show the salient points of the dynamics of innovative creation up to FEI.

7.3. Conclusion

At the primordial stage, the question arises as to how to take into account the NE with EI or FEI and, respectively, a dividing line of sophistication versus frugality. Indeed, innovation can take place in sophisticated places mobilizing digital technologies, such as 3D printing[5] (within a FabLab or, more broadly, a makerspace and/or an innovation platform), but can also be part of a frugal approach. Therefore, in the first instance, more sober in technology or, more exactly, *mobilizing a satisfactory level of technology: satisficing* in the sense of Simon (1976, 1978).

In this last case of sobriety, innovation can take place in sometimes very rudimentary workshops.

Bricolage (basic and/or technological) is essential in creation (and co-creation), as much for intellectual and/or artistic works as for the conception (and/or co-conception) of artifacts. Bricolage is a necessary practice, from the primitive ages of civilization to modern makers, to search for and find the solution(s) to problems arising in the elaboration of projects and/or objects in an individual or collective setting. Bricolage is inseparable from experimentation during the course of a practice and calls upon intuition, creativity, learning, acquired experience: interactivity, the mobilization of tips and tricks to elaborate, repair and circumvent the use of objects (already existing or invented), therefore with the means at hand, as well as including sophisticated technological means. Bricolage is also a distinct concept, but linked to improvisation. The art of bricolage and/or improvisation exists in every company: from the individual company to the very large company, as

5 As a reminder, three-dimensional (3D) printing is an additive manufacturing method – adding material layer by layer – as opposed to the usual subtractive manufacturing method known in the manufacturing industry since the beginning of the Industrial Revolution, by progressive removal of material or deformation of material. All known 3D printing technologies are based on the formation of the 3D virtual object in successive 2D thin film layers. For a synthetic presentation of the issue, see Berchon (2014) and/or in an economic and managerial re-contextualization, Bouvier-Patron (2014).

well as the start-up. As we have tried to show, the art of bricolage and/or improvisation are two key factors in the dynamics of innovative creation. The synthetic diagram proposed in Figure 7.1 is likely to explain, as well as to open up new research perspectives concerning innovative creation. Moreover, from a certain point of view, bricolage and/or improvisation can be seen as practices that contribute to the reduction of uncertainty. Indeed, if radical uncertainty is inherent to economic activity, the organization is constructed as an uncertainty reducer (Knight 1921), thus enabling nothing less than entrepreneurship.

The *uncertainty-reducing organization* is an essential ontological theoretical orientation of Knight (Bouvier-Patron 1996a) to grasp *the nature of the firm*.

The reduction of uncertainty is indispensable to decision-making and to the realization of economic and commercial activities; by extension, the processes involved in organizational dynamics, essentially those of an informal nature, because they are flexible and adaptive, and relying in particular on bricolage and improvisation (and less so on formal instituted procedures), serve to promote lateral coordination and the realization of complex tasks indispensable to design and innovation.

Moreover, as corporate social responsibility (CSR) and the manager's responsibility (Bowen 1953) are now at the heart of the strategy, any internal initiative or need in this direction is more easily legitimized.

Bricolage and/or improvisation are practices that are used because they are indispensable in the functioning of a human organization, as well as doubly useful because they are particularly adapted to an approach that is compatible with CSR and to reduce the impact on the NE.

The central issue is the choice of a *satisfactory technological level* that is part of a consequentist approach leading to the FEI.

Let us recall that the *consequentist approach* can be defined as *taking into account* ex ante *in the design, the foreseeable consequences of the production and/or use of a good on the NE: it is thus to act economically without generating, consciously* ex ante *and/or without imputations, harmful* ex post *effects on the NE*. Consequently, innovative bricolage (and/or improvisation) is consistent with a consequentist approach (see Bouvier-Patron (2015a) and Chapter 1 and Appendix 2 of this book) insofar as making do with the means at hand, and even the scarcity of resources, to find clever solutions (within a given time frame or not), first denotes a respectful mastery of materials and/or tools and then ensures the avoidance of possible waste and scrap, as well as the potential elimination of any impact on the NE. The approach to do this is important and must mobilize a *satisfactory level of technology*. Frugality is an appropriate path if it takes the form of FEI (see Chapters 5 and 6, referring to back the PPG concept in Chapter 1).

Such a consideration of the NE then obviously implies the integration of the complete life cycle (both materials or inputs and artifacts to be realized) from the design upstream (*ex ante*), starting with bio-sourced elements (even if derived from recycling).

Conclusion

Taking into account the Natural Environment (NE) is nowadays essential to innovate. Innovation that respects the NE has environmental innovation (EI) as its primary target. EI can be achieved through technology or through frugality. In the perspective we have proposed, it can be EI but with a weighted degree of technological sophistication. In fact, there are two possible ways to innovate.

Thus, in a logic of high sophistication, the FabLab is an interesting option: it is a technical-organizational place open to makers and/or hackers allowing permanent interactions, within communities of practice whose members are passionate, combining decentralized expertise and mobilizing ICT and DT. The FabLab, in itself, can appear as a certain way of considering frugality. However, since technological hubris leads to a race to the front in terms of marketing value creation, it invites us to reflect on the *satisfactory technological level* and on a frugal approach to IE. But frugality is not enough in itself. A specific frugal approach is needed: one that is compatible with the respect of the NE. Hence, we propose the concept of *frugal environmental innovation* (FEI) in line with a *consequentist* approach and generating *positive private goods* (PPG).

From the point of view of innovative creation (of which a conceptual map is presented, see Figure 7.1), what prevails at a high degree of sophistication exists at least as much at a lower degree of sophistication. Thus, bricolage and improvisation are more naturally mobilized in a frugal approach, but these two dynamic springs of innovative creation are at play whatever the type of innovation.

To conclude this analysis, let us summarize the seven chapters of this book.

Chapter 1 explains in detail the constraint of taking into account the NE as a challenge to be met by the company through the concept of *positive private good* in a *consequentist approach.*

Chapter 2 focuses on the design by sophisticated technological means: those of the FabLab allowing *a priori* to rise to the level of the challenge. The technological ambition is the usual solution in the West. Moreover, the importance of bricolage and improvisation, in an underlying way, is already revealed here.

Chapter 3 consciously explores the technological orientation by focusing on the *communitization of innovation* (upstream through communities of practice and downstream through communities of use) and the *creation of value*. This leads to a shift towards symbolic value.

Chapter 4 examines more precisely the consequences of sophistication through technological excess at the perceptible level of use (but therefore also, consequently, of the upstream offer). Here again, bricolage and improvisation (starting with technological objects among hackers, then geeks and, ultimately, for everyone) respond to a claim of self-affirmation through marking. The techno-marketing that makes this possible relies on technical factors of emergence: places of creation; interactions between creative milieus (including through informal and links to artistic universes); socialization through online gaming (with the societal importance of gaming); means of virtualization of entities (including ourselves through the avatar); objects, symbols, values, and available tools (smartphone and/or laptop). All this is connected to the social networks that now structure the technologized social life or the development of digital by the Cloud of Big Data (feeding the Deep Learning of AI). AI opens, moreover, a spectrum of new possibilities for marketing, such as the virtual influencer. Nevertheless, the more technology structures social life, the more we witness appropriations and/or detour showing that bricolage and improvisation are key springs that manifest themselves both at the level of creation and use. In spite of this salient fact, all of these considerations generate a technological excess and lead to pleading for a counter-model.

Chapter 5 invites a return to common sense and puts forward the alternative of frugality as a possible path to a solution that can achieve positive private goods (PPGs). This is characterized by an orientation of the analysis on the concept of frugal environmental innovation (FEI), because frugality alone does not lead, intrinsically, to the consideration of the NE.

Chapter 6 reinforces the previous point by showing, among the environmental innovations (EI) – often mobilizing a high technological orientation – the importance of the FEI as a possible strategy of enterprise mobilizing an adapted technological degree in a path most likely to lead to a viable solution and coherent with a consequentist approach.

Chapter 7 intends to make explicit the key role of bricolage and improvisation as the mainsprings of innovative creation in general: this makes it possible to draw up a conceptual map of innovative creation. In short, bricolage and improvisation are consubstantial to the frugal approach and, in particular, to a frugal innovation respectful of the NE, called frugal environmental innovation (FEI).

Innovation (whatever the technological degree) is an interesting possibility for the company if it chooses the appropriate organizational modalities, but its planning (except in certain special cases) is almost impossible. The essential key to innovative creation lies in bricolage and improvisation. Moreover, technological hubris, with its sophistication, significant R&D costs and consequences in terms of use, reinforces the need to reflect on the appropriate technological level, which can be measured with the frugal approach. Bricolage and improvisation are required in any case (even with a high level of sophistication) but the specific form of frugality compatible with the consideration of the NE, the FEI, is the way suggested here in a consequentist approach. Bricolage and improvisation put resourcefulness and serendipity back at the heart of the analysis (independently of the level of sophistication and/or the investments made). This leads to a more global reflection on organizational functioning (in its complexity and dynamics) as well as on the use of technology. Furthermore, consequentism brings into question and transcends the *precautionary/preventive* opposition (see Kast (2003) on this opposition): it is not a question of orienting ourselves towards one or the other but, simply, of considering the activities of companies as they exist and claiming the necessity of taking into account the consequences of these activities in the calculation of profitability in order to allow for the commensurability of choices (of purchase, of use, of production, of investment, of technological option) by encouraging the realization of PPG.

Appendices

Appendix 1

Informal Barrier to Mobility

The contract between partners is based on the principle of mutual benefit without preventing a possible deviation (always possible in a framework of radical uncertainty), hence the proposed concept of an *informal barrier to mobility*. In line with the work on the concept of *plan* by Selten (1978) and Van Damme (1989), which is based on Kohlberg and Mertens (1986), the aim is to deal with the question of the collective strategy of actors in the inter-organizational sphere. The challenge, beyond the proposal of a formalization, is to operationalize a discourse. In the network perspective (mentioned in Chapter 2), the aim here is to characterize the behaviors of three actors (in double-sourcing supply: with one client and two suppliers) during coordination in the game: will the actors converge towards the initially designated partnership solution or deviate from this negotiated solution? Thus, from coordination generating trust, the trust established allows cooperation to continue (with or without taking into account an external opportunity, sometimes leading to a concerted exit). Within this framework, there are many reasons for deviation, including self-interest, voluntary failure (or opportunism) and involuntary failure. The issue of deviation is distinct from that of opportunism. This variety of behavior is linked to the introduction of two distinct types of hazard: the appearance of new information (major hazard or uncertainty); the effective capacity of supplier 2 to replace supplier 1 (probabilistic hazard).

In other words, despite a partnership relationship, mobility is possible. Only the *informal barrier to mobility*, established in a particular case of deviation, preserves the collective strategy (an idea captured during formalization by ε).

We will first present the concepts (section A1.1) before proposing a qualitative model (based on game theory at the level of formalization but proposing a resolution that does not resemble the usual methodology and procedures) (section A1.2) and, finally, engaging in a discussion of the game's solutions and opening the analysis to the transition from the relationship to the network (section A1.3).

A1.1. Conceptual presentation: partnership and contract

For Farrell and Scotchmer (1988), *partnership* corresponds to equality, in the sharing of the result, between members with complementary activities, and this even when there is inequality in the contribution of each (because what matters is the obtaining of the result while each of the actors is indispensable for the obtaining of it). On this basis, we propose a definition, consistent with the previous one, but more specific. Thus, with the aim of realizing a common product, the industrial partnership consists, after negotiation, of the inception of a mutually advantageous long-term contractual relation and not accompanied by *property rights* between actors having complementary activities[1]; *complementary activities* by opposition to *similar activities* in Richardson's (1972) terminology.

Complementarity of one activity with respect to another (or others) simply means that the first activity is required at the same time as the second to produce a given product. We will thus examine the *relational quality of the contract* (section A1.1.1), the *proposed solution concept* (section A1.1.2) and then *double sourcing with a leader premium* (section A1.1.3).

A1.1.1. *Quality of the contractual relationship*

Partnership is at least as much a theoretical concept as a concrete practice, which is tending to become widespread within the industrial organization of western economies. The new practices linked to the partnership approach can be analyzed as responses to *Japanese-style* conceptions of production organization methods (Aoki 1986, 1988); the objective being, for both, in an uncertain framework, to promote product quality while reducing their cost. It is easy to understand that this perspective must be extended to the whole chain of actors who participate in the manufacture of this product: i.e. also to the suppliers of the client firm who wish to develop a product. Considering the required competencies distributed between several suppliers, the co-design of a product is essential with the partnership: we seek henceforth to integrate, at the level of the co-design of the product, a form of

1 Let us recall the analytical definition given by Hart and Moore (1990, p. 1135): "Two assets a_m and a_n are strictly complementary if they are unproductive unless they are used together". If we replace *asset* by *competency*, we come back to a key idea in the argument, namely the replaceability, or not, of a competency. What is not replaceable is indispensable. This raises the question of the coordination of indispensable competencies: we arrive at the complementarity of competencies in the sense of Richardson (1972). Hart and Moore (1990) focus on the concept of replaceability (*dispensability*), which applies to an agent with respect to an *asset* but not to an *asset* with respect to another *asset*. The reason for this is that, for Hart and Moore (1990), it allows us to distinguish a productive structure composed of *asset*(s) with individuals who are, or are not, replaceable from the point of view of access to these *asset*(s).

rationalization *ex ante*, which will make it possible to eliminate costs, of various natures, at the level of the production, the assembly, the quality control, the sale and the after-sales (or consequences on the NE). As we have already pointed out, partnership is explained by the need to coordinate complementary competencies in an uncertain world (Knight 1921). This is increasingly true for more and more complex products (hence the importance of design). The mimetism of competitive strategic behavior accelerates the trend. Organizational innovation (here inter-organizational) induced by technological innovation requiring complex distributed competencies induces a constant mobilization of partners and an association, in the long term, to make the efforts made profitable concerning material investments as well as immaterial investments: the committed relationship has a cost that is measured first of all by the quality of the construction of the relationship and by the appreciation of the cost generated by the loss of the established relationship. Thus, the partnership is based as much on the initial negotiation phase (where a *plan of action* is set up to establish a collective strategy) as on the coordination phase (in order to achieve this *plan*).

A1.1.2. *Plan concept and focal point solution*

The behavior (of the actors involved in such a process) is naturally fundamental. Given the fact that the actors considered do not evolve in a fixed universe, we will try to determine under which conditions the deviation of the *plan*[2] can participate, or not, in the collective strategy of the linked partners.

The analysis of deviation has been the subject of considerable development in game theory since the formalization of the Nash equilibrium (1951), which is, in fact, the mathematical generalization, through axiomatics, of the solution proposed to the duopoly by Cournot (1838): Nash equilibrium is precisely *a solution of a game where, this point being reached, no unilateral deviation of a player allows access to a better gain* (this type of equilibrium where none of the players has an interest in deviating unilaterally is said to be *self-enforcing*). The central issue here is the sensitivity to unilateral deviations as soon as the rational player perceives that they have the possibility of taking a unilateral action that would allow them to obtain a better payoff. By the same token, no stable equilibrium can be selected as long as a player has an interest in deviating.

It is the constraints on behavior, the procedures for solving the games or the game framework itself that allow us to propose concepts for selecting a particular type of solution. At the same time, the selected equilibrium is therefore an

2 The concept of *plan* used here is basically inspired by Van Damme (1989) and thus mobilizes the concept of *forward induction* of Kohlberg and Mertens (1986).

equilibrium from a certain point of view: the analysis of the "credibility" of threats in a game is furthermore revealing of this (Tirole 1983). Taking into account *sequential games* has only led to a multiplication of the number of possible solutions (even though considerable research has been carried out to try to resolve the question following Kreps and Wilson (1982b)).

The reasons for selecting an *ex ante* equilibrium are in fact based on very mixed arguments. Among other things, it is worth emphasizing the influence of several important factors: the sensitivity of actors' judgments to *contextual conditions* (this analysis has very old roots, see Zeuthen (1933)); the importance of the *common culture* between actors (Schelling 1956, 1960); and also the dependence of the actors' common past on the present outcomes through a phenomenon of *reputation* (Selten 1978; Kreps and Wilson 1982a; Axelrod 1984; Kreps 1990). Moreover, in support of the idea of *ex ante* equilibrium selection, *common-interest* games have the distinction of having a Nash equilibrium designated *ex ante* by the players and preferred, by all, to any other Nash equilibrium in the game. However, even more important is the consideration of the possibility for each player to form plans in order to influence others and reach a (best) private (Selten 1978) or collective goal: in the latter case, either by negotiating a common outcome beforehand to avoid a conflict with disastrous consequences for the (opposing) parties (Moulin 1981, 1984); or, even more significantly, when there is an *a priori* advantage in negotiating and then coordinating individual behaviors in order to select the *most satisfactory collective equilibrium* for each of the parties (Van Damme (1989), by mobilizing Simon's satisficing) without preventing any possible deviation.

A1.1.2.1. *Practical functioning of the plan*

The concept of a plan is characterized by a multiplayer game whose successive actions are coordinated, first *ex ante*, by a consultation before the game (preplay phase of negotiation: this makes it possible, in particular, to make explicit the common objective or *focal point* (see below), the rules and the possible outcomes), and then, during the course of the game (intraplay phase), by sending *signals* between the players in the form of an *irreversible temporal action towards a node of the game*. The argument is legitimate in the following way: in order to reach a certain node in the game, a sequence from the beginning of the game must have led to that node (Kohlberg and Mertens 1986).

Kohlberg and Mertens (1986) illustrate the nature of the *signal* sent: it consists of the renunciation of a certain individual gain in order to collectively obtain a higher (but hypothetical) gain for each of the players. It is the interpretation of this signal by the other players that will lead to a better solution for all.

In a game with two players, the first player tries to confront the second player with a *fait accompli* (or self-commitment) in order to push the latter to understand the benefits of opting for a collectively advantageous solution. The issue at stake will then be the credibility of the action of implementing this *fait accompli*.

– In the first stage, during the negotiation phase, the first player exposes to the second player the advantages of coordinating towards a certain solution (and the possible alteration of the relationship resulting from a deviation).

– In the second stage, the first player sends a signal to the second player: the second player can consider whether or not to respond favorably to the first player. Deviating here is voluntary and the signal is not the result of an error but a deliberate act (Kohlberg and Mertens 1986). Deviating symmetrically places the other in front of a *fait accompli* (for the benefit of the community or for their own satisfaction).

All in all, communication (possible before the game) is thus reestablished during the game by sending signals between the players.

The existence and analysis of signals reveal how each player follows what was planned during the negotiation phase. In particular, the respect of the initial commitments allows the convergence towards the solution desired by the players during the preplay phase.

It must be emphasized that the desire to reach the same unique solution is expressed before the game and that the realization of this solution depends exclusively on the interest that each player has in obtaining this solution.

The establishment of a negotiation before the game, on the basis of the mutual advantage and the free adhesion of each of the players, makes it possible to designate a *point of rendez-vous* or *focal point* (Schelling 1956, 1960), which will be reached except if a deviation proves to be more advantageous for at least one of the players. Indeed, because of the radical uncertainty, the general context can change, and, if it is going to be imposed on all, the perception of each one can differ. At any moment, depending on the radical uncertainty, a player may leave the relationship (momentarily or permanently) if they feel that it is no longer in their interest. Thus, a partnership relationship must in fact reconcile two *a priori* contradictory elements: relational stability over time (which favors learning between two or more actors) and potential deviation. Stability cannot prevent each of the actors from changing strategy if a new situation requires it. In the problem we are considering, the stability of an equilibrium designated *ex ante* can only be threatened by the deviation of one of the players.

In addition, as the partnership must be a freely consented relationship, it is excluded that restrictive means of surveillance are authoritatively implemented by one of the parties. This does not prevent rules and procedures from being negotiated jointly to indicate what is involved and the consequences that follow. Mutual benefit appears to be the best guarantee against deviation. However, this guarantee cannot constitute an optimal insurance because nothing can prevent a player from deviating (except their own interest) according to the radical uncertainty that prevails.

Moreover, anticipating everything *ex ante* seems difficult unless individual behavior is extraordinarily constrained (which does not prevent us from considering the foreseeable consequences without necessarily being able to give to them a probability to occur). Fines/penalties negotiated *ex ante* between private actors, and imposed on the effective deviant player, can only play a secondary role: firstly, because a fine will never be a deterrent if a player really wants to deviate; secondly, because a partnership relationship where coercive actions predominate is no longer a partnership relationship.

The partnership must be entered into while accepting the possibility of a deviation: a deviation that can later only be subsequently sanctioned under certain conditions, especially if it can lead to a collective benefit.

The point of view developed here is not shared in analyses such as that of Abreu et al. (1991), which refer to the principal–agent theory: which is out of scope (see the Introduction) for dealing with the partnership question and/or, moreover, many other contractual situations.

A1.1.2.2. *Nature of the equilibrium sought: the focal point*

According to Schelling (1960), the *focal point*, selected by the actors (without prior negotiation but based solely on their *common culture*), must allow for the coordination of actions: as such, there would be an endogenous procedure for convergence towards an equilibrium without this procedure being made explicit by the actors concerned.

The *focal point* is sensitive to the conditions of place and time, as well as to the common knowledge shared between the actors: the selection of an equilibrium thus depends strongly on a phenomenon of contextualization. *Contextualization* is a set of information (generally qualitative in nature), outside of the payoff matrix, which, by combining the two, makes sense of the decision by informing each player's choice of action.

If the degree of common knowledge about this context shared between the two players makes it possible for actions to converge (Schelling 1960), this convergence can be made even more certain by allowing for negotiation during a pregame phase (or preplay). There is then an elaboration of a code (Crémer 1990) between players that is specific to them (a code that is not independent of the common knowledge, particularly concerning the general principles to be respected).

A solution explicitly elaborated during the preliminary negotiation phase, and dependent on coordination during the game, is only a sophistication of Schelling's concept of *focal point*.

The definition to be retained is the following: the *focal point* results from the designation, thanks to a *common culture* of the players (implicit and/or explicit), of a solution before the beginning of the game, with these players showing that they intend to meet at a given *rendez-vous* point (solution related/linked to the satisficing of Simon (1976, 1978), see Bouvier-Patron (1998a)).

Concerning double-sourcing procurement, we can refer to Anton and Yao (1987), Demski et al. (1987), Farrell and Gallini (1988) and, for a critical view, Riordan and Sappington (1989). However, with the exception of Farrell and Gallini (1988), the authors cited situate the problem in the case of public market procurement.

The additional transaction costs generated by having two suppliers nevertheless allow the buyer to protect themself against two levels of risk: the immediate risk (first level of risk) of opportunism and/or involuntary failure of one of the two suppliers, and the second level of risk (linked to the first) consisting of having to call upon (i.e. find, select and negotiate), at the last moment, a new supplier (if the one chosen *a priori* does not honor, voluntarily or involuntarily, its commitments).

This cost of changing supplier(s) *ex post* (or *switching costs*) is important in the sense that it expresses the waste of resources necessary to compensate for the absence of a minimal insurance (via the initial implementation of the double-sourcing principle) taken by the buyer *ex ante*. However, it is clear that such insurance cannot cover the risk of opportunism or the simultaneous involuntary failure of both suppliers: but it can be estimated, on the one hand, that the probability of such an event is relatively low and, on the other hand, that, basically, economic activity is risky and that it is up to the buyer to take out insurance compatible with the level of risk they believe they are incurring (if the security of their supply is priceless and their financial resources are high, they can always buy a priority privilege at full price). However, if they have the choice, the buyer can/should select at least two competent suppliers per supply market.

What is decisive for the partnership is not so much the instantaneous efficiency (i.e. in terms of price, costs, competition of supply and services offered) as the quality of the link between two actors in the long term. The problem of the contract as a barrier to entry has been raised by other authors (Aghion and Bolton 1987).

Basically, the establishment of a partnership depends on the trust of individual A towards individual B and vice versa (Breton and Wintrobe 1982): *trust is individual*

A's belief in the respect at t1 of the commitment initially made at t0 by individual B (and vice versa). Trust between partners is an essential key to building a good relationship between them.

This trust cannot exist when the client is authoritarian.

Furthermore, trust can also be altered or destroyed if one or the other of the suppliers (in the case of double sourcing) fails (involuntarily by overestimating its capacities or voluntarily by opportunism).

However, without destroying confidence, it is quite essential to be able to take into account new information linked to *radical uncertainty* (Knight 1921) and, consequently, any possible deviation is feasible and must be anticipated as much as possible.

Will this possible deviation, when it occurs, ultimately destroy trust? Our answer is negative if the concept of an *informal mobility barrier* (a distant extension of the *mobility barrier* concept of Caves and Porter (1977)) applies. The *informal mobility barrier makes it possible to characterize a situation where a collective strategy is negotiated, in an initial period, and where the coordination of the actors is effective even though a deviation has occurred but without deteriorating the partnership* (see solution VIII of the game).

More generally, in this partnership framework, the potential mobility of the actors is preserved even though a stable, but not binding, link is established between these same actors.

A1.1.3. *Contractual relationship and double sourcing*

The economic objective, from the point of view of a firm (called the client firm), will consist here of realizing a product based on the combination of several required components, all of these components being of different competencies not available within the same firm.

The necessary components, not available internally, will have to be obtained through procurement from suppliers. We assume, for simplicity, that each supplier sells only one of the necessary components and only needs one competency (to make that component).

As regards the possible vertical integration of a supplier, the explanation generally adopted is that the client firm makes its decision on the basis of the minimization of its costs by appreciating the cost of vertical integration compared to the cost of contracting with the supplier according to the classic trade-off introduced by Coase (1937) between *make and/or buy*. If we admit, for the sake of convenience, that this transactional approach is indeed the one that is relevant at first reading, the decision of the potentially integrating client firm must above all take into account its effective capacity to carry out the component after internalization (obtained initially thanks to the supplier) at a more advantageous cost. We will make the (very realistic) assumption here that the competency required to develop this component, held by the supplier, is too difficult for the integrating client to appropriate (even though the latter had the financial means for such an operation).

All in all, integration, at a prohibitive cost (given the competencies to be acquired), would be accompanied here, in addition, by a realization cost much higher than that of the market. Thus, the cost of vertical integration is too high and the client prefers to continue the contractual relationship with its supplier.

In fact, this limit of vertical integration (which we do not want to go into here) lies essentially in the impossibility for the client to circumvent the *bargaining power* of the supplier, based on the high level of competency held (Asanuma 1989) and the difficulty of replacing it (Bouvier-Patron 1994a, 1995, 1998b, 2002, 2011a, 2013, 2017a). Competency is then untransferable or strongly altered in the case of vertical integration, even at the cost of a dizzying increase in costs for the acquirer. In this case, the best solution is to set up a contractual relationship called industrial partnership.

The client firm needs, if possible, several suppliers for the same type of supply and is bound to each of its suppliers by a contract in a bilateral relationship.

What will matter now is the type of supply: double sourcing offers the best alternative.

The client buys from two suppliers or *double-sourcing* procurement (Farrell and Gallini 1988) for the same type of supply. The additional finesse consists of a particular rule known as *double sourcing* with *leader premium* (where, for example, the first supplier has 75% of the supply market and the second supplier has 25%).

Double-sourcing procurement is used to provide greater security of supply than single-source procurement. Double sourcing is also a practice that allows for an elaborate supply strategy, such as alternating, in an agreed-upon manner, the leadership of the business volume to be achieved (at *t0*, supplier 1 achieves 75% of the market and, at *t1*, this role is taken over by supplier 2).

There is thus a periodic change of role between supplier 1 and supplier 2, which stimulates them and maintains an equal status between them. In reality, practitioners developing client–supplier contracts are well aware of the importance of creating incentive mechanisms to favor emulation, limit dependency and keep the relationship attractive to all partners.

This general thinking on double-sourcing procurement can also be specifically adapted.

For very complex and rare products, the principle of double-sourcing procurement can be introduced at a very early stage and only at the design stage of a component in order to create initial emulation and to allow the client to select the only supplier (who will therefore design and produce the component concerned). Here, the cost of the design is such that there is no question of making one or more prototypes per component. Only the design plan proposed by the selected supplier will be binding and constitutes the reference document for the production phase. This said, the supplier is selected for a certain period of time (which can be set as equivalent to the coverage of its *sunk costs*: Baumol and Willig (1981)). In the end, the client can either continue with the same supplier or issue a new invitation to tender. The competency and the reputation effect of the supplier are not to be neglected: in the case of civil aircraft, for example, it should not be neglected that if the implementation cost is high, the life of an aircraft is about 30 years and the supplier retained on a component with high value will thus have a real interest in *keeping its place*. For the assembly of complex products, the practice of *double sourcing* at a very early stage (with periodic review) is preferable to *single sourcing*.

Thus, the practice of *double sourcing* is adaptable to almost any situation, but also offers great security against voluntary behavioral drifts or poorly controlled or uncontrollable contingencies.

It is therefore the exception (presence of a monopoly) or the technical choice (flow control) that determines the use of a *single-source* practice, as *double sourcing*, for all or part of the production stages of a product and/or the components of this same product, offers all the advantages (*quality*[3], *economies of scale* and/or

3 There is a line of American–Japanese influence on quality and flow management since the 1950s (W. Deming, *Plan Do Check Act*; J. Juran, *improvement through quality and cost of non-quality*; A. Feigenbaum, *Total Quality Control*; T. Ohno, synthesizing the contributions of KanBan at Toyota). Building on this foundation, Womack and Jones (1990, 1996) propose *lean management*, which is based on five principles: 1) identify the client's needs; 2) identify the value chain (value-creating stages); 3) optimize flows and eliminate losses; 4) control from the bottom up; 5) continuous improvement and employee involvement via *total quality management*. From a flow optimization perspective (minimizing inventories and *just-in-time* supply), for the production of a final product, the main justification for choosing *single sourcing* is the possibility of controlling flows and benefiting from a return, in terms of cost, due to the *economies of scale* obtained by the sole (and/or *leader*) supplier. However, such a result is also available in *double sourcing*.

learning effects of Arrow (1962b)), and this, especially when a leader who carries out 75% of the supply and for a comparative cost is designated, which, all things considered, is not higher than that of the single source with its supposed returns.

A1.2. The qualitative model

The model (see Figure A1.1) illustrates the pattern of a negotiation between potential partners in a noncooperative game setting. The explanation provided here refers to the game tree (the outcomes, measured in payoffs). The objective is simply to consider the behavior of the players in the partnership context just presented. We thus have a client and two suppliers, i.e. three players.

The client and the suppliers seek to set up a mutually advantageous association with a view to pursuing a long-term partnership. As a result, a collective strategy is negotiated *ex ante* (a *plan* of action is then constructed) ensuring the selection of a specific solution, called the coordination solution (or *focal point* (Schelling 1960)), but the coordination is only effective if this solution is actually selected, as the plan can and should provide for other eventualities. Each of the players individually maximizes their gains. This allows a player to select a solution outside the collective plan of action defined during the preliminary negotiation.

We can represent the strategic action of this contextualization of the *partnership with double sourcing and leader premium* (i.e. three players: a client and two suppliers selected for their competencies, but one of the two is the leader) in the form of a sequential game with the challenge of finding a *focal point* within the framework of the realization of a plan discussed collectively and reflecting the strategic possibilities given new information. This new information includes the existence of radical uncertainty (as is the case in business life), which is not probabilizable but relates to a value that can be interpreted by the players and that they cannot know in advance.

The proposed modeling is qualitative in that the objective is not to proceed to the calculation and selection of equilibria (as would be indicated by the usual methods of resolution), but is based on the articulation of several principles (*forward induction* (Kohlberg and Mertens 1986), *focal point* (Schelling 1960), *plan* (Selten 1978; Van Damme 1989)) allowing to render, as well as possible, the life of the business and the dynamics of change inherent in it.

The game tree is shown in Figure A1.1.

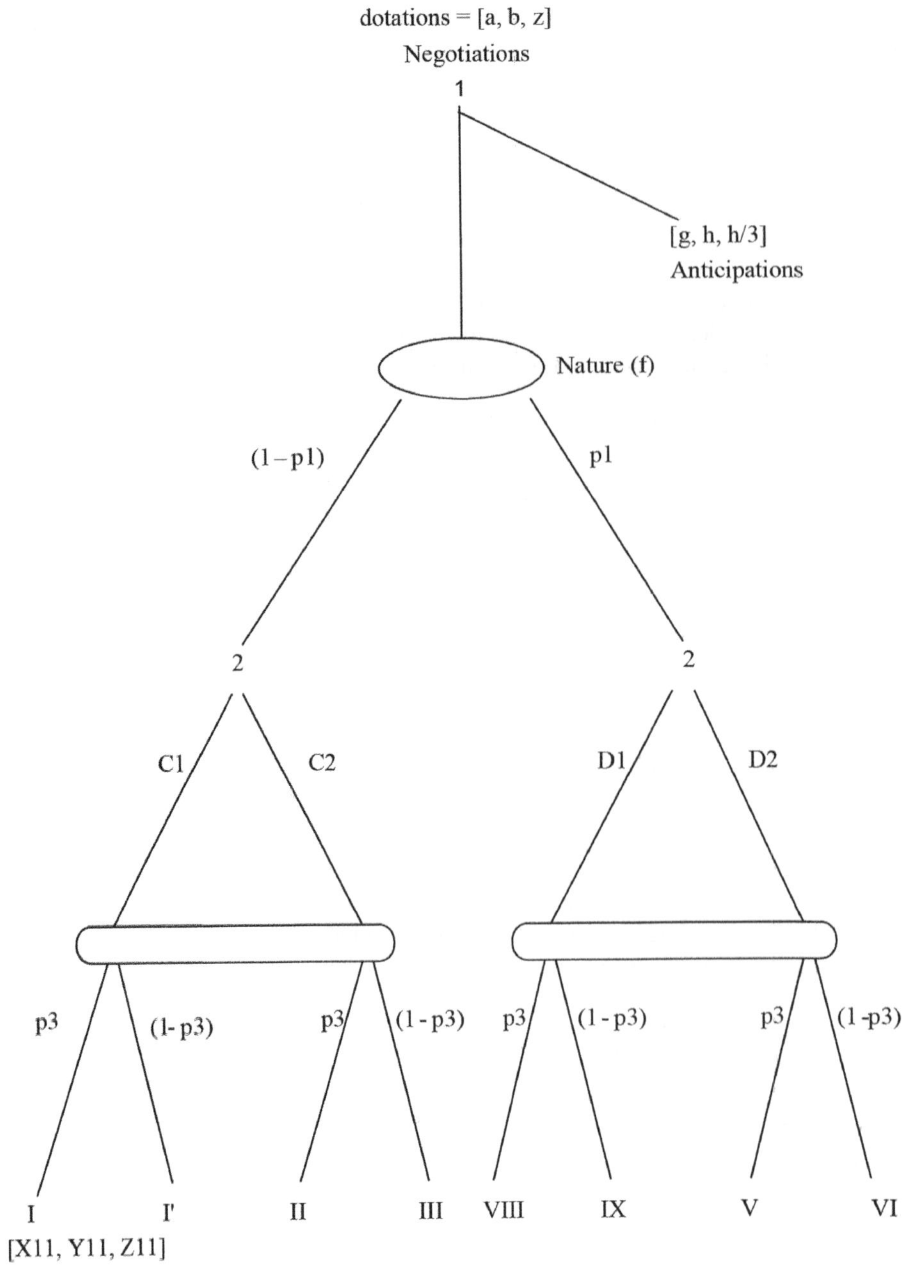

Figure A1.1. *Game tree (source: author 2014)*

The possible solutions are formulated below:

[I] = [X11, Y11, Z11]

[I’] = [I]

[II] = [X11, 0, Y11 + Z11]

[III] = [X11 – (|*f* – Y11|), Y11 + (|*f* – Y11|), Z11]

[V] = [X11,*f*,Y11 + Z11]

[VI] = [1/4 X11, *f*, Z11]

[VIII] = [X11 + (1/2 (|*f* – Y11|)), *f* – (1/2 (|*f* – Y11|)) + ε, Y11 + Z11)]

[IX] = [1/4 X11 + (1/2 (|*f* – Y11|)), *f* – (1/2 (|*f* – Y11|)) + ε, Z11)]

Or by indicating the qualitative translation:

– **Non-deviation (1 – p2):**

Cooperation (*focal point*) [I] = [X11, Y11, Z11]

Cooperation / 3 failing [I’] = [I]

Opportunism / bad bet [II] = [X11, 0, Y11 + Z11]

Opportunism / good bet [III] = [X11 – (|*f* – Y11|), Y11 + (|*f* – Y11|), Z11] (2 requires the bonus)

– **Deviation (p2):**

Individualist / 3 capable [V] = [X11, *f*, Y11 + Z11]

Individualist / 3 failing [VI] = [1/4 X11, *f*, Z11]

Concerted / 3 capable:

[VIII] = [X11 + 1/2 (|*f* – Y11|), *f* – 1/2 (|*f* – Y11| + ε), Y11 + Z11)]

Concerted / 3 failing: [IX] = [1/4 X11 + 1/2 (|*f* – Y11|), *f* – (1/2 |*f* – Y11| + ε), Z11)]

The game can be repeated and this perspective is integrated into the players’ reasoning (the number of repetitions not being known by the players in the same way as the future in terms of finality is not conceivable).

Therefore, in the case of repetition, *reputation* is essential (Selten 1978; Kreps and Wilson 1982a): it is based on the memorization of past actions as shown experimentally by Axelrod (1984).

The different possible solutions of the game (I, I', II, III, V, VI, VIII and IX) are viewed in relation to the initially negotiated coordination solution (i.e. I) and given the opportunity f offered to player 2. The value f is a random exogenous variable (determined by nature).

The first solution I, constituted by the triplet [X11, Y11, Z11] (corresponding to the payoffs, respectively, of players 1, 2 and 3), is based on the hypothesis of the doubling of the initial assets (of these players) that are going to be involved in the association.

Now, since the initial assets are given by the triplet [a, b, z] (respectively, for players 1, 2 and 3), we have: X11 = 2a, Y11 = 2b and Z11 = 2z:

[a, b, z] = [12, 12, 4], or [X11, Y11, Z11] = [24, 24, 8]

with p1 = 0.5 and p3 = 0.5 and the values of f:

– for f > Y11: f = 18 and f = 22;

– for f < Y11: f = 42, f = 50 and f = 60.

Knowing f = 42, the value allowing 1 to gain at least as much as 3 in case of a successful deviation:

	f = 18	f = 22	f = 30	**f = 42**	f = 50	f = 60
[I]	[24,24,8]	[24,24,8]	[24,24,8]	...	[24,24,8]	...
[II]	[24,0,32]	[24,0,32]	[24,0,32]	...	[24,0,32]	...
[III]	[18,30,8]	[22,26,8]	[18,30,8]	...	[-2,50,8]	...
[V]	[24,18,32]	[24,22,32]	[24,30,32]	...	[24, 50,32]	...
[VI]	[6, 18, 8]	[6, 22, 8]	[6, 30, 8]	...	[6, 50, 8]	...
[VIII]	[27,18+ε,32]	[25,22+ε,32]	[27,30+ε,32]	**[33,42+ε,32]**	[37,50+ε,32]	[42,60+ε,32]
[IX]	[9, 18, 8]	[7, 22, 8]	[9, 30, 8]	[15,42, 8]	[19, 50, 8]	[24, 60, 8]

The respective strategy of each player is as follows.

– **Player 1:** given that we admit that g < X11 and, moreover, g < 1/4(X11) (i.e. the value of g is even less than the worst solution of the game for player 1), then player 1 cooperates and runs the game (hoping to get at least X11).

– **Player 2:**

- if they are a non-deviant type, player 2's interest in opportunism[4] is tempered by the nullity of gains that this may entail if they choose such a strategy; so they will rather cooperate in all loyalty by playing C1 which gives, on average, between I and I', a better result compared to the opportunistic temptation (an average of between II and III);

- if they are of a deviant type, then the interest of player 2 in an individualistic exit by playing D2 is tempered by possible negative consequences in the long run.

Knowing that $\varepsilon = 1/2(|f - Y11|)$, the cost of an irrevocable decision on their side is too high and the preference is for a collective strategy: player 2 can expect from maintaining the association a satisfaction at least equivalent to that provided by the individualistic deviation strategy. This satisfaction is measured by ε.

Under this hypothesis, which we retain, player 2 will therefore choose D1 (i.e. the alternative VIII versus IX rather than V versus VI).

Thus, if they are a deviant type, because of the fear of regretting the deterioration of the partnership in the long run (roughly estimated by the value $\varepsilon \geq 1/2(|f - Y11|)$, the cost of an irrevocable exit is too high in a long-run projection and, strategically, not being selfish may be more advantageous (implying the choice of a concerted deviation D1): D1 > D2.

– **Player 3:** as for player 3, their fate improves when they are able to replace player 2 (which corresponds to solutions II, V and VIII); the situation of deviation is preferable to that of non-deviation because the average of their gains is 8 (knowing C1) while it increases to 20 (knowing D1).

The results obtained are presented below.

If we take into account the fact that, for convenience, in this sequential coordination game with radical uncertainty, only player 2 is active and seeks to maximize their payoffs.

– When $Y11 = f$, the equilibrium of the game is solution I. This is the solution initially anticipated (player 2 gets 24, player 1 also gets 24 and player 3 gets 8): the plan is respected. The anticipation is based on a stable convention that allows, in a way, to predict the future.

– When $f > Y11$, the equilibrium of the game is given by solution VIII. The plan is also respected in the sense that player 1, who can do nothing about player 2's deviation,

4 Note also that when player 2 does not deviate, player 1 tolerates player 2's opportunism if $X11 - |f - Y11| > 1/4(X11)$ or, in any case, as long as they can still afford it (i.e. $X11 - |f - Y11| = 0$).

does expect player 2, as in the case mentioned here, to act in the spirit of partnership (choosing D1 over D2) even though, for player 2, this option is made credible by ε, i.e. the perceived benefit of participating in a long-run strategy within the association.

Thus, it can be argued that player 2 maximizes their payoffs by choosing the cooperative-type coordination strategy, and that this unique strategy is applied by taking into account a parameter f that takes two sets of values $Y11 \geq f$ (case where there is no deviation) and $f > Y11$ (case where there is deviation): the strategy is unique but is relative to the context (i.e. C1 on the one hand and D1 on the other hand).

Moreover, concerning player 1, we can see that, according to our hypotheses, as soon as $f \geq 42$, player 1 obtains (on average) at least as much as in the case of non-deviation (knowing D1). Indeed, concerning player 1, their expectation of winning is (when $f = 42$):

$$0.5\,(0.5(24) + 0.5(24)) + 0.5\,(0.5(33) + 0.5(15)) = 24$$

Beyond that, for $f \geq 42$, player 1 obtains, on average and in one move, at least one situation of indifference between player 2's deviation or non-deviation, and even, player 1 can see an absolute advantage when player 2 deviates and $f > 42$.

Thus, when $f > 42$, player 1's satisfaction is increasing.

For $24 < f < 42$, player 1's gains (while player 2 deviates) provide them with increasing satisfaction only in pure strategy, but, on average, their risk of loss relative to the reservation value (i.e. in this case, the collective solution negotiated *ex ante* and obtained when player 2 does not deviate) is evident when player 3 cannot replace player 2.

From a general point of view, it should be stressed that, for player 1, the calculation of their payoffs is hypothetical. Indeed, their decision to enter the game is in fact based on an *ex ante* calculation that only allows them to anticipate on the basis of confidence and not to maximize by calculation. To perform the maximization calculation, this player needs the value of the information f that they cannot know *ex ante.* On the contrary, when they know this information, such a maximization calculation is no longer necessary.

The decision pathway procedure is a staged sequence.

– **Stage 0:** a *focal point* is selected *ex ante* (solution I).

– **Stage 1:** player 1 (or the client) initiates the cooperative coordination sequence in accordance with the negotiation phase; we assume that player 1 renounces g (of the triplet [g, h, h/3], which corresponds to the respective gains of players (1, 2 and 3) concerning an immediate individual valuation of each player's assets on the short-term market).

The triplet linked to the (*ex ante*) *anticipations* of facing the market alone is therefore assumed to be lower in gains than the expectations linked to the collective action plan symbolized by solution I.

– **Stage 2:** player 2 (or the first supplier) must then make a decision about their commitment, but they must wait for new information f that is unknown to all of the players during the negotiation phase (and which is made public once the type of player 2 has been chosen by nature).

This information f concerns an opportunity for player 2 to seize a market outside the game and thus realize the corresponding value f.

Nature can choose two types of player 2: a non-deviating type of player 2 (with probability (1 - p1)) or a deviating type of player 2 (with probability p1). This probability p1 is the probability of obtaining a payoff greater than the *ex ante* negotiated coordination solution (i.e. $f > Y11$). The probability p1 is set to 0.5 (i.e. p1 = 0.5). We consider that the value of f, which is non-probabilizable, corresponds here to the radical uncertainty in the sense of Knight (1921).

Once their type is known, player 2 can now make a decision and choose: if they are non-deviant, between C1 (cooperative coordination strategy on the *focal point*) and C2 (feigning cooperation while being opportunistic); if they are deviant, between D1 (concerted deviation) and D2 (individualistic deviation).

– **Stage 3:** if they are a deviant type, player 2 can therefore:

- deviate in a concerted manner[5], symbolized by D1 (which remains consistent with the agreement made at the time of the initial negotiation and also consistent with the partnership perspective insofar as the players are to meet again in later periods), with the possible consequences of solutions VIII and IX;

- deviate in an individualistic way, symbolized by D2 (against their initial partnership commitments), with the possible consequences of solutions V and VI.

5 The result is an agreement to pay a bonus from player 2 to player 1 when player 2 deviates. Player 2 thus shows, by an explicit signal, their desire to continue the partnership despite their deviation. This bonus (paid to 1) is estimated as follows in case of deviation of player 2: $1/2(|f - Y11|)$. As compensation for this relative disutility to them, player 2 sees the satisfaction of remaining in the collective (at least equivalent to the apparent loss incurred, i.e. $\varepsilon \geq 1/2(|f - Y11|)$). In fact, ε symbolizes the benefit to player 2 of participating in a long-term collective strategy where ε *measures the regret of losing the relationship formed*. For player 2, a concerted deviation is thus equivalent to paying a bonus showing their willingness to continue the partnership. However, the disutility consented to by player 2 in paying the bonus is "compensated" relationally by this qualitative value ε. The continuation of a long-term partnership collaboration and the fear of deteriorating or losing it is a *satisfactory level of aspiration* (or *satisficing* (Simon 1976, 1978)).

– **Stage 4:** player 3, whose potential role is to replace player 2 in the event that the latter deviates, can effectively achieve, in all cases, at least 25% of the supply market (the level which binds them contractually to the client), but there is uncertainty about their capacity to go beyond this and thus to be able to replace player 2 (who, when they do not deviate, ensures 75% of the supply market).

This uncertainty about player 3's ability to achieve 100% of the market is not the result of an intentional concealment on the part of player 3, but of a lack of knowledge about their true ability to suddenly move from 25% to 100% (of the supply market). Bricolage or improvisation are key elements because they can make things possible.

At the same time, we combine a probability p3 concerning the ability of player 3 to replace player 2 and a probability of (1 - p3) in the opposite case. As player 3 does not have the information about their ability to move from 25% to 100% of the supply market, the probability p3 is set to 0.5 (p3 = 0.5).

– **Stage 3':** at the same time, this uncertainty about player 3's abilities can be the object of a bet by player 2. By doing so, they can try to take advantage of the situation by betting on the inability of player 3 to replace them. Player 2's *bargaining power* becomes high when player 3 is caught short (i.e. when player 3 is unable to replace player 2 at a moment's notice).

When there is a non-deviant type of player 2, this player can, by choosing C2, catch player 3 in default. With a deviant type of player 2, the individualistic strategy of player 2 consists simply of choosing D2 for the sole reason of seizing *f* for themselves.

Both of these selfish strategies (C2 and D2) can be (a) effective (in the case of solution III, on the one hand, and solution VI, on the other hand) but can be (b) ineffective (at least, in the case of non-deviation, in the case of solution II); it all hinges on whether player 3 is unable (case a) or capable (case b) of replacing player 2.

Thus, in the case of a non-deviation with an opportunistic attempt and a successful bet by player 2 that player 3 is unable to replace them (solution III), player 2 will be able to act opportunistically[6] and show their *bargaining power* by obtaining more than the coordinating solution.

However, player 2 can also see their bet defeated by player 3's ability to replace them: solution II corresponding to this situation is very prejudicial for player 2. Even more, when they deviate in an individualistic way (solution VI), player 2 will completely destroy the collective when player 3 is unable to replace them.

6 The transfer occurs from player 1 to player 2 due to player 2's *bargaining power* in the following way: $X11 - (|f - Y11|)$, at least as long as $X11 - (|f - Y11|) \geq 0$.

Note that in the case of individualistic deviation, it is not a question of a bet (check or win) by speculating on the uncertainty of the potential capacity of others but of a particular belief in the interest of an association.

In contrast to the situation presented by solution VI, where player 3 proves unable to replace player 2, the situation represented by solution V, when player 3 can replace player 2, corresponds to one of the best solutions in the game (in the short term) but significant (despite the apparent satisfaction of the players) of the exit from the plan and, at the very least, of the end of the *double-sourcing partnership* (in any case with player 2 as a member).

A long-term horizon and the consideration of the long term in the calculations of the players (in particular those of player 2) should normally make it possible to discredit such a solution V (unless there is an extremely high value *f*).

A1.3. From relationship to network

The association between the client and the supplier(s), without constraints other than those accepted by themselves during the negotiation phase, amounts (when the players respect, through their effective coordination, the collective action plan defined *ex ante*) to setting up an *informal mobility barrier* (solution I in the case without deviation or VIII in the case with deviation). This is equivalent (in both cases I and VIII) to generating an immediately advantageous solution (individually and collectively), sealing a profitable collaboration in the long term and defining, within the framework of analysis opened up by solution VIII, a strategy for occupying the market (in the double dimension of defending the advantage provided by the establishment and continuation of the association, and of preventing the entry of new suppliers into related markets, which are accessible here only to player 2). These related markets symbolize either stage before the market position occupied by the associated players, or new markets where it is necessary to be present in order to remain in the competitive race. Thus defined, the plan put in place (as well as its maintenance) will prove to be successful and robust, whatever the disturbances in the game, unless an exceptionally high value *f* is reached (materializing the situation of a strong radical uncertainty drastically disturbing expectations and behavior).

We can thus see that it is at least as much the deviation of player 2 (following new information linked to the radical uncertainty) as the question of the capacity of player 3 to replace player 2 that leads, or not, to the obtaining of solution VIII.

From the presented game, our conclusions are that player 1 would have no interest in dissuading player 2 from deviating when the values of *f* are high (the threshold here is given by $f \geq 42$); player 2 has no interest in being opportunistic; player 3 has no advantage in being unable to replace player 2.

Yet, it is important to emphasize that these findings are sufficient conditions for this *informal mobility barrier* to be in place in the *double-sourcing partnership* studied. The equilibrium of the game corresponds to *the cooperative coordination strategy*, summarized here as that of player 2 (the only active player for ease of representation). This strategy is declined in two modalities (C1, D1) according to the unknown *ex ante* value of the parameter f (information given by nature), thus: either the solution I in the case of non-deviation when $Y11 \geq f$; or the solution VIII in the case of deviation when $f > Y11$. Satisfaction for player 1 increases when $f \geq 42$, especially as their payoff is then no longer lower than that of player 3.

Solution VIII is the archetype of a good collective solution combining efficiency, flexibility and remuneration in the short term and strategic control of the market in the long term: there is a sharing of roles between the two suppliers according to their strategic competencies because while supplier 2 temporarily occupies the place of supplier 1, the latter, in the name of the network in which it is situated (with the two other players), can seize an opportunity that would otherwise be seized by a competing network. This sharing of roles is favorable to each of the players, as well as to the community to which they belong. This makes it possible to establish a very high quality of links that serves as relational cement. This is the idea that we defend with the concept of *informal mobility barrier*.

It is a central concept for understanding growth dynamics not in reference to a static equilibrium but by integrating strategic movements linked to the business opportunities necessary for long-term developments such as the development of new competencies. This is an essential mechanism for a good quality industrial configuration. We have insisted (Bouvier-Patron 1994, 1996b, 2002, 2017b) on network configurations by focusing on their relative stability and, as a result, on the potential existence of a *network life cycle* that can oscillate either around the equilibrium zone, as well as either tend towards *hyperstability* (rigidification of links) or towards *hyperplasticity* (unraveling of links).

The balanced evolutionary form of the network, in order to maintain a stable dynamic state, is governed by the *incentive mechanism for stability* representing a series of necessary conditions whose non-observance, in whole or in part, generates relational deformations (more or less large) leading eventually to drifts towards the extremes (*hyperplasticity* and *hyperstability*). Following this qualitative formalization, we therefore present the concepts of an informal barrier to mobility (section A1.3.1) and an *incentive mechanism for stability* (section A1.3.2).

A1.3.1. *Informal barrier to mobility*

In a very instructive commentary[7] by Gilbert (1989), it appears that mobility barriers (Caves and Porter 1977) are the antithesis of contestable markets, and, more subtly, that the analysis of barriers is not possible (as it is too descriptive) and that it is therefore more certain to succeed in defining a world without barriers as that of *contestable markets* (Baumol et al. 1977; Baumol 1982). The concept of *mobility barriers* as an antithesis to contestable markets is a fundamental point for our analysis. However, what is important is the existence of *informal barriers to mobility* that explain the relational specificity involved, while at the same time seeing it as the source of a relational stabilizer (as opposed to the *hyperplasticity* of a contestable market or the *hyperstability* of a sclerotic organization). The nature of the contract as a barrier is an idea already mobilized by Aghion and Bolton (1987).

Inter-organization is a spectral category that includes unusual partnerships (as the highest relational quality). This makes it possible to consider networks as a relevant level of understanding of the dynamics of firms. This dynamic includes a phase of stability that is conducive to change. We can rely on the concept of *institution* in the sense of Schotter (1981)[8]: an institution has a relative stability that allows for bifurcations linked to the strategies of actors, which characterizes the normal life of a network of firms (NoF).

---

7 Gilbert (1989, p. 479): "If it is not possible to provide an exhaustive list of the determinants of barriers to entry, it is at least possible to describe a market in which barriers to capital mobility do not exist. This is the world of perfectly contestable markets [...] Firms are equally efficient, and each firm can imitate the products and services of any other firm. Cost functions need not be convex, but all expenditures are potentially reversible [...] The result is a market that performs as close as possible to the competitive ideal. Price equals marginal cost unless the industry is a natural monopoly, in which case price equals average cost. A key characteristic of a perfectly contestable market is that each firm acts as if it faces a perfectly horizontal demand function for any increase in price. This condition can serve as a definition for the absence of barriers to entry [...] Mobility barriers arise for reasons of technology and consumer tastes [...] in an imperfectly competitive economy. Indeed, there are many circumstances where welfare is strictly improved by impeding entry into an industry".

8 As already mentioned, Schotter (1981) develops the concept of social institution, allowing for a deviation that can lead to a stable configuration producing a regularity accepted by all (convention) until the next deviation. From a stability appears one or more deviations that can be transformed again into regularities accepted by all (conventions) until the next deviation. This makes it possible to establish a procedure of endogenization of institutions: we find this in the concept of *plan*.

Nevertheless, certain actor strategies lead to institutional blockages and prevent the redeployment of the organization under consideration (extreme cases of *hyperstability* and *hyperplasticity*).

This is why network configurations are constantly evolving in a continuum of hybrid situations[9] (we can speak here of the *life cycle of networks*). The balanced situation ensures the preservation of learning under the constraint of increasing information, but a degenerative evolution leads to two opposite extremes.

Let the axis of typical configurations be:

<-hyperplasticity [10] balanced form hyperstability[11]->

(eccentric hyperplasticity) (eccentric hyperstability[12])

9 Our analysis thus also encompasses, without having to subscribe to it, Chandler–Williamson's thesis stipulating the evolution of hybrid forms towards the vertically integrated form.

10 In practice, this situation is unmanageable because it corresponds to hyper-competition with homogeneity of actors and products as envisaged by the liberal fiction. More subtly, the installed firm practices a so-called *sustainability of price*. If this price cannot be called into question (following the example of *contestable markets* (Baumol et al. 1977, p. 352): "If every price–output combination for a potential entrant will force it to incur losses, we say that the announced monopoly price–output vector is sustainable […] The announced prices of a monopolist […] are sustainable if the monopoly is financially viable at these prices"). That is, the announced price must allow a profit greater than or equal to zero for the installed firm and, at this price, any entry must lead to a loss for the entrant. A natural monopoly practices a sustainable price.

11 It seems to us that the sectors of French industry that suffered in the 1970s were the victims of a lock-in effect extended to the whole of industry. We can cite, in no particular order, a series of factors such as the failure to take into account changes in demand, the failure to anticipate international competition, the lack of modernization of infrastructures, the routinization of activity, the lock-in of the industrial fabric structured around a few large establishments in the same sector, the exclusive orientation of activity towards the mass production of standardized products in order to benefit from returns on scale by using a low-skilled workforce, the centralization of competencies towards a corporate trade with limited (or no) redeployment. For the concepts of competency and profession in relation to the observed reality, see Teece (1980, 1988) and Dosi et al. (1990).

12 The Aoki (1986, 1988) or J-Group network is an intermediate case, between balanced and eccentric towards hyperstability, because of the hierarchical structuring in the network and the exclusivity imposed on the partners: a disadvantage that can be compensated by a very horizontal intra-firm structuring.

Chapter 2 shows that *network* analysis (Bouvier-Patron 1994b, 1996b, 2002, 2014) was initiated by Aoki (1986) or Thorelli (1986).

The network, from a practical point of view, is consecutive to the management of the relational portfolio from the client's point of view: networks of firms (NoF; and not of the company-network or firm-network F-N).

The equilibrium position (balanced network) is fragile because it requires constant effort on the part of each of the actors who contribute to it. However, deviations are possible: they result from individual behavior and have an impact on the system.

Although the metaphor may appear deterministic, the intuitive idea that we must have of the overall deviations of the system (starting from the reference point that is the equilibrium situation) is the apparent movement of the pendulum correlated, positively or negatively, with the *bargaining power* of the coordinating actor: the importance of the *bargaining power* of the coordinating actor (by default or by excess) influences the functioning of the network.

The equilibrium position is a dynamic of movement that generates an evolution driven by a fictitious pendulum describing a potentially chaotic trajectory towards two extreme poles (*hyperstability* and *hyperplasticity*) between which a continuum of situations is possible. The two extreme attractors are catastrophic points[13]: a form of accelerated sedimentation leading to an increasingly rigid trend structuring with *hyperstability*; a form of vertiginous softening of fading and/or bursting of the links with *hyperplasticity*. Navigating towards these extreme poles, a shift of recovery, although difficult, is not to be excluded: an evolution is therefore always possible positively in the direction of the dynamic equilibrium zone (and also negatively in the direction of the extremes). A symmetrical deviation is possible towards one or the other of the two attractors; reversibility towards the equilibrium zone is more delicate (even an absolute difficulty[14]), except in the very vicinity of the equilibrium zone.

If we place ourselves from the point of view of the equilibrium situation (which is accessible, see Figure A1.1), it is a question of explaining the conditions that make it possible to prevent the change in the behavior of actors in the direction of the two opposite polar situations.

---

13 Thom (1980, p. 6): "The word catastrophe here does not have the negative connotation that it has in everyday language [...] quite simply at each point v of the catastrophic set K the things change". Here, the extreme situation of *hyperplasticity* or *hyperstability* is catastrophic in both senses of the term.

14 The outcome of the sectors devastated by a crisis since the end of the 1960s has been closure, abandonment, reconversion, but never a restart.

Some actors (the coordinating actor or the actors straddling several competing networks (Bouvier-Patron 1994a, 1996b)) have a decisive influence on the network and its evolution.

The possible extreme deviations can often be explained by precisely designating the role of the actors and the induced evolutionary dynamics (with possible situations of degeneration with respect to the conditions for obtaining a controlled evolutionary dynamics (see Bouvier-Patron 1994a, 1996b, 2002)). It is therefore important to inspect each contractual upstream supply market in the network and, in particular, the existence of straddling players serving several competing networks (and also different clients, which, on the other hand, indicates a high level of competency beneficial in the industrial organization). Networks, competitors or not, are rarely disjointed. In cascade, by amplification of the resonance, the negative evolutions can reverberate to an entire sector of activity, a region or, by propagation effect, to the whole economy.

A1.3.2. *The incentive mechanism for stability*

The *incentive mechanism for stability* is a contractual procedure whose challenge is to preserve evolving relational stability without any of the contracting parties having to renounce their free will or suffer from any renunciation in order to support the collective effort. In the strategic vocabulary of Schelling (1960), the analogy is, between at least two actors, that of a freely agreed and mutually advantageous *rendez-vous*; and, unless revised to take into account increasing information (radical uncertainty), the designated *focal point* will be the same today or tomorrow. The *incentive mechanism for stability* specifies that, by nature, in addition to free membership and, during the relationship, the absence of any *a priori* deprivation of mobility (and/or strong constraint inscribed by materiality: specific investment supported by only one party), there is a mutual benefit of engaging and maintaining the relationship with a constant perspective of learning and continuous improvement.

Operating in a reciprocal mode leads to learning based on *routine efficiency*[15] without, however, causing blindness due to the ability to take into account the increasing information. This efficiency is then self-sustaining as long as the continuation of the relationship is seen as in everyone's interest.

15 Routine efficiency results from the advantages perceived by each of the actors of maintaining a stable relationship over time (which is an empirical strategic behavior perceived very early by Valla (1982)).

The deviance of one of the parties is possible and will be the consequence of new information unknown *ex ante* and not probable expressing either the need for a temporary exit or the loss of the community of interests. The growing information constraint must be expressed as such because the radical uncertainty (Knight 1921) that it embodies is present in business life and proves to be fundamentally indomitable. Insofar as these characteristics presented have no material counterpart in terms of potential hindrance to the mobility of the actors (Caves and Porter 1977), the *incentive mechanism for stability* does refer to an *informal barrier to mobility*. From a normative point of view, the contractual form[16] corresponding to *an incentive mechanism for stability* must respect the following seven (six + one) conditions in the client–supplier framework (adaptable for a relationship between peers, in the NoF).

1) A bilateral/multilateral commitment where everyone freely adheres to the relationship (*guarantee of non-coercion*) following a mutual audit within the framework of a long negotiation procedure.

2) An *ex ante* commitment of proportionality between the turnover achieved *ex post* by the client actor (downstream) and the volume of orders entrusted to a particular supplier (*guarantee of reciprocity*): this serves as an objective basis for the existence of a mutual advantage in establishing and then preserving the relationship.

3) A commitment of non-dependence (symmetrical) so that the stability (over time) of the relationship does not generate a perverse effect of *relational lock-in* for one, the other or both actors (*guarantee of potential mobility*). One way to do this is to permanently preserve potential competition: in particular through the practice of *double-sourcing* procurement for the client (and the policy of multi-clientelism for the supplier) and also by resorting to calls for tenders for each new supply upstream market and/or at the end of a contract.

4) A stable mutual commitment based as little as possible, especially unilaterally, on specific material investments (*sunk costs*: irrecoverable costs (Baumol et al. 1981)) in favor of an informal relationship (*informal relationship guarantee*). This does not mean that there is no investment, but that the investment is made by everyone on their competencies in the very name of their ability to be efficient, to defend their reputation and to innovate.

5) A temporal commitment aimed at promoting symmetrical learning under increasing information constraints (*guarantee of a stability/plasticity trade-off*)[17].

---

16 The six conditions delimit a theoretical zone of existence of the good bilateral partnership relationship by displaying a set of required rules, but this does not mean that the resulting contract is a complete contract.

17 Stability is favorable to learning and improvement, but plasticity ensures a deformation or even an opening of the constraints defined within the framework of existing routines, which makes it possible to introduce the conditions for an evolution.

6) A commitment to the specificity of the supply upstream market paid by a supplier to the client (*specificity guarantee*) based on a generic competency that can be redeployed to several different, possibly competing, clients. The object is to avoid the existence of straddling players (i.e. holding a monopoly on an upstream supply market and providing an identical service to many clients; who may find themselves competing downstream on products that tend to look alike), especially if the specificity held by the supplier serving several competing clients represents a significant part of the specificity of each competitor's product. The possible existence of a *natural monopoly* (Baumol et al. 1977; Baumol 1982) will make it impossible to apply this rule.

7) A requirement of remedies for possible voluntary or involuntary ruptures (*guarantee of non-infringement*). Thanks to this rule no. 7, the penalties linked to the different eventualities of rupture must be foreseen. In case, respectively, of voluntary or involuntary rupture of one of the parties, there are direct penalties (explicit clauses of the contract imposing financial penalties in both cases) and indirect (loss of the relationship). In the partnership case, the main antidote is the implicit threat, and internalized *ex ante,* expressed as an *a priori* regret of losing the relationship, as well as *the relational quality*.

Remedies for breaches of contract have been analyzed by Shavell (1984). We believe that it is possible to internalize the remedies for infringements insofar as a good client–supplier relationship plays a considerable role here (often ignored by the theory).

Note two things:

– an involuntary termination (default of the supplier) highlights above all the inadequacy of the *ex ante* supplier selection procedure;

– if the *ex ante* selection of the partner (basically based on its *reputation*) turns out to be insufficient to guard against any eventual failure, which is always possible, the common objectives and the positive externalities of beneficial joint work will, in fact, function as a reciprocity clause to be preserved (to preserve mutual learning and co-evolution).

In the latter case, the fear of the nonrenewal of the relationship is an implicit threat, which is internalized *ex ante* by the two protagonists and serves as a powerful incentive factor.

It is important to note that rule no. 7, necessary in the general case, is almost superfluous in the partnership framework because, in addition to the choice of the partner and the existence of a common objective, the clearly understood advantage of the parties consists of a common long-term projection: the continuation of the relationship beneficial to both parties is a natural source of incentive within the framework of periodic renegotiation (generally a four-year period).

Thus, in addition to the nonrenewal of the mutually advantageous contract, it is the *ex ante* fear of the loss of the relationship, which will act as a safeguard clause: *the* a priori *regret of the loss of the relational quality established* in a partnership framework seems to be a decisive and dissuasive factor systematically obliging the parties to seek an arrangement before any rupture and/or any recourse to penalties. This is generally the case because the protagonists seek to avoid conflict and, *a fortiori*, recourse to the courts (moreover, the problem which then arises is the difficulty of determining responsibilities, see Tirole (1986)).

It is important to take into account all of these seven conditions (which also have an effective operational scope) and to not isolate one of them. This is particularly true for the industrial player who wishes to develop a product but who, not having all the competencies and/or all the ingredients in-house, must call on suppliers. The *coordinating actor*, with the required competencies and/or ingredients, has an essential role in the contractualization. If the analysis can focus on the elementary bilateral relationship of the client–supplier transaction, we can consider a space of higher relevance, which is that of the *double-sourcing partnership with a premium to the leader* (case studied in the qualitative modeling above) and beyond the network of firms (NoF).

A good network of firms (or *balanced star network*[18]: Bouvier-Patron 1994a, 1996b) will have, without loss of generality, the advantages of the bilateral level if there is duplication for each bilateral partnership relationship of the *incentive mechanism for stability*. As the analysis of complexity shows, the whole has its own coherence, but a decomposability of this whole into a unitary element allows meticulous auscultation. Good unit quality can only mean, at the very least, a positive potential at the level of the whole and, more likely, a multiplied potential. Alterations, deformations or possible deteriorations will affect the form of equilibrium for any displacement below or beyond, but a robust core makes it possible not to deviate from the position of equilibrium and/or to return to it more easily.

18 The *star network* is the most structuring elementary network of the industrial organization: it is both its elementary form and the most widespread. Moreover, it does not prevent and even allows for more sophisticated forms (increase in complexity with clusters of networks where there is more than one coordinating actor as for multipolar innovation networks) or much more rigid (case of subcontracting networks with a strong pyramidal hierarchical form) or even more anarchic (perpetual modifications of the links/relationships).

The network of firms is an essential organizational form in the sense that the policy of refocusing on the core business and of outsourcing, mobilized since the beginning of the 1980s, imposes itself as a relatively stable mode of operation whatever the nature and quality of the services required (instead of being transitory – pending vertical integration as is still often suggested in economics at the analytical level). Moreover, the creation of the network responds to an imperative to access one or more required upstream supply market, and this logic generates a search for *relational proximity* (which also does not prevent *geographical proximity* (see Bouvier-Patron 2016): apart from the ambition of a local circular economy, the network has a coherent economic relevance with *relational proximity* and has, *a priori*, no reason to adopt a geographical logic (geographical proximity) except for a deliberate industrial choice (encouraging localization: example of Aérospatiale in Toulouse) and/or ethics (consistency with an SD allowing the preservation of the NE). The network is therefore not a geographical concept in itself without ever prohibiting it. More generally, the connection between the industrial logic of the network of firms and SD mainly operates at the level of product design (Bouvier-Patron 2010, 2015b), especially by adopting a frugal environmental approach (Bouvier-Patron 2017b, 2020).

Appendix 2

Philosophy and Consequentist Approach

Semantically, it is already important not to confuse *consequentism* and *consequentialism philosophy* (the last term being introduced by Anscombe (1958)) and associated (abusively) with *utilitarianism* (by J. Bentham in his *Traité des Peines et des Récomenses* (treatise on punishments and rewards) published first in 1811, where he advocates the greatest happiness for all through quantitative maximization; then by J.S. Mill in *Utilitarianism*, published in 1861, substituting quality for quantity by maximizing pleasures and minimizing pains). For all utilitarians since Bentham, only the consequences of our actions matter, regardless of the motivations.

However, in a *consequentist* approach, there can (and there must) be coherence between the motivation, the actions and the consequences of the actions: thus, to illustrate the point, if we have to innovate in a radical way, no irrevocable impact is acceptable.

There is not, in itself, a school of *consequentist philosophy*. As a group of thinking/acting actors, B. Spinoza would be their potential founding father based on a methodological rule present in the *Ethics* (post-mortem publication of this work from 1661 to 1677) and which we will summarize in the following way: *potential human freedom cannot rest simply on the consciousness that we have of a thing but on the knowledge (non-ignorance) of the determinism of this thing.*

Human freedom thus consists of knowing the causes which determine us.

This methodological perspective takes us away from authors usually considered as references on this issue: Singer (1975), presented as a figurehead of modern *consequentialism*, on a principle of purely moral individual conscience (of the type becoming vegetarian to eliminate animal suffering); Jonas (1979), with his moral *principle of responsibility* and, if necessary, by authoritarianism. Moreover, it is in no way a question here of comparing things to the state of nature and of projecting, in a contractualist and differentialist logic, a *just society* (Rawls 1971) and, *a fortiori* even less, of referring to a *pluralist*, or even *communitarian* vision (Walzer 1984). In addition, to go on the theme of economics and management, even though Knight (1921) establishes a link between *property rights* and *consequentism* (from the point of view of responsibility and effective incentive), the consequent action cannot be summed up either in the pure logic of *property rights* (the absence of which would lead to all abuses (Hardin 1968)), nor in the opposite thesis (where *property rights* induce a Malthusianism beneficial to the owners alone), whereas, ideally, the solution favorable to the community lies rather in *respected common rules of reciprocity* (Ostrom 1990).

The challenge we are talking about is to choose and then adopt, in a methodological practice of analysis and then action, a *consequentist approach*. The *consequentism* evoked is therefore not an *a priori* category of Kantian obedience, but rather a universal methodological tool that is practical and applicable to any object considered: a universalism of method. By decentering *consequentism* – from the individual to the method (as suggested by Harsanyi (1982)) – we can therefore free ourselves from the initial utilitarian logic and wonder about the only *procedural rule* to follow, as Simon suggests (1976, 1978) through the *How*. The individual decision will take precedence, based on a universal method, making it possible to *measure* a priori *the consequences on others and/or third-party goods of all types*. This decision does not exclude a maximization of a profit, but without this subordinate criterion governs the decision. *Consequentism* is indeed a practical methodology and not deontology (deontology being *a body of rules of conduct establishing* a priori *what to do without necessarily studying the consequences*). From the consequentist point of view adopted here, an action is bad if it generates harmful negative externalities (to the Natural Environment, others and/or the community or third-party goods).

We could object that it is impossible to control the sequence of causes and consequences, which is true in absolute terms (except teleological interpretation), but it turns out that any entity making a decision has a proven ability to measure the future impact of their decision, but their pure selfishness leads them to ignore it (and this too often knowingly).

Appendix 3

Inter-organization and Patents

The protection of invention and innovation is not simple. From strong appropriability (exclusive, linked to the supposed effectiveness of the patent as protection: Arrow (1962a)), it was necessary to consider weak appropriability (presence of uncontrollable externalities, specific and tacit knowledge, differentiated absorptive capacities companies present on a market or the fragmentation of knowledge). Furthermore, the question arises of reconciling the protection of the pioneering innovator and dissemination to competitors (Ordover 1991).

An essential criterion for filing a patent is based on the concept of *novelty* (implying a difference between a before and an after: because it did not exist before). The alleged novelty therefore lapses when a third party can assert anteriority materialized by any publicity emanating from a public (and not secret) source, even though it is in a segmented or disseminated way. In addition, there is a gradation of novelty via the criterion of the degree of comparative inventiveness in relation to what exists or is proposed. All in all, it should be admitted that assessing who the "pioneer" is contains an element of subjectivity.

The patent is granted according to three criteria of appreciation: social utility, nonobviousness, and novelty by non-anteriority. However, the formal recognition of an invention by the patent does not provide information on the effectiveness of the induced novelty. To assess the effectiveness of the novelty of the patent, we must measure the *degree of generality* (degree of diffusion of the patent in different technologies), the *degree of originality* (number of citations of other patents in the act of the patent filed) and the *value of the patent* (number of patent citations and payment of patent renewal fees).

This can hardly be achieved at the time of filing, except assuming that the patent is distributed and adopted even before being filed.

Furthermore, this mode of taking into account favors what is objectifiable and quantifiable and neglects what is informal and tacit (elements that are difficult to patent), but which are decisive in an innovation.

For the high-tech sectors, information is part of an unlimited, porous and rapid technological horizon because knowledge is in perpetual renewal, fragmented, not necessarily codified, disseminated and absorbed. Moreover, the patent race becomes an issue in itself for various reasons: the patent is a means of visibility on the market or with third parties (as valuable assets); a means of direct economic valuation (through the collection of royalties); a means of exchange due to the impossibility, for a single company, of covering the extent of the knowledge required to achieve a project and/or a product; even a means of developing new cooperative areas given the extent of disparate competencies and resources to be mobilized.

Generally, the motives, nature, durations and forms of these new patent collaborations are given a lot of consideration (Chesbrough 2003; Faems et al. 2005; Cohendet et al. 2006; Pisano 2006; Hamdouch et al. 2008; Bosch-Sijtsema and Postma (2009); Gambardella and McGahan 2009).

The resulting profusion of patent filings, especially in high-tech sectors, is largely due to the difficulty of monetary and/or market evaluation of patents: it is then a question of patenting the slightest invention (regardless of the intrinsic value[1]) to possibly have a potential currency of exchange (Hall and Ziedonis 2001) and/or to engage directly in negotiations with other companies (including competitors).

The role of the patent as protection (theoretically allowing the exclusion of competitors) has been relativized by the study by Levin et al. (1987) on the practices and mechanisms used by companies to capture the economic spinoffs of their innovations: it turns out that companies are filing more and more patents, but paradoxically consider patents to be a relatively inefficient means of securing the spinoffs.

The sectors consider that the speed of change, as well as the extent of the necessary knowledge, are decisive in the study of the reasons mentioned.

1 During negotiations, the intrinsic value of a patent depends on the degree of novelty and inventiveness.

However, the two main arguments cited on the ineffectiveness of patent protection are:

– the patent is easy to circumvent (its degree of potential or actual novelty being questionable or disputed) or, in a counter-productive way, more or less reveals the information (information which should, however, be kept secret);

– knowledge evolving too quickly, which disqualifies the interest of filing a patent.

The effectiveness of patent protection turns out to be overestimated for its primary objective (strong appropriability), but the maintenance and/or increasing recourse to the practice of filing a patent clearly indicates an interest in doing so and the existence of reasons other than the exclusion of competitors or the desire to erect a barrier to entry. In fact, manufacturers quite systematically resort to a policy of filing patents by combining two complementary aspects: creating and/or mobilizing new knowledge by providing themselves with a minimum shield; taking advantage of the publicity of the patent to negotiate with other firms within the framework of contracts and/or license agreements.

Ayerbe and Mitkova (2005) insist on the double importance of an internal valuation of patents in coherence with a strategic business unit (SBU) of the company and simultaneously of an external exploitation of patents by the license.

To sweep a spectrum of possibilities, Arundel (2001) and Hall and Ziedonis (2001) mention different uses concerning the patent:

– access to complementarities (Teece 1986; Jacquemin 1988; Kogut 1989; Reitzig 2004; Pisano 2006) between potential or effective partners;

– creation of new competencies (Teece 1980);

– reduction of costs by the collective (Jacquemin 1988);

– sending a signal[2] (Hall and Ziedonis 2001; Blind et al. 2006, 2009) on competencies. Indeed, the patent constitutes a valuable signal: active communication with markets, suppliers and clients, or preventively to dissuade a rival, and also and above all to negotiate and operate patent exchanges.

It is therefore necessary to integrate the patent into a broad strategic panoply, from confidentiality (or non-patent secrecy strategy) to the filing of a patent (*a priori* as part of the defense of assets and/or in a more offensive way) without

2 On the very origin of this concept, see Spence (1973) and Tirole (1988).

necessarily aiming for a strong appropriability. In total, the possible strategic facets of the patent are numerous:

– interest in patenting, even without the actual use of the patent by its owner, to dissuade, slow down or block competition;

– signal on competencies to find partners (while protecting existing knowledge) or to obtain new resources;

– bargaining chip when knowledge is fragmented and complex;

– way of piloting, managing and promoting a collective innovation;

– creation of a knowledge market, the patent revealing the information (and more or less effectively protecting the holder).

In summary, the patent can be seen in several ways through defensive, offensive, mixed (defensive/offensive) and reputational means:

– **rather passive defensive strategy (defense of the acquired heritage):**

- maintain the legal monopoly (logic of appropriability and create a barrier to entry),

- patrimonial evaluation of intangible assets and management of these assets for renewal, extension of application (to new areas, new territories, new actors) or the transfer of license,

- institutional evaluation (corporate) and/or marketing of the company,

- signaling and attracting capital for a new project,

- creation of *bargaining power* to better negotiate an agreement, sale or acquisition,

- crutch for the renewal of the range and rapid access to innovation (reduction of time to market) by acquiring a license (use of a third-party patent);

– **offensive strategy: strategic action versus subversive guerrilla:**

- creation of a barrier to mobility making it possible to control competitors by filing successive patents before and instead of others,

- disinformation guerrillas to influence, direct or even mislead the environment, either through institutional communication or through decoys;

– **mixed defensive/offensive strategies in the high-tech sectors:** given the high-tech complexity and the fragmentation of knowledge, the nature of the products to be developed and the diversity of the technologies required, each company can do nothing alone and comes up against the patents from other companies. This implies two structuring possibilities:

- carrying out barter or cross-exchange (cross-licensing),

- engaging in genuine institutionalized cooperation (patent pool);

– **reputational strategy:** in an economic and managerial universe where the logic of value becomes decisive, the most significant synthetic strategic weapon – both defensive and offensive – is based on the reputation effect (Kreps and Wilson 1982a). It is a global multi-faceted strategy based on patent filing:

- make known to actively protect[3], and at best, an invention and send signals to deter/encourage (to enter, innovate, imitate, cooperate, buy, put on the market) as well as to brandish a credible threat,

- report proven competency (to suppliers, clients or capital markets),

- communicate before negotiations with other key players and before exchanges or cooperation,

- building value through corporate image.

Intangible capital should not be neglected because it represents an appreciable source of valuation, sometimes more important than company results: to raise funds, negotiate in the event of sale and/or acquisition, even to resist a takeover bid (via a high stock exchange listing, preventing a takeover).

In case of imitation[4] (ranging from elements obtained and used by business intelligence, to the degree and nature of imitation to counterfeiting), this statistically leads (except for the major prestigious brands concerning counterfeiting) to little recourse in court (Lanjouw and Shankerman 2001), the explanation lies in the cost and delays of legal action and/or even in the uncertainty about the eventual result of a proceeding. The observed practice, for various reasons (costs, deadlines, confidentiality, reputation), is therefore to favor an amicable settlement.

3 Active protection aims to have: a temporary monopoly to benefit from the exploitation of a creation and, at the very least, to recover the costly investment made – while being relatively sheltered from the capture of the creation by competitors – to have a weapon to fight against counterfeiting in a context of globalization; products from emerging countries inducing a considerable competitive bias.

4 Mansfield et al. (1981) shows that most patented innovations are imitated within four years. That said, note that imitating a patent never means capturing all the specificity of a company (competencies, tacit knowledge, technologies, organization, commercial network, etc.).

Intoxicating competitors (actual/potential), bluffing or forcing them to react can be part of a strategy without being a strategy in itself.

All the possibilities considered above lead to several possible typical cases (which will be summarized in Table A3.1):

– Case 1, proprietary strategy with patent filing: strong closed appropriability (theoretical case) based on the primacy of the intra-organization; knowing, however, that there are externalities and absorption capacities limited by the amount of knowledge (including tacit) available; network externalities requiring, at the very least, inter-organizational coordination to disseminate a standard (type 1).

– Case 1', proprietary strategy with patent filing and need for inter-firm coordination (high-tech sectors) through cross patent exchanges (cross licensing) up to a form of strong institutionalized cooperation (patent pool) (type 1').

– Case 2, pseudo-proprietary strategy but without necessarily filing a patent: specific open appropriability (type 2). Such a strategy is centrally based on confidentiality (at least upstream) – or *secrecy strategy* – within the framework of privileged client–supplier relationships (partnerships). Pseudo-proprietary appropriation is a proprietary logic, but the securing of which does not primarily, and voluntarily, pass through legal protection; not out of lack of interest in legal protection but out of risk aversion linked to the dissemination of information to third parties (due to a patent filing).

– Case 3, proprietary strategy with patent filing by open appropriation (open innovation design: Chesbrough (2003); Dittrich and Duysters (2007)[5]) (type 3). For Chesbrough, the company remains centered on itself but opens, by necessity, to multiple forms of collaboration or cooperation (horizontal or vertical) in order to manage and develop a portfolio of innovations (Faems et al. 2005) and this in the uncertainty about the actual value of the patents; knowing that it is less the intrinsic value of patents and more the business model used by the company that explains commercial success. An open innovation system, according to Chesbrough, is therefore a complex inter-organizational network of relationships that change over time where each company absorbs external knowledge and/or develops internal knowledge by relying on the economic environment (with rapidity of dissemination of knowledge and adoption). This is essential for any company holding a patent and/or wishing to use the patent of others. As inspired by Chesbrough et al. (2009) we should think of innovation as a value chain: suppliers, upstream, sell patents to other players, downstream, who carry out technology development; in this division of labor, technology suppliers appear as specialized, implementing potential

5 In open innovation (as opposed to close innovation within the firm), innovations are increasingly the result of the collaboration of several legally distinct moral and/or physical parties giving blurred organizational boundaries to the development of new products.

technological applications without having the competencies or capacities to finalize them, thus supplying an intermediate technology market. This situation is not necessarily fixed as suppliers, through *mobility*, end up mastering suppliers and finalization competencies (e.g. Samsung, supplier to Apple; Asus, supplier to Sony). Client firms, downstream, acquire and assemble complementary knowledge and competencies, allowing the commercial development of technologies. In the value chain of technological products, downstream is decisive. Instead of Chesbrough's concept of *open innovation* (2003), we may prefer to rely on Allen's concept of *collective invention* (1983) and on the work of Lessig (2001) to distinguish *strong openness* from *weak openness*.

– Case 3', access opening with authorization (type 3').

Weak openness (type 3') relates to the situation of an open resource insofar as it is accessible to all, without discrimination and at a non-confiscatory cost, simply by means of an authorization in the form of an accepted license as in the case of open source.

In contrast, strong openness (which may constitute another case: case 4 (type 4)) generates the absence of authorization for the use of a resource, which indeed becomes unappropriable by anyone.

If the license is free, as in the case of free software (open source), access to the source code is open free of charge and the modifications made – even for subsequent commercial use – also remain free consistent with the rights associated with this type of license[6], namely a tacit authorization of use subject to compliance with the rules enacted. This does not then prevent us from being able to market a product from open source.

In the *new economy*, filing patents aims at a reputation effect (see above) but the issue is open source (Tirole and Lerner 2002), which is mainly beneficial because of the active existence of a highly expert community of practice (Brown and Duguid 1991, 1998; Wenger and Snyder 2000). This community of practice explains and justifies the circulation of knowledge while respecting the associated license. The example of Netscape–Mozilla (Hammerly et al. 1999) is emblematic: the (temporary) abandonment of proprietary logic makes it possible, free of charge for the company, via the community of practice, to make the product efficient and to benefit from incorporated innovation. This particularity makes a comparison between high-tech sectors tricky, even though, in all cases, the material expenditure on R&D is considerable. In the pharmaceutical sector, for example, there are few

6 Free software is based on the General Public License called copyleft (as opposed to copyright), allowing accessibility to the source code and use: anyone can access, use, modify, copy and even distribute software under this license on the condition that they respect the terms.

enlightened amateurs who can, at home and/or interact with others, perfect a molecule, develop it, and also experiment with it and, moreover, find an easy way to communicate on an equal basis with scientific experts working within companies or on behalf of private laboratories and/or large pharmaceutical firms.

More generally, given the costs of innovation, the use of an off-patent strategy involving confidentiality cannot be ruled out, including within the inter-organizational space, in order to protect ourselves from competing networks: this secrecy strategy consists of not wanting to reveal anything to third parties (Brouwer and Kleinknecht 1999; Arundel 2001).

In this logic of secrecy, the patent in itself can be dangerous by conveying strategic information to competitors both on innovations and on research programs. This implies in particular a need for contractualization of exclusivity between partners in order to develop, secretly at first upstream, research programs and innovations (Levin et al. 1987).

Once in the market[7], the new products can then certainly be copied, but the company can prepare to fight back and, above all, to anticipate.

In particular, this involves anticipating the launch on the market, as well as the renewal of the product (or range) one step ahead of the others and/or also according to the effective competitive reaction.

Be that as it may (filing of a patent versus secrecy strategy), given the high costs and the volume of knowledge required, the collaborative and, *a fortiori*, cooperative dimension is essential in terms of R&D (Harigan 1985a, 1985b; Contractor and Lorange 1988; Jacquemin 1988; Kogut 1989; Mowery 1998; Stuart and Podolny 1996; Powell et al. 1996; Brouwer and Kleinknecht 1999; Arundel 2001; Hall and Ziedonis 2001; Hagedoorn 2002). It is a question of accessing all the necessary complementary knowledge, reducing the cost of access to it, and also increasing the effectiveness of research expenditure. Aoki (1986, 1988) thus largely insisted on the

7 Abernathy and Clark (1985) then Henderson and Clark (1990) showed the importance, for the firm, of the link to the market and the need for recombining technologies as well as commercial and technical competencies (architectural innovation) in terms of synchronic (between those already existing) and diachronic (between old and new). Furthermore, other authors (Rosenberg 1982; Kline and Rosenberg 1986) established the importance of the innovation process as interactive and based on the articulation between incremental and radical innovations. This seems to be confirmed by the success of Japanese companies, of which Aoki (1986, 1988) showed the essential source: namely inter-firms structuring. Radical innovation cannot be overlooked but is less common. However, it seems preferable and relevant to reason in terms of continuity and positioning at a given moment (Kline and Rosenberg 1986) rather than in dichotomous and hierarchical terms.

importance of network functioning for innovation. The business network (Hamdouch et al. 2008) is the place where knowledge exchanges are combined for innovation.

Inter-organization is today the main receptacle for the genesis, design, management and marketing of innovation.

Moreover, the collaborative and/or cooperative purpose can result in different forms of coordination (which may correspond to different phases) in a rather proprietary logic with possibly a weak openness mobilizing:

– upstream confidentiality (for the subsequent development of innovative programs and products);

– the barter of means or knowledge with free temporary or permanent access;

– the negotiations[8] on cross-exchanges (cross-licensing);

– market transactions (on patents, knowledge or competencies);

– joint patent filing (joint ventures);

– the institutionalization of collective innovation (patent pool).

The managerial trade-off is thus to be found between the necessary confidentiality, not legally protectable, and the acceptable level of risk of dissemination of information by the patent (whose protection efficiency is relative, but is mainly used for negotiations or as currency exchanges).

Some firms may be in competition upstream through their R&D programs (Levin et al. 1987). This is not necessarily the case in high-tech sectors with fragmented knowledge (and a potential patent race). Downstream, the coordination (collaborations or cooperation) of complementarities allowing access to the missing dimensions of knowledge very often repels competition upstream (Pisano 2006; Gambardella and McGahan 2009) with suppliers (specialized in knowledge creation or renewal) but not necessarily having intrinsic means of valuating. In addition, globally, the necessary cooperation between competitors (d'Aspremont and Jacquemin 1987) promotes the internalization of R&D externalities through appropriate forms in a continuum of possibilities (barter, exchanges, agreements,

8 Negotiation is necessary because without an exchange agreement, companies cannot advance in their programs, but, above all, they can, in a sterile process, counter each other (blockage) or sue for counterfeit (which can be an end in itself because it is profitable and keeps competitors in check). This encourages each company to file multitudes of patents as a precaution. It is this very fact that also induces, to break the impasse, the interest of a negotiation to proceed to exchanges.

alliance, joint ventures, consortia). That said, without delimitation of individual property rights and in a situation of relational or informational asymmetry, this can generate the problems of stowaway (free rider), or even in the extreme case, of a hold-up (Schelling 1956, 1960). Thus, in a closed appropriability regime, the whole question would focus on this risk (very exaggerated by the theory) of potential unilateral capture by a third party (hold-up) with the recommendation to resort to vertical integration (or internalization) for all high-value, high-specificity activities (Williamson 1975, 1985; Klein et al. 1978; Teece 1980).

However, Schelling (1956, 1960) calls for a bilateral equilibrium through the taking of symmetrical hostages and the very anticipation of the risk of a hold-up. The absence of eventual convergence towards a collectively acceptable solution will therefore only result from substantial asymmetries in the capacities to dispose of credible threats (in the event of conflict) or from not having a common knowledge to be able to carry out coordination by appointment (in the nonconfrontational case) on the *focal point*.

The applicability of Schelling's work (1956, 1960) to design, analyze and understand strategic cooperative issues corresponds to the implementation of weak appropriability, with open innovation being potentially beneficial to all parties.

In practice, the filing of a patent confers less of a monopoly of exploitation (fragile and relative because the appropriation is imperfect) than a useful *market power* to obtain income and also, more fundamentally, a *bargaining power* in order to obtain the missing complementarities.

For high-tech sectors where the complexity of knowledge is great and in constant renewal (speed of evolution and race for knowledge), the patent is obvious if it is unavoidable on a key aspect of the field of knowledge and necessarily as a means of exchange to access the other knowledge required.

In a universe of complex knowledge, a single company must coordinate with others to move forward. The need for coordination, due to the fragmentation of knowledge, leads to inter-organizational functioning on the basis of cross-patent exchanges or, on a much more cooperative level, to consider a way of governance of the constituted collective in consortium.

Thus, alongside the traditional role of protection, the patent is a means of negotiation (Cohendet et al. 2006). Otherwise, the proliferation of property rights in an area that interests several legally distinct actors amounts to noting, de facto, the absence of usable and profitable rights individually and collectively.

To go even further (Heller and Eisenberg 1998), common goods shared and accessible to all (strong openness) are doomed to disappear (in an analysis filiation with Hardin (1968)): this is the case of type 4, as already mentioned.

Regime \ Form	Intra-organization (company/environment)	Inter-organization
(T1) Closed appropriability	(Alpha) Strict delimitation of ownership and supposed effectiveness of the patent	Externalities and absorption with network externalities involving coordination to distribute a standard
(T1') Collective appropriability	Patent proprietary strategy and avoid the risk of unilateral hold-up	Coordination in high tech: patent barter, exchange or consortium agreements
(T2) Specific open appropriability	Intra-organization not functional without the associated network (without or with patent filing)	Coordination from upstream design: tacit exchanges and upstream confidentiality and/or downstream patent
(T3) Appropriability in open innovation	Open organization but also recovering double flow intra/inter and open innovation without preeminence of the offer side	Openness to multifaceted collaborations
(T3') Appropriability with opening access	Community first and open source	Collective invention Access with community authorization
(T4) Non-appropriability	Non-defendable potential rights	Absence of rights: copies and/or counterfeits

Table A3.1. *Conceptual patent approach synthesis (source: author)*

To synthesize the classificatory approach proposed on the different forms of appropriability (Table A3.1), we first apprehend the traditional approach of the innovative company centered on the intra-organization and the externalities (type 1, alpha proposition). From this initial framework, several possibilities of understanding the inter-organization are possible.

– A logic inherent in high-tech sectors (type 1') where inter-organization results, taking into account fragmented knowledge, from coordination by negotiation concerning exchanges of patents (cross-licensing) or from cooperative pooling in a single structure (patent pool).

– A logic (type 2) of upstream design where the inter-organization mobilized by confidentiality is of the client–supplier type managed by a coordinating actor (network head) producing/assembling the final product and able to exploit it alone downstream and/or be part of a commercial (sales agreement) or strategic (production and/or research) alliance: either therefore, a design/sales logic, upstream–downstream, where the inter-organization is based on a common for joint research (joint ventures) and/or joint sale (trade agreement).

– An open business logic (type 3), centered on itself, but embedded in multifaceted collaborations.

– A relatively open logic of access (type 3') where the inter-organization corresponds rather to a community self-organization resulting from the free use of the same technology while respecting the community rules (as can be illustrated by Chapter 3, Business EcoSystems (BES)).

– The strong openness (type 4) generates the absence of authorization for the use of a resource, which becomes, in fact, unappropriated by anyone and prevents a defense of a mark, an invention or a possible innovation. In addition, some countries may have legislation but do not apply it or provide the means to apply it, leaving the field open to copying and/or counterfeiting, for example.

To go beyond the proposed classification, inter-organizational patent relations correspond to complex logics. Inter-organization is not only linked to symmetrical or asymmetrical pooling but can, because of the refocusing on the core business of each firm, lead to partial or total recourse to the outsourcing of R&D.

Empirical measurements have been carried out in France, in particular via the *Enquête sur les relations inter-entreprises* (ERIE) survey (Survey on inter-company relations) at the instigation of the SESSI. We already have two indicators or aggregates at this level: domestic R&D expenditure by companies called DIRD and external R&D expenditure by companies called DERD.

The level of DIRD is in relationship with the *absorptive capacities* (Cohen and Levinthal 1990).

The level of DERD refers above all to an acquisition of R&D from outside such as the purchase of a service or supply within the framework of a client–supplier relationship (which may correspond to outsourcing).

For the same company, the amount of the DIRD can be significant and the amount of the DERD can be just as much: this is not contradictory.

In a network approach, everyone being refocused on their profession and having to be efficient, substantial amounts must be spent to innovate and remain at the forefront in their field. However, everything that does not fall within the profession is nevertheless essential and must be at the highest level of innovation.

It is therefore not surprising that the data shows *an increasing relationship between the level of internal R&D expenditure and outsourcing*. This only reinforces the earlier results of Colombo and Garrone (1996).

We can summarize the use of outsourcing by the argument of the need for complementary competencies[9] (Richardson 1972). In addition, the maintenance of absorptive capacities (Cohen and Levinthal 1990) as the use of external suppliers is affirmed and imposed.

It is not certain that the probability of forging external links by outsourcing is systematically higher when the company belongs to a sector considered high tech compared to a sector that would be considered less so (Veugelers 1997).

In addition, the high levels of R&D expenditure are indeed due to large firms (Corbel 2005, 2007), but creativity and inventiveness often come from other actors, such as start-ups. In a network, the size of the company is not necessarily the most discriminating factor when it comes first to the production and exchange of knowledge, as well as competencies and their renewal.

9 Dhont-Peltrault and Pfister (2006) mention, in order of importance based on empirical data, the reasons for selecting the supplier for outsourcing: 1) recognition of the supplier's competency; 2) the complementarity of activity with it; 3) the quality provided in the supply and the service; 4) the price of the supply; 5) the geographical proximity of the contractors. The geographic location of the supplier breaks down statistically into thirds: local, national, foreign.

References

Aaker, J. (1997). Dimensions of brand personality. *Journal of Marketing Research*, 24, 347–356.

Abecassis-Moedas, C. and Mahmoud-Jouini, S. (2008). Absorptive capacity and source-recipient complementarity in designing new products: An empirically derived framework. *Journal of Product Innovation Management*, 25(5), 473–490.

Abernathy, W. and Clark, K. (1985). Innovation: Mapping the winds of creative destruction. *Research Policy*, 14, 3–22.

Abreu, D., Milgrom, P., Pearce, D. (1991). Information and timing in repeated partnerships. *Econometrica*, 59(6), 1713–1733.

Achs, Z. and Audretsch, D. (1988). Innovation in large and small firms: An empirical analysis. *American Economic Review*, 78(4), 678–690.

Adner, R. and Kapoor, R. (2010). Value creation in innovation ecosystems: How the structure of technological interdependence affects firm performance in new technology generations. *Strategic Management Journal*, 31(3), 306–333.

Aghion, P. and Bolton, P. (1987). Contracts as a barrier to entry. *American Economic Review*, 77(3), 388–401.

Akerlof, G. (1970). The market for lemons: Quality uncertainty and the market mechanism. *Quarterly Journal of Economics*, 84, 488–500.

Alchian, A. and Demsetz, H. (1972). Production information costs and economic organization. *American Economic Review*, 62(5), 777–785.

Allen, R. (1983). Collective inventions. *Journal of Economic Behaviour and Organization*, 4, 1–24.

Alonso-Ugaglia, A., Ferru, M., Guimond, B. (2016). Stratégies et trajectoires environnementales des établissements de Poitou-Charentes. *Revue d'économie industrielle*, 53(1), 9–45.

Altenburg, T. and Lundvall, B. (2009). Building inclusive innovation systems in developing countries: Challenges for IS research. In *Handbook of Innovation Systems and Developing Countries: Building Domestic Capabilities in a Global Setting*, Lundvall, B.A., Joseph, K.J, Chaminade, C., Vang, J. (eds). Edward Elgar, Cheltenham.

Altshuller, G. (1988). *Creativity as an Exact Science*. Gordon & Breach, Philadelphia.

Ambec, S. and Barla, P. (2002). Theoretical foundation of the Porter hypothesis. *Economics Letters*, 75(3), 355–360.

Ambec, S. and Lanoie, P. (2008). Does it pay to be green? *Academy of Management Perspectives*, 22(4), 45–62.

Amin, A. and Roberts, J. (2008). Knowing in action: Beyond communities of practice. *Research Policy*, 37, 353–369.

Anderson, P. (1999). Complexity theory and organization science. Special issue: Application of complexity theory to organization science. *Organization Science*, 10(3), 215–376.

Anderson, C. (2012). *Makers: The New Industrial Revolution*. Crown Business Book, New York.

Anscombe, G. (1958). Modern moral philosophy. *Philosophy*, 33, 1–19.

Ansoff, I. (1965). *Corporate Strategy*. Wiley, New York.

Ansoff, I. (1979). *Strategic Management*. Macmillan Press, London.

Ansoff, I., Declerck, R., Hayes, R. (1976). *From Strategic Planning to Strategic Management*. Wiley, New York.

Anton, J. and Yao, D. (1987). Second sourcing and the experience curve: Price competition in defense procurement. *The RAND Journal of Economics*, 18, 57–76.

Aoki, M. (1986). Horizontal vs vertical information structure of the firm. *American Economic Review*, 5, 971–983.

Aoki, M. (1988). *Information, Incentives and Bargaining in the Japanese Economy*. Cambridge University Press, Cambridge.

Aoki, M. (1990a). The participatory generation of information rents and the theory of the firm. In *The Firm as a Nexus of Treaties*, Aoki, M., Gustafsson, B., Williamson, O.E. (eds). Sage, London.

Aoki, M. (1990b). Toward an economic model of the Japanese firm. *Journal of Economic Literature*, 28, 1–27.

Aoki, M. (1991). Aspects of conventions within the firm. In *Colloque sur l'économie des conventions*, volume 2, Orléan, A. (ed.). CREA, Paris.

Argyris, C. and Schön, D. (1978). *Organizational Learning*. Addisson-Wesley, Boston.

Arrow, K. (1962a). Economic welfare and the allocation of resources for invention. In *The Rate and Direction of Inventive Activity*, Nelson, R. (ed.). Princeton University Press, Princeton.

Arrow, K. (1962b). The economic implication of learning by doing. *Review of Economic Studies*, 9(2), 155–173.

Arrow, K. (ed.) (1969). The organization of economic activity: Issues pertinent to the choice of market versus nonmarket allocation. The analysis and evaluation of public expenditures. In *Collected Papers of K.J. Arrow, Volume 2: General Equilibrium*. The Belknap Press of Harvard University Press, Cambridge.

Arrow, K. and Fischer, A. (1974). Environmental preservation, uncertainty and irreversibility. *Quarterly Journal of Economics*, 88, 312–319.

Arthur, B. (1989). Competing technologies, increasing returns and lock-in by historical events. *The Economic Journal*, 99, 116–131.

Arundel, A. (2001). The relative effectiveness of patents and secrecy for appropriation. *Research Policy*, 30, 611–624.

Arundel, A. and Kemp, R. (2009). *Measuring Eco-Innovation*. United Nations University, Maastricht.

Arvidsson, A. (2007). Creative class or administrative class? On advertising and the "underground". *Ephemera: Theory & Politics in Organization*, 7(1), 8–23.

Asanuma, B. (1989). Manufacturer–supplier relationships in Japan and the concept of relation-specific skill. *Journal of the Japanese and International Economies*, 3, 1–30.

Ashby, W. (1952). *Design for a Brain*. Wiley, New York.

Ashby, W. (1958). Requisite variety and its implications for the control of complex systems. *Cybernetica*, 2.

d'Aspremont, C. and Jacquemin, A. (1987). A note on cooperative and noncooperative R&D in duopoly. Working document, C.O.R.E., Louvain, 87–42.

Auriol, E. and Benaïm, M. (2000). Standardization in decentralized economies. *American Economic Review*, 90(3), 550–570.

Auriol, E. and Benaïm, M. (2001). Convergence and oscillation in standardization games. *European Journal of Economic and Social Systems*, 15(1), 39–55.

Axelrod, R. (1984). *The Evolution of Cooperation*. Basic Books, New York.

Ayerbe, C. and Mitkova, L. (2005). Quelle organisation pour la valorisation des brevets d'invention ? Le cas d'Air Liquide. *Revue française de gestion*, 155, 191–206.

Bailey, P. (1991). Full cost accounting for life cycle costs – A guide for engineers and financial analysts. *Environmental Finance*, 13–29.

Bain, J. (1956). *Barriers to New Competition*. Harvard University Press, Cambridge.

Baker, T. and Nelson, R. (2005). Creating something out of nothing: Resource construction through entrepreneurial bricolage. *Administrative Science Quarterly*, 50, 329–366.

Baker, T., Miner, A., Eesley, D. (2003). Improvising firms: Bricolage, retrospective interpretation & improvisational competencies in the founding process. *Research Policy*, 32, 255–276.

Banerjee, S. (2001). Managerial perceptions of corporate environmentalism interpretations from industry and strategic implications for organizations. *Journal of Management Studies*, 38(4), 489–513.

Bansal, P. and Roth, K. (2000). Why companies go green: A model of ecological responsiveness. *Academy of Management Journal*, 43(4), 717–736.

Barnosky, A., Matzke, N., Tomiya, S., Wogan, G., Swartz, B., Quental, T., Marshall, C., McGuire, J., Lindsey, E., Maguire, K. et al. (2011). Has the earth's sixth mass extinction already arrived? *Nature*, 471, 51–57.

Barodawala, B., Banerjee, R., Roy, S., Kapur, V. (2015). Jugaad – The perennial short-term solution. *World Journal of Social Sciences*, 5(2), 163–176.

Bartle, R. (1996). Hearts, clubs, diamonds, spades: Players who suit MUDs [Online]. Available at: http://www.mud.co.uk/richard/hcds.htm.

Base Carbone (2014). Documentation des facteurs d'émissions de la Base Carbone®. Working document, ADEME.

Basu, R., Banerjee, P., Sweeny, E. (2013). Frugal innovation: Core competencies to address global sustainability. *Journal of Management for Global Sustainability*, 1(2), 63–82.

Baudrillard, J. (1968). *Le système des objets*. Gallimard, Paris.

Baudrillard, J. (1970). *La société de consommation*. Gallimard, Paris.

Baumol, W. (1982). Contestable markets: An uprising in the theory of industry structure. *American Economic Review*, 1, 1–15.

Baumol, W. and Willig, R. (1981). Fixed costs, sunk costs, entry barriers, and sustainability of monopoly. *Quarterly Journal of Economics*, 405–431.

Baumol, W., Bailey, E., Willig, R. (1977). Weak invisible hand theorems on the sustainability of multiptoduct natural monopoly. *American Economic Review*, 3, 351–365.

Bazerman, C. (1999). *The Languages of Edison Light*. MIT Press, Cambridge.

Beamon, B. (1999). Designing the green supply chain. *Logistics Information Management*, 14(4), 332–342.

Bebbington, J., Brown, J., Frame, B. (2007). Accounting technologies and sustainability assessment models. *Ecological Economics*, 61(2–3), 224–236.

Belk, R. (1988). Possessions and the extended self. *Journal of Consumer Research*, 15(2), 139–168.

Bénézech, D., Karcher, T., Garcia, C. (2013). Dans quelle mesure l'orientation entrepreneuriale se traduit-elle en activités d'innovation dans les PME ? *Revue de l'entrepreneuriat*, 12(4), 35–58.

Benghozi, P.J. (2000). Le développement des NTIC dans les entreprises françaises : premiers constats. *Réseaux*, 18(104), 31–57.

Benner, M. and Tushman, M. (2003). Exploitation, exploration, and process management: The productivity dilemma revisited. *Academy of Management Review*, 28(2), 238–256.

Bennett, S. (1991). *Ecopreneuring: The Complete Guide to Small Business Opportunities from the Environmental Revolution*. Wiley, New York.

Benyus, J. (1997). *Biomimicry, Innovation Inspired by Nature*. Harper Collins, New York.

Berchon, M. (2014). Impression 3D. *Pour la science*, 36(4), 22–28.

Berle, G. (1991). *The Green Entrepreneur: Business Opportunities that Can Save the Earth & Make You Money*. Liberty Hall Press, Albany.

Berle, A. and Means, G. (1932). *The Modern Corporation and Private Property*. Harcourt, New York.

von Bertalanffy, L. (1968). *General System Theory*. Braziller, New York.

Black, L. (2006). Corporate social responsibility as capability: The case of BHP Billiton. *Journal of Corporate Citizenship*, 23, 25–38.

Black, F. and Scholes, M. (1973). Theory of rational option pricing. *Journal of Political Economy*, 81, 637–654.

Blind, K. (2012). The influence of regulations on innovation: A quantitative assessment for OECD countries. *Research Policy*, 41, 391–400.

Blind, K., Edler, J., Frietsch, R., Schmoch, U. (2006). Motives to patent: Empirical evidence from Germany. *Research Policy*, 35(5), 655–672.

Blind, K., Cremers, K., Mueller, E. (2009). The influence of strategic patenting on companies' patent portfolios. *Research Policy*, 38(2), 428–436.

Blue, R. (1990). *Ecopreneuring: Managing for Results*. Scott Foresman, Glenview.

Boiral, O. (2006). Corporate response to global warming: For a proactive strategy. *International Journal of Business and Economics Perspectives*, 1(1), 79–95.

Boisot, M. and Child, J. (1999). Organizations as adaptative systems in complex environments, special issue: Application of complexity theory. *Organization Science*, 10(3).

Boiteux, M. (2001). Transport : choix des investissements et coûts des nuisances. Report, Commissariat Général au Plan, Paris.

Bosch-Sijtsema, P. and Postma T. (2009). Cooperative innovation projects: Capabilities and governance mechanisms. *Journal of Product Innovation Management*, 26(1), 58–70.

Bourdieu, P. (1997). *Méditations pascaliennes*. Le Seuil, Paris.

Bouvier-Patron, P. (1993). Les formes d'organisation des entreprises : limites de l'approche transactionnelle et genèse de l'inter-organisation. *Économie appliquée*, 4, 7–40.

Bouvier-Patron, P. (1994a). La dimension interentreprises de production dans le modèle "J" d'Aoki. *Revue d'économie politique*, 1, 119–144.

Bouvier-Patron, P. (1994b). L'application des concepts de "Lock-In" et de "Barrières à la Mobilité" à une théorie des réseaux d'entreprises. *Revue française d'économie*, 1, 205–232.

Bouvier-Patron, P. (1995). Asymétrie et symétrie relationnelle dans la relation bilatérale client-fournisseur. *Économies et Sociétés*, 2, 51–68.

Bouvier-Patron, P. (1996a). La question de la réduction d'incertitude chez F. Knight. *L'Actualité économique*, 4, 397–415.

Bouvier-Patron, P. (1996b). Un concept de réseau pour analyser l'organisation industrielle. In *Coopération entre les entreprises et organisation industrielle*, Ravix, J.L. (ed.). CNRS Éditions, Paris.

Bouvier-Patron, P. (1998a). Quelle relation possible entre niveau d'aspiration satisfaisant et point focal ? *Revue internationale de systémique*, 2, 177–201.

Bouvier-Patron, P. (1998b). Stratégies relationnelles entre les enseignes de grande distribution et leurs fournisseurs. *Économie rurale*, 45(2), 69–83.

Bouvier-Patron, P. (1999). Coordination et réduction d'incertitude. In *Les approches évolutionnistes de la firme et de l'industrie*, Baslé, M., Delorme, R., Lemoigne, J.L., Paulré, B. (eds). L'Harmattan, Paris.

Bouvier-Patron, P. (2001). Analysis of change within and between firms embedded in their environment in the context of increasing interactions: Understanding complexity of organizations. *European Journal of Economic and Social Systems*, 15(1), 1–38.

Bouvier-Patron, P. (2002). La stabilité des relations clients-fournisseurs : un essai d'interprétation. *Sciences de gestion*, 4(3), 11–44.

Bouvier-Patron, P. (2003). La marque dans la marque. *Revue internationale des PME*, 16(1), 75–104.

Bouvier-Patron, P. (2007). Gouvernance environnementale et proximité relationnelle : vers une innovation économique et managériale ? *Sciences de gestion*, 9(5), 19–40.

Bouvier-Patron, P. (2009). Externalisation de la R&D : vers une gestion partenariale ? *Revue française de gestion industrielle*, 28(3), 99–119.

Bouvier-Patron, P. (2010). Le lien SPI-industrie, problème ou solution pour innover en développement durable. *European Journal of Economic and Social Systems*, 23(2), 33–48.

Bouvier-Patron, P. (2011a). *Entreprise et innovation : vers l'inter-organisation innovante responsable ?* L'Harmattan, Paris.

Bouvier-Patron, P. (2011b). *Inter-organisation et brevet : une proposition de classification.* De Boeck, Brussels.

Bouvier-Patron, P. (2013). La dimension stratégique du cahier des charges dans la relation client-fournisseur. *Revue recherches en sciences de gestion*, 95, 21–42.

Bouvier-Patron, P. (2014). *Économie et management de l'entreprise innovante : réseaux, territoire et développement durable.* L'Harmattan, Paris.

Bouvier-Patron, P. (2015a). Coût global, conséquentisme et stratégie de développement durable. *Management international*, 20(1), 114–122.

Bouvier-Patron, P. (2015b). *FabLab et extension de la forme réseau : vers une nouvelle dynamique industrielle ?* De Boeck, Brussels.

Bouvier-Patron, P. (2016). Vers la coordination interne et externe de la PME "banale" localisée dans un contexte d'innovation et de développement durable. *Géographie, économie, société*, 18, 189–210.

Bouvier-Patron, P. (2017a). Cahier des charges et relation client-fournisseurs : une tentative de synthèse. *Gérer & comprendre*, 129, 33–43.

Bouvier-Patron, P. (2017b). Innovation frugale environnementale : futur avantage concurrentiel de la firme ? *Revue recherches en sciences de gestion*, 118(1), 23–41.

Bouvier-Patron, P. (2019). Influenceur, marketing stratégique et intelligence artificielle. *Survey-magazine*, 802(1).

Bouvier-Patron, P. (2020). Stratégies d'entreprise & innovation frugale environnementale : proposition d'une matrice stratégique. *Recherches en sciences de gestion*, 136(1), 39–65.

Bouvier-Patron, P. (2021a). Bricolage et improvisation, deux clefs fondamentales de la création innovant. *Technologie et innovation*, 21, 6.

Bouvier-Patron, P. (2021b). From improvisation to innovation: The key role of "bricolage". In *Innovation Economics, Engineering and Management Handbook 2*, Uzunidis, D., Kasmi, F., Adatto, L. (eds). ISTE Ltd, London, and John Wiley & Sons, New York.

Bouvier-Patron, P. (2021c). Co-creation and innovation: Strategic issues for the company. In *Innovation Economics, Engineering and Management Handbook 2*, Uzunidis, D., Kasmi, F., Adatto, L. (eds). ISTE Ltd, London, and John Wiley & Sons, New York.

Bouvier-Patron, P. and Chatelain, Y. (2001). Le hacking appliqué au marketing. *Revue française de gestion*, 135, 5–17.

Bowen, H. (1953). *Social Responsibilities of the Businessman.* Harper & Brother, New York.

Bower, J. and Christensen, C. (1995). Disruptive technologies: Catching the wave. *Harvard Business Review*, January–February.

Bowman, E. and Hurry, D. (1993). Strategy through the option lens: An integrated view of resource investments and incremental choice process. *Academy of Management Review*, 18(4), 760–782.

Braungart, M. and McDonough, W. (2002). *Cradle to Cradle: Remaking the Way We Make Things*. North Point Press, New York.

Brem, A. and Wolfram, P. (2014). Research and development from the bottom up: Introduction of terminologies for new product development in emerging markets. *Journal of Innovation and Entrepreneurship*, 3(9), 1–22.

Breton, A. and Wintrobe, R. (1982). *The Logic of Bureaucratic Conduct*. Cambridge University Press, Cambridge.

Brouwer, E. and Kleinknecht, A. (1999). Innovative output, and a firm's propensity to patent. An exploration of CIS micro data. *Research Policy*, 28, 615–624.

Brown, T. (2008). Design thinking. *Harvard Business Review*, 85–92.

Brown, J. and Duguid, P. (1991). Organizational learning and communities of practice: Towards a unified view of working, learning and innovation. *Organization Science*, 2, 40–57.

Brown, J. and Duguid, P. (1998). Organizing knowledge. *California Management Review*, 40(3), 90–111.

Brown, S. and Eisenhardt, K. (1998). *Competing on the Edge: Strategy as Structured Chaos*. Harvard Business School Press, Boston.

Brunnermeier, S. and Cohen, M. (2003). Determinants of environmental innovation in US manufacturing industries. *Journal of Environmental Economics and Management*, 45, 278–293.

Bruntland, G. (1987). Our common future. Report, The World Commission on Environment and Development – United Nations. Oxford University Press, Oxford.

Buchanan, J. (1965). An economic theory of clubs. *Economica*, 32(125), 1–14.

Buchanan, J. and Tullock, G. (1962). *The Calculus of Consent: Logical Foundations of Constitutional Democracy*. University of Michigan Press, Ann Arbor.

Burns, T. and Stalker, G. (1961). *The Management of Innovation*. Tavistock, London.

Buysse, K. and Verbeke, A. (2003). Proactive environmental strategies: A stakeholder management perspective. *Strategic Management Journal*, 24, 453–470.

Byrne, J. (1993). The virtual corporation. *Business Week*, 3304, 98–104.

Cabeza Gutés, M. (1996). The concept of weak sustainability. *Ecological Economics*, 17, 147–156.

Capdevila, I. (2015). Co-working spaces and the localised dynamics of innovation in Barcelona. *International Journal of Innovation Management*, 19(3), 1540004.

Carlile, P. (2004). Integrative framework for managing knowledge across boundaries. *Organization Science*, 15(5), 555–568.

Carroll, A. (1979). A three dimensional conceptual model of corporate performance. *Academy of Management Review*, 4(4), 497–505.

Cavalli, N. (2007). The symbolic dimension of innovation processes. *American Behavioral Scientist*, 50(7), 958–969.

Caves, R. and Porter, M. (1977). From entry barriers to mobility barriers: Conjectural decisions and contrived deterrence to new competition. *Quarterly Journal of Economics*, 91(2), 241–261.

Chamberlin, E. (1933). *The Theory of Monopolistic Competition*. Harvard University Press, Cambridge.

Chandler, A. (1962). *Strategy and Structure: Chapters in the History of Industrial Enterprise*. MIT Press, Cambridge.

Chandler, A. (1977). *The Visible Hand*. Harvard University Press, Cambridge.

Chang, R. (ed.) (1997). *Incommensurability, Incomparability, and Practical Reason*. Harvard University Press, Cambridge.

Chatterjee, S. and Kumar, K. (2009). Effective electronic waste management and recycling process involving formal and non-formal sectors. *International Journal of Physical Sciences*, 4(13), 893–905.

Chesbrough, H. (2003). *Open Innovation: The New Imperative for Creating & Profiting from Technology*. Harvard Business School Press, Boston.

Chevassus-au-Louis, B. (2009). Approche économique de la biodiversité et des services liés aux écosystèmes : contribution à la décision publique. Report, Rapport du Centre d'Analyse Stratégique, La Documentation française.

Chevassus-au-Louis, N. (2014). *Théories du complot*. Éditions First, Paris.

Child, J. (1972). Organization structure and strategies of control: A replication of the Aston study. *Administrative Science Quarterly*, 17, 163–177.

Choquet, G. (1953–1954). Theory of capacities. *Annales de l'institut Fourier*, 5, 131–295.

Christensen, C. (1997). *The Innovator's Dilemma*. Harvard Business School Press, Boston.

Coase, R. (1937). The nature of the firm. *Economica*, 4, 386–405.

Coase, R. (1960). The problem of social cost. *Journal of Law and Economics*, 3, 1–44.

Cohen, W. and Levinthal, D. (1990). Absorptive capacity: A new perspective on learning and innovation. *Administrative Science Quarterly*, 35, 128–152.

Cohendet, P. and Zapata, S. (2009). Innovation and creativity: Is there economic significance to the creative city? *International Management*, 13, 23–36.

Cohendet, P., Farcot, M., Pénin, J. (2006). Entre incitation et coordination : repenser le rôle économique du brevet d'invention dans une économie fondée sur la connaissance. *Management International*, 10, 65–84.

Cohendet, P., Grandadam, D., Simon, L. (2010). The anatomy of the creative city. *Industry & Innovation*, 17(1), 91–111.

Cohendet, P., Grandadam, D., Simon, L. (2011). Rethinking urban creativity: Lessons from Barcelona and Montreal. *City, Culture and Society*, 2, 151–158.

Cohendet, P., Grandadam, D., Simon, L. (2013). Places, spaces and the dynamics of creativity: The video game industry in Montreal. *Regional Studies*, 47(10), 1701–1714.

Collectif (2013). FabLab, hackingspace, les lieux de fabrication numérique collaboratif. Working document, December.

Colombo, M. and Garrone, P. (1996). Technological cooperative agreements and firm's R&D intensity: A note on causality relations. *Research Policy*, 25, 923–932.

Contractor, F. and Lorange, P. (1988). *Cooperatives Strategies in International Business*. Lexington Books, Lanham.

Corbel, P. (2005). Collaborer pour innover : un partenariat privé-public souvent de proximité. *SESSI*, 12(2).

Corbel, P. (2007). *Management stratégique des droits de la propriété intellectuelle*. Gualino, Paris.

Cosnard, M. (1991). Dynamique chaotique déterministe. In *Les théories de la complexité*, Fogelman Soulié, F. (ed.). Le Seuil, Paris.

Costanza, R. and Daly, H. (1992). Natural capital and sustainable development. *Conservation Biology*, 6(1), 37–46.

Costanza, R., Cumberland, J., Daly, H., Goodland, R., Norgaard, R. (eds) (1997a). *An Introduction to Ecological Economics*. St. Lucie Press, Boca Raton.

Costanza, R., d'Arge, R., de Groot, R. (1997b). The value of the world's ecosystem services and natural capital. *Nature*, 87(3), 253–260.

Cournot, A. (1838). *Recherches sur les principes mathématiques de la théorie des richesses*. Marcel Rivière, Paris.

Cova, B. (1995). *Au delà du marché : quand le lien importe plus que le bien*. L'Harmattan, Paris.

Cova, B. and Cova, V. (2002). Tribal marketing: The tribalisation of society and its impact on the conduct of marketing. *European Journal of Marketing*, 36(5–6), 595–620.

Crémer, J. (1980). A partial theory of the optimal organization of a bureaucracy. *The Bell Journal of Economics*, 11(2), 683–693.

Crémer, J. (1990). Common knowledge and the co-ordination of economic activities. In *The Firm as a Nexus of Treaties*, Aoki, M., Gustafsson, B., Williamson, O.E. (eds). Sage, London.

Crémer, J. (1993). Corporate culture and shared knowledge. *Industrial and Corporate Change*, 2(3), 351–386.

Crocker, T. (1966). The structuring of atmospheric pollution control systems. In *The Economics of Air Pollution*, Wolozin, H. (ed.). Norton, New York.

Cropper, M. and Oates, W. (1992). Environmental economies: A survey. *Journal of Economic Literature*, 30(2), 675–740.

Cropper, M., Evans, W., Berardi, S., Ducla-Soares, M., Portney, P. (1992). The determinants of pesticide regulation: A statistical analysis of EPA decision making. *Journal of Political Economy*, 100, 175–197.

Cunha, M., Rego, A., Oliveira, P., Habib, N. (2014). Product innovation in resource-poor environments: Three research streams. *Journal of Product Innovation Management*, 31(2), 202–210.

Cyert, R. and March, J. (1963). *A Behavioral Theory of the Firm*. Prentice Hall, Hoboken.

Dahlander, L. and Magnusson, M. (2005). Relationships between open source software companies and communities: Observations from Nordic firms. *Research Policy*, 34(4), 481–493.

Dahlander, L. and Magnusson, M. (2008). How do firms make use of open source communities? *Long Range Planning*, 41(6), 629–649.

Dahlander, L., Frederiksen, L., Rullani, F. (2008). Online communities and open innovation: Governance and symbolic value creation. *Industry & Innovation*, 15(2), 115–123.

Dahlander, L., Frederiksen, L., Rullani, F. (2014). *Online Communities and Open Innovation: Governance and Symbolic Value Creation*. Routledge, Abingdon.

Daily, G. (ed.) (1997). *Nature's Services: Societal Dependence on Natural Ecosystems*. Island Press, Washington.

Dales, J. (1968). Land, water and ownership. *Canadian Journal of Economics*, 1, 797–804.

Dalle, J.M. (1995). Dynamiques d'adoption, coordination et diversité. La diffusion des standards technologiques. *Revue économique*, 46(4), 1081–1098.

Daly, H. (1990). Toward some operational principles of sustainable development. *Ecological Economics*, 2, 1–6.

Dasgupta, P. and Heal, G. (1974). The optimal depletion of exhaustible resources. *The Review of Economic Studies*, 41, 3–28.

DATALAB (2019). Chiffres clefs du climat. Report, Commissariat Général au Développement Durable, Paris.

David, P. (1985). Clio and the economics of QWERTY. *American Economic Review*, 75(2), 332–337.

Davidow, W. and Malone, M. (1992). *The Virtual Corporation*. Harper Business, New York.

Davis, K. (1973). The case for and against business assumption of social responsibilities. *Academy of Management Review*, 2(3), 70–76.

De Marchi, V. (2012). Environmental innovation and R&D cooperation: Empirical evidence from Spanish manufacturing firm. *Research Policy*, 41(3), 614–623.

Dean, T. and McMullen, J. (2007). Toward a theory of sustainable entrepreneurship: Reducing environmental degradation through entrepreneurial action. *Journal of Business Venturing*, 22, 50–76.

Debord, G. (1967). *La société du spectacle*. Buchet-Chastel, Paris.

Demski, J., Sappington, D., Spiller, P. (1987). Managing supplier switching. *The RAND Journal of Economics*, 18, 77–97.

Depret, M. and Hamdouch, A. (2009). Quelles politiques de l'innovation et de l'environnement pour quelle dynamique d'innovation environnementale ? *Innovations*, 9(2), 127–147.

Deschamps, L. (1998). L'investissement de l'éthique : vers une réconciliation de l'économie et de l'éthique. *Futuribles*, 125, 39–45.

DGCIS (2010). Le tableau de bord des NTIC dans les entreprises. Report, Direction Générale de la Compétitivité et de l'Industrie et des Services, Paris.

Dhillon, B. (1989). *Life Cycle Costing: Techniques, Models and Applications*. Gordon & Breach, Philadelphia.

Dhont-Peltrault, E. and Pfister, E. (2006). L'externalisation de la R&D : quel arbitrage entre sous-traitance et coopération ? Research note 06–02, MEN Direction de l'Evaluation et de la Prospective.

Di Maria, E. and Finotto, V. (2008). Communities of consumption and made in Italy. *Industry and Innovation*, 15(2), 179–197.

DiBona, C. and Ockman, S. (1999). *Open Sources: Voices From the Open Source Revolution*. O'Reilly Media, Newton.

Dittrich, K. and Duysters, G. (2007). Networking as a means to strategy change: The case of open innovation in mobile telephony. *Journal of Product Innovation Management*, 24(6), 510–521.

Dittrich, K., Duysters, G., de Man, A. (2007). Strategic repositioning by means of alliances networks: The case of IBM. *Research Policy*, 36, 1496–1511.

Dobers, P., Strannegard, L., Wolff, R. (2001). Knowledge interests in corporate environmental management. *Business Strategy and the Environment*, 10, 335–343.

Donaldson, T. and Preston, L. (1995). The stakeholder theory of the corporation: Concepts, evidence and implications. *Academy of Management Review*, 20(1), 65–91.

Dooley, K. and Van de Ven, A. (1999). Explaining complex organizational dynamics. Special issue: Application of complexity theory to organization science. *Organization Science*, 10(3), 353–372.

Dosi, G., Teece, D., Winter, S. (1990). Les frontières des entreprises : vers une théorie de la cohérence de la grande entreprise. *Revue d'économie industrielle*, 1(5), 238–254.

Doz, Y. (1994). Les dilemmes de la gestion du renouvellement des compétences clés. *Revue française de gestion*, 7(9), 92–104.

Drèze, J. (1962). L'utilité sociale d'une vie humaine. *Revue française de recherche opérationnelle*, 23, 3–28.

Ducheneaut, N., Nickell, E., Moore, R., Yee, N. (2007). Une solitude collective ? In *Culture d'univers : jeux en réseau, mondes virtuels, le nouvel âge de la société numérique*, Beau, F. (ed.). FYP Éditions, Limoges.

Dussauge, P., Garette, B., Ramanantsoa, B. (1988). Stratégies relationnelles et stratégies d'alliances technologiques. *Revue française de gestion*, 8(6), 7–19.

Dutton, J. and Jackson, S. (1987). Categorizing strategic issues: Links to organizational action. *Academy of Management Review*, 12(1), 76–90.

Dwyer, P. (2007). Measuring the value of electronic word of mouth and it's impact in consumer communities. *Journal of Interactive Marketing*, 21(2), 63–79.

Elliott, R. (1994). Exploring the symbolic meaning of brands. *British Journal of Management*, 5, 13–19.

Elliott, R. and Leonard, C. (2004). Peer pressure and poverty: Exploring fashion brands and consumption symbolism among of the "British poor". *Journal of Consumer Behaviour*, 3(4), 347–359.

Elliott, R. and Wattanasuwan, K. (1998). Brand as symbolic resources for the construction of identity. *International Journal of Advertising*, 17(2), 131–144.

Ellsberg, D. (1961). Risk, ambiguity, and the savage axioms. *Quarterly Journal of Economics*, 75, 643–669.

Eychenne, F. (2012). Fab Labs : Tour d'Horizon. Report, FING.

Fabricky, W. and Blanchard, B. (1991). *Life Cycle Cost and Economic Analysis*. Prentice Hall, Hoboken.

Faems, D., Van Looy, B., Debackere, K. (2005). Interorganizational collaboration and innovation: Toward a portfolio approach. *Journal of Product Innovation Management*, 22(3), 238–250.

Farrell, J. and Gallini, N. (1988). Second-sourcing as a commitment: Monopoly incentives to attract competition. *Quarterly Journal of Economics*, 103(4), 673–694.

Farrell, J. and Saloner, G. (1986). Installed base and compatibility. *American Economic Review*, 76, 940–955.

Farrell, J. and Scotchmer, S. (1988). Partnerships. *Quarterly Journal of Economics*, 103, 279–297.

Fava, J. (1991). Product life cycle assessment: Improving environmental quality. *Integrated Environmental Management*, 3, 19–21.

Fayol, H. (1916). *Administration générale et industrielle*. Dunod, Paris.

Ferru, M., Liberat, N., Guimond, B., Depret, M.H. (2015). Deconstructing the collective process of environmental innovation: A case study of Poitou-Charentes companies. *Journal of Innovation Economics & Management*, 1(16), 139–170.

FING (2014). État des lieux et typologie des ateliers de fabrication numérique. Report, Ministère de l'économie de l'industrie et du numérique/Direction générale des entreprises, Paris.

Fleming, L. and Waguespack, D. (2007). Brokerage, boundary spanning, and leadership in open innovation communities. *Organization Science*, 18(2), 165–180.

Flichy, P. (2001). La place de l'imaginaire dans l'action technique, le cas de l'internet. *Réseaux*, 5(109), 52–73.

Florida, R. (1996). Lean and green: The move to environmentally conscious manufacturing. *California Management Review*, 39(1), 80–105.

Florida, R. (2002). *The Rise of the Creative Class*. Basic Books, New York.

Florida, R. (2005). *The Flight of the Creative Class: The New Global Competition for Talent*. Harper Collins, New York.

Foxon, T. and Pearson, P. (2008). Overcoming barriers to innovation and diffusion of cleaner technologies: Some features of a sustainable innovation policy regime. *Journal of Cleaner Production*, 16(1), 148–161.

Franke, N. and Shah, S. (2003). How communities support innovative activities: An exploration of assistance and sharing among end-users. *Research Policy*, 32(1), 157–178.

Freeman, R. (1984). *Strategic Management: A Stakeholder Approach*. Pitman, Boston.

Frondel, M., Horbach, J., Rennings, K. (2007). End-of-pipe or cleaner production? An empirical comparison of environmental innovation decisions across OECD countries. *Business Strategy and the Environment*, 16(8), 571–584.

Fussler, C. and James, P. (1996). *Driving Eco-Innovation: A Breakthrough Discipline for Innovation and Sustainability*. Pitman, Boston.

Galbraith, J.R. (1971). Matrix organization designs: How to combine functional and project forms. *Business Horizons*, 14(1), 2–96.

Gallini, N. (2002). The economics of patents: Lessons from recent US patent reform. *Journal of Economic Perspectives*, 16(2), 131–154.

Gambardella, A. and McGahan, A. (2009). Business-model innovation: General purpose technologies and their implications for industry structure. *Long Range Planning*, 43(2–3), 262–271.

Gaon, T. and Stora, M. (2008). Critique de la notion d'addiction au jeu vidéo. *Quaderni*, 7(6), 33–42.

Garnier, M. and Poncin, I. (2013). L'avatar en marketing : synthèse, cadre intégrateur et perspectives. *Recherche et applications en marketing*, 28(1), 92–123.

Gawer, A. and Cusumano, M. (2002). *Platform Leadership: How Intel, Microsoft, and Cisco Drive Industry Innovation*. Harvard Business School Press, Boston.

Gayer, T., Hamilton, J., Viscusi, W. (2000). Private values of risk trade-offs at Superfund sites: Housing market evidence on learning about risk. *The Review of Economics and Statistics*, 82, 439–451.

Georgescu-Roegen, N. (1971). *The Entropy Law and the Economic Process*. Harvard University Press, Cambridge.

Gershenfeld, N. (2005). *FabLab: The Coming Revolution on Your Desktop: From Personal Computers to Personal Fabrication*. Basic Books, New York.

Geyer, R. and Jackson, T. (2004). Supply loops & their constraints: The industrial ecology of recycling & reuse. *California Management Review*, 46(2), 55–73.

Gilbert, R. (1989). Mobility barriers and the value of incumbency. In *Handbook of Industrial Organization*, Schmalensee, R. and Willig, R. (eds). Elsevier, Amsterdam.

Girard, R. (1972). *La violence et le sacré*. Éditions Grasset, Paris.

Gómez-Baggethun, E., de Groot, R., Lomas, P., Montes, C. (2010). The history of ecosystem services in economic theory and practice: From early notions to markets and payment schemes. *Ecological Economics*, 69(6), 1209–1218.

Govindarajan, V. and Ramamurti, R. (2011). Reverse innovation, emerging markets, and global strategy. *Global Strategy Journal*, 1, 191–205.

Granovetter, M. (1985). Economic actions and social structures: The problem of embeddedness. *American Journal of Sociology*, 91, 481–510.

Granovetter, M. (1994). Business groups. In *The Handbook of Economic Sociology*, Smelser, N. and Swedberg, R. (eds). Princeton University Press, Princeton.

Granstrand, O. (1999). *The Economics and Management of Intellectual Property*. Edward Elgar, Cheltenham.

Green, K., McMeekin, A., Irwin, A. (1994). Technological trajectories and R&D for environmental innovation in UK firms. *Futures*, 26(10), 1047–1059.

Grossman, S. and Hart, O. (1986). The cost and benefits of ownership: A theory of vertical and lateral integration. *Journal of Political Economy*, 94(4), 691–719.

Grubb, E. and Grathwohl, H. (1967). Consumer self-concept, symbolism and market behavior: A theoretical approach. *Journal of Marketing*, 31, 22–27.

Guillaume, H. (1972). L'analyse coûts-avantages et la préparation des décisions publiques. *Revue économique*, 23(3), 358–409.

Gumuchian, H. and Pecqueur, B. (2006). *La ressource territoriale*. Éditions Economica, Paris.

Gustafsson, B. (1998). Scope and limits of the market mechanism in environmental management. *Ecological Economics*, 24(2), 259–274.

Gyrd-Jones, R. and Kornum, N. (2013). Managing the co-created brand: Value and cultural complementarity in online and offline multistakeholder ecosystems. *Journal of Business Research*, 66(9), 1484–1493.

Hagedoorn, J. (2002). Inter-firm R&D partnerships: An overview of major trends and patterns since 1960. *Research Policy*, 31(4), 477–492.

Hahn, R. (1984). Market power and transferable property rights. *The Quarterly Journal of Economics*, 99, 753–765.

Hahn, R. (1989). Economic prescriptions for environmental problems: How the patient followed the doctor's orders. *Journal of Economic Perspectives*, 3, 95–114.

Hakansson, H. (1982). *International Marketing and Purchasing of Industrial Goods: An Interaction Approach*. Wiley, New York.

Hakansson, H. (1988). Formal and informal cooperative strategies in international networks. In *Cooperative Strategies in International Business*, Contractor, F.J. and Lorange, P. (eds). Lexington Books, Lanham.

Hakansson, H. (1989). *Corporate Technological Behaviour*. Routledge, Abingdon.

Hall, R. (1992). The strategic analysis of intangible resources. *Strategic Management Journal*, 13, 135–144.

Hall, B. and Ziedonis, R. (2001). The patent paradox revisited: An empirical study of patenting in the U.S. semiconductor industry, 1979–1995. *The RAND Journal of Economics*, 32(1), 101–128.

Halme, M., Lindeman, S., Linna, P. (2012). Innovation for inclusive business: Intrapreneurial bricolage in multinational corporations. *Journal of Management Studies*, 49(4), 743–784.

Hamdouch, A., Laperche, B., Munier, F. (2008). The collective innovation process and the need for dynamic coordination: General presentation. *Journal of Innovation Economics Management*, 2, 3–13.

Hammerly, J., Paquin, T., Walton, S. (1999). Freeing the source: The story of Mozilla. In *Open Sources: Voices from the Open Source Revolution*, DiBona, C., Ockman, S., Stone, M. (eds). O'Reilly Media, Cambridge.

Handy, C. (1995). Trust and the virtual organization. *Harvard Business Review*, 73(3), 40–50.

Hansen, E., Große-Dunker, F., Reichwald, R. (2009). Sustainability innovation cube – A framework to evaluate sustainability-oriented innovations. *International Journal of Innovation Management*, 13(4), 683–713.

Hardelin, J., Katossky, A., Marical, F. (2010). Pourquoi et comment monétariser l'environnement ? In *Donner une valeur à l'environnement : la monétarisation, un exercice délicat mais nécessaire*, Pappalardo, M. (ed.). Ministère de l'écologie, Paris.

Hardin, G. (1968). The tragedy of the commons. *Science*, 162, 1243–1248.

Harrigan, K. (1985a). *Joint Ventures, Alliances and Corporate Strategy*. Beard Books, Frederick.

Harrigan, K. (1985b). *Strategies for Joint Ventures*. Lexington Books, Lanham.

Harsanyi, J. (1956). Approaches to the bargaining problem before and after the theory of games. *Econometrica*, 24, 144–157.

Harsanyi, J. (1965). Bargaining and conflict situations in the light of a new approach to game theory. *American Economic Review*, 55, 447–471.

Harsanyi, J. (1982). Morality and the theory of rational behaviour. In *Utilitarianism and Beyond*, Sen, A. and Williams, B. (eds). Cambridge University Press, Cambridge.

Hart, S. (1995). A natural-resource-based view of the firm. *Academy of Management Review*, 20(4), 986–1014.

Hart, S. (1997). Beyond greening: Strategies for a sustainable world. *Harvard Business Review*, 75, 66–77.

Hart, O. and Moore, J. (1990). Property rights and the nature of the firm. *Journal of Political Economy*, 98(6), 119–158.

Hart, S. and Shrivastava, P. (1995). Creating sustainable corporations. *Business Strategy & the Environment*, 4(3), 154–165.

Hartje, V. and Laurie, L. (1984). Adoption rules for pollution control innovations: End-of-pipe versus integrated technologies. Working document, International Institute for Environment and Society.

Hartwick, J. (1977). Intergenerational equity and the investing of rents from exhaustible resources. *The American Economic Review*, 67(5), 972–974.

Hayek, F. (1945). The use of knowledge in society. *American Economic Review*, 4, 519–530.

Hayes, R. and Wheelwright, S. (1979). The dynamics of process-product life cycles. *Harvard Business Review*, 57(2), 127–136.

Heilbrunn, B. (2010). Les marques, entre valeur d'image et valeur d'usage. *L'Expansion Management Review*, 2010/2(137), 72–78.

Heilbrunn, B. (2017). Ré-jouir : pour une esth/éthique de la marque. *Rue Descartes*, 2017/1(91), 141–149.

Heller, M. and Eisenberg, R. (1998). Can patents deter innovation? The Anticommons in biomedical research. *Science*, 280, 698–701.

Hellström, T. (2007). Dimensions of environmentally sustainable innovation: The structure of eco-innovation concepts. *Sustainable Development*, 15, 148–159.

Hemmelskamp, J. (1997). Environmental policy instruments & their effect on innovation. *European Planning Studies*, 5(2), 177–194.

Henderson, R. and Clark, K. (1990). Architectural innovation. *Administrative Science Quarterly*, 35, 9–30.

Henriques, I. and Sadorsky, P. (1999). The relationship between environmental commitment and managerial perceptions of stakeholder importance. *Academy of Management Journal*, 42(1), 47–99.

Henry, C. (1974a). Investment decisions under uncertainty: The irreversibility effect. *American Economic Review*, 64, 1006–1012.

Henry, C. (1974b). Option values in the economics of irreplaceable assets. *Symposium on the Economics of Exhaustible Resources. Review of Economic Studies*, 89–104.

Hillary, R. (ed.) (2000). *Small and Medium-Sized Enterprises and the Environment: Business Imperatives*. Greenleaf Publishing, Sheffield.

Hofstra, N. and Huisingh, D. (2014). Eco-innovations characterized: A taxonomic classification of relationships between humans and nature. *Journal of Cleaner Production*, 66, 459–468.

Holland, L. (2003). Can the principle of the ecological footprint be applied to measure the environmental sustainability of business? *Corporate Social Responsibility and Environmental Management*, 10, 224–232.

Holling, C. (1973). Resilience and stability of ecological systems. *Annual Review of Ecological Systems*, 4(1), 1–23.

Holling, C. (2001). Understanding the complexity of economic, ecological, and social systems. *Ecosystems*, 4, 390–405.

Holmstrom, B. and Tirole, J. (1989). The theory of the firm. In *Handbook of Industrial Organization*, volume 1, Schmalensee, R. and Willig, R. (eds). Elsevier, Amsterdam.

Holt, D. (2004). *How Brands Become Icons: The Principles of Cultural Branding*. Harvard Business School Press, Boston.

Horbach, J. (2008). Determinants of environmental innovation – New evidence from German panel data sources. *Research Policy*, 37(1), 163–173.

Hotelling, H. (1929). Stability in competition. *Economic Journal*, 39, 41–57.

Hotelling, H. (1931). The economics of exhaustible resources. *Journal of Political Economy*, 39(2), 137–175.

Houssiaux, J. (1957). Le concept de quasi-intégration et le rôle des sous-traitants dans l'industrie. *Revue économique*, 2, 220–247.

Howe, J. (2008). *Crowdsourcing*. Crown Publishing Group, New York.

Huber, J. (2004). *New Technologies and Environmental Innovation*. Edward Elgar, Cheltenham.

Hunt, C. and Auster, E. (1990). Proactive environmental management: Avoiding the toxic trap. *Sloan Management Review*, 31, 7–18.

Hutchinson, A. and Hutchinson, F. (1997). *Environmental Business Management*. McGraw Hill, New York.

Imai, K. and Itami, H. (1984). Interpenetration of organization and market. *International Journal of Industrial Organization*, 2(4), 285–310.

Ingelaere, R. (2015). Innovations technologiques et performance industrielle globale : l'exemple de l'impression 3D. Report, Conseil économique social et environmental, Paris.

INSEE (2010). Les sociétés innovantes de 10 salariés ou plus : quatre sur dix entre 2006 et 2008. *INSEE Première*, 1314.

Irwin, A. and Hooper, P. (1992). Clean technology, successful innovation and the greening of industry: A case study analysis. *Business Strategy and the Environment*, 1(2), 1–11.

Itoh, H. (1987). Information processing capacities of the firm. *Journal of the Japanese and International Economies*, 1(3), 299–326.

Jacquemin, A. (1985). *Sélection et pouvoir dans la nouvelle économie industrielle*. Economica, Paris.

Jacquemin, A. (1988). Coopération entre les entreprises et droit économique. In *Coopération entre entreprises*, Jacquemin, A. and Remiche, B. (eds). De Boek, Brussels.

Jaffe, A. and Palmer, K. (1997). Environmental regulation and innovation: A panel data study. *Review of Economics and Statistics*, 79(4), 610–619.

James, P. (1997). The sustainability circle: A new tool for product design. *Journal of Sustainable Product Design*, 2, 52–57.

Jean, A. (2021). *Les algorithmes font-ils la loi ?* Éditions de l'Observatoire, Paris.

Jensen, M. and Meckling, W. (1976). Theory of the firm, managerial behaviour, agency costs and ownership structure. *Journal of Financial Economics*, 3(4), 305–360.

Jonas, H. (1979). *Prinzip Verantwortung: Versuch einer Ethik für die technologische Zivilisation*. Insel-Verlag, Francfort-sur-le-Main.

Judge, W. and Douglas, T. (1998). Performance implications of incorporating natural environmental issues into the strategic planning process: An empirical assessment. *Journal of Management Studies*, 35(2), 241–262.

Kamien, M. and Schwartz, L. (1982). Market structure and innovation: A survey. *Journal of Economic Literature*, 1, 1–37.

Kamoche, K. and Cunha, M. (2001). Minimal structures: From jazz improvisation to product innovation. *Organization Studies*, 22, 733–764.

Kapferer, J.N. (1998). *Les marques Capital de l'entreprise*. Éditions d'Organisation, Paris.

Kapferer, J.N. and Bastien, V. (2008). *Luxe oblige*. Éditions d'Organisation, Paris.

Kapferer, J.N. and Laurent, G. (1983). *La sensibilité aux marques : un nouveau concept pour gérer les marques*. Éditions d'Organisation, Paris.

Kast, R. (2003). Calcul d'un coût économiquement acceptable pour la mise en pratique du principe de précaution. *Revue économique*, 54(6), 1307–1334.

Katz, M. and Shapiro, C. (1985). Network externalities, competition and compatibility. *American Economic Review*, 75, 424–440.

Kauffman, S. (1993). *The Origins of Order*. Oxford University Press, Oxford.

Kauffman, S. (1995). *The Search for Law of Self Organization and Complexity*. Oxford University Press, Oxford.

Kemp, R. (2010). Eco-innovation: Definition, measurement and open research issues. *Economia Politica*, 27(3), 397–420.

Kemp, R. and Foxon, T. (2007). *Typology of Eco-Innovation*. United Nations University, Maastricht.

Kemp, R. and Pearson, P. (2007). Final report of the MEI project. Report, MEI Measuring Eco-innovation, UNU-Merit – Maastricht Working Paper Series.

Keynes, J.M. (1921). *A Treatise on Probability*. Macmillan, London.

Keynes, J.M. (1936). *The General Theory of Employment Interest and Money*. Macmillan, London.

Kim, A. and Ko, E. (2012). Do social media marketing activities enhance customer equity? An empirical study of luxury fashion brand. *Journal of Business Research*, 65(10), 1480–1486.

Kimberly, J. and Bouchikhi, H. (1995). The dynamics of organizational development and change: How the past shapes the present and constrains the future. *Organization Science*, 6(1), 9–18.

Kindleberger, C. (1986). International public goods without international government. *American Economic Review*, 76(1), 1–13.

Klein, J.-L. and Pecqueur, B. (2017). Living labs, innovation sociale et territoire. *Canadian Journal of Regional Science/Revue canadienne des sciences régionales*, 40(1), 1–4.

Klein, B., Crawford, R., Alchian, A. (1978). Vertical integration, appropriable rents, and the competitive contracting process. *Journal of Law and Economics*, 21, 297–326.

Kline, S. and Rosenberg, N. (1986). An overview of innovation. In *The Positive Sum Strategy*, Landau, R. and Rosenberg, N. (eds). Academy of Engineering Press, London.

Knight, F. (1921). *Risk, Uncertainty and Profit.* The Riverside Press, Cambridge.

Knight, P. and Jenkins, J. (2009). Adopting and applying eco-design techniques: A practitioners perspective. *Journal of Cleaner Production*, 17(5), 549–558.

Kogut, B. (1989). The stability of joint ventures. *The Journal of Industrial Economics*, 38(2), 183–198.

Kohlberg, E. and Mertens, J.F. (1986). On the strategic stability of equilibria. *Econometrica*, 1003–1037.

Kohn, M. (2010). Totem et tabou de Freud et l'origine du langage. *Figures de la psychanalyse*, 2010/1(19), 251–260.

Kozinets, R. (1999). E-tribalized marketing? The strategic implications of virtual communities of consumption. *European Management Journal*, 17(3), 252–264.

Kozinets, R. (2002). The field behind the screen: Using netnography for marketing research in online communities. *Journal of Marketing Research*, 39, 61–72.

Kreps, D. (1990). Corporate culture and economic theory. In *Perspective on Positive Political Economy*, Alt, J. and Shepsle, K. (eds). Cambridge University Press, Cambridge.

Kreps, D. and Wilson, R. (1982a). Reputation and imperfect information. *Journal of Economic Theory*, 27, 253–279.

Kreps, D. and Wilson, R. (1982b). Sequential equilibria. *Econometrica*, 863–894.

Krutilla, J. (1961). Welfare aspects of benefit-cost analysis. *Journal of Political Economy*, 69(3), 226–235.

Krutilla, J. (1967). Conservation reconsidered. *American Economic Review*, 57, 777–786.

Kuhn, T. (1962). *La structure des révolutions scientifiques*. Flammarion, Paris.

Laffont, J.J. (1988). *Fondements de l'économie publique. Cours de théorie microéconomique*, volume 1. Éditions Economica, Paris.

Lancaster, K. (1975). Socially optimal product differentiation. *American Economic Review*, 65(4), 567–585.

Lanjouw, J. and Shankerman, M. (2001). Characteristics of patent litigation: A window on competition. *The RAND Journal of Economics*, 32(1), 129–151.

Lave, J. and Wenger, E. (1991), *Situated Learning. Legitimate Peripheral Participation*. Cambridge University Press, Cambridge.

Lawrence, P. and Lorsch, J. (1967). *Organization and Environment: Managing Differenciation and Integration*. Harvard Business School Press, Boston.

Lecoq, X., Demilx, B., Warnier, V. (2006). Le business model, un outil d'analyse stratégique. *L'Expansion Management Review*, 123, 96–109.

Lessig, L. (2001). *The Future of Ideas*. Vintage Books, New York.

Levi-Strauss, C. (1962a). *La pensée sauvage*. Plon, Paris.

Levi-Strauss, C. (1962b). *Le totémisme aujourd'hui*. PUF, Paris.

Levin, R., Klevorick, A., Nelson, R., Winter, S. (1987). Appropriating the returns from industrial research and development. *Brookings Papers on Economic Activity*, 3, 783–820.

Levy, S. (1959). Symbols for sale. *Harvard Business Review*, 37(4), 117–124.

Lewin, K. (1948). *Resolving Social Conflicts: Selected Papers on Group Dynamics*. Harper & Brothers, New York.

Lewin, A.Y. (1999). Application of complexity theory to organization science. *Organization Science*, 10(3), 233–236.

Lewin, A.Y. and Volberda, H.W. (1999). Co-evolution. *Organization Science*, 10(5), 519–534.

Lieberman, M. and Montgomery, D. (1988). First-mover advantages. *Strategic Management Journal*, 9, 45–58.

Lipnack, J. and Stamps, J. (1997). *Virtual Teams: Reaching Across Space, Time, and Organizations with Technology*. Wiley, New York.

Lipovetsky, G. (1987). *L'Empire de l'éphémère*. Gallimard, Paris.

Lundvall, B. (1988). Innovation as an interactive process. In *Technical Change and Economic Theory*, Dosi, G., Freeman, C., Nelson, R., Silverberg, G., Soete, L. (eds). Pinter Publishers, London.

Lyotard, J.F. (1979). *La condition post-moderne*. Éditions de Minuit, Paris.

Maffesoli, M. (1988). *Le temps des tribus, le déclin de l'individualisme dans les sociétés de masse*. Méridiens Klincksieck, Paris.

Mansfield, E. (1984). R&D and innovation: Some empirical findings. In *R&D, Patents, and Productivity*, Griliches, Z. (ed.). University of Chicago Press, Chicago.

Mansfield, E., Schwartz, M., Wagner, S. (1981). Imitation costs and patents: An empirical study. *Economic Journal*, 91, 907–918.

March, J. (1991). Exploration and exploitation in organizational learning. *Organization Science*, 2(1), 1–13.

March, J. and Simon, H. (1958). *Organizations*. Wiley, New York.

Marion, G. (2003). Apparence et identité : une approche sémiotique du discours des adolescentes à propos de leur expérience de la mode. *Recherche et applications en marketing*, 18, 1–27.

Marshall, A. (1890). *Principles of Economics*. Macmillan, London.

Martinet, A.C. and Savall, H. (1978). Dysfonctionnements, coûts et performances cachés. *Revue d'économie industrielle*, 5, 82–94.

Martinez-Alier, J. (1995). The environment as a luxury good or "too poor to be green"? *Ecological Economics*, 13, 1–10.

Massé, P. (1968). *Le choix des investissements*. Dunod, Paris.

Mauss, M. (1923). *Essai sur le don, forme archaïque de l'échange*. Librairie Félix Alcan, Paris.

Mazzanti, M. and Zoboli, R. (2008). Waste generation, waste disposal and policy effectiveness: Evidence on decoupling from the European Union. *Resources, Conservation & Recycling*, 52(10), 1221–1234.

McCracken, G. and Roth, V. (1989). Does clothing have a code? Empirical findings and theoretical implications in the study of clothing as a means of communication. *International Journal of Research in Marketing*, 6(1), 13–33.

McKim, R. (1972). *Experiences in Visual Thinking*. Wadsworth Publishing, Belmont.

McLuhan, M. (1962). *The Gutenberg Galaxy: The Making of the Typographic Man*. University of Toronto Press, Toronto.

McLuhan, M. (1967). *The Medium is the Massage: An Inventory of Effects*. Bantam Books, New York.

Meade, J. (1952). External economies and diseconomies in a competitive situation. *Economic Journal*, 62, 54–67.

Meadows, D., Meadows, D., Randers, J., Behrens, W. (1972). *The Limits to Growth*. Universe Books, New York.

Meek, W., Pacheco, D., York, J. (2010). The impact of social norms on entrepreneurial action: Evidence from the environmental entrepreneurship context. *Journal of Business Venturing*, 25(5), 493–509.

Mendez, A. and Mercier, D. (2006). Compétences-clés de territoires. Le rôle des relations inter-organisationnelles. *Revue française de gestion*, 2006/5(164), 253–275.

Merindol, V. and Versailles, D. (2017). Créer et innover aujourd'hui en Île de France : le rôle des plateformes d'innovations. Report, Le HubBpifrance, Innovation Factory and Paris&Co, Paris.

Merton, R. (1973). Theory of rational option pricing. *Bell Journal of Economics and Management Science*, 4, 141–183.

Meyer, H. (1995). Organizational environments and organizational discourse: Bureaucracy between two worlds. *Organization Science*, 6(1), 33–43.

Miles, R. and Snow, C. (1978). *Organization Strategy, Structure and Process*. McGraw Hill, New York.

Miles, R. and Snow, C. (1992). Causes of failures in network organizations. *California Management Review*, 34(4), 53–72.

Milgram, S. (1967). The small world problem. *Psychology Today*, 2, 60–67.

Miner, A., Bassoff, P., Moorman, C. (2001). Organizational improvisation and learning: A field study. *Administrative Science Quarterly*, 46, 304–337.

Miniard, P. and Cohen, J. (1983). Modeling personal and normative influences on behavior. *Journal of Consumer Research*, 10(2), 169–180.

Mintzberg, H. (1979). *The Structuring of Organizations*. Prentice-Hall, Hoboken.

Mitchell, R., Agle, B., Wood, D. (1997). Toward a theory of stakeholder identification and salience: Defining the principle of who and what really counts. *Academy of Management Review*, 22(4), 853–886.

Monfreda, C., Wackernagel, M., Deumling, D. (2004). Establishing national natural capital accounts based on detailed ecological footprint and biological capacity accounts. *Land Use Policy*, 21, 231–246.

Montgomery, D. (1972). Markets in licences and efficient pollution control programs. *Journal of Economic Theory*, 5, 395–418.

Moore, J. (1993). Predators and prey: A new ecology of competition. *Harvard Business Review*, 71, 75–86.

Moore, J. (1996). *The Death of Competition: Leadership and Strategy in the Age of Business Ecosystems*. HarperCollins, New York.

Moore, J. (2006). Business ecosystems and the view from the firm. *The Antitrust Bulletin*, 51(1), 31–75.

Moorman, C. and Miner, A. (1998a). The convergence between planning and execution: Improvisation in new product development. *Journal of Marketing*, 62, 1–20.

Moorman, C. and Miner, A. (1998b). Organizational improvisation and organizational memory. *Academy of Management Review*, 23(4), 698–723.

Morel, B. and Ramanujam, R. (1999). Through the looking glass of complexity: The dynamics of organizations as adaptative and evolving systems. Special issue: Application of complexity theory to organization science. *Organization Science*, 10(3), 278–293.

Morgan, G., Frost, P., Pondy, L. (1983). Organizational symbolism. In *Organizational Symbolism*, Pondy, L., Frost, P., Morgan, G., Dandridge, T. (eds). JAI Press, Stamford.

Moulin, H. (1981). *Théorie des jeux pour l'économie et la politique*. Éditions Hermann, Paris.

Moulin, H. (1984). Comportement stratégique et communication conflictuelle : le cas non-coopératif. *Revue économique*, 1, 109–145.

Mowery, D. (1998). The changing structure of the US national innovation system: Implications for international conflict and cooperation in R&D policy. *Research Policy*, 7(2), 639–654.

Mowery, D., Oxley, J., Silverman, B. (1996). Strategic alliances and interfirm knowledge transfer. *Strategic Management Journal*, 17, 77–91.

Muniz, A. and O'Guinn, T. (2001). Brand community. *Journal of Consumer Research*, 27(4), 412–432.

Musso, P. (2000). Le cyberespace, figure de l'utopie technologique réticulaire. *Sociologie et Sociétés*, 32(2), 31–56.

Musso, P. (2005). *Fabriquer le futur, l'imaginaire au service de l'innovation*. Édition Village Mondial, Paris.

Musso, P. (2009). Usages et imaginaires des TIC. In *L'évolution des usages et des cultures numériques : de la mutation du lien*, Licoppe, C. (ed.). FYP éditions, Limoges.

Myers, S. (1977). Determinants of corporate borrowing. *Journal of Financial Economics*, 5, 147–175.

Nash, J. (1951). Non cooperative games. *Annals of Mathematics*, 54(2), 286–295.

Nelson, R. and Winter, S. (1982). *An Evolutionary Theory of Economic Change*. The Belknap Press, Cambridge.

Nohria, N. and Berkley, J. (1994). Whatever happened to the take-charge manager? *Harvard Business Review*, 128–137.

Nonaka, I. (1991). The knowledge-creating company. *Harvard Business Review*, 69, 96–104.

Nonaka, I. (1994). A dynamic theory of organizational knowledge creation. *Organizational Science*, 5(1), 14–37.

Nordhaus, W. (1974). Resources as a constraint on growth. *American Economic Review*, 64, 22–26.

Nordhaus, W. (1991). To slow or not to slow: The economies of the greenhouse effect. *The Economic Journal*, 101, 920–937.

Nordhaus, W. (1998). Revised estimates of the impacts of climate change damages [Online]. Available at: http:www.econ.yale.edu./~nordhaus/homepage/impact.

Nordhaus, W. (2006). After Kyoto: Alternative mechanisms to control global warming. *American Economic Association (AEA)*, 96(2), 31–34.

North, D. (1990). *Institutions, Institutional Change and Economic Performance*. Cambridge University Press, Cambridge.

Obadia, L. (2012). Le totémisme, "aujourd'hui" ? *Anthropologie et sociétés*, 36(1–2), 279–295.

Olson, M. (1978). *La logique de l'action collective*. Presses Universitaires de France, Paris.

Oltra, V. and Saint Jean, M. (2009). Sectoral systems of environmental innovation: An application to the French automotive industry. *Technological Forecasting and Social Change*, 76(4), 567–583.

Ordover, J.A. (1991). A patent system for both diffusion and exclusion. *Journal of Economic Perspectives*, 5, 43–60.

Osborn, A. (1953). *Applied Imagination*. Scribner, Oxford.

Ostrom, E. (1990). *Governing the Commons: The Evolution of Institutions for Collective Action*. Cambridge University Press, Cambridge.

Ostrom, V. and Ostrom, E. (1977). Public goods and public choices. In *Alternatives for Delivering Public Services*, Savas, E.S. (ed.). Westview Press, Boulder.

Ouchi, W. (1981). *Theory Z: How American Business Can Meet the Japanese Challenge*. Addison Wiley, Boston.

Ouchi, W. (1984). *The M Form Society*. Addison Wiley, Boston.

Overcash, M. (1996). Cleaner production: Basic principles and development. *Clean Technology*, 2(1), 1–6.

Paché, G. and Paraponaris, C. (1993). *L'entreprise en réseau*. PUF, Paris.

Paché, G. and Paraponaris, C. (2006). L'entreprise en réseau : approches inter et intra organisationnelles. Éditions de l'ADREG [Online]. Available at: http://asso.nordnet.fr/adreg.

Pacheco, D., Dean, T., Payne, D. (2010). Escaping the green prison: Entrepreneurship and the creation of opportunities for sustainable development. *Journal of Business Venturing*, 25, 464–480.

Palmer, K., Oates, W., Portney, P. (1995). Tightening environmental standards: The benefit-cost or the no-cost paradigm? *Journal of Economic Perspectives*, 9(4), 119–132.

Paulré, B. (1993). Apprentissage et systémique. *Économies et sociétés*, 5/1993(1), 25–61.

Paulré, B. (1997). Évolutionnisme contemporain et auto-organisation. *Économie appliquée*, 50(3), 121–150.

Paulré, B. (1999). Introduction. In *Approches évolutionnistes de la firme et de l'industrie*, Baslé, M., Delorme, R., Lemoigne, J.L, Paulré, B. (eds). L'Harmattan, Paris.

Pearce, D. (1988). Economics, equity and sustainable development. *Futures*, 20, 598–605.

Pearce, D. and Atkinson, G. (1993). Capital theory and the measurement of sustainable development. *Ecological Economics*, 8, 103–108.

Pearce, D., Markandya, A., Barbier, E. (1989). *Blueprint for a Green Economy*. Earthscan, London.

Pechmann, C. and Knight, S. (2002). An experimental investigation of the joint effects of advertising and peers on adolescents' beliefs and intentions about cigarette consumption. *Journal of Consumer Research*, 29, 5–19.

Peirce, C. (1931–1958). *The Collected Works of Charles Saunders Peirce*, volumes 1–6 and 7–8. Hartshorne, C., Weiss, P., Burks, A.W. (eds). Harvard University Press, Camrbridge.

Pénin, J. (2010). Le problème des "patent trolls" : comment limiter la spéculation sur la propriété intellectuelle dans une économie fondée sur la connaissance. *Innovations*, 2(3), 35–53.

Penrose, E. (1959). *The Theory of the Growth of the Firm*. Oxford Blackwell, Hoboken.

Perrin, J. (2001). *Concevoir l'innovation industrielle*. Édition du CNRS, Paris.

Peters, T. and Waterman, R. (1982). *Search of Excellence*. Harper & Row, New York.

Pfeffer, J. and Salancik, G. (1978). *The External Control of Organizations: A Resource Dependence Perspective*. Harper & Row, New York.

Phau, I. and Prendergast, G. (2000). Consuming luxury brands: The relevance of the "rarity principle". *Journal of Brand Management*, 8(2), 122–137.

Philippette, T. (2015). La dimension sociocognitive de la jouabilité. *Interfaces numériques*, 4(1), 23–41.

Piacentini, M. and Mailer, G. (2005). Symbolic consumption in teenagers' clothing choices. *Journal of Consumer Behaviour*, 3(3), 251–262.

Pigou, A. (1920). *The Economics of Welfare*. Macmillan, London.

Pisano, G. (2006). Profiting from innovation and intellectual property revolution. *Research Policy*, 35, 1122–1130.

Polanyi, M. (1966). *The Tacit Dimension*. DoubleDay Anchor, New York.

Polonsky, M. and Ottman, J. (1988). Stakeholders' contribution to the green new development process. *Journal of Marketing Management*, 14, 533–557.

Porter, M. (1979). The structure within industries and companies performance. *Review of Economics and Statistics*, 2, 214–227.

Porter, M. (1980). *Competitive Strategy*. The Free Press, New York.

Porter, M. (1985). *Competitive Advantage*. The Free Press, New York.

Porter, M. (1990). *The Competitive Advantage of Nations*. The Free Press, New York.

Porter, M. (1991). America's Green strategy. *Scientific American*, 264, 168.

Porter, M. and van der Linde, C. (1995a). Green and competitive. *Harvard Business Review*, 120–134.

Porter, M. and van der Linde, C. (1995b). Towards a new conception of the environment–competitiveness relationship. *Journal of Economic Perspectives*, 9(4), 97–118.

Powell, W. (1990). Neither market nor hierarchy: Network forms of organization. *Research in Organization Behavior*, 12, 295–336.

Powell, W., Koput, K., Smith-Doerr, L. (1996). Interorganizational collaboration and the locus of innovation: Networks of learning in biotechnology. *Administrative Science Quarterly*, 41(1), 116–145.

Prahalad, C. (2005). *The Fortune at the Base of the Pyramid: Eradicating Poverty Through Profits*. Wharton School Publishing, Philadelphia.

Prahalad, C. and Hamel, G. (1990). The core competence of the corporation. *Harvard Business Review*, 3, 79–91.

Prahalad, C. and Mashelkar, R. (2010). Innovation's holy grail. *Harvard Business Review*, 132–141.

Prigogine, I. and Stenger, I. (1979). *La Nouvelle Alliance*. Gallimard, Paris.

Psillos, S. (2011). An explorer upon untrodden ground: Peirce on abduction. In *Handbook of the History of Logic, Inductive Logic*, Hartmann, S. and Woods, J. (eds). Elsevier, Amsterdam.

Radjou, N., Prabhu, J., Ahuja, S. (2012). *Jugaad Innovation: Think Frugal, Be Flexible, Generate Break Through Growth*. Jossey-Bass, San Francisco.

Radner, R. (1992). Hierarchy: The economics of managing. *Journal of Economic Literature*, 1392–1415.

Rawls, J. (1971). *A Theory of Justice*. Harvard University Press, Cambridge.

Raymond, E. (1999). *The Cathedral and the Bazaar*. O'ReillyMedia, Newton.

Rayport, J. and Sviokla, J. (1995). Exploiting the virtual value chain. *Harvard Business Review*, 73(6), 75–85.

Raz, J. (1986). *The Morality of Freedom*. Clarendon Press, Oxford.

Rehfeld, K.M., Rennings, K., Ziegler, A. (2007). Integrated product policy and environmental product innovations: An empirical analysis. *Ecological Economics*, 61(1), 91–100.

Reitzig, M. (2004). The private values of 'thickets' and 'fences': Towards an updated picture of the use of patents across industries. *Economics of Innovation & New Technology*, 13(5), 457–476.

Rennings, K. (2000). Redefining innovation: Eco-innovation research and the contribution from ecological economics. *Ecological Economics*, 32(2), 319–332.

Rheingold, H. (1993). *The Virtual Community*. Addison-Wesley, Boston.

Ribière, G. (2010). La gestion des aménités et le développement durable. *Revue française d'administration publique*, 2010/2(134), 373–383.

Ricard, P. (2015). *Le biomimétisme : s'inspirer de la nature pour innover durablement*. Conseil Economique et Social.

Richardson, G. (1972). The organization of industry. *Economic Journal*, 883–896.

Ricoeur, P. (1997). *L'idéologie et l'utopie*. Le Seuil, Paris.

Rifkin, J. (2011). *The Third Industrial Revolution: How Lateral Power is Transforming Energy, the Economy, and the World*. Palgrave Macmillan, London.

Ring, P. and Van de Ven, A. (1992). Structuring cooperative relationships between organizations. *Strategic Management Journal*, 13, 483–498.

Ring, P. and Van de Ven, A. (1994). Developmental processes of cooperative interorganizational relationships. *Academy of Management Review*, 19(1), 90–118.

Riordan, M. (1990). What is vertical integration? In *The Firm as a Nexus of Treaties*, Aoki, M., Gustafson, B., Williamson, O.E. (eds). Sage Publications, Thousand Oaks.

Riordan, M. and Sappington, D. (1989). Second sourcing. *The RAND Journal of Economics*, 20, 41–58.

Rogers, E. (1962). *Diffusion of Innovations*. The Free Press, New York.

Roome, N. (1992). Developing environmental management strategies. *Business Strategy and the Environment*, 1(1), 11–24.

Rosenberg, M. (1979). *Conceiving the Self*. Basic Books, New York.

Rosenberg, N. (1982). *Inside the Black Box*. Cambridge University Press, Cambridge.

Rouers, B. (2008). Les marques corporelles des sociétés traditionnelles : un éclairage pour les pratiques contemporaines. *Psychotropes*, 14(2008/2), 23–45.

Roy, M., Boiral, O., Lagacé, D. (2001). Environmental commitment and manufacturing excellence: A comparative study within Canadian industry. *Business Strategy and the Environment*, 10(5), 257–268.

Rueff, J. (2008). Où en sont les "Game Studies" ? *Réseaux*, 2008/5(151), 139–166.

Samuelson, P. (1954). The pure theory of public expenditure. *The Review of Economics and Statistics*, 36(4), 387–389.

Sappington, D. (1991). Incentives in principal-agent relationships. *Journal of Economic Perspectives*, 5(2), 45–66.

Saviotti, P. (1996). *Technological Evolution, Variety and the Economy*. Edward Elgar, Cheltenham.

Schaltegger, S. (2002). A framework for ecopreneurship: Leading bioneers and environmental managers to ecopreneurship. *Green Management International*, 8(3), 45–58.

Schaltegger, S. and Wagner, M. (2011). Sustainable entrepreneurship and sustainability innovation: Categories and interactions. *Business Strategy and the Environment*, 20(4), 222–237.

Schelling, T. (1956). An essay on bargaining. *American Economic Review*, 283–306.

Schelling, T. (1960). *The Strategy of Conflict*. Harvard University Press, Cambridge.

Schick, H., Marxen, S., Freimann, J. (2002). Sustainability issues for start-up entrepreneurs. *Green Management International*, 8(3), 59–70.

Schiederig, T., Tietze, F., Herstatt, C. (2012). Green innovation in technology and innovation management – An exploratory literature review. *R&D Management*, 42(2), 180–192.

Schmeidler, D. (1989). Subjective probability and expected utility without additivity. *Econometrica*, 57, 571–587.

Schotter, A. (1981). *The Economic Theory of Social Institution*. Cambridge University Press, Cambridge.

Schotter, A. and Schwödiauer, G. (1980). Economics and the theory of games: A survey. *Journal of Economic Literature*, 479–527.

Schouten, J. and McAlexander, J. (1995). Subcultures of consumption: An ethnography of the new bikers. *Journal of Consumer Research*, 22, 43–61.

Schumpeter, J. (1939). *Business Cycles*. McGraw Hill, New York.

Schumpeter, J. (1942). *Capitalism, Socialism and Democracy*. Harper & Row, New York.

Selten, R. (1978). The chain-store paradox. *Theory and Decision*, 9, 127–159.

SESSI (2005). L'utilisation des TIC dans les entreprises. *Les 4 pages des statistiques industrielles*, 1(2), 1–4.

Seyfang, G. and Smith, A. (2007). Grassroots innovations for sustainable development: Towards a new research and policy agenda. *Environmental Politics*, 16(4), 584–603.

Shackle, G. (1961). *Decision, Order and Time in Human Affairs*. Cambridge University Press, Cambridge.

Shackle, G. (1979). *Imagination and the Nature of Choice*. Edinburgh University Press, Edinburgh.

Sharma, S. and Vredenburg, H. (1998). Proactive corporate environmental strategy and the development of competitively valuable organizational capabilities. *Strategic Management Journal*, 19(8), 729–753.

Shavell, S. (1984). The design of contract and remedies for breach. *Quarterly Journal of Economics*, 99(1), 121–148.

Shrivastava, P. (1995a). Ecocentric management for a risk society. *Academy of Management Review*, 20(1), 118–137.

Shrivastava, P. (1995b). Environmental technologies and competitive advantage. *Strategic Management Journal*, 16, 183–200.

Shrivastava, P. (1995c). The role of corporations in achieving ecological sustainability. *Academy of Management Review*, 20(4), 936–960.

Simmons, C., Lewis, K., Barrett, J. (2000). Two feet – Two approaches: A component-based model of ecological footprinting. *Ecological Economics*, 32(3), 375–380.

Simon, H. (1947). *Administrative Behavior*. Macmillan, New York.

Simon, H. (1955). On class of skew distribution functions. *Biometrika*, 42(3–4), 425–440.

Simon, H. (1957). *Models of Man*. Wiley, New York.

Simon, H. (1958). The role of expectations in an adaptive or behavioristic model. In *Expectations, Uncertainty and Business Behavior*, Bowman, M.J. (ed.). Social Science Research Council, New York.

Simon, H. (1969). *The Sciences of the Artificial*. MIT Press, Cambridge.

Simon, H. (1972). Theories of bounded rationality. In *Decision and Organization*, Radner, C. and Radner, R. (eds). North-Holland, Amsterdam.

Simon, H. (1976). From substantive to procedural rationality. In *Method and Appraisal in Economics*, Latsis, S.J. (ed.). Cambridge University Press, Cambridge.

Simon, H. (1978). Rationality as process and as product of thought. *American Economic Review*, 68, 1–16.

Simon, H. (1979). Rational decision making in business organizations. *American Economic Review*, 69(4), 493–513.

Simon, H. (1980). *The Sciences of the Artificial*. MIT Press, Cambridge.

Simon, H. (1982). *Models of Bounded Rationality*, volume 2. MIT Press, Cambridge.

Simon, H. (1991). Organizations and markets. *Journal of Economic Perspectives*, 2, 25–44.

Simon, H. (1993). Altruism and economics. *American Economic Review*, 83(2), 156–161.

Simon, L. (2009). Underground, upperground et middle-ground : les collectifs créatifs et la capacité créative de la ville. *Management International*, 13, 37–51.

Singer, P. (1975). *Animal Liberation: A New Ethics for Our Treatment of Animals*. Random House, New York.

Solow, R. (1974a). The economics of resources or the resources of economics. *American Economic Review*, 64, 1–14.

Solow, R. (1974b). Intergenerational equity and exhaustible resources. *The Review of Economic Studies*, 41, 29–46.

Spence, M. (1973). Job market signaling. *Quarterly Journal of Economics*, 8, 355–374.

Spence, M., Gherib, J.B., Biwole, V. (2001). Sustainable entrepreneurship: Is entrepreneurial will enough? A north-south comparison. *Journal of Business Ethics*, 99(3), 335–367.

Spinoza, B. (1677). *L'Éthique*. Gallimard, Paris.

Stark, J. (ed.) (2015). *Product Lifecycle Management*. Springer International Publishing, Berlin.

Stead, I. (1976). The costs of technological innovation. *Research Policy*, 5(1), 2–9.

Stigler G. (1966). *The Theory of Price*. Macmillan, Paris.

Stigler, G. (1971). The theory of economic regulation. *Bell Journal of Economics and Management Science*, 3, 3–21.

Stiglitz, J., Sen, A., Fitoussi, J.-P. (eds) (2009). Rapport de la Commission sur la mesure des performances économiques et du progrès social. Report, Paris.

Stuart, T. and Podolny, J. (1996). Local search and the evolution of technological capabilities. *Strategic Management Journal*, 17, 21–38.

Suchman, M. (1995). Managing legitimacy: Strategic and institutional approaches. *Academy of Management Review*, 20(3), 571–610.

Sukhdev, P. (ed.) (2008). The Economics of Ecosystems and Biodiversity. Report, European Community, Cambridge.

Swanson, E. and Ramiller, N. (1997). The organizing vision in information systems innovation. *Organization Science*, 8(5), 458–474.

Swartz, T. (1983). Brand symbols and message differentiation. *Journal of Advertising Research*, 23(5), 59–64.

Taylor, F.W. (1911). *The Principles of Scientific Management*. Harper & Brothers, New York.

Teece, D. (1980). Economies of scope and the scope of the enterprise. *Journal of Economic Behavior and Organization*, 1(3), 223–247.

Teece, D. (1986). Profiting from technological innovation: Implications for integration, collaboration, licensing and public policy. *Research Policy*, 15, 285–305.

Teece, D. (1988). Technological change and the nature of the firm. In *Technical Change and Economic Theory*, Dosi, G. (ed.). Pinter Publishers, London.

Teece, D. (2007). Explicating dynamic capabilities: The nature and microfoundations of sustainable enterprise performance. *Strategic Management Journal*, 28(13), 1319–1350.

Thiétart, R.A. and Forgues, B. (1995). Chaos theory and organization. *Organization Science*, 6(1), 19–31.

Thiétart, R.A. and Koenig, C. (1987). Programmes aérospatiaux : la stratégie de l'organisation mutuelle. *Revue française de gestion*, 62, 42–53.

Thom, R. (1980). *Paraboles et catastrophes*. Flammarion, Paris.

Thorelli, H. (1986). Networks: Between markets and hierarchies. *Strategic Management Journal*, 7, 37–51.

Tietenberg, T. (1985). Emissions trading: An exercise in reforming pollution policy. Working document, Resources for the Future Inc., Washington D.C.

Tirole, J. (1983). Jeux dynamiques. *Revue d'économie politique*, 4, 551–575.

Tirole, J. (1986). Procurement and renegotiation. *Journal of Political Economy*, 94, 235–259.

Tirole, J. (1988). *The Theory of Industrial Organization*. MIT Press, Cambridge.

Tirole, J. and Lerner, J. (2002). Some simple economics of open source. *Journal of Industrial Economics*, 50(2), 197–234.

Tiwari, R. and Herstatt, C. (2012). India – A lead market for frugal innovations? Extending the lead market theory to emerging economies. TIM/TUHH Working Paper, 7(6).

Tiwari, R. and Kalogerakis, K. (2017). Innovation pathways & trajectories in India's auto component indus. Working document, TIM/TUHH, Hamburg, 8(9).

Tocci, J. (2007). The well-dressed geek: Media appropriation & subcultural style. MiT5, MIT [Online]. Available at: http://web.mit.edu/comm-forum/mit5/papers/Tocci.pdf.

Tocci, J. (2009). Geek cultures: Media and identity in the digital age [Online]. Available at: http://repository.upenn.edu/edissertations/953.

Troxler, P. (2013). Making the third industrial revolution. The struggle for polycentric structures and a new peer production commons in the FabLab community. In *FabLabs: Of Machines, Makers & Inventors*, Walter-Herrmann, J. and Büching, C. (eds). Transcript Publishers, Bielefeld.

Turkle, S. (1995). *Life on the Screen: Identity in the Age of the Internet*. Simon & Schuster, New York.

Turner Schenk, C. and Holman, R. (1980). A sociological approach to brand choice: The concept of situational self-image. *Advances in Consumer Research*, 7, 610–614.

Tushman, M. and O'Reilly, C. (1996). The ambidextrous organizations: Managing evolutionary and revolutionary change. *California Management Review*, 38(4), 8–30.

Urban, G. and Hauser, J. (1993). *Design and Marketing of New Products*. Prentice Hall, Hoboken.

Valla, J.P. (1982). Éléments d'une approche marketing du concept de filière. *Revue d'économie industrielle*, 1(2), 76–92.

Van Damme, E. (1989). Stable equilibria and forward induction. *Journal of Economic Theory*, 48(2), 476–496.

Vernon, R. (1966). International investment and international trade in the product cycle. *Quarterly Journal of Economics*, 80(2), 190–207.

Veugelers, R. (1997). Internal R&D expenditures and external technology sourcing. *Research Policy*, 26, 303–315.

Veugelers, R. (2012). Which policy instruments to induce clean innovating? *Research Policy*, 41(10), 1770–1778.

Von Hippel, E. (1976). The dominant role of users in the scientific instrument innovation process. *Research Policy*, 5, 212–225.

Von Hippel, E. (1988). *The Sources of Innovation*. Oxford University Press, New York.

Von Hippel, E. (2005). *Democratizing Innovation*. MIT Press, Cambridge.

Wackernagel, M. and Rees, W. (1996). *Our Ecological Footprint, Reducing Human Impacts on the Earth*. New Society Publishers, Île Gabriola.

Wackernagel, M. and Rees, W. (1999). *Notre empreinte écologique*. Éditions Écosociété, Montreal/Quebec.

Wackernagel, M. and Yount, J. (1998). The ecological footprint: An indicator of progress toward regional sustainability. *Environmental Monitoring and Assessment*, 51, 511–529.

Wackernagel, M. and Yount, J. (2000). Footprints for sustainability: The next steps. *Environment, Development and Sustainability*, 2, 21–42.

Wagner, M. (2007). On the relationship between environmental management, environmental innovation and patenting: Evidence from German manufacturing firms. *Research Policy*, 36, 1587–1602.

Walley, E. and Taylor, D. (2002). Opportunists, champions, mavericks? A typology of green entrepreneurs. *Green Management International*, 8(3), 31–43.

Walras, L. (1874). *Éléments d'économie politique pure*. Guillaumin & Cie, Paris.

Walzer, M. (1984). *Spheres of Justice: A Defense of Pluralism and Equality*. Basic Books, New York.

Weber, M. (1922). *Wirtschaft und Gesellschaft*. Mohr Siebeck, Tübingen.

Weick, K. (1977). Organization design. *Organizational Dynamics*, 6(6), 31–46.

Weick, K. (1979). *The Social Psychology of Organizing*. Addisson-Wesley, Boston.

Weick, K. (1993). The collapse of sensemaking in organizations: The Mann Gulch disaster. *Administrative Science Quarterly*, 38, 628–652.

Weick, K., Sutcliffe, K., Obsfeld, D. (2005). Organizing and the process of sensemaking. *Organization Science*, 16(4), 409–421.

Weisbrod, B. (1964). Collective-consumption services of individual Lacy consumption goods. *Quarterly Journal of Economics*, 78(3), 471–477.

Weisbuch, G. (1991). *Complex System Dynamics*. Addisson-Wesley, Boston.

Weitzman, M. (1974). Prices vs. quantities. *Review of Economic Studies*, 41(4), 477–491.

Wenger, E. and Snyder, W. (2000). Communities of practice. *Harvard Business Review*, 78, 139–145.

Wernerfelt, B. (1984). A resource based view of the firm. *Strategic Management Journal*, 5, 171–180.

Weyrauch, T. and Herstatt, C. (2016). What is frugal innovation? Three defining criteria. *Journal of Frugal Innovation*, 1(2), 1–18.

Wiener, N. (1948). *Cybernetics*. Éditions Hermann, Paris.

Wiertz, C. and de Ruyter, K. (2007). Beyond the call of duty: Why customers contribute to firm-hosted commercial online communities. *Organization Studies*, 28(3), 347–376.

Williamson, O. (1975). *Markets and Hierarchies: Analysis and Antitrust Implications*. The Free Press, New York.

Williamson, O. (1985). *The Economic Institutions of Capitalism*. The Free Press, New York.

Wisner, P., Epstein, M., Bagozzi, R. (2010). Environmental proactivity and performance. *Advances in Environmental Accounting and Management*, 4, 105–127.

Womack, J. and Jones, D. (1990). *The Machine that Changed the World: The Story of Lean Production*. Harper & Collins, New York.

Womack, J. and Jones, D. (1996). *Lean Thinking: Banish Waste and Create Wealth in Your Corporation*. Simon & Schuster, New York.

Woodside, A. (2010). Brand-consumer storytelling theory and research: Introduction to a psychology & marketing. Special issue. *Psychology & Marketing*, 27(6), 531–540.

Wooten, D. (2006). From labeling possessions to possessing labels: Ridicule and socialization among adolescents. *Journal of Consumer Research*, 33, 188–198.

Yee, N. (2002). Ariadne – Understanding MMORPG addiction [Online]. Available at: http://www.nickyee.com/hub/addiction/addiction.pdf.

Yee, N. (2007). Motivations for play in online games. *CyberPsychology & Behavior*, 9, 772–775.

Yu, J. (2007). Looking inside out: A sociological of knowledge and ignorance of geekness. *Human Architecture: Journal of the Sociology of Self-Knowledge*, 5(2), 40–49.

Zabban, V. (2012). Retour sur les Game Studies : comprendre et dépasser les approches formelles et culturelles du jeu vidéo. *Réseaux*, 73–174(1), 137–176.

Zeschky, M., Widenmayer, B., Gassmann, O. (2011). Frugal innovation in emerging markets. *Research-Technology Management*, 54(4), 38–45.

Zeschky, M., Winterhalter, S., Gassmann, O. (2014). From cost to frugal and reverse innovation: Mapping the field and implications for global competitiveness. *Research-Technology Management*, 57(4), 20–27.

Zeuthen, F. (1933). Du monopole bilatéral. *Revue d'économie politique*, 47, 1651–1670.

Index

A, B

C, D

E, F

G, H

I, J

K, L

M, N

O, P

R, S

T, U

V, W

Other titles from

iSTE

in

Innovation, Entrepreneurship and Management

2023

DARTIGUEPEYROU Carine, SALOFF-COSTE Michel
Futures: The Great Turn (Innovation and Technology Set – Volume 18)

PEYROUX Élisabeth, RAIMOND Christine, VIEL Vincent
Development and Territorial Restructuring in an Era of Global Change: Theories, Approaches and Future Research Perspectives

SAULAIS Pierre
Knowledge and Ideation: Inventive Knowledge Analysis for Ideation Stimulation (Innovation and Technology Set – Volume 17)

2022

AOUINAÏT Camille
Open Innovation Strategies (Smart Innovation Set – Volume 39)

BOUCHÉ Geneviève
Productive Economy, Contributory Economy: Governance Tools for the Third Millennium (Innovation and Technology Set – Volume 15)

BRUYÈRE Christelle
Caring Management in Health Organizations: A Lever for Crisis Management (Health and Innovation Set – Volume 3)

HELLER David
Valuation of the Liability Structure by Real Options (Modern Finance, Management Innovation and Economic Growth Set – Volume 5)

MATHIEU Valérie
A Customer-oriented Manager for B2B Services: Principles and Implementation

MORALES Lucía, DZEVER Sam, TAYLOR Robert
Asia-Europe Industrial Connectivity in Times of Crisis (Innovation and Technology Set – Volume 16)

NOËL Florent, SCHMIDT Géraldine
Employability and Industrial Mutations: Between Individual Trajectories and Organizational Strategic Planning (Technological Changes and Human Resources Set – Volume 4)

DE SAINT JULIEN Odile
The Innovation Ecosystem as a Source of Value Creation: A Value Creation Lever for Open Innovation (Diverse and Global Perspectives on Value Creation Set – Volume 4)

SALOFF-COSTE Michel
Innovation Ecosystems: The Future of Civilizations and the Civilization of the Future (Innovation and Technology Set – Volume 14)

VAYRE Emilie
Digitalization of Work: New Spaces and New Working Times (Technological Changes and Human Resources Set – Volume 5)

ZAFEIRIS Konstantinos N, SKIADIS Christos H, DIMOTIKALIS Yannis, KARAGRIGORIOU Alex, KARAGRIGORIOU-VONTA Christina
Data Analysis and Related Applications 1: Computational, Algorithmic and Applied Economic Data Analysis (Big Data, Artificial Intelligence and Data Analysis Set – Volume 9)
Data Analysis and Related Applications 2: Multivariate, Health and Demographic Data Analysis (Big Data, Artificial Intelligence and Data Analysis Set – Volume 10)

2021

ARCADE Jacques
Strategic Engineering (Innovation and Technology Set – Volume 11)

BÉRANGER Jérôme, RIZOULIÈRES Roland
The Digital Revolution in Health (Health and Innovation Set – Volume 2)

BOBILLIER CHAUMON Marc-Eric
Digital Transformations in the Challenge of Activity and Work: Understanding and Supporting Technological Changes (Technological Changes and Human Resources Set – Volume 3)

BUCLET Nicolas
Territorial Ecology and Socio-ecological Transition (Smart Innovation Set – Volume 34)

DIMOTIKALIS Yannis, KARAGRIGORIOU Alex, PARPOULA Christina, SKIADIS Christos H
Applied Modeling Techniques and Data Analysis 1: Computational Data Analysis Methods and Tools (Big Data, Artificial Intelligence and Data Analysis Set - Volume 7)
Applied Modeling Techniques and Data Analysis 2: Financial, Demographic, Stochastic and Statistical Models and Methods (Big Data, Artificial Intelligence and Data Analysis Set – Volume 8)

DISPAS Christophe, KAYANAKIS Georges, SERVEL Nicolas, STRIUKOVA Ludmila
Innovation and Financial Markets (Innovation between Risk and Reward Set – Volume 7)

ENJOLRAS Manon
Innovation and Export: The Joint Challenge of the Small Company (Smart Innovation Set – Volume 37)

FLEURY Sylvain, RICHIR Simon
Immersive Technologies to Accelerate Innovation: How Virtual and Augmented Reality Enables the Co-Creation of Concepts (Smart Innovation Set – Volume 38)

GIORGINI Pierre
The Contributory Revolution (Innovation and Technology Set – Volume 13)

GOGLIN Christian
Emotions and Values in Equity Crowdfunding Investment Choices 2: Modeling and Empirical Study

GRENIER Corinne, OIRY Ewan
Altering Frontiers: Organizational Innovations in Healthcare (Health and Innovation Set – Volume 1)

GUERRIER Claudine
Security and Its Challenges in the 21st Century (Innovation and Technology Set – Volume 12)

HELLER David
Performance of Valuation Methods in Financial Transactions (Modern Finance, Management Innovation and Economic Growth Set – Volume 4)

LEHMANN Paul-Jacques
Liberalism and Capitalism Today

SOULÉ Bastien, HALLÉ Julie, VIGNAL Bénédicte, BOUTROY Éric, NIER Olivier
Innovation in Sport: Innovation Trajectories and Process Optimization (Smart Innovation Set – Volume 35)

UZUNIDIS Dimitri, KASMI Fedoua, ADATTO Laurent
Innovation Economics, Engineering and Management Handbook 1: Main Themes
Innovation Economics, Engineering and Management Handbook 2: Special Themes

VALLIER Estelle
Innovation in Clusters: Science–Industry Relationships in the Face of Forced Advancement (Smart Innovation Set – Volume 36)

2020

ACH Yves-Alain, RMADI-SAÏD Sandra
Financial Information and Brand Value: Reflections, Challenges and Limitations

ANDREOSSO-O'CALLAGHAN Bernadette, DZEVER Sam, JAUSSAUD Jacques, TAYLOR Robert
Sustainable Development and Energy Transition in Europe and Asia (Innovation and Technology Set – Volume 9)

BEN SLIMANE Sonia, M'HENNI Hatem
Entrepreneurship and Development: Realities and Future Prospects (Smart Innovation Set – Volume 30)

CHOUTEAU Marianne, FOREST Joëlle, NGUYEN Céline
Innovation for Society: The P.S.I. Approach (Smart Innovation Set – Volume 28)

CORON Clotilde
Quantifying Human Resources: Uses and Analysis (Technological Changes and Human Resources Set – Volume 2)

CORON Clotilde, GILBERT Patrick
Technological Change (Technological Changes and Human Resources Set – Volume 1)

CERDIN Jean-Luc, PERETTI Jean-Marie
The Success of Apprenticeships: Views of Stakeholders on Training and Learning (Human Resources Management Set – Volume 3)

DELCHET-COCHET Karen
Circular Economy: From Waste Reduction to Value Creation (Economic Growth Set – Volume 2)

DIDAY Edwin, GUAN Rong, SAPORTA Gilbert, WANG Huiwen
Advances in Data Science
(Big Data, Artificial Intelligence and Data Analysis Set – Volume 4)

DOS SANTOS PAULINO Victor
Innovation Trends in the Space Industry
(Smart Innovation Set – Volume 25)

GASMI Nacer
Corporate Innovation Strategies: Corporate Social Responsibility and Shared Value Creation
(Smart Innovation Set – Volume 33)

GOGLIN Christian
Emotions and Values in Equity Crowdfunding Investment Choices 1: Transdisciplinary Theoretical Approach

GUILHON Bernard
Venture Capital and the Financing of Innovation
(Innovation Between Risk and Reward Set – Volume 6)

LATOUCHE Pascal
Open Innovation: Human Set-up
(Innovation and Technology Set – Volume 10)

LIMA Marcos
Entrepreneurship and Innovation Education: Frameworks and Tools
(Smart Innovation Set – Volume 32)

MACHADO Carolina, DAVIM J. Paulo
Sustainable Management for Managers and Engineers

MAKRIDES Andreas, KARAGRIGORIOU Alex, SKIADAS Christos H.
Data Analysis and Applications 3: Computational, Classification, Financial, Statistical and Stochastic Methods
(Big Data, Artificial Intelligence and Data Analysis Set – Volume 5)
Data Analysis and Applications 4: Financial Data Analysis and Methods
(Big Data, Artificial Intelligence and Data Analysis Set – Volume 6)

MASSOTTE Pierre, CORSI Patrick
Complex Decision-Making in Economy and Finance

MEUNIER François-Xavier
Dual Innovation Systems: Concepts, Tools and Methods (Smart Innovation Set – Volume 31)

MICHAUD Thomas
Science Fiction and Innovation Design (Innovation in Engineering and Technology Set – Volume 6)

MONINO Jean-Louis
Data Control: Major Challenge for the Digital Society (Smart Innovation Set – Volume 29)

MORLAT Clément
Sustainable Productive System: Eco-development versus Sustainable Development (Smart Innovation Set – Volume 26)

SAULAIS Pierre, ERMINE Jean-Louis
Knowledge Management in Innovative Companies 2: Understanding and Deploying a KM Plan within a Learning Organization (Smart Innovation Set – Volume 27)

2019

AMENDOLA Mario, GAFFARD Jean-Luc
Disorder and Public Concern Around Globalization

BARBAROUX Pierre
Disruptive Technology and Defence Innovation Ecosystems (Innovation in Engineering and Technology Set – Volume 5)

DOU Henri, JUILLET Alain, CLERC Philippe
Strategic Intelligence for the Future 1: A New Strategic and Operational Approach
Strategic Intelligence for the Future 2: A New Information Function Approach

FRIKHA Azza
Measurement in Marketing: Operationalization of Latent Constructs

FRIMOUSSE Soufyane
Innovation and Agility in the Digital Age
(Human Resources Management Set – Volume 2)

GAY Claudine, SZOSTAK Bérangère L.
Innovation and Creativity in SMEs: Challenges, Evolutions and Prospects
(Smart Innovation Set – Volume 21)

GORIA Stéphane, HUMBERT Pierre, ROUSSEL Benoît
Information, Knowledge and Agile Creativity
(Smart Innovation Set – Volume 22)

HELLER David
Investment Decision-making Using Optional Models
(Economic Growth Set – Volume 2)

HELLER David, DE CHADIRAC Sylvain, HALAOUI Lana, JOUVET Camille
The Emergence of Start-ups
(Economic Growth Set – Volume 1)

HÉRAUD Jean-Alain, KERR Fiona, BURGER-HELMCHEN Thierry
Creative Management of Complex Systems
(Smart Innovation Set – Volume 19)

LATOUCHE Pascal
Open Innovation: Corporate Incubator
(Innovation and Technology Set – Volume 7)

LEHMANN Paul-Jacques
The Future of the Euro Currency

LEIGNEL Jean-Louis, MÉNAGER Emmanuel, YABLONSKY Serge
Sustainable Enterprise Performance: A Comprehensive Evaluation Method

LIÈVRE Pascal, AUBRY Monique, GAREL Gilles
Management of Extreme Situations: From Polar Expeditions to Exploration-Oriented Organizations

MILLOT Michel
Embarrassment of Product Choices 2: Towards a Society of Well-being

N'GOALA Gilles, PEZ-PÉRARD Virginie, PRIM-ALLAZ Isabelle
Augmented Customer Strategy: CRM in the Digital Age

NIKOLOVA Blagovesta
The RRI Challenge: Responsibilization in a State of Tension with Market Regulation
(Innovation and Responsibility Set – Volume 3)

PELLEGRIN-BOUCHER Estelle, ROY Pierre
Innovation in the Cultural and Creative Industries
(Innovation and Technology Set – Volume 8)

PRIOLON Joël
Financial Markets for Commodities

QUINIOU Matthieu
Blockchain: The Advent of Disintermediation

RAVIX Joël-Thomas, DESCHAMPS Marc
Innovation and Industrial Policies
(Innovation between Risk and Reward Set – Volume 5)

ROGER Alain, VINOT Didier
Skills Management: New Applications, New Questions
(Human Resources Management Set – Volume 1)

SAULAIS Pierre, ERMINE Jean-Louis
Knowledge Management in Innovative Companies 1: Understanding and Deploying a KM Plan within a Learning Organization
(Smart Innovation Set – Volume 23)

SERVAJEAN-HILST Romaric
Co-innovation Dynamics: The Management of Client-Supplier Interactions for Open Innovation
(Smart Innovation Set – Volume 20)

SKIADAS Christos H., BOZEMAN James R.
Data Analysis and Applications 1: Clustering and Regression, Modeling-estimating, Forecasting and Data Mining
(Big Data, Artificial Intelligence and Data Analysis Set – Volume 2)
Data Analysis and Applications 2: Utilization of Results in Europe and Other Topics
(Big Data, Artificial Intelligence and Data Analysis Set – Volume 3)

UZUNIDIS Dimitri
Systemic Innovation: Entrepreneurial Strategies and Market Dynamics

VIGEZZI Michel
World Industrialization: Shared Inventions, Competitive Innovations and Social Dynamics
(Smart Innovation Set – Volume 24)

2018

BURKHARDT Kirsten
Private Equity Firms: Their Role in the Formation of Strategic Alliances

CALLENS Stéphane
Creative Globalization
(Smart Innovation Set – Volume 16)

CASADELLA Vanessa
Innovation Systems in Emerging Economies: MINT – Mexico, Indonesia, Nigeria, Turkey
(Smart Innovation Set – Volume 18)

CHOUTEAU Marianne, FOREST Joëlle, NGUYEN Céline
Science, Technology and Innovation Culture
(Innovation in Engineering and Technology Set – Volume 3)

CORLOSQUET-HABART Marine, JANSSEN Jacques
Big Data for Insurance Companies
(Big Data, Artificial Intelligence and Data Analysis Set – Volume 1)

CROS Françoise
Innovation and Society
(Smart Innovation Set – Volume 15)

DEBREF Romain
Environmental Innovation and Ecodesign: Certainties and Controversies
(Smart Innovation Set – Volume 17)

DOMINGUEZ Noémie
SME Internationalization Strategies: Innovation to Conquer New Markets

ERMINE Jean-Louis
Knowledge Management: The Creative Loop
(Innovation and Technology Set – Volume 5)

GILBERT Patrick, BOBADILLA Natalia, GASTALDI Lise,
LE BOULAIRE Martine, LELEBINA Olga
Innovation, Research and Development Management

IBRAHIMI Mohammed
Mergers & Acquisitions: Theory, Strategy, Finance

LEMAÎTRE Denis
Training Engineers for Innovation

LÉVY Aldo, BEN BOUHENI Faten, AMMI Chantal
Financial Management: USGAAP and IFRS Standards
(Innovation and Technology Set – Volume 6)

MILLOT Michel
Embarrassment of Product Choices 1: How to Consume Differently

PANSERA Mario, OWEN Richard
Innovation and Development: The Politics at the Bottom of the Pyramid
(Innovation and Responsibility Set – Volume 2)

RICHEZ Yves
Corporate Talent Detection and Development

SACHETTI Philippe, ZUPPINGER Thibaud
New Technologies and Branding
(Innovation and Technology Set – Volume 4)

SAMIER Henri
Intuition, Creativity, Innovation

TEMPLE Ludovic, COMPAORÉ SAWADOGO Eveline M.F.W.
Innovation Processes in Agro-Ecological Transitions in Developing Countries
(Innovation in Engineering and Technology Set – Volume 2)

UZUNIDIS Dimitri
Collective Innovation Processes: Principles and Practices
(Innovation in Engineering and Technology Set – Volume 4)

VAN HOOREBEKE Delphine
The Management of Living Beings or Emo-management

2017

AÏT-EL-HADJ Smaïl
The Ongoing Technological System
(Smart Innovation Set – Volume 11)

BAUDRY Marc, DUMONT Béatrice
Patents: Prompting or Restricting Innovation?
(Smart Innovation Set – Volume 12)

BÉRARD Céline, TEYSSIER Christine
Risk Management: Lever for SME Development and Stakeholder Value Creation

CHALENÇON Ludivine
Location Strategies and Value Creation of International Mergers and Acquisitions

CHAUVEL Danièle, BORZILLO Stefano
The Innovative Company: An Ill-defined Object
(Innovation between Risk and Reward Set – Volume 1)

CORSI Patrick
Going Past Limits To Growth

D'ANDRIA Aude, GABARRET Inés
Building 21st Century Entrepreneurship
(Innovation and Technology Set – Volume 2)

DAIDJ Nabyla
Cooperation, Coopetition and Innovation
(Innovation and Technology Set – Volume 3)

FERNEZ-WALCH Sandrine
The Multiple Facets of Innovation Project Management
(Innovation between Risk and Reward Set – Volume 4)

FOREST Joëlle
Creative Rationality and Innovation
(Smart Innovation Set – Volume 14)

GUILHON Bernard
Innovation and Production Ecosystems
(Innovation between Risk and Reward Set – Volume 2)

HAMMOUDI Abdelhakim, DAIDJ Nabyla
Game Theory Approach to Managerial Strategies and Value Creation
(Diverse and Global Perspectives on Value Creation Set – Volume 3)

LALLEMENT Rémi
Intellectual Property and Innovation Protection: New Practices and New Policy Issues
(Innovation between Risk and Reward Set – Volume 3)

LAPERCHE Blandine
Enterprise Knowledge Capital
(Smart Innovation Set – Volume 13)

LEBERT Didier, EL YOUNSI Hafida
International Specialization Dynamics
(Smart Innovation Set – Volume 9)

MAESSCHALCK Marc
Reflexive Governance for Research and Innovative Knowledge
(Responsible Research and Innovation Set – Volume 6)

MASSOTTE Pierre
Ethics in Social Networking and Business 1: Theory, Practice and Current Recommendations
Ethics in Social Networking and Business 2: The Future and Changing Paradigms

MASSOTTE Pierre, CORSI Patrick
Smart Decisions in Complex Systems

MEDINA Mercedes, HERRERO Mónica, URGELLÉS Alicia
Current and Emerging Issues in the Audiovisual Industry
(Diverse and Global Perspectives on Value Creation Set – Volume 1)

MICHAUD Thomas
Innovation, Between Science and Science Fiction
(Smart Innovation Set – Volume 10)

PELLÉ Sophie
Business, Innovation and Responsibility
(Responsible Research and Innovation Set – Volume 7)

SAVIGNAC Emmanuelle
The Gamification of Work: The Use of Games in the Workplace

SUGAHARA Satoshi, DAIDJ Nabyla, USHIO Sumitaka
Value Creation in Management Accounting and Strategic Management: An Integrated Approach
(Diverse and Global Perspectives on Value Creation Set –Volume 2)

UZUNIDIS Dimitri, SAULAIS Pierre
Innovation Engines: Entrepreneurs and Enterprises in a Turbulent World
(Innovation in Engineering and Technology Set – Volume 1)

2016

BARBAROUX Pierre, ATTOUR Amel, SCHENK Eric
Knowledge Management and Innovation
(Smart Innovation Set – Volume 6)

BEN BOUHENI Faten, AMMI Chantal, LEVY Aldo
Banking Governance, Performance And Risk-Taking: Conventional Banks Vs Islamic Banks

BOUTILLIER Sophie, CARRÉ Denis, LEVRATTO Nadine
Entrepreneurial Ecosystems (Smart Innovation Set – Volume 2)

BOUTILLIER Sophie, UZUNIDIS Dimitri
The Entrepreneur (Smart Innovation Set – Volume 8)

BOUVARD Patricia, SUZANNE Hervé
Collective Intelligence Development in Business

GALLAUD Delphine, LAPERCHE Blandine
Circular Economy, Industrial Ecology and Short Supply Chains (Smart Innovation Set – Volume 4)

GUERRIER Claudine
Security and Privacy in the Digital Era (Innovation and Technology Set – Volume 1)

MEGHOUAR Hicham
Corporate Takeover Targets

MONINO Jean-Louis, SEDKAOUI Soraya
Big Data, Open Data and Data Development (Smart Innovation Set – Volume 3)

MOREL Laure, LE ROUX Serge
Fab Labs: Innovative User (Smart Innovation Set – Volume 5)

PICARD Fabienne, TANGUY Corinne
Innovations and Techno-ecological Transition (Smart Innovation Set – Volume 7)

2015

CASADELLA Vanessa, LIU Zeting, DIMITRI Uzunidis
Innovation Capabilities and Economic Development in Open Economies (Smart Innovation Set – Volume 1)

CORSI Patrick, MORIN Dominique
Sequencing Apple's DNA

CORSI Patrick, NEAU Erwan
Innovation Capability Maturity Model

FAIVRE-TAVIGNOT Bénédicte
Social Business and Base of the Pyramid

GODÉ Cécile
Team Coordination in Extreme Environments

MAILLARD Pierre
Competitive Quality and Innovation

MASSOTTE Pierre, CORSI Patrick
Operationalizing Sustainability

MASSOTTE Pierre, CORSI Patrick
Sustainability Calling

2014

DUBÉ Jean, LEGROS Diègo
Spatial Econometrics Using Microdata

LESCA Humbert, LESCA Nicolas
Strategic Decisions and Weak Signals

2013

HABART-CORLOSQUET Marine, JANSSEN Jacques, MANCA Raimondo
VaR Methodology for Non-Gaussian Finance

2012

DAL PONT Jean-Pierre
Process Engineering and Industrial Management

MAILLARD Pierre
Competitive Quality Strategies

POMEROL Jean-Charles
Decision-Making and Action

SZYLAR Christian
UCITS Handbook

2011

LESCA Nicolas
Environmental Scanning and Sustainable Development

LESCA Nicolas, LESCA Humbert
Weak Signals for Strategic Intelligence: Anticipation Tool for Managers

MERCIER-LAURENT Eunika
Innovation Ecosystems

2010

SZYLAR Christian
Risk Management under UCITS III/IV

2009

COHEN Corine
Business Intelligence

ZANINETTI Jean-Marc
Sustainable Development in the USA

2008

CORSI Patrick, DULIEU Mike
The Marketing of Technology Intensive Products and Services

DZEVER Sam, JAUSSAUD Jacques, ANDREOSSO Bernadette
Evolving Corporate Structures and Cultures in Asia: Impact of Globalization

2007

AMMI Chantal
Global Consumer Behavior

2006

BOUGHZALA Imed, ERMINE Jean-Louis
Trends in Enterprise Knowledge Management

CORSI Patrick *et al.*
Innovation Engineering: the Power of Intangible Networks

Printed and bound by CPI Group (UK) Ltd, Croydon, CR0 4YY
13/09/2026
14961039-0007